CW00968171

Germany's Asia-Pacific Empire

Colonialism and Naval Policy
1885–1914

This book examines German attempts to acquire colonial territories in East Asia and the Pacific, and discusses the huge impact this had on local and other international powers. It covers the German acquisition of Kiautschou in 1897, which had profound consequences for China, beginning a 'scramble for concessions' by other western powers; the formation of the powerful German East Asiatic Cruiser Squadron which was seen by the British as a major threat, and which resulted in the advent of the Fleet-Unit concept and the birth of the Royal Australian Navy; the Japanese siege and capture of the key German base of Tsingtau in 1914, and the fate of the various former German colonies after Germany's defeat in 1918. The book contains many illustrations from the author's extensive private collection.

Germany's Asia-Pacific Empire

Colonialism and Naval Policy
1885–1914

Charles Stephenson

THE BOYDELL PRESS

© Charles Stephenson 2009

All Rights Reserved. Except as permitted under current legislation
no part of this work may be photocopied, stored in a retrieval system,
published, performed in public, adapted, broadcast,
transmitted, recorded or reproduced in any form or by any means,
without the prior permission of the copyright owner

The right of Charles Stephenson to be identified as
the author of this work has been asserted in accordance with
sections 77 and 78 of the Copyright, Designs and Patents Act 1988

First published 2009
The Boydell Press, Woodbridge

ISBN 978 1 84383 518 9

The Boydell Press is an imprint of Boydell & Brewer Ltd
PO Box 9, Woodbridge, Suffolk IP12 3DF, UK
and of Boydell & Brewer Inc.
668 Mount Hope Ave, Rochester, NY 14604, USA
website: www.boydellandbrewer.com

A CIP catalogue record for this book is available
from the British Library

All URLs were verified on 17 July 2009.
However, the publisher has no responsibility for the continued existence
or accuracy of URLs for external or third-party internet websites
referred to in this book, and does not guarantee that any content
on such websites is, or will remain, accurate or appropriate.

This publication is printed on acid-free paper

Printed in Great Britain by
CPI Antony Rowe, Chippenham and Eastbourne

This work is dedicated to the memory of

'Nain'

my maternal great-grandmother

Ruth Greenwood (1875–1959)

A steadfast and much loved lady

Contents

Illustrations

Maps and Tables

Introduction

Perhaps the first thing to say about this work is that it is not founded on original research based upon the careful scrutiny of primary sources; or rather it is, but none of this research is mine. No, this is a work of synthesis, which takes, or perhaps ruthlessly plunders would be a more apt description, the original research of many eminent scholars and attempts to weave it into a narrative concerning the colonial and naval policy of Imperial Germany in the Asia-Pacific region over the given period of 1885 to 1914. There are also few, if any, new interpretations of existing material to be found here. Any potential reader is then entitled to ask, 'what is the purpose of this work? Why does it exist?'

I would answer it thus; there is very little currently in print, at least in English, concerning Imperial Germany and her Asia-Pacific colonies. There has never been anything in print, to my knowledge, that examines this subject holistically. Those attracted to colonial and naval history in general, and in the Asia-Pacific area during the given period in particular, form then the target readership. It is hoped that it may also interest those whose area of interest concerns late Imperial Germany and the role of Kaiser Wilhelm II, *Weltpolitik*, and indeed the pre-Great War period generally. Many of the matters and incidents investigated and explained have received little or no coverage in generally accessible works. However, while I am confident that this work will make no concessions academically, I have tried to pitch it at a popular level.

It was, I think, Winston Churchill who codified common sense by opining that 'Chronology is the key to narrative.' I have attempted to adhere to this sage advice throughout the bulk of the work, though it has proven necessary to adopt thematic approach in chapters 3 (China 1897–1914: Colonial Development and Political Turbulence) and 7 (Naval Plans and Operations 1897–1914). Apart from these two instances however the story proceeds from the formal acquisition of Kaiser Wilhelmsland in 1885 to the fall of Tsingtau in late 1914.

A word or two needs to be said about language usage. The current methodology for Romanising the Chinese language is the Hanyu Pinyin system, which was generally adopted in the late 1970s. This replaced the Wade-Giles method that had been commonly used since the nineteenth century. Under the latter, the Chinese territory occupied by Germany in 1897 was known in English as, among other variations, Kiao-chou, Kiao-Chow, Kiao-chow and Kiaochow. To the Germans it was normally rendered as Kiautschou, and this, for the sake of consistency, is the term used throughout the work, the modern rendition being Jiāozhōu.

Similarly with the city in the Kiautschou Territory, today Romanised as Qīngdǎo; this was subject to variations such as Tsingtao and Tsing-tao. Again, I have adopted the German usage of Tsingtau for the sake of consistency. Other variations and changes in nomenclature that have occurred over time for various reasons have, hopefully, been identified in the text, including the names of several of the Pacific islands and territories. The object of the exercise has been, in general terms, to provide some consistency, though this has been freely sacrificed where it has been thought appropriate. In short, I have tried to apply common sense in respect of the matter and any offence caused to purists, or indeed anyone else, is accidental.

Information relating to the various naval vessels mentioned in the text has been taken from various editions of *Jane's Fighting Ships* and *Conway's All the World's Fighting Ships*, which are invaluable reference sources, and have been my first port of call concerning naval technical matters.

There are also a great number of people to whom I am indebted for their generous assistance in putting together this work. These include but are not limited to: Lisa L Crane, the Special Collections Digital Projects Coordinator at The Claremont Colleges, California, Randal Gray, whose eagle-eye and vast store of knowledge made him an invaluable copy-editor, Fran Hezel of Micronesian Seminar, Sam Markham, Assistant Archivist at Associated Press, Carrie Marsh, Special Collections Librarian at Honnold/Mudd Library (Claremont Colleges), Katie Morgan, Beloit College Archives (Wisconsin) summer manager, Adam Rosenkranz, the Reference Librarian/Bibliographer of The Claremont Colleges, Adrienne and Dennis Quarmby, Philip Sims of US Naval Sea Systems Command (NAVSEA), Martha Smalley, of Yale University (New Haven, Connecticut), Teru-kazu Takahashi of Okayama University, Japan, Graham Thompson of Shanghai and Carol Varas of Micronesian Seminar.

I have found myself particularly grateful to Peter Sowden, the editor who handles Boydell & Brewer's modern and early modern history list. His unfailing patience and pertinent suggestions have greatly improved the original draft of this work. Thanks Peter.

It goes almost without saying that although all of the above have been of the greatest help imaginable, any errors contained in this work are mine and mine alone. I can only hope that they are not too numerous.

Map 1. East Asia, Australasia, and the Pacific

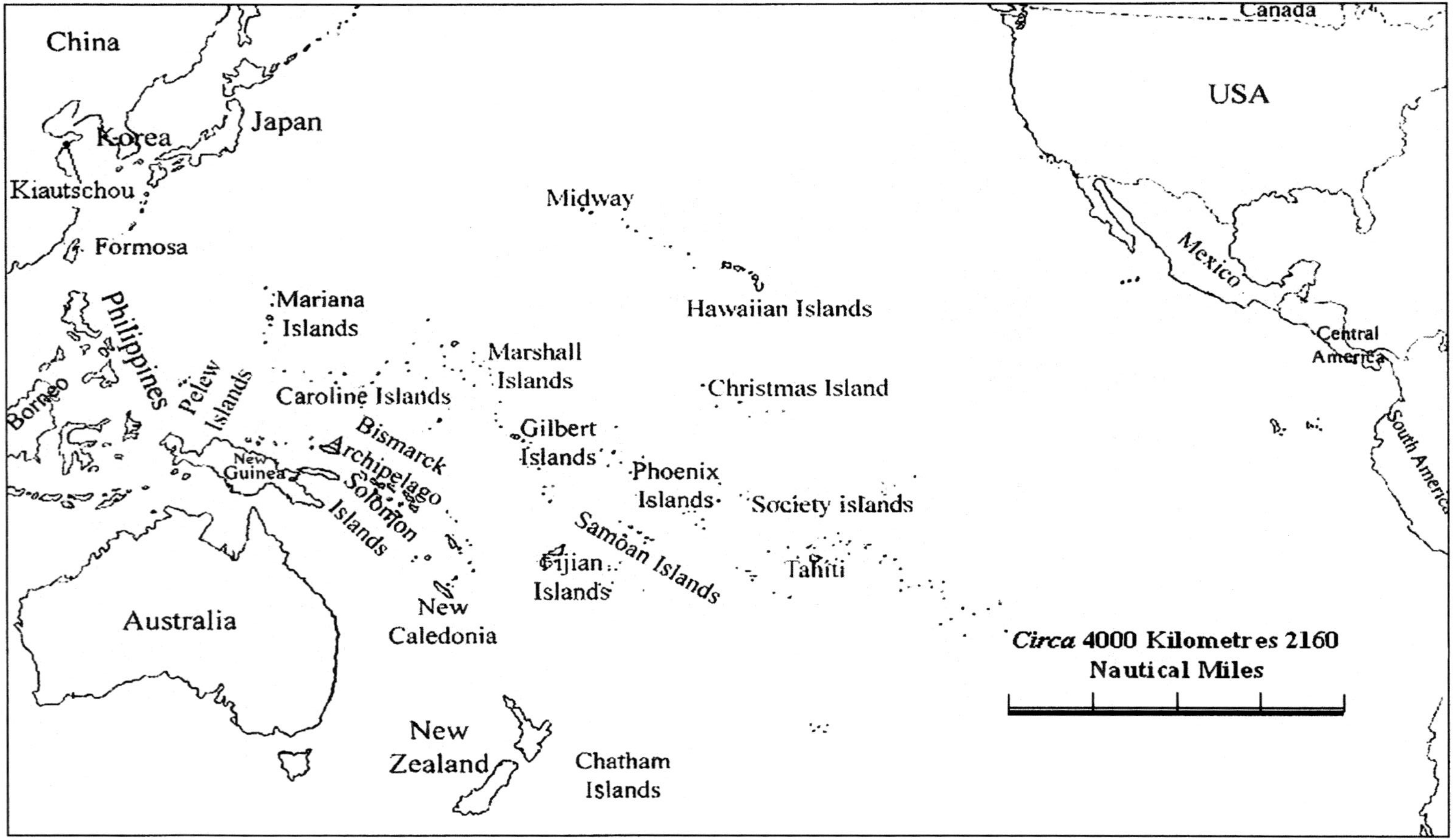

I

Bismarck and Empire: 1885–1888
Kaiser Wilhelm's Land, the Bismarck
Archipelago, the Marshall Islands and Nauru

The extra-European colonial history of Imperial Germany was very different from that of other European powers, not least because of its relative brevity. Sir John Robert Seeley, writing of the British Empire in 1883, commented that 'we seem, as it were, to have conquered and peopled half the world in a fit of absence of mind.'[1] The entry of Imperial Germany into colonialism cannot be attributed to 'absent mindedness', but rather to cold Bismarckian calculation. Having said that, we do not know exactly what that calculation was, indeed the Imperial Chancellor Otto von Bismarck's apparently sudden interest in the acquisition of African colonial territory in 1884 has given rise to a great deal of debate.

Some have seen it as designed to provoke a quarrel with the British just at the moment when the Anglophile Crown Prince Frederick William, who was married to 'Vicky', formerly Britain's Princess Royal, might have succeeded his father Kaiser Wilhelm I. For example Herbert Bismarck, speaking in 1890, apparently confirms such an argument:

> When we started our colonial policy we had to assume that the Crown Prince's reign would be a long one with English influence predominant. To prevent this we had to embark on a colonial policy because it was popular and also able to provoke conflict with England at any given moment.[2]

The Crown Princess, writing contemporaneously in 1884, saw it as an act of what we might now call social-imperialism; an attempt to focus the electorate on foreign policy rather than domestic issues: 'I am almost certain that the whole agitation about colonial enterprise would not have been cooked up if it were not a useful handle for the elections.'[3]

Elections in Imperial Germany were problematic for the ruling elite for reasons pertaining to the constitution, under which the King of Prussia filled the position of German Kaiser. The Kaiser was responsible for appointing the Imperial Chancellor, who was responsible only to him, and who in turn appointed ministers (State Secretaries) to head the various government departments. The component parts of the Empire were twenty-five polities, which were sovereignties in their own right,[4] as well as the two former French territories, the entire province of Alsace and a large portion of Lorraine. These were incorporated into the Empire as the province of Elsass-Lothringen; the only common Imperial jurisdiction, and governed from Berlin, the Imperial capital.[5]

There were two Imperial assemblies; the Federal Council (*Bundesrat*) and the National Assembly (*Reichstag*), the former, consisting of the rulers, or their delegates, of the various states that made up the Empire, had fifty-eight seats, and the latter was made up of 397 deputies, who were the representatives of the people. These were, under Article 20 of the constitution, chosen by 'universal and direct election by a secret ballot'.[6] These constitutional arrangements might appear to confer a degree of democratic control over government decisions, but there was more form than substance in this, as the elected deputies, while free to debate, could not instigate legislation. Bills and so forth were initiated by the government, the Kaiser, Chancellor, and State Secretaries, and sent to the Federal Council. They were then sent to the National Assembly, which could debate them and then, by a majority vote, pass or reject them. The Assembly could also propose amendments. One of the tasks of the Chancellor then was to construct majorities in the Assembly so that the government could get its legislation through.

Since the formation of Imperial Germany in 1871 there had been groups that had been characterised by Bismarck as 'enemies of the realm', which included, most particularly, the German Social Democratic Party (SPD) and the Trades Unions, though Catholics and liberals also figured in the category in varying degrees and at various times. The advance of the SPD, a party with an avowedly Marxist outlook, seemed inexorable, and it advanced both in terms of numbers and organisation as Imperial Germany became more industrialised. Yet there was no flexibility in the social structure or constitution to accommodate the rise of such a grouping, and the concomitant social change thus implied. In effect, any reform of the constitution would have been revolutionary, for it was designed to preserve an agrarian neo-feudal system, and could find no place for mass, particularly working-class, participation.[7]

Indeed, under the system of checks and balances inherent in the constitutional arrangements, a power of veto over change was guaranteed to the largest contingent in the Federal Council. This was held by delegates of the state of Prussia, which formed some two-thirds of both the Empire's area and population.[8] Prussia's constitution had been amended in 1849, from universal franchise, to a three-class franchise.[9] Thus the Prussian aristocracy, the Junkers, were in a position to maintain their privileged position in a society that was experiencing great change; scientific, industrial, economic, and demographic among others. This resistance was undertaken in an effort to perpetuate both their social and functional ascendancy, based on land ownership, and domination of the bureaucracy and the army respectively. This connection between social position and administrative power basically defines the 'old ways' and 'values', products of their collective historical memory, which they epitomised, and sought to preserve. The means, whereby this was to be achieved, involved preserving the status quo, as regards the Prussian Army and bureaucracy, and maintaining the authority of the Prussian King over the German Empire, through his position as German Kaiser and Commander-of-Chief of the military forces of that Empire.

Indeed one of the institutions of state that was absolutely outside the remit of almost any form of civil control was the Army.[10] This requires some qualification, as there was no 'German' Army as such. The constitution of the Second Reich combined the armies of all the constituent states with the Prussian Army, with the exception of the armies of the Kingdoms of Bavaria, Saxony and Württemberg. The King of Bavaria retained command of the Bavarian forces during peacetime, and Saxony and Württemberg kept their own General Staffs. The secondment of staff officers from the ex-Prussian, now Great, General Staff ensured consistency between the various forces in all contexts. The four armies combined constituted the Imperial German Army, and under Article 64 of the constitution all of them were obliged to obey the orders of the Kaiser, who had the authority to appoint commanding officers and whose approval was required for the appointment of general officers.[11] This meant of course that the Great General Staff exercised effective control of military matters, which was of course, as most things in the Empire were, dominated by Prussia. This situation was one of the legacies bequeathed by the Iron Chancellor to his successors.

In order try and curb the electoral success of the 'enemies of the Empire', Bismarck had resort to various stratagems, including of course the diversion of attention to colonies and enemies abroad. Hence, between 1884 and 1885 Germany acquired significant African territory; Togo, the Cameroons, German East Africa and German South West Africa. In any event, Bismarck's desire for extra-European colonies did not long endure. On 5 December 1888 he was to tell the explorer Eugen Wolf: 'on my map Africa is located in Europe. Here is Russia, here is France, and we are situated in the centre; that is my map of Africa.'[12] Indeed, one of the few scholars to have delved into German colonial policy in the region discerns three distinct phases with regards to it; first a policy, adopted under, and thus inherited from, Bismarck, of disinterest, then 'active interventionism', culminating in 'a quest for advantageous disengagement' in 1899.[13]

The acquisition of overseas territory under Bismarck can be viewed then as foreign policy conducted with a view to influencing domestic opinion. That the territories acquired were, to the Chancellor, disposable or otherwise of little consequence was made plain to the future Kaiser Wilhelm II during his period of education at the foreign ministry. As he later recalled it:

> I spoke often with the Prince about the colonial question and always found in him the intention to utilize the colonies as commercial objects, or objects for swapping purposes, other than to make them useful to the fatherland or utilize them as sources of raw materials.[14]

Another facet of Bismarck's foreign policy, and one upon which the safety of the German Empire was predicated, was the isolation of France. Deemed a military necessity by Field Marshal Helmuth, Count von Moltke (Chief of the Great General, Staff) Wilhelm I, and the German military in general, one of the consequences of the creation of the Empire was the permanent alienation of France, through the annexation of her territory.

There was then a perpetual balancing act for Germany to perform, inasmuch as any enemy, potential or actual, of Germany could be almost certain to have the support of France. Bismarck's foreign policy then pursued the desiderata of being, at least, on friendly terms with two of the other three European 'Great Powers' of Russia, Austria-Hungary and Britain. British foreign policy during the late nineteenth century tended towards isolation, usually described as splendid, leaving by default only Russia and Austria-Hungary, both of which had mutual antagonisms. Bismarck's attempts to get around this included the 1881 'League of the Three Emperors' and the Reinsurance Treaty of 1887; the latter being necessary due to the collapse of the former because of antagonism in the Balkans between Russia and Austria-Hungary.[15] As Kaiser Wilhelm I is supposed to have put it: 'Bismarck was the one man who could juggle five balls of which at least two were always in the air.'[16]

That there were ambiguities and contradictions in Bismarck's foreign policies is undoubted, as is the minor importance with which the Chancellor viewed such matters. Bismarck's vision was broad, and in furtherance of it he went so far as to get his son, Herbert, made State Secretary for Foreign Affairs in 1886. This was not a case of nepotism pure and simple, for Herbert had carried out important missions on behalf of his father, most particularly the negotiations with Britain; over South West Africa in 1884, and the settlement of potential colonial disputes elsewhere during 1885, the latter leading to German acquisitions in the Pacific area. These territories, officially known as the 'Protectorate of German New Guinea,' consisted of: Kaiser Wilhelm's Land (*Kaiserwilhelmsland*) (the north-eastern part of New Guinea), the Bismarck Archipelago (the Admiralty Islands, Duke of York Islands, Mussau Islands, New Britain, New Hanover, New Ireland, and the Vitu Islands) and the German Solomon Islands (Buka Island, Bougainville) totalling a land area of some 240,000 square kilometres, of which Kaiser Wilhelm's Land accounted for the majority at 179,000 square kilometres. These parts eventually, following acquisitions in later years and the reorganisation of German colonial administration in the Pacific in 1906, became known as the 'Old Protectorate.'[17]

The method of initial acquisition smacks of old-style colonialism; in the middle of 1884 four German gunboats appeared in New Guinea waters and on 3 November the German flag was hoisted at New Britain, followed by similar occurrences in other places throughout the month. The British government was notified officially of these actions only on 19 December.

On 17 May 1885, Wilhelm I granted an Imperial charter to the German New Guinea Company (*Deutsche Neuguinea-Kompanie*) to occupy:

> [...] as 'Kaiser Wilhelm's Land, that portion of New Guinea not under British or Dutch suzerainty, together with the Bismarck Archipelago; subject to the maintenance of the political institutions agreed upon, as well as to the payment of the expenses of administration, the Company was to exercise the corresponding rights of sovereignty.[18]

This exercise in colonial expansion was popular; indeed the German Colonial

Union (Kolonialverein) founded in 1882 had an influence out of proportion to the size of its membership, which in 1884 numbered some 9,000.[19] There were societies with similar aims, including the Society for German Colonisation (Gesellschaft für deutsche Kolonisation), the founding manifesto of which was promulgated in March 1885 by the African explorer Carl Peters. Described by Craig as a 'curious mixture of mountebank, patriot and Jew-baiter', Peters was inspired by a desire to emulate British achievements in the colonial sphere.[20] His manifesto set out the problems, as perceived, and solutions:

> The German nation has been left empty-handed in the partitioning of the world as it has taken place from the beginning of the fifteenth century up to today. All the other civilized nations of Europe have outposts beyond our continent where their language and customs can take firm root and flourish. As soon as the German emigrant has left the borders of the Reich behind him, he is a stranger on foreign territory. The German Empire, mighty and strong through a unity won by blood, has become the leading power on the European continent; but everywhere her sons abroad have to adapt to nations that are either indifferent or even hostile to ours. For centuries, the great stream of German emigration has become assimilated into foreign races and disappeared within them. Germandom outside Europe is constantly in national decline.
>
> In this fact – so incredibly distressing to national pride – lies an enormous economic disadvantage for our people! Year after year, the strength of about 200,000 Germans is lost to our Fatherland! This massive concentration of power usually flows directly into the camp of our economic competitors and increases the strength of our opponents. Foreign branches carry out the German import of products from tropical zones, which causes many millions in German capital to be lost to foreign nations each year! German exports are dependent on the arbitrariness of foreign tariff policies. Our industry lacks a market that is secure under all circumstances, because our nation lacks colonies of its own.
>
> In order to remedy this deplorable national state of affairs, practical and vigorous action is necessary.
>
> With this as a starting point, a society has convened in Berlin whose objective is the practical initiation of such action. The Society for German Colonisation intends to take up the realisation of carefully planned colonizing projects in a resolute and sweeping manner, thus supporting and supplementing the efforts of other organisations with similar aims.
>
> The society has set the following tasks for itself as priorities:
>
> 1. Acquisition of appropriate colonial capital.
> 2. Finding and purchasing suitable territories for colonisation.
> 3. Directing German emigration to these areas.
>
> Filled with the conviction that the energetic launch of this great national mission must not be postponed any longer, we venture to turn to the German people with the request that they actively support the efforts of our society! The German nation has proven repeatedly that it is prepared to make sacrifices for general patriotic endeavours – may it also participate resourcefully in the solution of this great historical question.

Every German whose heart beats for the greatness and honour of our nation is asked to join our society. It is necessary to make up for centuries of oversight and to prove to the world that the German people have inherited not only ancient imperial glory from our forefathers but also their old German-national spirit![21]

There was alas little in the way of 'imperial glory' to be garnered in Kaiser Wilhelm's Land, as the German New Guinea Company was unable to make the venture profitable. Neither did it succeed in attracting any significant emigration from Germany; indeed its activities attracted only opprobrium and the German government was obliged to assume control of the territory in 1899, by which time 'nine million marks had been buried, like the dead, in the soil of Kaiser Wilhelmsland'.[22]

That was for the future of course, and there was a further addition to German territory in 1886 with the acquisition of the Marshall Islands. These had been Spanish territory, but had been somewhat neglected by their 'owner' and both Britain and Germany had began diplomatic moves to safeguard their interests in the area. This had taken the form of a joint note to Spain refusing to acknowledge her sovereignty over the Caroline and Palau islands. On 24 September 1885 Bismarck proposed referring the matter to the arbitration of the Pope, Leo XIII, which was accepted by all parties. The Pope announced his findings on 22 October in a masterful judgement that succeeded in mediating all the conflicting claims, and Germany and Spain, Britain having withdrawn from the dispute, signed an agreement at the Vatican on 17 December 1885. The agreement meant that Spain's claim to the Caroline Islands was formally recognised, though Germany's right to establish naval stations and trading posts there was conceded, while Germany's claim to the Marshall Islands was agreed.[23] This territory, consisting of the Ratak Group in the east and the Ralik Group in the west, number overall some 353 individual islands, which have a total land area of about 400 square kilometres. A German protectorate was formally declared on 13 September 1886.[24]

On 16 April 1888, following an agreement on delineation with Britain – the Anglo-German Convention of 1886 – that placed the territory within its purview, Germany annexed the island of Nauru. This tiny island, with a total area of some 21 square kilometres, was placed, administratively, within the Protectorate of the Marshall Islands.[25]

The Marshall Islands were, like German New Guinea, also to be run by a private company, though in a 'condominium' arrangement with the German government. The agreement was signed on 21 January 1888 granting the Jaluit Company (*Jaluit-Gesselschaft AG*), which had been created a year earlier by the same two companies that had formed the New Guinea Company – Robertson & Hernsheim and the German Trading and Commercial Company – a trading monopoly and obliging it to underwrite administrative duties in the islands. This meant that while the German government appointed officials to administer the territory, the Jaluit Company paid their salaries and all associated administrative costs. This was not a particularly onerous duty; by 1906 the total number of administrative staff had doubled from its original number, and amounted to four personnel. The downside, from the administrator's point of view, was that the company regarded the Marshall Islands very much as its own colony.[26]

Despite these acquisitions being made in the Kaiser's name, it was the Chancellor that directed foreign policy in furtherance of his grand designs.[27] Indeed, Bismarck reserved to himself the 'the main deciding voice in everything' according to the memoirs of Wilhelm II.[28] While these memoirs are decidedly partial and not to be relied on, the ex-Kaiser does make some valid points, as when, for example, he reflects on the relationship between Bismarck and the Imperial German constitution: '[T]he Constitution of the Empire was drawn up so as to fit in with Bismarck's extraordinary preponderance as a statesman; the big cuirassier boots did not fit every man.'[29] That Bismarck had designed the Imperial constitution around the personalities of himself and Kaiser Wilhelm I, a powerful Chancellor and a largely compliant Kaiser, is an un-contentious point to make. How the arrangement was to survive, when one or other of the personalities was to change, as must eventually come to pass via human mortality if nothing else, was not, apparently, an issue that Bismarck had addressed himself to. Indeed, the issue was avoided for a great deal of time simply through the longevity of Wilhelm I, who was not to leave this world until 9 March 1888 aged 91, at which time he had been King of Prussia and Kaiser for 27 and 17 years respectively.

The new King of Prussia, and thus Kaiser, was Frederick III, the former Crown Prince Frederick William. Bismarck distrusted him through a perhaps misplaced fear of his, and his wife's, supposed liberalism, and ensured that, when he was Crown Prince, his influence was minimal. How his personality would have engaged with Bismarck's will never be known, for the year 1888 was the year of the three Kaisers. Frederick, already terminally ill with throat cancer, was to live only 99 days following his accession,[30] being succeeded by his eldest son, who became Kaiser Wilhelm II. The personality of the new Kaiser was quite different to that of his grandfather, and, though only twenty-nine years old upon accession, his reign 'began, as it was to continue, with bombast and swagger'.[31] These were not new characteristics, indeed his own father had, in 1886, noted several unsavoury aspects of Wilhelm's personality, including a 'tendency to brag' and 'overwhelming conceit'.[32] He had been Kaiser for only a little over two years when, in 1891, Baron Frederick von Holstein, the senior counsellor at the Foreign Ministry, wrote: 'I do not put much reliance on the Kaiser's constancy [...] Let us hope he will reach maturity before there is any serious testing time. In any case if we don't want a republic we must take our princes as Providence sends them.'[33]

It was not that Wilhelm was without talent or intelligence. Indeed James W Gerard, the US Ambassador to Germany 1913–17, who was certainly no uncritical admirer, noted his 'extraordinary versatility':

He commands his armies in person. He has won distinction as a writer and a public speaker. He is an excellent shot. He has composed music, written verses, superintended the production of a ballet, painted a picture; the beautiful Byzantine chapel in the Castle of Posen shows his genius for architecture; and, clothed in a clergyman's surplice, he has preached a sermon in Jerusalem.[34]

Gerard, though exaggerating somewhat in his list, also noted another trait, 'Wilhelm [...] might well be called the Restless Emperor. He is never satisfied to remain more than a few days in any place or in any occupation.'[35] Winston Churchill, who had also seen Wilhelm at first hand, included an appreciation of him in his 1937 work *Great Contemporaries*.

> His undeniable cleverness and versatility, his personal grace and vivacity, only aggravated his dangers by concealing his inadequacy. [...] in his own Memoirs [...] he has naively revealed to us his true measure. No more disarming revelation of inherent triviality, lack of understanding and sense of proportion [...] can be imagined. It is shocking to reflect that upon the word or nod of a being so limited there stood attentive and obedient for thirty years the forces which, whenever released, could devastate the world.[36]

Churchill concluded the quoted passage by observing that 'it was not his fault; it was his fate' to be in such a position, but there is another sense in which the turbulence and instability that Wilhelm displayed might not have been his fault. The circumstances surrounding his birth, which left him suffering from Erb's palsy of the left arm, and the effect this had on his development have been commented on often. For example:

> Wilhelm had as much intelligence as any European sovereign and more than most, but his lack of discipline, his self-indulgence, his overdeveloped sense of theatre, and his fundamental misreading of history prevented him from putting it to effective use. [...] his formal education had been neither thorough nor balanced, partly because he was preoccupied in his youth by his determination to overcome the physical handicap of having been born with an almost useless left arm and partly because of differences with his parents. But he never admitted any deficiency in this respect or tried seriously to repair it.[37]

Physical handicap is no bar to the development of intellect, or the successful holding of high political office. Lord Halifax, Franklin Roosevelt and Josef Stalin spring to mind in this regard, though the latter two were not born handicapped. However it might be the case that the birth trauma suffered by Wilhelm left him suffering from 'minimal brain damage' caused by oxygen starvation: 'It is likely that the future Kaiser was hypoxic (deprived of adequate supply of oxygen) for eight to ten minutes, possibly even longer [...].'[38] This hypothesis explains a great deal if correct, but there is of course no way of confirming it.

The reign of Wilhelm II continues to provoke strong interest among historians of Germany, manifested by the continuing appearance of hugely impressive works on the subject, such as for example those by J. C. G. Röhl, Lamar Cecil, Roderick R. McLean, Volker Berghahn, James Retallack, Christoper Clark and others. Despite, or perhaps because of, the breadth and depth of the studies devoted to his rule and personality, there is no real consensus on his exact responsibility for the direction Germany took under his auspices. His impulsive comments, actions, and orders created misunderstandings, diplomatic crises, and personal insults, which in turn led to estrangement and suspicion in the relations between Germany and the Great Powers.[39]

The new Kaiser wanted to rule as well as reign; unlike his grandfather he was not content with the constitutional fiction that the Kaiser made the decisions while the Chancellor put them into effect. Indeed, there was no space within the constitution Bismarck had designed for two people to be in charge of policy, and since only death could remove the Kaiser, it was the Chancellor that had to go. Bismarck resigned on 17 March 1890, at age 75, to be succeeded as Imperial Chancellor and Minister-President of Prussia by General Count Georg Leo von Caprivi.

With Bismarck's removal the way now lay open for Kaiser Wilhelm II to take over personal control of German policy. In the foreign sphere this was aided by the resignation of Herbert Bismarck from the position of State Secretary, being replaced by the Ambassador of the Grand Duchy of Baden in Berlin, Baron Adolf Marshall von Bieberstein. The dangers which this step entailed for the monarchy were clearly recognised by some, among them Wilhelm's former tutor Dr Georg Ernst Hinzpeter, who wrote some five years after Bismarck's dismissal:

> That catastrophe was nothing other than an attempt by the monarchy to free itself from the suffocating hold of the bureaucracy. It seems that by an extraordinary effort of strength the attempt succeeded. The responsibility which the monarchy thereby took upon itself is very great. If it does not prove itself equal to this responsibility, it has incurred a danger which may bring about its destruction.[40]

Count Caprivi had been a career officer in the Prussian Army, seeing action in Bismarck's 'Wars of [German] Unification' – the 1864 Schleswig-Holstein War of Succession (German–Danish War), the Austro-Prussian War of 1866 and the Franco-Prussian War of 1870–71 – and had served as Chief of the Admiralty from 1883 to 1888, an appointment greeted with dismay by the naval officer corps.[41]

During Lieutenant General Caprivi's tenure, and under his direction, Imperial Germany began construction of its first five modern steel cruisers, including the 4,300-tonne protected cruisers *Prinzess Wilhelm* (1887) and *Irene* (1888). Caprivi rejected cruiser warfare as being of minimal benefit to Germany in terms of conflict with France or Russia. Where he did see them of utility was in policing and, if necessary, defending the colonial empire that Bismarck had acquired. He also created the Torpedo Inspection section in Kiel and appointed one Alfred Tirpitz as its head. Caprivi was not interested in acquiring a large navy, adjudging that any such establishment would drain resources from the Army, which was the key to Germany's survival in his view.[42] He had resigned in 1888, following the accession of Wilhelm II, after the new Kaiser decided to split the command of the Navy and thus downgrade somewhat his position.[43] General Caprivi's next command was of Prussia's X Army Corps at Hanover, where he remained until March 1890, when he was appointed Chancellor.

The new Chancellor's appointment it seems came as something of a surprise to many, not least of all to Caprivi himself.[44] In domestic policy Caprivi was to pursue what was termed the 'New Course', inasmuch as, broadly speaking, he sought to conciliate the 'enemies of the realm' rather than attempt to marginalise or diminish them like his predecessor.

In foreign policy terms Bieberstein, who had no foreign diplomatic experience beyond representing his Duchy in Berlin, ostensibly, guided Caprivi. In reality however the new director of German foreign policy was Friedrich von Holstein, the head of the political department of the German Foreign Office.[45] Holstein is something of a shadowy figure in the history of Imperial Germany. He disdained publicity and lived a life of almost total anonymity, preferring to wield his influence, which was at times considerable, from behind the scenes as it were. As a young man, aged twenty-nine, he had been on the staff of the embassy in Washington where, during the winter months of 1866–67, Holstein had developed a friendship with Alice Mason Hooper, the twenty-eight-year-old wife of US Senator Charles Sumner. Sumner, who was some thirty years senior, had only married Hooper in October 1866, and so her being seen publicly with Holstein caused much gossip and provided ammunition his for political opponents. It seems that when confronted with this Hooper refused to terminate the friendship, and when Holstein was then recalled to Prussia in early 1867, she held her husband responsible for engineering his removal.[46] The true nature of the relationship will never be known, but in any event Holstein never married and lived only for his work, though he had a passionate taste for exotic gourmet food, and *Schnitzel à la Holstein*, 'the most elegant of all the *schnitzels*' was created for him.[47]

Holstein, the 'Grey Eminence', supposed himself the inheritor of Bismarck's mantle, but was burdened by preconceptions regarding the interests of other nations; or rather how those nations might have viewed their interests within a given context. He was sure that there could be no understanding between Britain and France. He was even more convinced of the implausibility of any Anglo-Russian understanding.[48]

As it happened, 1890 was the year when Bismarck's Reinsurance Treaty with Russia was due for renewal, and it was an agreement that Holstein opposed. Accordingly, he approached Caprivi, who probably had no knowledge of it, and advised against renewal; not only did Holstein see Russia as a threat in herself, but he feared that if Austria-Hungary learned of such an agreement then Germany's relations with her would be harmed. Holstein felt that Germany needed Austria-Hungary as a balance to Russia, and that the treaty, which he characterised as a 'bigamous relationship', prevented Germany developing an understanding with Britain.[49]

Caprivi, confident in Holstein's mastery of the subject, then advised Wilhelm that the treaty should be allowed to lapse, a point with which the Kaiser concurred despite having previously intimated to the Russian ambassador that it would be renewed. The non-extension of the Reinsurance Treaty with Russia has been seen as one of the turning points of German history, setting in train the process of diplomatic isolation that was to become more pronounced over the next two decades.[50] One of the balls that Bismarck had been credited with successfully juggling had fallen to the ground, and France was only too keen to pick it up. Within three years Russia joined France in an alliance.

It has been convincingly argued that the changed, and changing, circumstances within which German foreign policy was conducted in the 1890s, as compared to those that had pertained during Bismarck's earlier years, made a realignment inevitable in any event.[51] Indeed, Bismarck's 'system' as a whole was decrepit before the departure of its architect. As J. C. G. Röhl most elegantly stated it:

> As Bismarck grew older, the Government's dilemma presented itself with increasing clarity. Bismarck's autocracy was intolerable and his pedantic insistence on formal distinctions seriously hindered efficient government. There was a widespread feeling that the Government must accustom itself to take decisions collectively, as other governments did. And yet Bismarck's autocracy was necessary to hold the conglomerate departments together.[52]

Thus is delineated one of the abiding problems and contradictions of Bismarck's system. However, whatever the faults with that system, Holstein, Caprivi and the Kaiser, had gratuitously knocked away one of the cornerstones of Bismarckian diplomacy without having anything to put in its place.

One notable achievement of Caprivi's Chancellorship was the negotiation of the Anglo-German Treaty, signed at Berlin on 1 July 1890. The treaty codi-fied agreements reached 'on various issues pertaining to the colonial interests of Germany and Great Britain'. It settled respective 'spheres of influence' and borders in East Africa (Articles I–II), South West Africa (Article III), and West Africa (Article IV). However, perhaps the most notable feature of this accord were Articles XI and XII. Under the former Germany agreed 'to recognise the British protectorate over the remaining territories of the Sultan of Zanzibar, including the islands of Zanzibar and Pemba', while the latter granted 'sovereignty over the Island of Heligoland [in the North Sea] and all its facilities to His Majesty the German Kaiser'. It was through this exchange of territory that the agreement became popularly known as the 'Heligoland–Zanzibar Treaty'.[53]

Bismarck had prepared the groundwork for the treaty with the object of allevi-ating any areas of tension with Britain. He was not, as has been noted, interested in acquiring further territory in Africa, and because the agreement settled 'spheres of interest' and thus precluded Germany from expanding its colonial territory it was condemned in 'chauvinist circles of the German bourgeoisie' and led to the formation of the General German League, later to become the Pan German League.[54] Their view of the treaty was vitriolic: 'With one stroke of the pen – the hope of a great German colonial empire was ruined.'[55]

Despite the chauvinistic sentiments of some, it would be hard to argue that the agreement, particularly in relation to Heligoland, was not favourable to Germany; the island being strategically placed in relation to the important German ports of Bremerhaven and Cuxhaven, situated at the mouths of the River Weser and Elbe respectively. Brunsbüttel, on the northern bank of the Elbe, was also to become the western terminus of the Kaiser Wilhelm Canal. Constructed from 1887 to 1895, and widened and improved between 1907 and 1918, this waterway from Kiel was of crucial strategic importance for any German Fleet, inasmuch as it facilitated the passage of warships from the Baltic to the North Sea.[56] Had the British retained control of Heligoland, and thus the potential ability to exercise control over the German Bight sea area, the activities of the future High Seas Fleet might have been severely circumscribed.

One of the most curious aspects of the 1890 treaty was the creation of what became known as the 'Caprivi Strip'. Article III had stipulated that 'Germany shall be granted free access from its protectorate to the Zambezi by means of a strip of land not less than twenty English miles (32km) wide at any point'.[57] The purpose of this 460-kilometre corridor, squeezed between Bechuanaland (Botswana) to the south and Northern Rhodesia (Zambia) and Angola to the north, is not mentioned in the treaty, and the rationale behind its acquisition remains obscure.[58]

Caprivi, despite the increasing discomfiture he felt filling the role of Chancellor, remained in the position for four years. Holstein's policy of seeking a closer relationship with Britain was, if it had any chance of success at all, damaged by the 'Chancellor Crisis' that occurred in 1894. Simplistically put, the 'crisis' arose from a conservative backlash against the perceived liberalism of Caprivi's policies. The Count's position had been greatly eroded in 1892 when he had resigned from the post of Minister-President of Prussia after failing to have an educational bill passed by the Prussian Diet, though he retained the Imperial Chancellorship.

This reaction was not instigated by any one particular policy, but was certainly exacerbated by the results of the 1893 Reichstag elections, which saw advances in the vote for the Social Democrats. The 'New Course' seemed to have failed and, far from being conciliated, the 'enemies of the realm' appeared to be gaining in popularity. Terrified by the potential threat these subversive forces represented to state and society, a coalition of conservative groupings, headed by Count Botho zu Eulenburg, Caprivi's replacement as Prussian Minister-President, powerfully represented the dangers as they saw them to the Kaiser. The Kaiser was receptive to such overtures and plans for the legal suppression of Social Democracy, and even a top-down coup d'état, were discussed within his circle. Both were opposed by Caprivi, and faced with such an impasse the Kaiser dismissed both Caprivi and Eulenburg. The event demonstrated the Kaiser's autocratic tendencies and, in hindsight, marked the beginning of his 'personal rule'.59

Caprivi's successor was another, on the face of it, somewhat unlikely candidate; Chlodwig Karl Victor, Prince of Hohenlohe-Schillingsfürst, more familiarly known as Prince Chlodwig zu Hohenlohe-Schillingsfürst, or simply Hohenlohe. Aged 75 and somewhat infirm in health, Hohenlohe did however bring immense administrative skill to the job.[60] All his considerable political skills were to be required in his handling of the Kaiser, who was determined to raise Germany to the status of a world power. In this determination he was acting in line with 'public opinion'.[61] In 1896 the German government openly adopted a global foreign policy, entitled World Policy or *Weltpolitik*, that was reoriented away from Europe; Bismarck's 'map of Africa' had been shifted.[62]

It was however events in East Asia that were to provide the impetus for German colonial expansion, and to cause difficulties with Japan. Japanese–German relations were, following initial diplomatic exchanges in 1861, friendly, and, on the

German side, influential. These influences have been discerned in the Japanese Constitution of 1889 and in the military field.[63] This friendliness, and concomitant influence, was however severely dented by the actions and utterances of Germany, and her Imperial Ruler respectively, in the aftermath of the Sino-Japanese War of 1894–95.

The causes and course of this conflict, ostensibly over the status of Korea, need not overmuch concern us here, but it was to radically alter the geopolitical situation in the East Asia/Western Pacific, and in its outcome engineer a complete reversal of the Far Eastern balance of power.[64] The hostilities began officially on 1 August 1894 with mutual declarations of war, though serious fighting had been taking place previously, and was swiftly followed by severe Chinese setbacks both military and naval. By 21 November the Japanese had driven the Chinese forces out of Korea and taken the strategically important Port Arthur (Lüshun) and the Liaotung (Liaodong) Peninsula, which, potentially, gave them strategic control of the northern Yellow Sea. By March 1895 the Japanese had severely mauled the Chinese Imperial Navy during the Battle of Yalu River on 17 September 1894, which had then retired to Weihaiwei. This naval base fell to the Japanese Second Army, following a campaign lasting from 20 January to 12 February 1895. Japan also seized the Pescadore Islands[65] forcing the Chinese to the realisation that a negotiated settlement was urgently required.[66]

Forced thus to the negotiating table China signed a treaty with Japan on 17 April, known from the location of its settlement as the Treaty of Shimonoseki. This treaty, ratified on 8 May 1895, removed Korea from Chinese influence, ostensibly at least guaranteeing it absolute independence, and ceded the Liaodong Peninsula, together with Port Arthur, Formosa and the Pescadore Islands to Japan. There was also a large indemnity, and the victory led to a great upsurge of nationalistic feeling in Japan.[67]

This feeling was then greatly inflamed by the actions of Russia, Germany and France when, on 23 April, their representatives called on the Japanese Foreign Ministry to offer some 'friendly advice'. They recommended that Japan return the Liaodong Peninsula to China on the grounds that Japanese possession of it 'would be a constant menace to the capital of China, would at the same time render illusory the independence of Korea, and would henceforth be a perpetual obstacle to the peace in the Far East'.[68]

This intervention had been instigated by Russia with Germany supporting the move for reasons of 'high policy'.[69] Hohenlohe was to receive the thanks of the Tsar for this support, as he recorded in his journal: '[T]he [Tsar] expressed his satisfaction that we had acted in concert with him, and was pleased when I told him that were guided therein by the desire of manifesting our good relations with Russia'.[70]

Russian motives for not wishing to see Japan in possession of Port Arthur were obvious and, to the Japanese, comprehensible even if unwelcome; at a meeting on 11 April 1895 Russian Finance Minister Count Sergei Witte stated that if action were not taken he foresaw the day when 'the Mikado might become the Chinese emperor and Russia would need hundreds of thousands of troops [...] to defend

Map 2. Kaiser Wilhelm's Land, the Bismarck Archipelago and the Island Territories

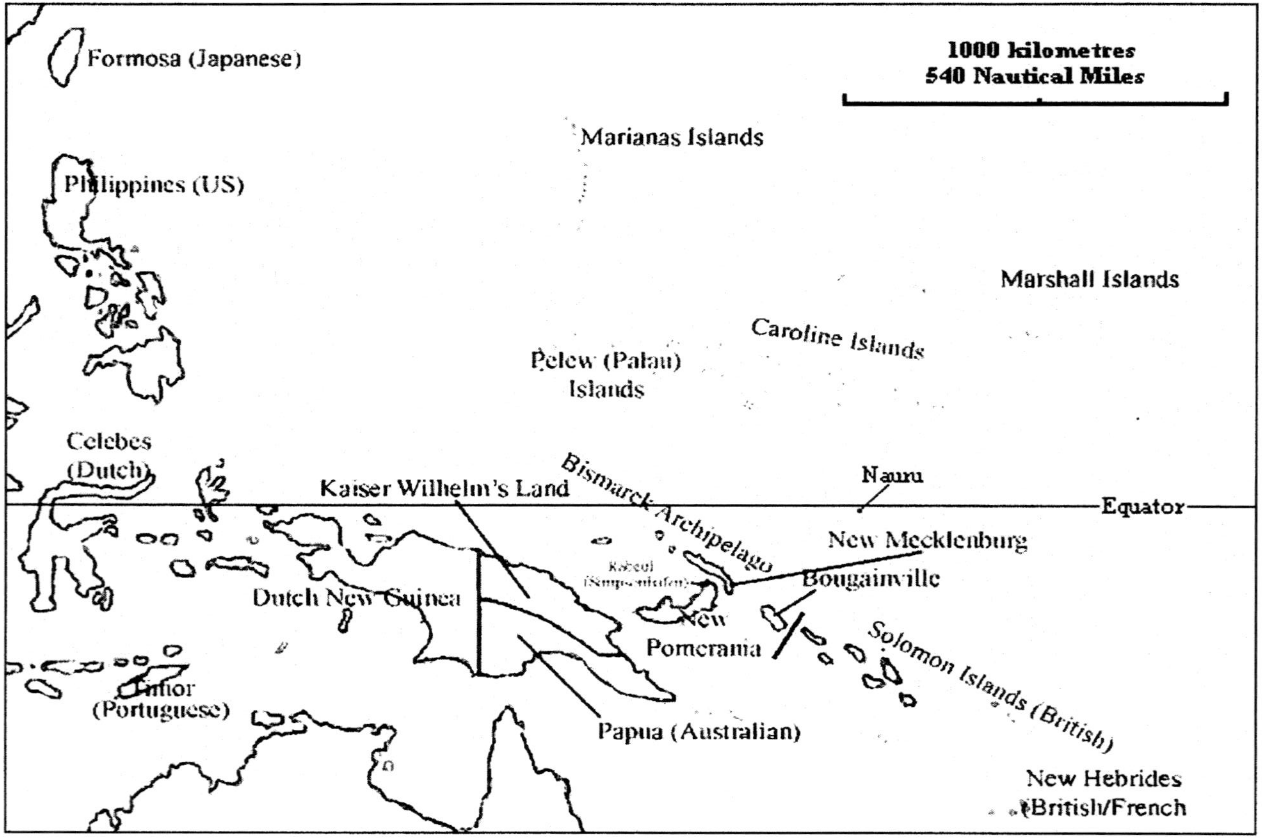

1000 kilometres
540 Nautical Miles

Formosa (Japanese)

Philippines (US)

Celebes (Dutch)

Timor (Portuguese)

Dutch New Guinea

Kaiser Wilhelm's Land

Bismarck Archipelago

Kabaul (Simpsonhafen)

New Pomerania

Papua (Australian)

New Mecklenburg

Bougainville

Nauru

Marianas Islands

Pelew (Palau) Islands

Caroline Islands

Marshall Islands

Solomon Islands (British)

Equator

New Hebrides (British/French)

her possessions'.[71] Germany's motives were unclear, and delivered in an abrupt and intimidating way by Felix von Gutschmid, Germany's representative in Japan 1892–97. The Japanese, it has been argued, considered Germany to have been the prime mover behind the advice, indeed Gutschmid's tone was such that the advice could hardly be reckoned on as friendly.[72] That this had, to some extent, affected Japanese–German relations was acknowledged by Prince Bernhard von Bülow, the Chancellor some years later:

> Our relations with [Japan] received a severe shock when, in 1895, we together with France and Russia forced victorious Japan to reduce her demands on China. When we thus interfered with Japan we lost much of the sympathy which she had for many years accorded us, and we did not earn particular gratitude from France and Russia.[73]

Bülow was to argue, in 1907, that Gutschmid had exceeded his instructions. This followed upon him receiving a report of the encounter and the way in which the message had been delivered, sent to him by one of Gutschmid's successors, Alfons Mumm von Schwarzenstein, German representative in Japan 1906–11. Schwarzenstein informed the Chancellor that the Japanese had told him that Gutschmid initially threatened war if they did not comply:

> feeling in Japan against Germany dated from the time of Germany's joint intervention with France and Russia in 1895. It was a misfortune that Baron Gutschmid, with his violent character, was the German representative just then.

> [Gutschmid] enjoyed the opportunity for humiliating Japan. [The] Vice-Minister for Foreign Affairs, [...] had received the declarations from the three Ministers [...] The declarations were identical in form, but the French Minister [...] and even the Russian, [...] had used conciliatory expressions throughout [...] while Baron Gutschmid added to his own a long written statement, in which he – and he alone – baldly threatened war.[74]

No doubt influenced, whether wittingly or not, by the doctrine popularly associated with Lord Palmerston whereby a state does not have friends, only interests, the Japanese, according to Schwarzenstein, kept the document that Gutschmid, a most un-diplomatic diplomat it seems, had presented to them a secret.[75]

Whatever the manner in which the matter was put to them however, it was clear to Japan that they could not hope to prevail against the combined naval power of the three powers should it come to conflict. Resistance was therefore futile, and might even have led to the loss of the other territory Japan had gained.[76] The humiliation to Japan was perhaps mitigated by the formulation of an appropriate form of words by which to announce the step down. On 10 May 1895 the emperor issued an Imperial Rescript:

> By concluding the Treaty of Peace, China has already shown her sincerity of regret for the violation of her engagements and thereby the justice of our cause has been proclaimed to the world. Under these circumstances, we can find nothing to impair

the honour and dignity of our empire if we now yield to the dictates of magnanimity and, taking into consideration the general situation, accept the advice of
the friendly powers.[77]

The treaty of retrocession was signed in Peking on 7–8 November 1895, and the
Japanese completed their evacuation of the Liaodong Peninsula and Port Arthur
on Christmas Day. Despite the 'magnanimity' of the withdrawal, it was clear to
Japan that what had prevailed was military force and that if Japan wished to
compete with the European powers then she could only do so by being equally as
powerful. Foreign Minister Count Munemitsu Mutsu concluded that 'diplomacy
shorn of military support will not succeed, however legitimate its aims might be'.[78]

   Kaiser Wilhelm also drew lessons from the conflict; he became obsessed with
the threat that he saw emanating in the East, terming it, though he did not coin
the phrase, the 'Yellow Peril'. As a graphic illustration of this perceived threat he
penned a sketch, and commissioned his favourite artist, Hermann Knackfuss, to
produce a full-scale version. Knackfuss, categorised as a 'mediocre painter', duly
obliged with an effort entitled *Völker Europas, wahrt eure heiligsten Güter!* (Peoples
of Europe, Protect your Holiest Goods!). The painting depicts the Archangel
Michael exhorting a cohort of feminine warriors representing the peoples of
Europe, Britannia, Marianne, etc., to do battle with the 'Yellow Peril' approaching
from the East, depicted as a Buddha figure riding a dragon.[79] Copies of this
painting were widely distributed, to royal relatives all over Europe as well as every
embassy in Berlin. While both the composition and subject matter tell us more
about the instigator than they do about the reality of the situation, those at whom
it was aimed did not necessarily appreciate this at the time.

   Indeed it has been argued that the Kaiser's pronouncements 'completely
changed' the Japanese perception of Germany, a state previously regarded both
as a mentor and friend, a view reinforced by the continuing statements of the
Kaiser regarding the 'Yellow Peril'.[80] Although the Kaiser's pronouncements were
not always in accordance with the policies pursued by 'his' foreign office, contemporary Japanese opinion was, on occasion, unable to discern this and so feelings
of antagonism were unnecessarily caused.[81] German diplomatic interference in the
area, and the Kaiser's pronouncements, however bizarre, did not however count
for as much as German action, and that Germany was capable of action in the
area was to be demonstrated to all within two years of the diplomatic intervention
with the seizure, at the point of a gun, of Chinese territory.

2

The Acquisition of Kiautschou: 1897

There was a pressing need, as viewed from the German Admiralty, for a permanent base in the Pacific area to accommodate the vessels of the East Asiatic Cruiser Division. A precursor to this force had been formed in the early 1880s, and its importance had grown commensurately with the acquisition of colonial territories. It became a permanently constituted unit in September 1894 following the outbreak of the Sino-Japanese War the previous August. Contemporary practice designated a division as a four-ship unit under the command of a rear admiral; the first holder being Paul Hoffman who took up position in November. The four warships in the command comprised three *Carola*-class iron flush-decked corvettes, *Alexandrine*, *Arcona* and *Marie*, and the newer *Irene II*-class protected cruiser-corvette *Irene*. Hoffman's orders enjoined him to protect German interests in the region generally, and to seek out potential sites for a permanent base.[1]

Both the composition of the Cruiser Division, the *Carola*-class vessels were obsolete when constructed, and the lack of dedicated facilities greatly hampered the operational efficiency of the unit. It was however easier to increase the potency of the division by attaching more powerful vessels to it, *Alexandrine* and *Marie* being replaced by the *Kaiser*-class central battery ironclad *Kaiser* and *Prinzess Wilhelm*, sister of *Irene*, in January 1895, than it was to establish a permanent base. Hoffman's successor, from 1896, was Rear Admiral Alfred von Tirpitz, and as he was to later put it: 'The lack of a base hampered us because the sole factor of power [...] was our flying squadron [*sic*], and the existence of this depended upon the Hong-Kong docks and consequently upon the favour of Britain.'[2] The docks, Tirpitz noted, had to be booked nine months in advance[3] and 'our Eastern Asiatic Squadron [*sic*] could be rendered useless on the slightest provocation by [their] refusal'.[4] Alternative facilities in Japan and China had been refused to Hoffman during the Sino-Japanese conflict.[5]

Though Tirpitz was later to claim that he came to the conclusion that Kiautschou Bay was the ideal site for a German naval base, the matter was undecided when he was recalled to Berlin to become Navy Secretary and begin planning a German battle-fleet. The future Grand Admiral handed over his command to the next most senior officer in the squadron, Captain Hugo Zeye,[6] and returned to Berlin in March 1897, a time that coincided with a change in personnel at the Foreign Office. State Secretary Adolf Marschall von Bieberstein, who had succeeded Herbert Bismarck in 1890 under Caprivi's chancellorship, resigned and was replaced, in June, by Bernhard von Bülow, who was expected to follow a more expansionist policy.

Tirpitz's successor was Rear Admiral Otto von Diederichs, a former instructor of naval history and strategy at the Kiel Marine Academy.[7] Diederichs left Berlin on 1 May 1897, finally arriving at Shanghai on 10 June whereupon he was compelled to wait three days pending the arrival of the divisional flagship *Kaiser*. During this sojourn he discovered he was sharing the hotel with a colleague; the chief of engineering at Kiel, Georg Ludwig Franzius, who was later to design the 128-metre span transporter bridge at the seaport constructed in 1909–10. Franzius had been dispatched to China to survey the various locales deemed potential sites for Germany's proposed naval base, and had, in May 1897, decided that Kiaut-schou offered the best prospects on several counts, including the potential for economic development.

The economic potential of the area had already been discovered, and enumerated, by the German geologist, geographer and explorer Ferdinand Baron von Richthofen. The uncle of the 'Red Baron' of Great War fame, and 'the most important Western researcher on China of his time',[8] Richthofen had undertaken several far-reaching journeys through China during the 1860s and 1870s, with the results being recorded in a massive six-volume work that appeared between 1877 and 1912; the final volumes posthumously. The area had become directly known to Germany, or at least Prussia, in 1860 when three Prussian warships, *Arkona*, *Frauenlob* and *Thetis*, had anchored in Kiautschou Bay as part of an attempt, successful as it turned out, to open trade links with China. The resultant treaty, giving the parties most favoured nation status, was dated 2 September 1861.[9]

Following his return to Germany in August 1897, Franzius therefore recommended Kiautschou as the best site for the base.[10] There was, as far as Germany was concerned, one potential problem; it was possible that the Russians had a prior claim through the concept of 'first anchoring', though this entire principle was dismissed retrospectively by Tirpitz. If this principle were adhered to, he stated, it would mean that 'England could claim not only Tsingtau, but the whole world, because Englishmen had at one time or another anchored everywhere.'[11] That the Chinese might have an opinion on the matter was not a factor that featured in the calculation.

While the various organs of the German government, Foreign Office, Navy and Kaiser, were now singing from the same, metaphorical, hymn sheet, there was another grouping, singing from a literal hymn sheet, that held more or less identical views and sought to implement them; the German missionaries of the Society of the Divine Word (SVD). There were different German missionary groupings in Shantung (Shandong) Province and Esherick, who has studied the matter deeply, categorises them thus: 'Protestants were on the whole a good deal less disruptive than the Catholics [...] and of the Catholics, none were more disruptive than the new order which entered the field in the 1880s – the German missionaries of the Society of the Divine Word (S.V.D.).'[12]

Otherwise known as the Steyler Mission, the local head of this organization was Johann Baptist von Anzer, who had been in China since 1879. He was appointed Bishop of Shantung in 1886, and he has been described as 'the most powerful and most vigorously colonialist' of all the German missionaries in the province.[13] Anzer had a close relationship with the German Foreign Office, and in March 1896, he complained to them that the Chinese, due to their perception of Germany's weakness, no longer respected him.[14] Indeed, it has been argued, his policy during his tenure up until 1897 was designed to engineer German military intervention through provoking an incident with the indigenous population.[15]

This policy was ultimately successful when, on 1 November 1897, two German missionaries, Richard Henle and Francis Xavier Nies, were hacked to death by a band of twenty to thirty armed men at Yen-chu-fu in Shantung Province.[16]

When this news reached Berlin the Kaiser sprang into action, writing to the Foreign Office on 6 November:

> I have just read in the press the news of the attack on the German Catholic Mission in Shantung, which is under my protection. Full atonement for this must be exacted through vigorous intervention by the fleet [...] I am now quite determined to give up our excessively cautious policy, which is already regarded as weak throughout East Asia, and to use all severity and if necessary the most brutal ruthlessness towards the Chinese, to show at long last that the German Kaiser is not to be trifled with, and that it is a bad thing to have him as an enemy [...] Energetic action is all the more called for because it will enable me to prove once again to my Catholic subjects, including the ultramontanes, that their well being is as close to my heart as that of, and they can count on my protection as much as, my other subjects.[17]

The 'vigorous intervention by the fleet' came in the form of an order Wilhelm commanded be transmitted to Diederichs. The order read: 'Proceed at once [to] Kiautschou with your whole squadron, occupy appropriate positions and places there and then exact full atonement in the way which seems the most appropriate to you. The greatest possible vigour is ordered. The goal of your voyage is to be kept secret.'[18]

Admiral Diederichs was at Shanghai with two of his vessels, *Kaiser* and *Prinzess Wilhelm*, when he received the order on 8 November. He replied to the head of the Navy High Command, Vice Admiral Eduard von Knorr, that he would 'immediately proceed against Kiautschou with [the] greatest energy'.[19] Two ships of the division were unavailable to him; *Arcona* was in dock at Shanghai and *Irene* similarly indisposed at Hong Kong. He could however call upon the services of the *Bussard*-class light cruiser *Cormoran*, which had been assigned to East Asia but was not formally a member of his command, though the vessel was far upriver of Shanghai, at Wuhan (Wuchang) and could not join him immediately.[20] Nevertheless, even with this attenuated force, Diederichs calculated that he could carry out his orders and, observing secrecy as per his orders, proceeded to sea with *Kaiser* on 10 November leaving the other two vessels to rendezvous with him later.

Meanwhile, in Berlin the Reich Chancellor, Hohenlohe, had been throwing cold water on the operation by putting some of the realities of the situation to the Kaiser:

If Your Majesty [...] wishes to give the squadron commander orders to take action at once, it might be necessary to choose somewhere other than Kiautschou, as in order to occupy Kiautschou in accordance with the agreement reached between Your majesty and the [Tsar] at Peterhof, Russian consent would have to be sought.[21]

Still in full flow, and at this time undeterred by diplomatic considerations, Wilhelm telegraphed to Tsar Nicholas II, seeking approval for the operation he had set in motion, and justifying it by recourse to a 'conversation' he recalled having taken place:

Chinese attacked German missions, Shantung, inflicting loss of life and property. I trust you approve according to our conversation Peterhof my sending German squadron to Kiautschou, as it is the only port available to operate from as a base against Marauders. I am under obligations to Catholic party in Germany to show that their missions are really safe under my protectorate.[22]

He received the following reply:

I am very grateful that you informed me personally. Regret attack by Chinese on German Catholic missions under your protectorate. Cannot approve nor disapprove your sending German squadron to Kiautschou as I lately learned that this harbour only had been temporarily ours in 1895–1896. I feel anxious lest perhaps severity may cause unrest and insecurity in Eastern China and widen the breach between Chinese and Christians.[23]

The Kaiser, taking this as approval of his behaviour fired off messages to his Chancellor, stating 'we must use this excellent opportunity without delay, before another great power provokes China or comes to her aid! Now or never';[24] and his recently appointed Foreign Secretary, who was in Rome:

Our conversation about [Kiautschou] [...] at the end of which you said that it was high time to stiffen up our tepid and vacillating policy in the Far East, has had a quick result, quicker than we imagined. Yesterday I received official information of an attack, with murder and robbery, on the German missionary station at Yen-chu-fu in Shantung. So the Chinese have at last given us the grounds and the 'incident' which your predecessor, [Baron Adolf Marschall von Bieberstein] so long desired. [...]

The message to the Admiral contains instructions to proceed at once to [Kiautschou] and seize it, threaten reprisals and act with energy.[25]

Wilhelm also reported the misgivings of his Reich Chancellor:

Today the Chancellor informed me that this intention would be a breach of the Peterhof Agreements, and that it must first be ascertained how the Russian Government would feel towards this enterprise. [...] However humiliating it may be for the German Empire to be obliged almost to obtain permission in St Petersburg to protect and avenge the Christians in China who are committed to its care, and also to help itself to a spot which it refrained from occupying three years ago out of excessive modesty – and to which there could have been no objection.[26]

Bülow was also apprised of the Tsar's anxieties vis-à-vis severe action causing a rift between the Chinese and Christians, but these concerns were utterly dismissed by the Kaiser:

> I do not share this anxiety. Thousands of German Christians will breathe a sigh of relief when they hear that the German Kaiser's ships are near by, hundreds of German traders will exult in the knowledge that the German Reich has won a firm foothold in Asia, hundred of thousands of Chinese will tremble when they feel the iron fist of the German Reich bearing down on their necks, and the whole German Reich will rejoice that its government has done a manly deed [...] but let the world learn the lesson once and for all from this incident, that where I am concerned: *Nemo me impune lacessit* ('No-one provokes me with impunity' – coincidentally(?) the motto of the British Royal Family in Scotland). [27]

The 'Peterhof Agreements', so called, mentioned by Hohenlohe were the outcome of diplomacy that had attended the Kaiser's visit to Russia, accompanied by the Chancellor and Bülow (then Acting Secretary of Foreign Affairs), from 7 to 10 August 1897. While on this visit the Germans had stayed at Peterhof, a site located south-west of the Russian capital St Petersburg. This 'palace, fountain and park ensemble' was begun at the behest of Peter the Great in 1714. [28]

We only have what transpired between Tsar and Kaiser at several removes, but it seems as if the Kaiser, at least to his own satisfaction, received the approval of the Tsar for Germany to take Kiautschou. Count Sergei Witte, at the time the Russian finance minister and later the constitutional prime minister of the Russian Empire 1905–6, put it thus in his memoirs:

> During the German Kaiser's stay at Peterhof there occurred an incident which was destined to have the most far-reaching effects upon the course of Russian history. It was afterwards related to me by Grand Duke Alezey Alexandrovich. Once when the two emperors were driving alone out in the country, so [the Tsar] told the Grand Duke, the German Kaiser asked his host whether Russia had any use for the Chinese Port of Kiautschou. He added that he would like to occupy that port and use it as a base for German shipping, but that he did not wish to take the step without his, [the Tsar's] consent. [The Tsar] did not tell the Grand Duke whether or not he actually gave his consent to the occupation of Kiautschou. What he did say was that his guest had placed him in an awkward position and the whole incident was extremely distasteful to him. I have but little doubt that [the Tsar], who is exceedingly well-mannered, found it impossible to refuse his guest's request point-blank and that the latter interpreted this attitude as indirect approval and implied consent. Some time later, Count Muraviev,[29] in discussing with me my opposition to the occupation of Port Arthur, let the cat out of the bag. He admitted that we had, in his words, 'rashly given our consent to the step which Germany had taken'.[30]

Whatever the Tsar had agreed with his cousin Wilhelm, or what Wilhelm thought he had agreed, the Russian government was, as Hohenlohe had warned, not acquiescent in the German manoeuvre. This was demonstrated on 10 November 1897 when the Kaiser was apprised of the views of that government via a telegram from the German chargé d'affaires in St Petersburg. This set out the views of Foreign Minister Count Mikhail Muraviev as expressed to the diplomat:

> As regards Russia's right to Kiautschou Bay, he had at the time (during 1895–96) received from China not only the right to use the harbour, but also the *droit du premier mouillage* [right of first anchoring], i.e., a promise that if the harbour was to be handed over to a foreign Power, Russia should under all circumstances be assured of the preference.
>
> For the safeguarding of these rights the Russian Commander of the squadron in the Far East had been commanded to send Russian ships into that harbour, the moment that any German ships entered it. But the Russian ships would not participate in our action in obtaining satisfaction for the murder of the missionaries. [...] Count Muraviev, deplored the Imperial Government's step. The result would be that the British, and perhaps even the French, would send ships into Kiautschou Bay, and this could not be prevented; so that what would happen would just be what least suited both our interests; the harbour would become open first to England, and then to all nations. Moreover it was an open question what China's attitude would be towards a forcible seizure of the harbour. Finally Count Muravieff said that so far he had discussed the matter with no one.
>
> The Russian Minister thus declares clearly enough that the Emperor Nicholas' Government has no intention of letting any other Power have Kiautschou, but wishes to take it itself, supposing China loses it.[31]

The last sentence was annotated by Wilhelm 'The direct contrary of what he and his Master both said to me at Peterhof.' The German Foreign Office now became alarmed at the turn events were taking, with Holstein warning the Chancellor on 9 November that 'the Russian declaration is so brutally explicit that it scarcely seems necessary to give the Kaiser any advice. He alone will know whether he wants war with Russia or not. We shall now have to be very careful with our action in China.'[32]

Hohenlohe was alarmed at the potentiality for the dispute to escalate into conflict, particularly if the Kaiser once again decided to intervene personally with the Russians. 'Things really look very bad' was the message he sent to Wolfgang von Rotenhan the under secretary of State at the Foreign Office on 10 November. He seemed not to think however that there was any imminence of war, provided nothing was done to inflame the situation: 'The Russians are [only] trying to frighten us. I cannot believe that the [Tsar] will declare war on us because of Kiautschou Bay.' The peril, as he perceived it, was his headstrong monarch: 'There is a danger that [the Kaiser] will send a telegram to the [Tsar] at once. And what will it say?'[33] It is perhaps remarkable that the Kaiser remained, by his standards, cool and collected and did not send an inflammatory telegram to the Russians. His logic was explained to the Foreign office on 11 November:

> Count Muraviev's note corresponds perfectly to the character of this mendacious gentleman [...] We should attempt to come to an arrangement with Russia to acquire the rights to Kiautschou, if necessary by purchase. Even Russia will yield

to a fait accompli, and will certainly not start a war on account of Kiautschou, as she needs us in the East.[34]

It was, in any case something of an academic debate, because Otto von Diederichs, having received his orders, could not be recalled once he had sailed on 10 November. The *Kaiser* rendezvoused with *Prinzess Wilhelm* and *Cormoran* at sea on 12 November, the latter two vessels having departed without arousing suspicion as to the nature of their mission, and set course north for Tsingtau, arriving in Kiautschou Bay on the morning of 13 November.

Diederichs determined on a reconnaissance of the area and accordingly landed at Tsingtau under the guise of a friendly visit later that day. His observations convinced him that even though there was a significant Chinese force in the vicinity, numbering some 3,000 men manning artillery positions and other fortifications, he could succeed in his mission. The Chinese had first become aware that Kiautschou Bay was a vulnerable point on the coast in 1891, and established and maintained the 3,000-strong garrison thereafter.[35] The most notable artillery position had been constructed on a 128-metre promontory that overlooked the bay, the coast and surrounding territory.[36]

The efficiency of this force was however judged to be low by Diederichs, who had also noted that their artillery, which should have covered the proposed landing site, was not operable.[37] Accordingly he re-entered Kiautschou Bay on the morning of 14 November 1897 and, at 8.00a.m. local time, set about landing a party of some 717 officers and ratings. Within an hour, and without fighting, these had gained several strategic points and put the telegraph out of commission. Backed by the guns of the three vessels in the Bay, an ultimatum was delivered to the local Chinese commander in the terms of; remove all your forces within three hours.

Faced with the superior force embodied in the 47 guns of the warships, the Chinese withdrew and at 2.20p.m. the German flag was hoisted. A twenty-one-gun salute, a symbolic demonstration reserved for the most imposing occasions, was ordered in commemoration of the bloodless victory. Diederichs, having made a speech to the Germans, then, in effect, declared himself Governor of the area and issued instructions to the inhabitants of the area occupied to the effect that they should continue as normal. He cautioned them that opposition was futile.[38]

The pretext for all this was of course the murder of Henle and Nies on 1 November, and, at least ostensibly, the German government was awaiting a reply from the Chinese government on the matter. Indeed, on 11 November Hohenlohe, at the urging of Tirpitz who had also become greatly alarmed at the potential consequences of the seizure, had advised the Kaiser that no occupation of Chinese territory should take place until such time as a reply arrived and was deemed unsatisfactory.[39] Perhaps realising that events might be spiralling out of control, Wilhelm accepted this advice. Accordingly, he had a telegram dispatched, via Admiral Hans von Koester, to Diederichs on 13 November telling him to suspend operations against Tsingtau and, if they had already taken place, to ensure that his occupation was deemed temporary.[40]

Diederichs had not received this message, and was unable to do so until, so as to enable him to report the success of his mission, he ordered the repair of the telegraph. Upon having the message decoded the Admiral could only reply that he had already proclaimed German occupation on a permanent basis and that going back on this was impossible.[41] Presentation of this fait accompli seems to have settled the matter in Berlin, and Knorr telegraphed him the following day offering congratulations and informing him that his proclamation remained in effect.[42]

This news galvanised the Kaiser, who made it perfectly clear on 15 November that he stood four-square behind Diederichs, and indeed wanted to go further. He argued that the demands to China should be set 'at such a level that they cannot be fulfilled and therefore justify further seizure' and that 'permanent occupation of [Kiautschou Bay] is to be envisaged'. The Kaiser also reiterated his mantra that he had the support of the Tsar:

> His Majesty remarked that he stood by the fact that [the Tsar] had given telegraphic approval. Two years ago the Tsar had had already expressed his agreement to Germany taking a port in China, while thanking him [the Kaiser] for our support for Russian policy in the Far East [...] His Majesty therefore does not believe that there will be a war with Russia [...] [43]

The reference to the Tsar's agreement of 'two years ago' was another example of Wilhelm's 'personal diplomacy'. The posthumously published memoirs of Hohenlohe record a diary entry of 11 September 1895 following the Chancellor's meeting with the Russian monarch:

> As regards the East Asiatic question,[44] the [Tsar] expressed his satisfaction that we had acted in concert with him, and was pleased when I told him that were guided therein by the desire of manifesting our good relations with Russia. [...] The [Tsar] then said that he had written in the spring to our [Kaiser], saying that he would have nothing against our acquiring something in that quarter, so as to have a fixed depot or coaling station. I told him that the [Kaiser] had mentioned this to me under the seal of secrecy [...].[45]

Despite this apparently unshakeable belief in the 'agreements' he had reached on a personal level with a brother emperor, the Kaiser still had to reckon with the Russian government, which continued to protest. As Hohenlohe wrote to the German Ambassador to Britain:

> A stiffening, if only temporary, of our relations with Russia is to be expected, since His Majesty the Emperor is not disposed to let Kiautschou go, While the exchange of views between here and St Petersburg, of which you know, show that Russia takes a lively interest in that spot [...][46]

On 18 November Hohenlohe informed Wilhelm that the Tsar placed a somewhat different interpretation on the telegraphic exchange that had occurred on 7 November:

The tone and content of the Russian document leave no room for doubt that the Tsar has been persuaded to take the view that [the Kaiser] intended to make improper use of his telegram, to the detriment of Russian rights, which it had never been [his] intention to relinquish.[47]

The Kaiser seemed however unconcerned, and to a suggestion of the Chancellor that delaying tactics be resorted to, and that the Tsar should be informed that Russian warships would be welcome to share Kiautschou Bay with the German navy, he noted:

Completely agree [...] Their famous right of *premier mouillage* will in no way be infringed by our occupation and later seizure. Russians can stay anchored there until they are blue in the face. But that cannot prevent us building a coaling station and docks there.[48]

This inflexible attitude – Bismarck, from retirement, noted that that Kiautschou was only '[...] a small piece of earth but large enough to encompass very big blunders'[49]– took material form in the arrangements to dispatch reinforcements to the area, one additional warship at first and then a second division plus a specially put together detachment of naval infantry and artillery personnel to garrison the territory. If the response of the Russian government was shouldered aside, then that of the Chinese was to be ignored completely. Wilhelm made this very clear in a message to the Foreign Office on 24 November:

That the Chinese know exactly what we want is certain; that they will wage war is highly unlikely, as they have neither ships nor money and the number of troops in Shantung is not great. The fact that Heinrich is being sent and the second division formed must of course be mentioned [in a telegram to China], as everyone knows it and it shows that the Imperial House does not for a moment hesitate to risk the lives of its members for the honour of Germany.[50]

The 'Heinrich' mentioned in the document was the Kaiser's younger brother Prince Heinrich of Prussia, a naval officer since 1877. On 23 November Diederichs had been promoted to Vice Admiral and his command formally rose from the status of a division to that of a squadron, the second, four ship, division[51] of which was to be commanded by Prince Heinrich; Wilhelm publicly announced this in a speech to the Reichstag on 30 November.[52] Meanwhile, four days earlier, Wilhelm had again written to Hohenloe displaying impatience with what he perceived as the slowness of the German government's response:

In about three weeks the *Kaiserin Augusta* will arrive in China; Prince Heinrich and the rest of the ships not until February [1898]. So that the crews do not remain away from their ships any longer than absolutely necessary, the moment has now come to form the colonial force, charter the steamer and embark them as soon as possible. I expect an answer tomorrow morning so that I can give my orders. No one is in any doubt about our intentions. A longer delay is impossible. That it is not for Russia to say anything in Kiautschou is as clear as daylight.[53]

Map 3. The Shantung Peninsula: the Kiautschou Protectorate,
the Neutral Zone and Weihaiwei

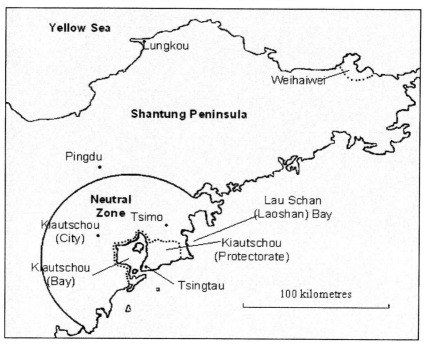

That the Kaiser had been engaged in personal rule was made evident to the Chancellor when Lieutenant General Heinrich von Gossler, the Prussian Minister of War, told him that he had received an order to put together a force to form the garrison, including artillery batteries. 'I know nothing about the dispatch of the batteries' the General conceded to his diary, noting further that 'if things continue as they are we shall have a war with China'.[54]

In fact the Kiautschou garrison was to be formed from naval personnel and resources, for two main reasons. First, the Navy was an Imperial institution, while the federal states of the German Empire retained, at least nominally, control of their own armies. Second, the territory was, uniquely among German overseas territory, to be run by the Navy rather than the Colonial Office.[55]

The Imperial German Navy had a body of personnel, trained as infantry and more or less ready to depart for overseas duty, in the form of I and II Naval Battalions (*See-Bataillons*) stationed at Kiel and Wilhelmshaven respectively.[56] On 3 December 1897 Admiral Knorr ordered a new unit, III Naval Battalion, to form by amalgamating the existing units. Accordingly, by the morning of 13 December 1897, the four companies at Kiel had amalgamated into two companies: the 1st and 3rd Companies of I Naval Battalion now formed the 1st Company III Naval Battalion, while the 2nd and 4th Companies formed the new 2nd Company. These two enlarged companies then travelled to Wilhelmshaven, where by a similar process the II Naval Battalion had formed 3rd and 4th Companies.[57]

On 15 December the 'All Highest Warlord' delivered a speech to the force, which was augmented by a detachment of Marine Artillery (*Matrosen Artillerie Abteilungen*) to set up and man the coastal artillery defences of the territory. The tone of the address was somewhat typically overblown, and the personal injunction to his brother included within it exemplifies this:

> If anyone [...] should ever venture to wish to hurt or harm us in the due exercise of our rights, smash him with an iron fist! And, if it be God's will, weave a laurel wreath around your young brow [Prince Heinrich was 35] which no one in the whole German Reich will begrudge you.[58]

Prince Heinrich replied that he would 'declare abroad the gospel of your Majesty's anointed person; to preach it to everyone who will hear it, and also to those who will not hear.'[59]

The Battalion and its auxiliaries[60] boarded the steamer *Darmstadt* of the Nord-Deutscher Line and in the afternoon of 16 December, embarked on their voyage halfway around the world. They arrived on 26 January 1898, and the next day Wilhelm issued an edict authorising the Imperial Navy to take charge of the administration of the area.[61] This force was augmented on 4 February when the steamship *Crefeld*, carrying 300 personnel of the Marine Artillery Detachment and a battery of field guns also arrived.[62]

On 1 March 1898, the Kaiser issued another decree, stating:

> At the head of the military and civil administration of the territory of Kiautschou will be a naval officer with the title of Governor. [...] The Secretary of the Navy Office has the right to inspect the naval infantry and the marine artillery in connection with the military garrisoning of the protectorate of Kiautschou.[63]

Thus was established the system whereby the German Protectorate of Kiautschou was to be governed and defended, somewhat pre-empting the formal confirmation of the seizure by the Sino-German 'Lease Agreement' that was not signed until 6 March 1898.

Article I
With the intention of both fortifying the amicable relations between China and Germany and strengthening the military readiness of the Chinese Empire, His Majesty the Emperor of China agrees to the following: while reserving all rights of sovereignty within a radius of fifty kilometres (100 Chinese li) from Kiautschou Bay, measured at high tide, His Majesty promises to allow the free march of German troops through this zone at all times, to refrain from any measures or directives in this zone without the prior agreement of the German government, and to place no obstacles in the way of any necessary regulation of these bodies of water. His Majesty the Emperor of China reserves the right to station troops and to take other military measures in this zone in cooperation with the German government.

Map 4. The Kiautschou Protectorate 1897–1914

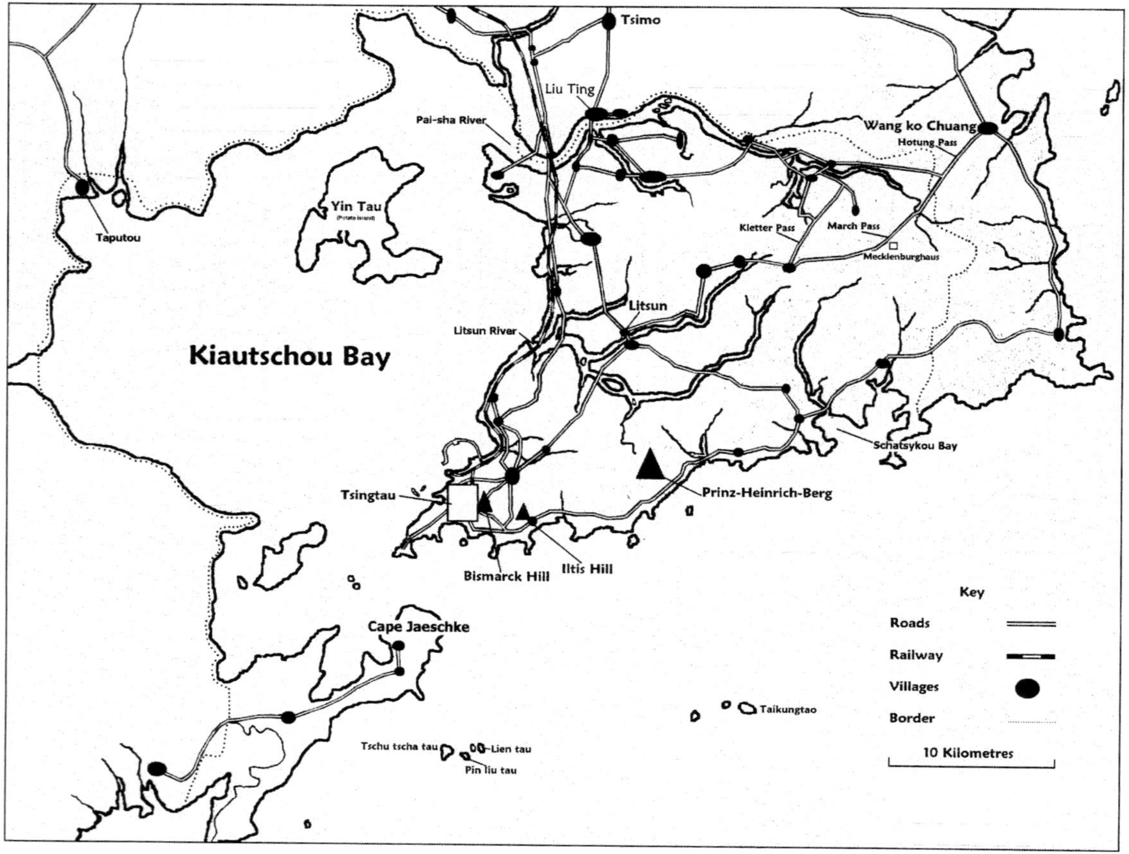

Key

Roads
Railway
Villages
Border

10 Kilometres

Wang ko Chuang
Hotung Pass
March Pass
Mecklenburghaus
Kletter Pass
Schatsykou Bay
Prinz-Heinrich-Berg
Tsimo
Litsun
Liu Ting
Pai-sha River
Litsun River
Iltis Hill
Bismarck Hill
Yin Tau
(Pramount)
Tsingtau
Kiautschou Bay
Cape Jaeschke
Tschu tscha tau
Lien tau
Pin liu tau
Taikungtao
Taputou

Article II
With the intention of fulfilling the justifiable request of His Majesty the German Kaiser, who wants Germany, like other powers, to have a place on the Chinese coast to repair and fit out ships, to store materials and supplies, and to maintain other related facilities, His Majesty the Emperor of China shall lease both sides of the entrance to Kiautschou Bay to Germany for a provisional period of 99 years. At an opportune time, Germany shall undertake to build fortifications in the leased area to protect both the planned structural works and the entrance to the bay.

Article III
To prevent any conflicts, the Imperial Chinese Government will not exercise sovereign rights in the leased area for the duration of the lease. It will surrender such rights to Germany for the following area:

1. On the northern side of the entrance to the bay: the area comprising the spit bounded to the north-east by the line drawn from the north-eastern corner of Potato Island to Loshan Harbour;

2. On the southern side of the entrance to the bay: the area comprising the spit bounded to the southwest by the line drawn to Tolosan Island from the south-western tip of the inlet south-west of Chiposan Island;

3. Chiposan Island and Potato Islands;

4. The entire water area of the bay up to the high water mark;

5. All islands lying off Kiautschou Bay as well as those needed for its defence from the sea, including Tolosan, Chaolian Dao, etc.

As regards the area leased to Germany and the fifty-kilometre zone around the bay, the supreme parties to this agreement reserve the right to define the boundaries more precisely in keeping with local conditions. This task will be carried out by commissioners appointed by both sides.

Chinese military and merchant vessels shall be granted the same privileges in Kiautschou Bay as those conferred on ships of other nations that are on friendly terms with Germany. The entry, departure and mooring of Chinese ships in the bay shall be subject to no restrictions other than those that the Imperial German Government shall deem necessary to impose at any time on the ships of other nations by virtue of the sovereign rights transferred to it.

Article IV
Germany agrees to place the necessary navigation marks both on the islands and in the shallows in front of the entrance to the bay.

No duties shall be levied on Chinese military and merchant vessels in Kiautschou Bay, with the exception of those to which other vessels are subject for the purpose of maintaining the necessary port and quay facilities.

Article V
If Germany at a subsequent date expresses the desire to return Kiautschou Bay to China before the expiration of the period of the lease, China shall compensate Germany for its outlays and provide Germany with a more suitable location.

Germany agrees never to sublease to another power the area it has leased from China.

As long as the Chinese living in the leased area abide by the law and local regulations, they shall at all times enjoy the protection of the German government. The Chinese residents may remain in the leased area provided their land is not claimed for other purposes. If property owned by Chinese residents is used for other purposes, the owners are entitled to compensation. Concerning the reinstatement of the Chinese customs stations once located outside the area leased to Germany but within the agreed-upon fifty-kilometre zone, the Imperial German Government intends to reach an agreement with the Chinese Government on ways to regulate both the customs border and customs revenue in a manner that protects all China's interests; it also reserves the right to enter into additional negotiations on this matter.[64]

On 27 April 1898 the Kaiser issued a Supreme Decree noting that the Chinese government had 'transferred possession of the area off Kiautschou Bay [...] to Germany, and we hereby place this area under imperial protection on behalf of the Empire'.[65] Via then 'a transaction in the old Prussian style' Germany had its place in the sun.[66]

3

China 1897–1914:
Colonial Development and Political Turbulence

The seizure of Kiautschou was to have profound and almost immediate conse-
quences for China, and indeed the peace of the whole East Asian region,
inasmuch as it was the first in a series of such manoeuvres characterised as the
'Scramble for Concessions'. In December 1897 Russian warships anchored at
Lushun (Port Arthur) and Darien (Talienwan) under the pretext of protecting
China against the Germans. Indeed, some scholars have contended that protests
in respect to German actions became somewhat muted when Foreign Minister
Count Muraviev realised that it would provide an excuse for Russian expansion in
a like manner. Russia had need of a warm-water naval base, such as Port Arthur,
and accordingly, following 'negotiations', the Chinese government signed a treaty
on 27 March 1898 ceding the Liaodong Peninsula, including Port Arthur and
Darien, to Russia for twenty-five years, and granting a concession for a railway to
be constructed from Harbin to Port Arthur.[1]

This Russian move prompted Britain to obtain additional Chinese territory
on the Kowloon Peninsula on a 99-year lease,[2] and at the same time acquire
Weihaiwei (Weihai), 'one of the least lustrous gems in Queen Victoria's imperial
tiara'.[3] The British occupation of the latter, a 738 square-kilometer area located
near the tip of the peninsula on the north-eastern coast of Shandong (Shantung)
Province, was to last, from 1 July 1898, 'for so long a period as Port Arthur shall
remain in the occupation of Russia'.[4]

On 2 May 1898 a French force occupied Zhanjiang (Chankiang, Lei Chow, Fort
Bayard) on the east side of the Leizhou Peninsula in Guangdong (Kwangtung)
province. The following year a 99-year lease was procured on an area of some
800 square kilometres, allowing the French strategic control of the Qiongzhou
(Hainan) Strait to the south. This body of water separates the peninsula from
Hainan Island, and connects the Gulf of Tonkin in the west to the South China
Sea in the east. Possession of Zhanjiang thus allowed the French greater strategic
control of the Gulf of Tonkin.

Even Italy, a member since 1882 of the Triple Alliance with Germany and
Austria-Hungary, and perhaps the least of the European 'Great Powers' attempted
to join in the scramble. Italy demanded, in February 1898, the cession of Sanmen
Bay in Zhejiang (Chehkiang) Province on the seacoast midway between Canton
and Peking. On this occasion however the Chinese government rejected the
demand out of hand and the Italians desisted.[5]

Of the European powers only Austria-Hungary abstained from attempting to gain Chinese territory, while the Pacific Powers of Japan and the USA, the latter embroiled in a colonial conflict of its own with Spain, did not physically annexe territory, or try to, though Japan did increase the size of its 'sphere of influence' in Fujian Province opposite Taiwan. The other powers also increased their pre-existing spheres; Britain in the Yangtze River Valley and around Canton; Russia in northern Manchuria; and France in Yunnan Province along the border of French Indochina. In both the leaseholds and their spheres of influence, the powers were permitted to maintain a military presence to protect their political, economic, and religious interests. As the Reverend Herbert H. Gowen, a noted scholar and authority on China and Japan, put it in 1913: 'By 1899 in all China's three thousand miles of coastline, there was not a harbour in which she could mobilise her own ships without the consent of the hated foreigner.'[6]

If the policy of the foreign powers in China at the macro-level was one of exploitation and disdain for the Chinese, their institutions and culture, then this was certainly replicated at the micro-level in Kiautschou and surrounding areas. The Kaiser's exhortation that the departing personnel of III Naval Battalion should 'smash with an iron fist' those who would impede 'the due exercise of our rights', combined with his previous exclamations in respect of the 'Yellow Peril', no doubt engendered a certain disdain for the indigenous population among the German colonisers. Indeed, German contemporary racial discourse designated them as inferior.[7]

Accordingly, shortly after taking over the Germans ensured that existing buildings at Tsingtau were demolished and a new town laid out for Europeans only. There was a buffer zone between Tsingtau and Tapautau, the European and Chinese area respectively, with the streets in the latter planned on a grid pattern to make crowd control easier if necessary.[8] Chinese were forbidden to reside in the European area, with domestic servants being the only exception. The Chinese however were not simply left to themselves, but rather were subject to a regime that regulated everything 'from the performance of Chinese theatrical productions to the size and cleanliness of Chinese dwellings'.[9] Racial distinction extended to health care, and was deliberate and institutionalised.[10]

Contemporary Western observers tended, in the main, to follow the German, and general European, perspective on the backwardness of China and the Chinese and focus on the benefits, as they saw them, of the German occupation. Approval of the growth and development of Kiautschou, and Tsingtau in particular, can be adjudged by the reports of eyewitnesses who visited the area at various stages of its development. For example the British Rear-Admiral Lord Charles Beresford, while on a fact-finding mission to China, was invited by Prince Heinrich of Prussia to journey there. According to his account of the matter, Beresford arrived at the port on 14 November 1898, the first anniversary of Diederichs' seizure, and therefore saw it before a great deal of development had occurred. He was of the opinion that:

This place would have great capabilities as a mercantile port in the future, provided very large sums of money are spent upon it. A breakwater will have to be built in order to make it a good anchorage and to defend it from easterly seas, and the inside harbour will have to be extensively dredged in order to give sufficient water. It is not an easy place for vessels to make, particularly in foggy weather.[11]

Beresford, being a naval man, also expressed interest in the military aspects of the colony, and he noted the industrious approach the Germans were adopting in respect of the defences:

The Germans were very actively employed on shore clearing the ground, building barracks, making parade-grounds, and preparing emplacements for guns in the most commanding positions. The place could be made into a very strong naval base, but this would entail a further large expenditure of money, owing to its configuration.[12]

The American clergyman, Arthur Judson Brown, who visited Tsingtau in 1901, noted that this expenditure had indeed been laid out: 'A large force of marines was on shore, and the hills commanding the city and harbour were bristling with cannon. The Germans were spending money without stint.'[13] He was also greatly impressed with the amount of civil work that had been undertaken:

Knowing how recently the city had been founded, I looked upon it with wonder. It was only three years and a half since the Germans had taken possession, but no boom city in the United States ever made more rapid progress in so short a period. Not a Chinese house could be seen, except a village in the distance. But along the shores rose a city of modern buildings with banks, department stores, public buildings, comfortable residences, a large church and imposing marine barracks. Landing, I found broad streets, some of them already well paved and others being paved by removing the dirt to a depth of twelve inches and then filling the excavation solid with broken rock. The gutters were wide and of stone, the sewers deep and, in some cases, cut through the solid rock.[14]

He also noted the separation of Tsingtau and Tapautau, and because the Germans had 'ruthlessly destroyed the old, unsanitary Chinese villages which they had found on their arrival' the strictness of the regime imposed upon the latter.[15]

The new Chinese city [at the time Tapautau had a population of 8,000] is about two and a half miles from [Tsingtau] and is connected with it by a splendid macadamised road for which the Germans filled ravines, cut through the solid rock of the hillsides and made retaining walls and culverts of solid masonry. Some of the old stone houses were allowed to remain, but many of the poorer houses were demolished, streets were straightened and the whole city placed under strict sanitary supervision. The Chinese as they came in were told where and how their houses must be erected on the regularly laid out streets.[16]

The Chinese population, and thus the accommodation required to house them was increasing rapidly however, and Brown noted that the work undertaken by the Germans was labour intensive with the result that 'from hundreds of outlying villages, the Chinese are flocking into Tsingtau, attracted by the remunerative employment which the Germans offer'.[17] As he put it, 'the thrifty Chinese are quite willing to take the foreigner's money, however much they may dislike him'.[18]

The eminent soil scientist Professor Franklin Hiram King visited Tsingtau in 1909 and noted the continuing improvements of the harbour:

> Tsingtau has a deep, commodious harbour always free from ice and Germany is constructing here very extensive and substantial harbour improvements which will be of lasting benefit to the province and the Empire. A pier four miles in length encloses the inner wharf, and a second wharf is nearing completion.[19]

Of particular interest to one of his profession however was the reforestation project being undertaken on the mountainous terrain to the north-east of Tsingtau and the experimentation with various flora in the Forest Garden: 'Germany [...] has established a large, comprehensive Forest Garden, under excellent management, which is showing remarkable developments for so short a time.' [20]

> The Forest Garden covers two hundred and seventy acres and the reforestation tract three thousand acres more. In the garden a great variety of forest and fruit trees and small fruits are being tried out with high promise of the most valuable results. [...] It was in the steep hills about Tsingtao that we first saw at close range serious soil erosion in China; and the returning of forest growth on hills nearly devoid of soil was here remarkable, in view of the long dry seasons, which prevail from November to June. [...] Most of the growth is volunteer, standing now protected by the German government in their effort to see what may be possible under careful supervision.[21]

Arthur Judson Brown's comment concerning the spending of money 'without stint' noted above is borne out somewhat in the statistics collected by the Germans.[22] The lease included concessions for the construction of railways, and for mineral rights within the German 'sphere of influence'. However before any exploitation of the area could be contemplated there was a pressing need to develop an infrastructure. Beresford noted that, whilst he was at Tsingtau, railway surveying was being undertaken with a view to connecting Tsingtau to the interior of the province.[23]

Indeed, a charter had been granted on 1 June 1899 to the Schantung-Eisenbahn-Gessellschaft, with a capital of 54,000,000 marks, whose brief was to construct a railway from the newly acquired port to the provincial capital Jinan (Tsinan), where it would eventually connect with the Tianjin–Pukou (Tientsin–Pukow) line.[24] With an eventual total length of some 435 kilometres what became known as the 'Shantung Railway' (now known as the Jiaoji Railway) was completed in 1904 at a cost of 52,900,000 marks.[25] Included in the total length was a branch at Changtien, of some 40 kilometres, to the valley containing the coalfield at Poshan, a large and important natural resource.[26] The first train completed the journey to Jinan on 23 February 1904 and the work was adjudged to be complete on 1 June. The railway disposed of 59 stations along its total length, serviced by 20 locomotives, 107 passenger coaches, used by 12,000–15,000 passengers per week, and 670 goods wagons.[27] In 1905 the Shantung Railway transported 280,000 tonnes of freight and more than 750,000 passengers, compared to 496,000 the previous year, while 413 ships visited Tsingtau. The port facilities there were augmented by the addition of a floating dock of 16,000 tonnes capacity.[28]

By 1908 the Tianjin–Pukou railway line was under construction, partly funded by German loans, which would massively increase the area available for economic penetration by German industry. [29] Indeed BASF, the chemical giant viewed China as clearly the 'most promising country' for dye exports; 'every [...] Chinese owned at least one blue jacket dyed with indigo.'[30] This was clearly a market of massive potential, and prior to the Great War the German chemical industry was pre-eminent globally. This superiority was, somewhat ironically, based on an 1856 British discovery; that of aniline, a coal tar derivative. From this arose a whole new business, the dyestuffs industry, which, for reasons outside the scope of this work, was particularly taken up by the scientists and businessmen of Germany. At the beginning of the twentieth century, these had achieved a dominant position in the world market through the IG cartel, or *interessen gemeinschaft* (community of interest), created in 1903:[31] 'In 1913 the world production of dyes reached approximately 150,000 tonnes, of which Germany controlled three-quarters, producing at the same time something over 85 per cent of the intermediates entering into the finished dyes.'[32]

Aside from the staple of dyestuffs, these corporations produced many other pioneering products, including heroin, and, perhaps of more lasting benefit, artificial fertilisers based on the synthetic production of nitrates.[33] By 1908 synthetic imported indigo was driving indigenous indigo planters out of business in coastal regions, and the improvements in the railway network could only increase the rate at which this occurred.[34]

The railway brought benefits in the other direction, as it were, and not just economically. For example, of great advantage to the German Navy was the discovery of coal deposits at the Hungschan open-cast coal mine at Wei Xian (Wei-hsien) that were of a quality sufficient to fuel warships. Prince Heinrich described the results of experiments with this coal to his brother in the summer of 1898:

> A few tonnes of Chinese coal that I had as samples from the much discussed coal basin, and with which I made parallel trials against British coal, have yielded a surprisingly good result. The best Poshan coal is equal to Cardiff! The poorer quality is incomparably better than the Japanese.[35]

As a result of these tests a contract was drawn up between the Shantung Mining Company (*Schantung-Bergbau-Gesellschaft*) and the Navy to supply the material to Tsingtau for the use of the East Asiatic Cruiser Squadron. This considerably eased the logistical burden on the squadron as the supply would make up 'its entire demand of coal, as far as it is loaded in Tsingtau.'[36]

A retrospective view of the year 1906 noted that work on the port facilities was ongoing, and would probably be completed in 1908, and that a 1,500-tonne crane had been installed, a device with a capacity exceeding that of any other along the

East Asian coast. Also commissioned during 1906 was the large floating dock and 24 ships used this on 216 days during that year.[37]

The Shantung Mining Company was the largest industrial undertaking in the leased area, however it was not to prove the most profitable; that honour went to the brewery constructed in 1903 by the Nordic Brewery Company. This was the first such facility built in China, utilising the water from the Laoshan Mountains, and it was something of an exception to the norm as most German companies, fearing for the security of their speculation, were unwilling to invest in the area.[38] It was indeed mostly public, rather than private, money that was expended in the territory, with the Navy expending some 23 million marks during the first two years. By 1913 this had risen to around 200 million marks, though the cost to the German taxpayer was reduced somewhat by the 36 million marks that had been raised locally. However the local economy was able to raise only some forty per cent of its necessary revenue, with the naval dockyard, still in government hands as no private investors could be induced to take it over, accounting for about half of the money. The annual subsidy necessary to maintain the territory was in the order of 10 million marks per year over the period of German occupation.[39]

Indeed, though trade with the hinterland was to expand massively over the lifetime of the German occupation, Chinese merchants largely dominated it and the German share was relatively small with even many of the mining concessions being taken over by Chinese enterprises in 1911.[40] In terms of shipping, it was the Japanese who came to dominate with around a 55 per cent share eventually and the Hamburg-Amerika Line reduced its sailings to the territory to once monthly.[41] The market for Tsingtao beer[42] was expanded somewhat when the ban on alcohol in other German territories, such as Samoa, was lifted; 'the need for a docile Samoan labour force had to adjust to Shandong's development'.[43]

Whist the economic and infrastructural facets of the German presence might have been superficially beneficial, at least potentially, to China, focusing on them to the exclusion of other factors is essentially to view the matter from a pro-colonialist perspective. Even foreigners who were, contemporaneously, essentially of a pro-Chinese viewpoint tended to adopt the colonialist viewpoint, inasmuch as they saw the technological benefits to China of Western-style development.

One such was William Alexander Parsons Martin, who devoted over sixty years of his life to China after arriving there in 1860. Martin learned to speak two Chinese dialects and to write classical Chinese and became the English teacher and later president of the Interpreters College formed to train Chinese diplomats. Despite viewing his primary responsibility as that of a Christian proselytiser he became the friend and confidant of many important officials, gaining the nickname *Kuan-hsi*, or first among Occidentals, and later the rank of governor.[44] Martin had a passion for science and technological advancement and believed that advocacy in this sphere was useful in his work; the subject of his graduation oration was 'The Uses of the Physical Sciences as an Equipment of the Missionary',[45] and a piece he contributed to *The Chinese Recorder* in 1897 was entitled 'Western Science as Auxiliary to the Spread of the Gospel'.[46] It is easy to categorise such people as 'God Botherers' in retrospect, and with some justification, but Martin at least seems to have had the interests of China and the Chinese very much at heart in his quest to improve their lot via scientific progress. His view of the German takeover of Tsingtau was thus coloured by his views on the role of Western ideas and techniques:

> At Kiautschou the Germans [...] have built a beautiful town opposite the Island of Tsingtao, presenting a fine model for imitation, which, however, the Chinese are not in haste to copy. They have constructed also a railway from the sea to Tsinanfu, very nearly bisecting the province. Weihen (Weifang) is destined to become a railroad centre; and several missionary societies are erecting colleges there to teach the people truths that Confucius never knew. More than half a century ago, when a missionary distributed Christian books in that region, the people brought them back saying, 'We have the works of our Sage, and they are sufficient for us.' Will not the new arts and sciences of the west convince them that their Sage was not omniscient?[47]

In fact the Confucian underpinnings of Chinese society and culture had been under question by individuals in the Chinese ruling elite for some time, and the foreign interventions following on Germany's seizure of Kiautschou gave this renewed impetus. One such reformer was Kang Youwei (K'ang Yu-wei 1858–1927) whose belief that China should adopt a constitutional system similar to that of Japan preceded the 'Scramble for Concessions'. Kang's petitioning for changes, first promulgated in 1888, polarised his colleagues in the scholarly class, many of whom regarded his ideas as heretical. This was particularly so because the reformers argued that a root and branch reform of the Chinese education system was required, which meant drastic changes to the Civil Examination system.[48]

The examination system had been a cornerstone of Chinese society for centuries, and it provided China with a literate elite constituted very differently from those of Europe and European emulators such as Japan. Under its auspices, any male adult in China, regardless of wealth, could, theoretically, become a high-ranking government official by taking and passing the exam. The meritocratic aspect of the system was diluted somewhat by the extremely time consuming and costly nature of the necessary study, which was based almost entirely on Confucian classics. Those who passed the extremely difficult process, they were held every other year when up to two million people from all levels of society attempted them, would thus know how to compose poems and write essays, but would not necessarily be skilled in mathematics or scientific subjects, which were considered intellectually inferior.[49] These latter skills were of course those that were of vital importance in establishing an industrial base, which in turn lead to wealth and power.[50]

The outcome of the Sino-Japanese War revealed that Japan, by adopting European ideas and methods, had become a powerful state capable of humiliating China, and many of the reformers concluded that unless change occurred this state of affairs would likely continue.[51] The depredations of the European powers shortly afterwards only served to confirm the relative weakness of Chinese institutions and gave new force to the arguments of the reformers.[52] The writings of two of these, the previously mentioned Kang and his follower, Liang Qichao, came to the attention of the Emperor Guangxu (Kwang Sü) and Kang travelled to Beijing (Peking) to present a series of petitions to him.[53] These proposals inspired the Emperor to begin, on 11 June 1898, what became known as the One Hundred Days of Reform, when, until 21 September, he issued edict after edict ordering a host of educational, military, economic, political and institutional reforms. To oversee these, Kang's disciple, Liang, was placed in charge of the transition bureau.[54]

The Emperor, the tenth of the Qing (Manchu) dynasty, and the ninth Qing emperor to rule over China, was however in a somewhat weak position. Zaitian, as he was known at his birth in 1871, had ascended the throne in 1875 aged four at the instigation of his aunt Cixi (Tz'u-hsi) the Dowager Empress, whereupon he was named the Guangxu Emperor, meaning 'Glorious Succession'. Cixi adopted the youngster as her son, and took the role of regent with the title of the 'Holy Mother Empress Dowager'. Until he achieved his majority in 1887 she ruled in his name, even delaying his taking over the government for two years after he came of age. Her influence was scarcely diminished after 1889, and, holding reactionary views as she did, she greatly opposed the corrupting effect of foreign influences as she saw them.[55] Accordingly she formed a focal point for those conservatives, to whom the departure from traditional ways was an aberration.

These conservative forces, with Cixi at their head were preoccupied with preserving the status quo at all costs. Accordingly they staged a *coup d'état* on 21 September 1898; the Emperor was abducted and placed under house arrest and six of the intellectual leaders of the movement were executed.[56] The Dowager Empress ordered Kang Youwei executed by leng t'che (língchí, otherwise known to Westerners as slow slicing or death by a thousand cuts) but both he and Liang Qichao managed to escape, first to Hong Kong and then to Japan.[57] They remained there for six years before travelling to Britain and Germany, promoting their ideas among the Chinese Diaspora. They were not to return to China until 1913.[58]

The convulsions at the top of the Chinese government were not the only conflicts that were to disturb the state however, for within a year a newer and much more consequential factor had emerged. On 9 October 1899 *The North-China Herald*, an English-language paper published in Shanghai, contained a report from Shantung:

> A sect has arisen whose only reason for existence is their hatred for foreigners and the foreign religion. For some occult reason they have taken the name of 'Boxers', and last spring they tried to drive out the missionaries in Siaochang [...] Like other uprisings in China this promises to die out.[59]

This reference to the so-called Boxers has been adjudged the first time the word appeared in print in relation to the organisation.[60] It was certainly not the last.

The causes and course of what became known as the Boxer War, also known as the Boxer Rebellion or Boxer Uprising, are complex and beyond adequate description in a few paragraphs because of the varying strands that led to it, and the differing stages of the conflict. Chinese nationalism and dislike of foreigners in general have been invoked as explanations, as has the presence and meddling of missionaries. Undoubtedly both played a part, but it seems likely that the most proximate causes were the depredations of foreign military forces and the weakness of the Chinese government in preventing these, together with the famine conditions that eventuated in parts of northern China at the time following extensive flooding.[61] The most recent scholarship is virtually unanimous in attributing the origin of the Boxer movement to Shantung, for although it later became widespread its origins were in the province; it was as Esherick states it 'really a regional movement'.[62] Certainly the German presence at Kiautschou and the habit, notable in 1899, of dispatching punitive military expeditions at the slightest provocation was much resented by the Chinese at every level.[63]

Because it was perceived as acquiescent in the humiliations visited by the foreign powers on Chinese culture, the Boxers originally directed their ire at the Qing court, but their cause seems to have been co-opted by the Empress Dowager. In any event the situation escalated greatly in June 1900 when the Boxers, together with Chinese Army troops, attacked and besieged the foreign legation compounds in Tianjin (Tientsin) and Beijing (Peking). The missions of Belgium, France, Japan, the Netherlands, Russia, Spain, the United Kingdom, and the United States were close enough together in Beijing that they were able to link their defences and provide a refuge for foreigners in the city. But the German legation, in another part of the city, was overrun, and the German envoy was taken captive and killed.

The response was to form the Eight-Nation Alliance, consisting of Austria-Hungary, France, Germany, Italy, Japan, Russia, the United Kingdom, and the United States, and organise a military expeditionary force to relieve the besieged legations and suppress the Boxers generally. Kaiser Wilhelm lobbied vigorously for the command of this expeditionary force to be the preserve of a German.

The Boxer War to Wilhelm was much more than a simple outbreak of violence in a faraway place; he considered it a struggle between Europe and Asia, a manifestation of the 'Yellow Peril'. The killing of the German envoy gave him the pretext to demand involvement of German forces and a German commander.[64] Upon this being, somewhat begrudgingly, agreed he appointed 68-year-old Field Marshal Count Alfred von Waldersee to the position.[65]

Waldersee, who has been described as 'reactionary', 'anti-Semitic' and a 'war fanatic', had been a close confidant of the Kaiser since 1885. He had assisted the young Prince of Prussia, as Wilhelm then was, in disengaging himself from the consequences of an illicit liaison, and, as an older man, was regarded as a kind of surrogate father to the headstrong future Kaiser.[66] Waldersee was also politically ambitious, and perceived the command as an opportunity to make a name for himself as a successful military leader. Military success would of course have virtually guaranteed the unalloyed approval of the Kaiser.[67]

When a portion of the East Asiatic Expeditionary Corps embarked at Bremerhaven on 2 July 1900 the Kaiser made an impromptu speech to them. While for obvious reason this was jingoistic in tone, it was nevertheless unremarkable. However on 27 July at a similar occasion, Wilhelm voiced what was regarded then, and is regarded similarly today, his most infamous utterance; the 'Hun Speech'.

Though there were attempts to suppress the relevant passage, which was changed to something rather more innocuous in the officially released version, the text had been taken down in shorthand by a reporter. When his words were released they invited worldwide ridicule. The relevant portion of the text has come down to us as follows:

> When you come upon the enemy, smite him. Pardon will not be given. Prisoners will not be taken. Whoever falls into your hands is forfeit. Once, a thousand years ago, the Huns under their King Attila made a name for themselves, one still potent in legend and tradition. May you in this way make the name German remembered in China for a thousand years so that no Chinaman will ever again dare to even squint at a German![68]

By the time Waldersee arrived in China in September 1900 the legations had been relieved by the multi-national force, minus the German expeditionary contingent, or indeed any German presence, under the command of a British officer, Major-General Sir Alfred Gaselee.[69] With the relief of the legations the settlement of the Boxer crisis was pursued on the political level by the imposition of an agreement and indemnity on the Chinese government. The allies had no wish, despite the involvement in the affair of that government to see it replaced; as Lord Salisbury put it, the Chinese were best equipped for 'the stupendous task of governing China'.[70]

At the local level, the troops of the relieving force were allowed, like some medieval horde, to murder, rape, and plunder within Beijing, which was effectively divided into zones of occupation.[71] This 'unregulated plunder' lasted for several days before the commands of the various contingents attempted to bring a degree of order to it. The Japanese having already made off with the bullion from the Chinese treasury, the need for some form of control, or 'regulated plunder', was perceived in order that the economy of the city could continue to function; a prerequisite to maintaining an effective military presence.[72]

When Field Marshal Waldersee finally reached the Chinese capital on 18 October 1900, he was thus too late by some two months to be considered the liberator, and so, in order to demonstrate the prowess of the German Army, could only carry out punitive expeditions against suspected Boxer sympathisers in the area around Beijing. By December 1900 the German force numbered some 17,000, the largest of the contingents that together now numbered some 64,000.[73] The area of operations was a rough triangle, the corners of which comprised Beijing, Tianjin, and Baodong, where allied troops were stationed, and expeditions proceeded from these to search for Boxers and pacify the area. Waldersee did not invent the tactics used, and in fairness to him it has been argued that his orders stated that women and children should not be killed.[74] However, he does stand accused of pursuing the matter with an hitherto unknown degree of thoroughness and enthusiasm; between December 1900 and April 1901, 46 expeditions were organised, of which 35 were purely German affairs.[75] In total, during his time in China, the forces under Waldersee launched some 75 expeditions.[76]

The scale of the savagery visited upon the Chinese population by the punitive expeditions mounted under Waldersee's command impressed itself even upon some of the missionaries upon whose behalf, and for whose protection, they were ostensibly mounted. To one, Dr Arthur Henderson Smith, [77] it seemed that the foreign forces had visited China 'for the express purpose of committing within the shortest time as many violations as possible of the sixth [*'Thou shalt not kill.'*], the seventh [*'Thou shalt not commit adultery.'*] and the eighth [*'Thou shalt not steal.'*] commandments'.[78]

The missionaries were not the only ones to note the barbarity of the foreign troops, plenty of journalists told the tale as well, including the American Thomas F. Millard of the *New York Herald*; in an article he had published in *Scribner's Magazine* in 1901 he wrote of the Chinese civilians being treated merely as 'living puppets for targets'.[79] The Anglo-Irish journalist and sometime foreign affairs commentator for the *Daily Telegraph*, Dr E. J. Dillon, wrote a particularly graphic piece for the Oxford published *Contemporary Review* in 1901. After describing the 'shoals' of dead Chinese either floating in the Hai (Pei-ho) River or washed up on its banks, he included the graphic account of just how barbaric the foreign expeditions were:

> I saw two bodies [...] [and] I should have glided past them but for the pathos of their story, which needed no articulate voice to tell. A father and his boy of eight had been shot down in the name of civilisation while holding each other's hands and praying for mercy. And there they lay, hand still holding hand, while a brown dog was slowly eating one of the arms of the father.[80]

Another graphic example came from J. Martin Miller, the war correspondent for *The Graphic*, a British journal and *Harper's Weekly* of New York: 'The spirit of revenge seized upon the soldiers of the allied armies, and the Russians, French and Germans particularly displayed a cruelty even less excusable than that of the Chinese, if the obligations of enlightenment be considered.'[81] Miller was also to write of the brutality of the German contingent in particular, of whom he stated 'the cruelties reported are becoming alarmingly numerous'.[82] There is evidence, it has been argued, that, with the greater vigour with which Waldersee pursued the anti-Boxer expeditions, the Germans were more brutal than other nationalities in their dealings with those Chinese citizenry that were unfortunate enough to come within their purview.[83]

Even the official war correspondent accompanying the German force, Baron Eugen Binder-Krieglstein, noted the readiness, compared with some of the other contingents, with which they resorted to violence at the slightest provocation.[84] This was not merely the soldiery being trigger happy, but rather a policy that came from the top; Waldersee noted in his diary on 7 December 1900 vis-à-vis the Chinese: 'Only if one behaves harshly and ruthlessly against them can one make progress with them.'[85]

It is no surprise to note that among Waldersee's brigade commanders was one Major General Lothar von Trotha.[86] Trotha has the distinction, if that is the correct word, of being the principal architect of the first genocide of the twentieth century.[87] This was earned by his actions, following appointment to command in German South West Africa (Namibia) in 1904, in the pursuit of quelling a rising by the Herero people, who had taken up arms in protest at land and cattle stealing by German settlers.[88] Large numbers of the Herero people, men, women, and children, were either killed directly or, with their water supplies poisoned, forced into desert areas to perish of thirst. The remainder were virtually enslaved, and it is estimated that by 1908 some eighty per cent of the estimated 60,000 population that had existed prior to 1904 had perished.[89] In chilling words Trothae had outlined his thoughts on the matter prior to taking command, echoing somewhat Waldersee's thoughts concerning the Chinese in 1900: 'My intimate knowledge of many central African tribes has everywhere convinced me of the necessity that the Negro does not respect treaties but only brute force.'[90]

Trotha's 'intimate knowledge' had been gained during campaigns in the Iringa Highlands region of German East Africa (Tanzania) where he commanded the Colonial Troops in 1896. These units conducted what we would today call a counter-insurgency campaign from 1891 to 1898 in an effort to subdue the Wehehe, who were resistant to German rule. It was a new kind of warfare; as Major General Eduard von Liebert, Governor and commander of German forces in the colony put it: 'For thirty years I have been continually engaged in the study of war and in the history of war in particular. But, what I experienced in Uhehe[91] existed beyond the parameters of all that had existed previously. It was truly African.'[92]

This 'African' type of war involved the isolation of those valley communities in the region that were considered rebellious, and the destruction of their food and water supplies. The men would be killed, shot if they had weapons, hanged if not, while young women and children were taken into custody and put to work as concubines or labourers.[93] The correspondent of the *Strassburger Neueste Nachrichten* put it bluntly: 'We did not take any prisoners. They were always hung.'[94] The operations in East Africa were the only significant combat operations undertaken by Germany between the Franco-Prussian War of 1870–71 and the Boxer War. It is then unsurprising that the methodologies resorted to in East Africa were utilised during the latter campaign, which in several ways it resembled.

A book written after the campaign, and encompassing the lessons learned during it, made the comparison between the combat in East Africa and that in China: 'The primitive and cunning characteristic of the Negroes appears also in the Chinese. They are evenly alike and equal, these natives; whether they are called Malayan or Zulu, Chinese or Indian.'[95]

Whilst there seems little doubt that that von Trotha's command, the 1st East Asiatic Infantry Brigade, played a full part in the expeditions, there is no evidence that it was noted as being particularly brutal in China.[96] Letters home from individual soldiers involved in the operations revealed the brutality of the operations generally, and these came to the notice of the newspapers, where large numbers were published. Known as 'Hun Letters' [*Hunnenbriefe*] these formed the basis of an indictment of German policy raised in the Reichstag by the opposition parties, particularly the SPD. The Chairman of the SPD, August Bebel, quoted from one:

You should have seen how we advanced into the town. Everything that came across our way, be it man, woman or child, everything was slaughtered. Now, how the women screamed! But the Kaiser's order stated: Show no mercy! – and we have sworn allegiance and obedience and that is what we are doing.[97]

Waldersee, who became, and astonishingly remains, a figure writ large in Chinese popular culture through his alleged liaison with Sai Jinhua, a Shanghai courtesan he is supposed to have originally consorted with in Berlin,[98] finally left China via Japan on 3 June 1901, before any peace agreement was signed, and returned to Germany.[99] The Kaiser however was no longer interested in him or his mission and he effectively vanished into something like obscurity until his death in 1904.[100]

The peace agreement itself, commonly known as the Boxer Protocol, was signed on 7 September 1901 between the Qing Empire of China and the Eight-Nation Alliance, plus Belgium, Spain and the Netherlands. The main features required the punishment of several named Chinese officials and the payment of a massive indemnity of 67.5 million pounds sterling over a period of 39 years. Further stipulations included the destruction of a number of fortifications between Beijing and the coast to facilitate any further movement of foreign forces to the capital if so required, the right to station foreign troops at various key point along the same route, the prohibition of arms importation into China for two years, and the suspension of the Civil Examination in some 45 cities where the Boxers had been active.[101]

There can be little doubt that the Boxer War, and the poisonous propaganda that accompanied it, widened a divide that already existed between the Europeans and the Chinese. To the Europeans, the Chinese became, if they were not already, the 'native', the 'other'. Carl Rosendahl, Diederichs' successor as Governor of Kiautschou, was in charge from March 1898 until February 1899, and both he and his successor Otto Ferdinand Paul Jäschke, who died in office in January 1901, seemed to share this view of the Chinese; it was under the auspices of Jäschke that the incursions of 1899 had taken place.[102] The permanent replacement for Jäschke was Oskar von Truppel, who took over from the acting governor, Max Rollmann, in June 1901.

Truppel seems to have been a man of a very different stamp from his predecessors, and he presided over what he termed the 'demilitarization of the colony'.[103] This involved an end to the provocative relations with the Chinese provincial government and the withdrawal of detachments of the Naval Battalion from Chinese territory.[104] Truppel was, as all the governors, a naval officer responsible to State Secretary Alfred von Tirpitz, and Tirpitz was keen that the territory should become financially secure. Accordingly, Truppel lobbied hard to achieve the goal of making Tsingtau the port through which the trade of Shantung and Honan provinces should pass.[105] In an attempt to make this an attractive option Tsingtau had initially been accorded the status of a free port, so that while goods remained within the port they were not liable for duties of any kind. However, by 1905 it was concluded that around half the goods that passed through the port were smuggled, so the decision was made to place the port under the authority of the Chinese Imperial Maritime Customs in return for 20 per cent of the revenues raised.[106] The Kiautschou territory was though never able to pay for itself, and remained a heavy drain on the naval budget (see Table 1).

Table 1. The Balance of Payments of the Kiautschou Territory 1901–1912 (expressed in millions of marks)[107]

Year	Imports	Exports	Difference
1901	13.45	5.28	- 8.17
1902	25.64	8.90	- 16.74
1903	34.97	14.74	- 20.23
1904	44.87	19.98	- 24.89
1905	69.17	24.71	- 44.46
1906	82.37	34.22	- 48.15
1907	55.38	32.59	- 22.79
1908	69.04	47.34	- 21.70
1909	65.46	54.73	- 10.73
1910	69.37	60.56	- 8.81
1911	114.93	80.29	- 34.64
1912	121.25	79.64	- 41.61
Totals	**765.90**	**462.98**	**- 302.92**

Directly under the Governor was the Chief of Staff, also Deputy Governor, who headed the military administration, and the Civil Commissioner, responsible, as the title suggests, for the civil administration of the territory. The first Civil Commissioner of Kiautschou was Dr Ludwig Wilhelm Schramaier, a Foreign Office official who had held consular positions in Shanghai and Canton and was seconded to Diederichs as an interpreter. Diederichs, as the first Governor of the territory, had firmly set his face against the evils of land speculation and was determined that it would not be allowed to occur. Schramaier drew up a memorandum on the matter, and, upon being appointed civil commissioner, drew up and became the driving force behind the regulatory framework pertaining.

These regulations, codified into a law in 1898, stipulated that all urban land the Governor deemed necessary for public works had to be sold to the authorities at pre-occupation prices. These areas were then divided up into parcels, and those not deemed to be of utility were then sold again at a profit. The rural areas were not generally affected by these rules.

All of the private land in the territory was subject to an annual tax at the rate of six per cent of its assessed value, and, if sold, a further thirty-three per cent increment tax was levied on the net profit. After twenty-five years there was to be a reassessment of its value, and the increment tax was then payable on any increase in value irrespective of whether or not it was to be sold. When any land was to be sold the Governor had the right to purchase it at the price reported, which of course provided a disincentive to those who sought to avoid or reduce their liability to the increment tax by reporting a low sale price.

After 1903 a tax on those who bought land but failed to develop it was introduced, whereby those individuals or organisations that tried to sit on land holdings were taxed at nine per cent per annum instead of the normal six per cent. Further, every three years of non-use would incur another three per cent increase, until a ceiling of twenty-four per cent per annum was reached. Improvements and development of the land would however ensure the tax reverted to six per cent. These anti-capitalist measures ensured that land speculation in Kiautschou was thus rendered economically impossible, and land utilisation and economic growth were very rapid.

The British Liberal Member of Parliament for Barnsley, Yorkshire, Sir Joseph Walton, a lawyer and member of the Royal Central Asian Society, whose interest in the region was so great that he was known as the 'Member for China',[108] approved of the measures. He visited Tsingtau during the gubernatorial tenure of Jäschke, and later remarked that: 'The regulations adopted by the Germans might with great advantage be put in force at places in our own Empire where new towns are being created. They are designed to stop land speculators buying up huge blocks of land and artificially running up prices.'[109] In another anti-capitalist move, the revenues raised by the land-tax measures were applied to the welfare of both the European and Chinese population of the territory.[110]

This move away from an overtly discriminatory regime in respect of the Chinese was a noteworthy feature of the colonial regime from 1904. In November of that year a German bank director, Hoffman, noted approvingly that under Truppel the Chinese residents of Kiautschou had become 'fully equal citizens of our colony' and had attained 'civil rights'.[111] Indeed, Steinmetz argues that from 1904 onwards the Chinese, 'especially the wealthier and more educated Chinese – were once again described as [...] a cultured or civilised people'.[112] He ascribes this attitudinal shift to the 'presence of educated Sinologists within the colonial government'.[113]

Certainly, in respect of the Pacific territories, it has been argued that the colonial officials tended to be better educated, younger, and more flexible in comparison with the Junker aristocrats associated with the African possessions.[114] There were exceptions to this as has already been noted, but of course the service providing the chief colonial officials for Kiautschou was not the Foreign Office, or the Colonial Office after 1907, but rather the Navy; an institution generally credited with being somewhat less dominated by 'Junker aristocrats' than, for example, the Army. To illustrate the case in point, Berghahn's analysis shows that in 1907 only eleven per cent of naval officers came from aristocratic backgrounds, as against thirty-four per cent in the Army.[115] It is perhaps worth noting at this point that not all the aristocratic army officers were, stereotypically, totally disconnected from education or culture in any event. For example Luiz Baron von Liliencron, who was an aide-de-camp to Jäschke and later rose to the rank of Major General, was the son of the eminent scholar, musicologist and liturgical specialist, Rochus Baron von Liliencron, and the cousin of the lyric poet Detlev Baron von Liliencron.[116] He was also an author in his own right.[117]

The bourgeois background of many naval officers did not however stop at least some of them from 'aping the mannerisms of the Prussian aristocracy'.[118] This point in the current context is reinforced when considering that Truppel's pred-ecessors had acted, vis-à-vis the 'natives', in a way that would have been familiar to their Africa- based counterparts. It seems then that the style of governance of Kiautschou under Truppel had rather less to do with his origins, it will not have gone unnoticed that he possessed the ennobling 'von', or naval background as such, and rather more to do with his own personality and style. It might also be pointed out that he was forty-seven years old upon taking up his appointment on 8 June 1901, and thus perhaps possessed a more considered 'world-view'. He had reached the age of fifty-seven when, for reasons that are unclear, he resigned the position on 19 August 1911. His replacement was to be his Chief of Staff Captain Alfred Meyer-Waldeck, who had held the position since 1908.[119] Truppel was thus the longest serving governor of the territory, and, as it happened, events conspired to ensure that Meyer-Waldeck was unable to exceed his tenure.

The period immediately following Meyer-Waldeck's appointment was tumul-tuous for China, though the direct effects on the Kiautschou Territory were more or less limited to an influx of Chinese. The population within Tsingtau's city limits, as compared to 1910, had increased by over 55 per cent some three years later – from 34,180 to 53,312, while the Chinese population outside the city, but within the borders of the protectorate, was estimated at 161,000, showing an increase of roughly the same magnitude over the period.[120]

Many of those Chinese who migrated to Kiautschou did so to avoid the upheaval occasioned by the revolution that broke out in September 1911. The Guangxu Emperor had died on 14 November 1908, a day before Empress Dowager Cixi, whose last edict named the former emperor's nephew, Pu Yi (Puyi), to the succes-sion. The Xuantong Emperor as he became known was just under three years old, thus a regency was exercised by his father Zaifeng (Prince Chun). The regent had a score to settle with the powerful commander of China's Beiyang Army (the first of the New Armies, created in 1901, and modelled on contemporary European lines in a systematic attempt to upgrade Chinese military capability), Yuan Shikai (Yuán Shìkǎi).[121]

This animus dated back to the One Hundred Days of 1898 when Yuan, so Zaifeng believed, had been among the conservative forces that had staged a *coup d'état* against his brother, and he accordingly forced him into retirement. Unfor-tunately it was to Yuan that he had to turn some three years later, following the Wuchang Uprising on 10 October 1911. This was a revolt by officers of the New Army stationed at that city (on the central Yangtze) who were also members of the United Alliance (Tongmenghui). Organised by Sun Yat-sen in 1905, the Alliance encompassed those with republican, nationalist and socialist objectives who wished an end to the Qing dynasty, the removal of foreign domination, and a reformation of land ownership.[122] The conflict quickly spread, becoming known as the Xinhai (Hsinhai) Revolution, whereby several provinces seceded from Qing rule.

Both sides of the conflict were aware that Yuan, who still commanded the loyalty of the Beiyang Army, held the balance of power; whichever side he supported would win. Yuan had it seems ideas of his own; he became Prime Minister under Zaifeng on 1 November 1911, then quickly manoeuvred the regent into abdicating his position, 6 December 1911, in favour of Empress Dowager Longyu, a niece of Cixi and former Empress Consort to the Guangxu Emperor.

Yuan also opened negotiations with the Alliance, which proclaimed the Republic of China on 1 January 1912 with Sun Yat-sen as the provisional president. The Republicans were militarily weak, and so were forced to compromise with Yuan who demanded the presidency for himself in exchange for arranging the abdication of the Emperor. This arrangement, despite many complications, was agreed to and on 12 February 1912 the Empress Dowager Longyu signed the edict of abdication on behalf of Pu Yi.[123] Two days later Yuan Shikai took the position of provisional president, after Sun resigned in the name of national unity and order,[124] and he was sworn in as President of the Republic of China on 10 March 1912.[125]

The constitution of the Republic of China was ostensibly democratic, and under it elections were conducted in February 1913, albeit the franchise was highly restrictive. The winner of these elections was the Kuomintang (Chinese Nationalist Party or KMT), which had been founded in August 1912 as an amalgam of the various groups, mainly the United Alliance, which had risen against the Qing dynasty. The leader and deputy leader were Sun Yat-sen and Huang Xing (Huang Hsing), but the dynamic force that mobilised support amongst the voting classes was Song Jiaoren, who became the parliamentary leader. Yuan began to exhibit dictatorial traits, inasmuch as he ignored parliament when negotiating a huge loan, the Reorganisation Loan, from the outside powers. In order to repay this loan he had to agree to foreign control of the Salt Tax and the presence of foreign administrators to ensure compliance – a complete betrayal of one of the main principles of the revolution. The parliament with its KMT majority attempted to call Yuan to account by impeaching him, whereas he dismissed several provincial governors and was strongly suspected of having Song killed in February 1913. These actions led to the Second Revolution of July 1913, in which attempts, poorly led by the KMT, were made to try and remove or restrict Yuan. They failed miserably, with the result that Yuan dissolved the Nationalist Party in November and dismissed the parliament early in 1914, ruling as an overt dictator from then on.[126]

Yuan's rule was unstable, and he was unable to effect centralised control from the capital Beijing (Peking). This tendency was to lead to the curse of 'warlordism' that was to bedevil China for the next thirty-odd years, but more immediately it had a direct effect on Japan. Japan's main foreign policy goal was to secure a dominant position in China via an expansion of economic and political influence.[127] In order to achieve this they had reached an accommodation with Sun Yat-sen who was prepared to concede considerable economic benefits to Japan, and a company to promote the exploitation of Chinese raw material using Japanese capital was set up. The China Industrial Company had Sun as president and a former Japanese Foreign Ministry official as his deputy. Sun however did not control China, and after the abortive rising in July 1913, and Yuan's successful suppression of it, he was not able to even remain in the country. Japan had, as it were, backed the wrong horse and was now more or less cut off from political influence, thus Japan's primary foreign policy goal was, for the moment, thwarted.[128]

Further difficulties loomed should China, as seemed all too likely, descend into political chaos. In that case the European Great Powers were likely to intervene in order to protect their investments and positions, which might well involve them dividing the country into spheres of influence. If that were to occur Japan could be blocked from access to Chinese markets and natural resources, such as coal and iron vital to Japanese heavy industry, and excluded from political influence.[129] This situation, where Japan was not only prevented from increasing its influence in China, but was also in danger of perhaps losing what it already had, was to have a significant effect on Japanese policy in August 1914. Then, the Japanese government found itself presented with an unsurpassed opportunity, not only to consolidate what it had, but to greatly enhance it, when it was presented with the prospect of relieving Germany of its colonial assets in the region.

4

Tectonic Shift 1: 1898–1899
Spain and the USA, Germany,
Micronesia and Samoa

Kiautschou was not the last territory Germany was to obtain in the Far East, though it was to be the last acquired by force of arms, or at least at first hand. The German interest in acquiring further territory coincided with an unrelated struggle between a long established imperial power and an up and coming one; the Spanish–American War of 1898. There were several factors entering into the American decision to go to war against Spain, including the Cuban struggle for independence, American imperialism, and, the ostensible trigger, the sinking of the US battleship *Maine* in Havana harbour on 15 February 1898.

Spain and the US went formally to war on 25 April, and on the 27th Commodore George Dewey of the US Navy sailed from a bay near Hong Kong, in command of his seven-ship Asiatic Squadron. He had left the British territory on 24 April, having received telegraphed orders from Secretary of the Navy John Davis Long (across the International Date Line) to attack the Spanish Navy in the Philippines: 'War has commenced between the United States and Spain. Proceed at once, particularly against Spanish fleet. You must capture vessels or destroy. Use utmost endeavors.'[1]

Dewey's squadron arrived at the mouth of Manila Bay on the night of 30 April and he planned to enter the bay and attack whatever Spanish warships he found there the next morning. It was a mission fraught with potential difficulties, including coastal defence batteries mounted on the islands of Corregidor and El Fraile covering the entrance, and the probability that that entrance was mined. Undeterred by these dangers, and in the full knowledge that he could do nothing to repair any damage caused to his squadron, Dewey entered the bay on the morning of 1 May 1898. There were no mines and the coastal artillery was ineffective, and by daybreak the squadron was well inside the bay and advancing towards the city of Manila.

The Americans dubbed the subsequent events as the Battle of Manila Bay, the Spanish termed it the Battle of Cavite (*Batalla de Cavite*), and it was an extraordinary affair. By 12.30p.m. the seven-ship Spanish squadron had ceased firing and the Spanish colours flying onshore were struck and replaced by the white flag of surrender. The Spanish commander, Admiral Patricio Montojo y Pasarón, ordered those of his ships remaining afloat to be scuttled, and the Americans burnt several of those that failed to disable themselves in this manner.

Dewey had won a famous, and decisive, victory; Spanish naval power in the Pacific had been utterly destroyed in a morning, with 371 men killed and wounded, while the American squadron had not had a single man killed, and only nine wounded, none of them seriously. None of the vessels had been damaged to any significant degree either. The next day the Americans took over the naval facilities at Cavite, and thus gained access to a dockyard that would be essential in maintaining the squadron so far from the continental US.

However, and despite his unequivocal victory, Dewey now found himself beset with difficulties. He had only a few hundred men to deploy militarily, yet garrisoned in Manila was a Spanish force numbering some 13,000. These were, in theory, able to manoeuvre and might conceivably have marched on Cavite to dispossess Dewey. The Spanish army in the Philippines had been fighting an insurrectionist movement for several years, and it was in order to bolster this insurrection, and thus 'assist me in my operations against the Spanish'[2] as Dewey put it, that he had the exiled leader of the insurrection, Emilio Aguinaldo, brought back to the Philippines from Singapore.[3]

Aguinaldo landed on 19 May and immediately rallied the insurgent forces behind him, then began the task of rounding up the Spanish garrisons in the islands. Manila though was still held by the Spanish. Aguinaldo believed, as of course did his followers, that what they and the Americans were fighting for was Filipino independence. He was only to be disabused of this notion at a later date.[4] For the moment he was useful in the absence of any US Army forces, which were not expected to arrive until June or July. The principal potential problem facing the US forces was that Aguinaldo might capture Manila before they could get their troops there.

Dewey also faced difficulties, or perceived difficulties, on the naval front from two directions. Most immediately, two German cruisers, the protected *Irene* and the light *Cormoran*, arrived at Manila Bay on 6 and 9 May respectively. On 10 May the commanders of the two warships called on the Spanish Governor-General and Admiral Montojo in Manila.[5] Rumours began to circulate to the effect that Germany would join with Spain and attempt to defeat Dewey's squadron. The rumour mill was fed still further on 6 June when the German liner *Darmstadt* sailed into the bay carrying some 1,400 German seamen. These were not however a landing party, but rather relief crews for the German East Asiatic Squadron that had been sent to Manila Bay to relieve a portion of the crews of *Irene* and *Cormoran*. The *Darmstadt* having departed on 9 June, three days later the protected cruiser SMS *Kaiserin Augusta* arrived with Vice Admiral Otto von Diederichs on board. The German vessels at Manila were further augmented by the arrival of the ironclad *Kaiser* on 18 June and the protected cruiser *Prinzess Wilhelm* two days later.[6]

The German warships at Manila Bay constituted a powerful squadron, probably as powerful as Dewey's force, and Dewey was profoundly suspicious of them, outnumbering, as they did, the contingents of Japan, France and Britain.[7] What, with perspective, can now be viewed as minor incidents assumed frightening proportions contemporaneously; incidents such as Diederichs visits to the

Spanish Governor-General and the apparent refusal of the German squadron to acknowledge the proclaimed US blockade. These incidents were much magnified by the popular American press.

Subsequent scholarly research has established that the 'confrontation' between Diederichs and Dewey was, largely, the product of the stressful situation Dewey, now promoted a rear admiral, found himself in following his destruction of the Spanish ships.[8] The American admiral was, both literally and figuratively, the man on the spot and his communications with his superiors were both slow, 'I was three days from any working cable station,'[9] and difficult since he was unable to make use of the Manila–Hong Kong cable.[10] Any decisions Dewey made could have had the most profound repercussions. It is hardly surprising then that the arrival of Diederichs, who was senior to him, was irksome in itself, but given that the German admiral was also known as the recent occupier of Kiautschou, and therefore as an accomplished annexationist at the head of a powerful force, then that Dewey was suspicious is hardly surprising.

The German Foreign Office, under Bernhard von Bülow, had no wish to antagonise the Americans as Bülow was later to claim: 'I only approved of sending our fleet to Manila to protect Germany's great economic interests there. Any enmity against America was distant from our minds.'[11] This position is confirmed by contemporaneous documents; on 14 May Bülow had informed the Kaiser that the Filipinos would be hardly likely to acquiesce in exchanging 'the Spanish yoke' for another set of European masters, and presciently, he foresaw that to subject them against their will to such foreign rule would probably be no easy task. He cautioned Wilhelm against any 'imprudent move' while remaining hopeful that territory would be gained through diplomatic means.[12] The German consul in Manila, Dr Friedrich Kruger, was instructed to 'remain negative' if approaches were made with a view to Germany becoming entangled in Philippine issues, and he was also told to 'observe unobtrusively and report any signs that may indicate that one or another power, for example England or America, is attempting to establish itself permanently through negotiations with the insurgents.'[13]

Diederichs' instructions from Vice Admiral Eduard von Knorr, Chief of the Naval High Command, were also clear as to what he was there to achieve; his remit was to 'protect German interests,' 'obtain a clear and correct picture' of what was happening and 'develop a personal appraisal of the Spanish position.'[14] Diederichs' actions during his time at the bay are evidence that he did not exceed these instructions as, for example, when the Spanish Governor-General asked him to mediate a truce between the Spanish military and the insurgent forces, and Diederichs declined as this would breach German neutrality.[15] The German admiral also considered that the blockade Dewey had declared was in fact illegal, inasmuch as it was ineffective.[16]

The relevant, indeed only, piece of International Law pertaining to blockades was the 16 April 1856 Declaration of Paris.[17] This had stated that 'Blockades, to be binding, must be effective – that is to say, maintained by a force sufficient in reality to prevent access to the coast of the enemy.'[18] Though the US was not a signatory, and there was in any event no international body that could enforce it, the United States declared that it would respect the principles of the declaration during hostilities with Spain.[19] Spain too declared its intention to abide by the declaration, but also gave notice that Madrid would reserve its right to issue letters of marque.[20]

Whatever the legal niceties, and however irritating Admiral Dewey found the German presence, the two squadrons did not come to blows, and in truth there was probably very little chance of that really happening. Neither commander was a fool, nor a knave, so it seems likely that some of the reports that found their way into the US public domain, both during and after the war, were much exaggerated. One such came from the captain of the cruiser *Raleigh*, who related, during a night of entertainment at the Union League Club House, a conversation he claimed to have overheard between Dewey and a German officer. Dewey is supposed to have said:

> Tell your admiral I am blockading here. Now note carefully what I say and tell your admiral that I say it [...] Tell your admiral that the slightest infraction of any rule will mean but one thing. That will be war. [...] If your people are ready for war with the United States they can have it at any time.[21]

Real, rather than fictional, fighting was something Dewey had to worry about in terms of Spanish naval reinforcements arriving. A relief expedition sailed from Cadiz on 16 June, commanded by Rear Admiral Manuel de la Cámara y Libermoore. The core of this relief consisted of the modernised second-class battleship *Pelayo* (1888) and the 'Reina Regente'-class cruiser *Carlos V* (1898). There were also three destroyers and, in order to reinforce Spanish forces in the Philippines, six vessels carrying troops and supplies. This squadron steamed on 16 June from Cadiz into the Mediterranean and, intending to pass through the Suez Canal, reached Port Said on 26 June intent on coaling. The British/Egyptian government however was dogmatic concerning enforcement of neutrality laws, and procrastinated to such an extent that it took over a week for the expedition to transit the canal.[22]

By sending their last naval reserves to the Philippines the Spanish government knew it was leaving itself open to naval attack, and that this might become a reality was brought home in no uncertain terms by the Battle of Santiago de Cuba, fought on 3 July 1898. It was a decisive victory, and the destruction of the Spanish navy in the western Atlantic meant that the Americans could now, if they wished, deploy their heavy ships on operations against mainland Spain, and the Spanish would be virtually defenceless. Indeed US propaganda and misinformation techniques had made an apparently convincing case that a US naval force would cross the Atlantic and attack the Spanish mainland and other holdings such as the Canary Islands.[23] On 7 July Cámara was ordered to return home.[24]

With the recall of the relieving force under Cámara the Spanish government had no cards left. Accordingly, on 26 July it asked France to mediate with the US and Jules-Martin Cambon, Ambassador to Washington 1897–1902, opened negotiations with William R. Day, the US Secretary of State, both 'possessing for this purpose full authority from the Government of the United States and the Government of Spain'.[25]

Cambon and Day negotiated a 'Protocol of Agreement' that was transmitted to Madrid for scrutiny, and, having been accepted on 11 August, was signed by both men the next day. There were six articles, but the key points were that Spain relinquished 'all claim of sovereignty over and title to Cuba' [Article I] and ceded to the US 'the island of Porto [*sic*] Rico and other islands now under Spanish sovereignty in the West Indies, and also an island in the Ladrones [Mariana, or Marianas, Islands] to be selected by the United States' [Article II]. The position as regards the Philippines was less clear cut: 'The United States will occupy and hold the city, bay and harbour of Manila, pending the conclusion of a treaty of peace which shall determine the control, disposition and government of the Philippines' [Article III].

Articles V and VI stipulated that peace negotiations would start in Paris 'not later than October 1, 1898' and that 'Upon the conclusion and signing of this protocol, hostilities between the two countries shall be suspended' respectively.[26] Because of the distances involved word only reached Manila on 16 August of the armistice terms, by which time they were rendered somewhat academic; the city had surrendered to the Americans at 5.45p.m. on 13 August.[27] This academic point was, however, to cost the US $20 million. During the formal peace negotiations that began at Paris on 1 October the Spanish were justified in pointing out that because Manila had surrendered after the armistice had been signed, when under the terms of that armistice the US should have stopped all operations, the conquest did not count. In recognition perhaps that the Spanish point had some validity, the US offered financial compensation, which the Spanish accepted, and on 10 December 1898 the US and Spain signed the Treaty of Paris.

The final form of the Treaty, while otherwise not differing greatly from the terms set out in the Protocol (Article II specified the 'island in the Ladrones' was to be Guam), demonstrated in no uncertain terms the change of heart that had occurred within the US administration vis-à-vis the Philippines. Article III stated that 'Spain cedes to the United States the archipelago known as the Philippine Islands [...] The United States will pay to Spain the sum of twenty million dollars ($20,000,000) within three months after the exchange of the ratifications of the present treaty'.[28]

Historians have achieved little in the way of consensus as regards when and why President William McKinley came to the decision to change his Philippine policy to one of annexation, though the President was later to claim that it was arrived at by supernatural means.[29]

Whatever the metaphysical input into the decision, there is little doubt that it was palatable to the European Great Powers. When the war started the Great Powers had accepted US intervention in Cuba, but Dewey's victory in Manila Bay raised the conflict from regional to global dimensions. Britain, France, Germany and Russia, and of course Japan, then became very interested in the fate of the Philippines. The Europeans were particularly concerned about the implications should the war proliferate, and the conflict spread to the eastern side of the Atlantic;

potential US naval bases in, say, the Canaries or Balearics, were not a prospect to be contemplated with equanimity. Accordingly they sought to encourage the peace process.[30] Had the US decided not to annex the Philippines then it seems probable that one or more of them, alone or in combination, would have claimed the archipelago or portions of it. Germany, or at least the Kaiser, seems to have been a firm proponent of acquiring territory there. Bülow records receiving a message from him in April 1898: 'Tirpitz is as firm as a rock in his conviction that we must have Manila and that this would be of enormous advantage to us. As soon as the revolution has torn Manila from Spain we must occupy it.'[31]

It seems unlikely that Alfred Tirpitz was particularly fixated on Manila in 1898, as that was the year the Navy State Secretary was campaigning for the first of his Fleet Acts to be adopted by the German Empire. In any event, once it became clear that the US intended to annex the Philippines, Germany set out a more realistic goal; that of acquiring the Spanish Pacific islands. Indeed, it was with US and British knowledge and approval that Germany approached Spain to open negotiations.[32] Spain, if shorn of the Philippines, would, in all likelihood, have had no end of difficulty in attempting to administer these remote and scattered territories. In any event, provisional agreement was reached in September 1898 that, subject to the final terms of the negotiations (the islands would remain under Spanish control until the treaty with the US was concluded)[33] that were due to start in Paris on 1 October, they would be transferred to Germany. The price was settled on 12 February 1899; 16.6 million marks (*circa* 25 million pesetas or $5 million).[34] The exchange was embodied in the Spanish–German Treaty of 30 June 1899 (*Tratado hispano-alemán de 30 junio de 1899*).[35]

President McKinley was able to include in his 1899 State of the Union Address his approval of the transaction:

> Subsequent to the exchange of our peace treaty with Spain, Germany acquired the Caroline Islands by purchase, paying therefore $5,000,000. Assurances have been received from the German Government that the rights of American missionaries and traders there will be considerably observed.[36]

Bernhard von Bülow records that he was also able to report positively on the matter:

> The acquisition of the Caroline and Marianne Islands turned our possessions in the western Pacific into a connected whole. With the Bismarck Archipelago and Kaiser Wilhelm Land in the south, the Marschall, Caroline, and Pelew Islands in the centre, and the Mariannes in the north, we now had a firm basis for our economic and general political development in Oceania. I was able also to point out in the Reichstag that the acquisition of the Carolines had in no way disturbed our good relations with Spain. For Spain they represented only fragments of a crumbled building, for us they were pillars and buttresses for a building with a future.[37]

Needless to say, the indigenous populations of these territories had no choice in the change of colonial masters, and probably only got to know that such a thing had occurred when the new rulers got around to telling them. For example, the people of Pohnpei (Ponape), who were to feature again in the story of Germany's Pacific territories, were informed only on 12 October 1899 that they now owed allegiance to Kaiser Wilhelm II. Rudolf von Bennigsen, Governor of German New Guinea, travelled there to proclaim the annexation thus:

> From now on, the flag of the German Empire shall fly over these islands for all time, to the honour of the Empire and as a warning towards the enemy. It shall bring the desired happiness and the long missed peace to these lands under German administration. It shall perpetually remind the population of this land to be faithful subjects to our beloved Emperor and King. At this solemn occasion let us join in the call to his honour: His Majesty, the German Emperor and King Wilhelm II, hooray![38]

Prince Heinrich thought that while the new German territories might have been of minimal economic value, they would nevertheless have value for the German Navy. Not only would it be possible to construct more coaling stations, but, because of their existence, they would 'help to increase our navy in general, as well as our squadron out here'.[39] This reasoning was exactly what Bismarck had feared; he opined in 1873 that 'colonies [...] would only be a source of weakness, because colonies could only be defended by powerful fleets, and Germany's geographical position did not necessitate her development into a first class maritime power'.[40]

These islands and island groups acquired by Germany were located within the region known as Micronesia (from the Greek 'small islands'). The term originated with the French explorer and navigator Jules Dumont d'Urville, who, in 1832, proposed differentiating the various island groups in the Pacific that had previously been aggregated as Polynesia. Henceforth, Micronesia described those islands inscribing an arc across the northern and central Pacific, while Melanesia (black islands) became the term for those to the north and east of Australia, including New Guinea, the Bismarck Archipelago, Fiji, the Solomon Islands and the Pelew (Palau) Islands. Polynesia then became the term for those islands roughly within the triangle Hawaii, New Zealand and Easter Island.[41]

Micronesia in general has been described as resembling 'a handful of chickpeas flung over the sea',[42] and the German territories in particular as 'a "cloud" of islands, stretching east and west between the parallels of 4° and 12°30' North, and the meridians of 134° and 172°30' East'.[43] In terms of distance, the area covered was over 3,700 kilometres east–west and 2,200 kilometres north–south, the extremities being Tobi (Hatohobei) and Mili Atoll in the Palau and Marshall Islands respectively, and the uninhabited volcano of Farallón de Pájaros in the Marianas and Kapingamarangi Atoll in the Carolines.[44]

In material terms the newly gained island territories were worthless; they were 'show colonies' acquired merely to boost Germany's prestige as a world power.[45] This was not a fact kept particularly well hidden at the time; indeed the precarious financial position of German New Guinea had been exemplified by the 'nationalisation' of that territory. The administration of the region had been in the hands of the German New Guinea Company until the Imperial government had been forced to take over the administration, appointing Rudolf von Bennigsen as governor on 1 April 1899.[46] The vice-governor, Albert Hahl, assumed the governorship in 1902 and put the economic status of the newly acquired islands quite clearly to the Reichstag the same year:

> Admittedly, Germany is unlikely to gain much economic advantage from this island territory. But I still think we can achieve a highly idealistic purpose there. This is to preserve the Polynesian [...] and gradually civilising them. Germany should hold tight to the idea that this purpose alone is enough to justify keeping and administering these islands.[47]

The Carolines and Marianas were, for administrative purposes, sub-divided into three districts; the Eastern Carolines, the Western Carolines including Palau [Belau], and the Marianas. Initially there were two district officers (*Bezirksamtmann*) stationed at Yap and Saipan under the vice-governor at Ponape. The whole was under the overall governance of the governor of German New Guinea based at Herbertshöhe in Neu Pommern (New Britain) in the Bismarck Archipelago. The vice-governorship was abolished in 1902 upon the then holder of the post, Albert Hahl, being elevated to gubernatorial level.[48] This entire area had, up until 1911, a total administrative workforce, spread across the three centres, of fourteen personnel, including three seamen for the government schooner.[49]

The territory purchased from Spain was not the last such to come to Germany however. That honour, if that is the correct term, went to German Samoa, a territory retrospectively dignified by Bülow as 'one of the finest brilliants in our colonial diadem'[50] Samoa is the native name of a group of volcanic islands in central Polynesia long known as the 'Navigators Islands'. The two largest islands are those in the western part of the archipelago, Savaii (Savai'i) and Upolu, the latter gaining some fame in Europe in the late nineteenth century for being the final home and last resting place of the Scots author, Robert Louis Stevenson. Stevenson and his wife Fanny had come to Samoa in 1889 and settled on Upolu the following year on land purchased on the slopes of Mount Vaea near Apia. Stevenson wrote numerous of works while in residence, including *The Bottle Imp*, *The Beach at Falesa*, *David Balfour*, and *The Ebb Tide*, but his most controversial work was *A Footnote to History: Eight Years of Trouble in Samoa*, which ridiculed the colonial officials and the way they ran affairs. He feared for a time it would result in his own deportation. Stevenson named his property 'Vailima' and it was while there on 3 December 1894 that he died from what is believed to have been a cerebral haemorrhage at the age of 44.[51]

The eastern portion of the archipelago consists, in the main, of Samoa's third largest island, Tutuila, and the three islands of the Manu'a Islands Group, Ofu, Olosega and Tau (Ta'u) located some 110 kilometres east of Tutuila. The unusual circular atoll of Swains Island is some 320 kilometres to the north of Tutuila and Rose Atoll, the easternmost of the Samoan islands, is located some 144 kilometres to the east of Tau.

European and American traders began visiting the islands during the 1830s, when, politically, they were divided into competing chieftainships. The various traders, mainly British, American and German, began backing, and arming, various of these factions in their disputes with each other, hoping thereby to achieve dominance if 'their' client won. The 1889 'Final Act of the Berlin Conference on Samoan Affairs', whereby Britain, the US and Germany all agreed to recognise Samoan independence, brought this process, immensely destructive in every sense of the word, to an end, at least temporarily. Under the terms of the 'Berlin General Act', as it became known, the Samoan king would be 'advised' by the consuls of the three powers.[52]

Problems arose when the succession came into question, and the election of a new king, according to the laws and customs of Samoa, was contested by force of arms. As President McKinley put it in his State of the Union address in December 1899:

> The active intervention of American and British war ships became imperative to restore order, at the cost of sanguinary encounters. In this emergency a joint commission of representatives of the United States, Germany, and Great Britain was sent to Samoa to investigate the situation and provide a temporary remedy. By its active efforts a peaceful solution was reached for the time being, the kingship being abolished and a provisional government established. Recommendations unanimously made by the commission for a permanent adjustment of the Samoan question were taken under consideration by the three powers parties to the General Act. But the more they were examined the more evident it became that a radical change was necessary in the relations of the powers to Samoa.[53]

The 'radical change' referred to was embodied in the 'Tripartite Treaty' of 2 December 1899, between the three powers. Under the Treaty, Germany assumed control of the western Samoan islands and the USA took over the eastern islands. Britain relinquished any claims and was compensated by German territory in the Solomons; the former German Solomon Islands (*Nördliche Salomon-Inseln*) territories of Santa Isabel, Choiseul and Ontong Java Atoll (Lord Howe Atoll), as well as the Shortland and Treasury archipelagos in the Bougainville Strait.[54] Thus came into existence the territory of German Samoa, the possession of which Admiral Tirpitz had deemed of great importance to Germany:

> The possession of the Samoan Islands would even now be of great strategic value to the German navy, as an important stopping place on the voyage from Kiautschou, via our possessions in the South Seas, to South America. A time will come when German control of the Samoan Islands will be still more important, since the Panama Canal will mean new routes for the world's trade, and new strategic military routes will result from it. An extension of the rights to a coaling station, which we now enjoy in the Tonga Islands (Vavau), by the cession to Germany of this island or another of the same group, would – although not quite without value – not constitute an equivalent. The already numerous and important German interests in Samoa (in comparison with Tonga) would be of inestimable assistance in the eventual conversion of a harbour in these islands into a highly valuable base.
>
> I must not fail also to point out the extraordinarily favourable situation of Samoa as a landing place and a station for a German world-cable (South America–Samoa–New Guinea–East Africa–West Africa), which we shall have to aim at in future.[55]

Map 5. Significant Islands, Island Groups, and Atolls comprising the German Pacific Island Territory 1885–1914

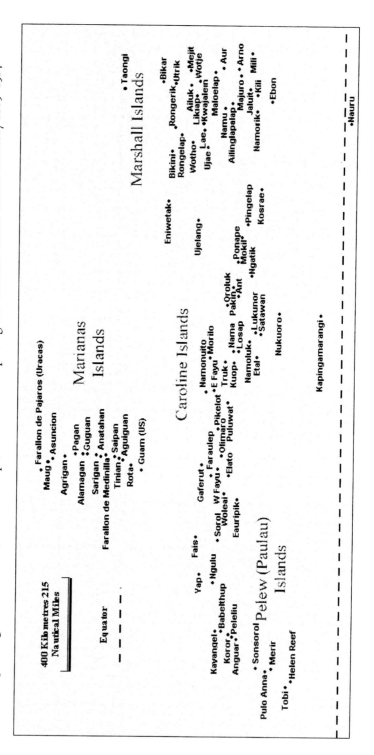

400 Kilometres 215
Nautical Miles

Equator

• Farallon de Pajaros (Uracas)
Maug •
• Asuncion
Agrigan •
Alamagan • Pagan
• Guguan
Sarigan • Anatahan
Farallon de Medinilla •
Tinian • Saipan
Rota • Aguiguan
• Guam (US)

Marianas
Islands

• Taongi

• Bikar
Bikini • Rongerik • Utrik
Rongelap • Ailuk • • Mejit
Wotho • Likiap • Wotje
Ujae Lae • Kwajalein
Maloelap
Namu • • Aur
Ailinglapalap • Majuro • • Arno
Jaluit •
Namorik • • Kili Mili •
• Ebon

Marshall Islands

Eniwetak •

Ujelang •

Ponape
Mokil •
• Ngatik

• Pingelap
Kosrae •

Caroline Islands

• Namonuito
• E Fayu • Morilo
• Olimaro • Pikelot
Gaferut • Faraulep
• Sorol W Fayu •
Woleai • Elato Puluwat •
Euripik •

Yap • Fais •
• Ngulu

• Nama
Kuop • • Losap
Namoluk •
Etal • • Lukunor
• Satawan

Truk • • Oroluk
Pakin •
• Ant

Nukuoro •

Kapingamarangi •

Pelew (Pałau)
Islands

Kavangel •
Koror • • Babetthup
Anguar • • Peleliu
• Sonsorol
Pulo Anna •
• Merir
Tobi • • Helen Reef

• Nauru

This was to be the last acquirement of colonial territory by Imperial Germany in the Pacific, and the penultimate acquirement anywhere if one counts the 1911 acquisition of the 275,000 square kilometres of *Neukamerun* in central Africa. This latter territory, largely worthless from the commercial viewpoint, was carved from France's possessions as a consequence of the Franco-German Agreement of 1911, signed between Imperial Germany and France following the Agadir Crisis of 1911.[56]

It is then somewhat ironic to note that during the period between these acquisitions, the man, other than Kaiser Wilhelm II, most associated with *Weltpolitik*, Bernhard von Bülow, was the Imperial German Chancellor. Hohenlohe, who complained that, particularly in foreign affairs, 'everything is settled by [the Kaiser] and Bülow' and that he had been told nothing of Waldersee's China Expedition, resigned on 16 October 1900.[57] Bülow succeeded him the same day in a move long planned and sought after by Wilhelm, who had remarked as far back as December 1895 that '[Hohenlohe] is too old, he can no longer handle foreign affairs and the Ministry of State [...] Bülow shall become my Bismarck [...]'.[58] Bülow's successor as Foreign Secretary was Oswald von Richthofen, a former director of the Colonial Department within the Foreign Office and a 'convinced colonialist'.[59]

In administrative terms, as well as geographically and politically, the German Pacific colonies, Kiautschou excepted, were at the periphery, and they largely escaped any close supervision from Berlin. They were also neglected in terms of defensive measures; there were no colonial troops or military forces in the territories and no defences were constructed on any of the islands. The administrators of the various territories, islands and groups of islands were largely left to manage their domains in their own way.[60]

According to the German Colonial Society, at the beginning of 1904 the territory of Kaiser-Wilhelmsland, an area of about 179,000 square kilometres, had a population that was estimated at 100,000, of which 113 were European but only 98 German. Some nine years later, in 1913, the European population had risen to 283, of which 264 were German; included in the figure for Europeans were 76 adult females.[61]

The Bismarck Archipelago of some 61,000 square kilometres had a population estimated at 200,000 in 1904, while the European element amounted on 1 January 1 to 320, of which 203 were Germans. By 1913 the European population had risen to 685, of which 482 were German with 134 adult females.[62]

During the year 1903 Kaiser-Wilhelmsland and the Bismarck Archipelago imported goods to the value of 2,913,814 marks, while exports over the same period totalled 1,206,720 marks.[63] By 1913 the value of exported goods had increased to 5,041,106 marks, as against imports amounting to 5,871,840 marks.[64] Exports from the territories consisted in the main of foodstuffs in the shape of copra (the dried meat, or kernel, of the coconut), cocoa, coffee, nuts and sea-cucumbers, Some rubber was also exported, as were decorative items such as mother-of-pearl, tortoise-shell and bird-of-paradise plumes, which were highly sought after in the European millinery industry. Imports consisted in the main of manufactured articles and raw materials such as metals and coal.[65]

The Caroline Islands, with a total area of some 1,600 square kilometres including the 450 square kilometres of the Palau Islands, had, in 1904, a European population of 135 of which only 43 were German. The population of the Marianas, a total land mass of 625 square kilometres, was adjudged to be 2,704, including 45 Japanese and 13 Europeans of which only 7 were German. The value of exports from the territories in 1903 amounted to 589,635 marks, while goods worth 514,099 were imported.

The Marshalls, some 353 islands divided into two archipelagos comprising a total land area of about 400 square kilometres , exported goods to the value of 521,598 marks in 1903, as against imports worth 497,794 marks. The indigenous population was reckoned to be around 15,000, with 51 Germans out of the European total of 77.[66]

The island territories underwent administrative reorganisation in 1906, and in May 1907 responsibility for colonial affairs was removed from Foreign Office control with the establishment of the Colonial Office as a Department of State in its own right. The first Colonial Secretary was Bernhard Dernburg, a former banker of Jewish extraction, who brought notions of efficiency to the job.[67] On 8 January 1907, while heading the Colonial Department of the Foreign Office, Dernburg had argued:

> Whereas colonisation was once carried out by means of destruction, today we are able to colonise by means of preservation. This includes the missionary and the doctor, the railway and the machine, that is to say, the advanced theoretical and applied sciences in all fields.[68]

Dernburg was, somewhat paradoxically, referring to the African colonies, most particularly German South West Africa (Namibia), where a colonial conflict of great brutality had been underway since 1904. The conflict, and the extensive means the Germans found necessary to deploy in order to conduct and eventually win it, propelled colonial matters into the forefront of the domestic sphere. These were paramount during the so-called 'Hottentot Election' of 1907, which, in a similar manner to the British 'Khaki Election' of 1900, saw politicians and parties of the right deploy a wave of chauvinistic hysteria in order to inflict losses on their opponents who had unpatriotically dared to criticise German excesses.[69]

Though obscured by the jingoism of the electoral and colonial campaigns, reforms to the colonial system were required, and, though they had hardly featured in the electoral furore, these were applicable to the Pacific colonies also. The administration of Micronesia was reorganised with, theoretically at least, a more central control exercised from the governor in New Guinea. The arrangement whereby the Jaluit Company effectively ran the Marshall Islands was cancelled, and the islands were integrated into the island territory with Jaluit Island itself becoming a district officer's post.[70]

A census was taken in the territories in 1911, which put the indigenous population at 15,400, suggesting that earlier estimates had been greatly inflated. The European population in 1913 was enumerated at 459, of which 259 were German and 75 adult females.[71] The total combined value of imports for the island groups in 1913 was computed at 3,335,219 marks, as compared with a total of 1,011,893 for 1903, while exports totalled 7,045,700 marks in comparison to 1,111,233 to the earlier year.[72] The main product exported from the islands was phosphate, though there was also a trade in food, such as copra, sea-cucumbers, nuts and sharks' fins, and decorative items like mother-of-pearl and tortoise-shell. Imports consisted of manufactured goods, alcohol, tobacco and food.[73]

The phosphate industry is worthy of further comment, inasmuch as it has been described as being the first example of large-scale capitalist production within the context of the colonial economy.[74] This followed the discovery of large-scale deposits of the mineral on Nauru and the adjacent Ocean Island (Banaba) in the Carolines by Albert Ellis, an Australian prospector, in 1900.[75] The following year the Jaluit Company established a jointly owned company, the Pacific Phosphate Company, with the British-owned Pacific Islands Company to exploit these deposits. The same resource was also discovered on Anguar in the Palau Islands, but a purely German concern, the *Deutsche Südseephosphat-AG*, was established in 1909 to undertake the exploitation there.[76]

The phosphate from Anguar, Ocean Island and Nauru was in much demand for enriching and fertilising the farmland of Australia and New Zealand, and exports of it replaced copra as Micronesia's major export by 1911. During the latter year phosphates contributed more than 80 per cent of the total exports from the German Island Territories, while copra accounted for 16 per cent.[77] It is probably the case that without the phosphate export trade the economy of the territories would have been wholly dependant upon subsidies from Germany. As it was, by 1908 the Pacific Island Territories began to register a small surplus (see Table 2).

Table 2. The Balance of Payments of the German Pacific Colonies 1901–1912 (expressed in millions of marks)[78]

Year	Imports	Exports	Difference
1901	4.45	3.56	- 0.89
1902	5.87	3.77	- 2.10
1903	6.94	3.88	- 3.06
1904	5.79	4.00	- 1.79
1905	8.85	4.39	- 4.46
1906	8.38	5.64	- 2.74
1907	8.54	5.24	- 3.30
1908	7.59	8.72	+ 1.13
1909	9.79	11.35	+ 1.56
1910	9.70	18.19	+ 8.49
1911	12.08	16.41	+ 4.33
1912	14.20	17.13	+ 2.93
Totals	102.18	102.28	+ 0.10

Map 6. The Samoan Archipelago

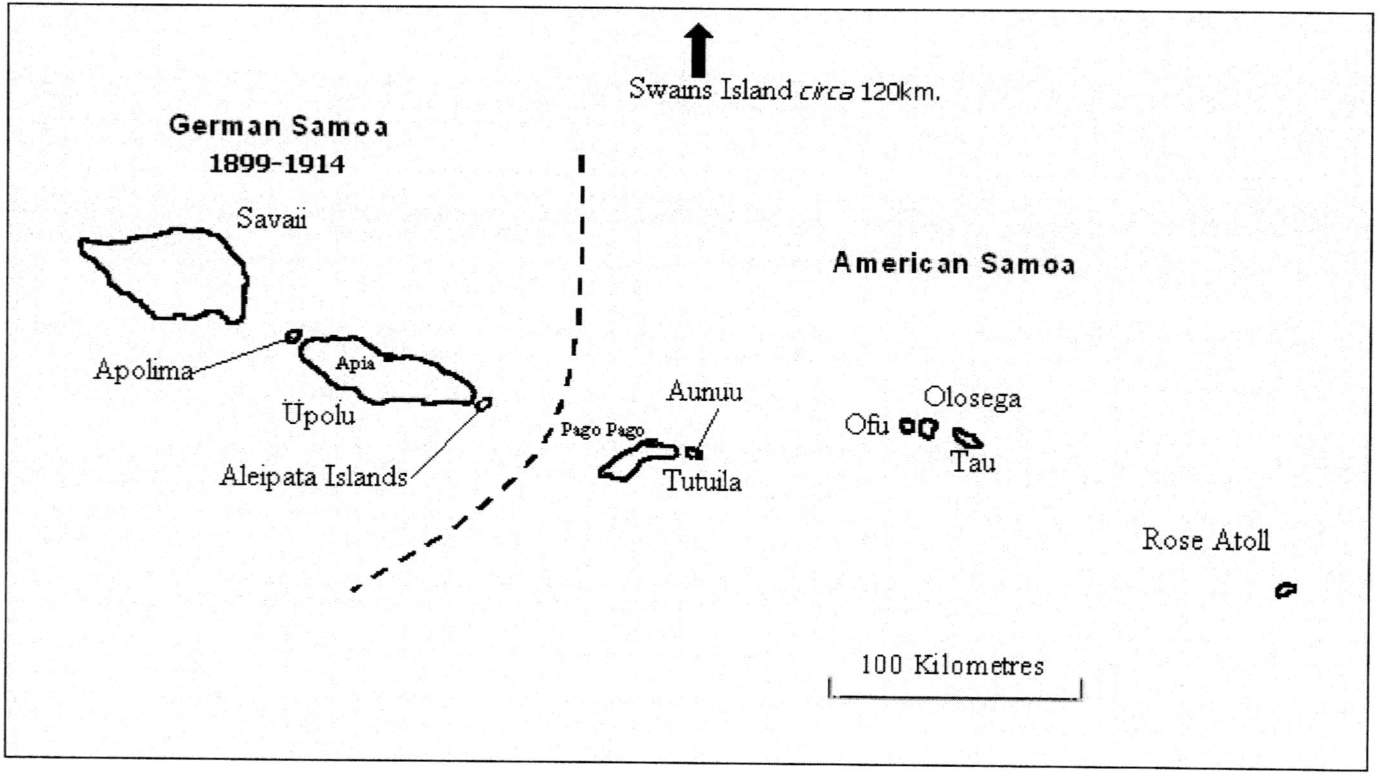

German Samoa
1899–1914

Savaii

Apolima

Apia

Upolu

Aleipata Islands

Swains Island *circa* 120km.

American Samoa

Pago Pago

Aunuu

Tutuila

Ofu

Olosega

Tau

Rose Atoll

100 Kilometres

The number of German administrative personnel increased as time passed, and further posts were established on several more islands. By 1912 there were district officers on Ponape and Yap, and stations had been established on Anguar, Belau, Jaluit Nauru, Saipan and Truk. The German presence in the latter case being sometimes restricted to a single person with a few locally recruited police; the total administrative staff in 1912 having risen to 25 German officials, including two German teachers at a government school on Saipan. With this level of presence nothing remotely approaching close administrative control was possible, and the most the officers could do was occasionally visit some of the islands on the schooner at their disposal, or perhaps on a trading vessel, where they might settle disputes or pass on their decrees.[79]

The four main islands of the protectorate of German Samoa, Sawaii, Upolu (the seat of the governor), Manono, and Apolima, comprised a land area of some 2,572 square kilometres, which supported a population of 32,512. This included, in 1904, 192 Germans out of a European total of 381, and around 600 of mixed ethnicity. Trade in 1903 consisted of exports worth 1,384,507 marks as against imports valued at 2,681,405 marks.[80] These had increased to 5,044,485 marks and 4,994,401 marks respectively in 1913.[81] A census carried out in 1911 established that the indigenous population was 33,554. In 1913 there were 329 Germans out of a total of 557 Europeans, including 99 adult females. Some 1,500 Chinese were also noted.[82]

The disparity between adult European males and females, noted in all the various territories and over the time period, had inevitable consequences. For example, the 1913 population count in German Samoa noted the presence of 1,025 persons of 'mixed descent'. This grouping had not arisen exclusively since formal German colonisation, and was it seems difficult in any event to classify.[83]

The small numbers of German residents recorded in the various censuses was not a feature unique to the Far Eastern colonies. While over a million Germans emigrated between 1887 and 1906, nearly all went to the USA, and by 1913, while the pace of emigration had greatly slackened, there were still only about 23,500 Germans residing in the overseas possessions. Around half of these were in South West Africa, and many were not settlers but rather soldiers, policemen and bureaucrats.[84]

The colonial officials sent out to the Pacific tended to be of a different stamp, better educated, younger, and more flexible, to those that administered Germany's African possessions.[85] One such was Dr Wilhelm Heinrich Solf, who became the first governor of German Samoa and was later appointed Colonial Secretary in 1911. An academic and a linguist, Solf was a philosophy graduate and was a scholar of Sanskrit, Urdu and Persian.[86] He based his policies on those of the British in Fiji and oversaw a regime that made great efforts to accommodate the indigenous population, so much that he was accused by his enemies of 'going native'.[87] Indeed he is said to have often presented himself as a traditional Samoan chief, even though this fooled no one but perhaps himself and invited ridicule from some German settlers.[88]

If German colonial rule can then be said to have been generally benevolent

Map 7. The island of Ponape, showing the five tribal areas or districts[1]

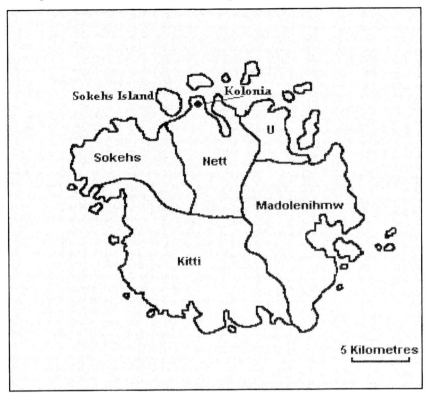

In translation, three of the districts are sometimes rendered as Uh, Net and Kiti. See Kenneth L Rehg and Damian G Sohl, *Ponapean Reference Grammar* (Honolulu, University Press of Hawaii, 1981), p. 360.

in the Pacific, it was not always so in particular instances. The appointment of District Officer Gustav Boeder to the island of Pohnpei in the eastern Carolines in 1910 being one such; he had previously served in German East Africa and was not a person of the tolerant variety in respect of 'natives'. Boeder put forcefully into action a 'labour tax' scheme whereby each Pohnpeian was required to provide fifteen days of unpaid labour per year for public projects. This system was however deeply unpopular with the Pohnpeians, who had, according to German perceptions, a somewhat relaxed attitude towards manual labour that some, particularly Boeder and his ilk, perceived as resistance to German rule.[89]

These conflicting expectations came to a head on 17 October 1910 when a member of the Sokehs chiefdom, which comprised the north-east quarter of Pohnpei and the island of Sokehs, was brutally flogged by Otto Hollborn, the German foreman, on Sokehs Island while undertaking a road-building project. The next day the islanders turned up dressed for war, and Hollborn together with another German were pursued into the house of a missionary where they were trapped. Boeder, accompanied by his secretary, hurried by boat to the scene, but was shot down before he could make his presence felt. His secretary attempted to regain the boat but was shot and stabbed before he could make it, as were Hollborn and his compatriot and four boatmen from another island.[90]

The Sokehs insurgents could have overrun virtually the entire island and killed all the German inhabitants, but the traditional leaders of other districts did not join in and indeed responded to appeals to protect the colonialists. Thus was set in motion what became known as the Sokehs Rebellion, as the insurgents besieged the Germans, who were only defended by 50 policemen for some 40 days. There were no Colonial Defence Forces (*Schutztruppe*) in the Pacific and so the manpower to defeat the rising had to come from the Navy and from the paramilitary police (*Polizeitruppe*) elsewhere in the territories. In January 1911 police troops sent from German New Guinea, with naval support from the light cruisers *Emden* and *Nürnberg*, the small 'Bussard'-class unprotected cruiser *Cormoran* and the survey ship *Planet*, landed. These were augmented with landing parties from the ships complete with artillery. The insurgents retreated to Sokehs Island, which is separated by small strait from the Pohnpei mainland (see Map 7), and entrenched themselves on Sokehs heights, a natural defensive position with steep sides and thickly forested top. Supported by gunfire from the cruisers, the sailors and police assaulted the position and quickly overran it.[91]

German retribution was swift, and on 24 February, known today on the island as Sokehs Rebellion Day, fifteen of the ringleaders were publicly shot. Two more who were on Yap were also executed, and the entire Sokehs population, some 462 men women and children, were exiled to Yap and then Palau, where the able-bodied men were assigned to punitive labour in the phosphate industry. Their land was confiscated and distributed among other islanders.[92]

If the Sokehs Rebellion was unique it was probably because of special factors. As has been noted, there were simply too few German administrative personnel and settlers to cause an intolerable degree of interference in the lives of the indigenous peoples of Micronesia. Exacerbating this was the atomised nature of the territory in question – literally hundreds of islands scattered over great distances. In the main then, and by default, the various island societies were effectively left to govern themselves on a day-to-day basis.

One advantage that accrued to Germany through possession of the islands was the ability to build stations at strategic points in order to expand the German Wireless Network. Until the advent of dependable wireless systems, intercontinental telecommunication relied on submarine telegraph cables. These were laid across oceans and provided a reliable means of communication between far-flung points. Britain, with a vast and distant empire to communicate with, was in the forefront of deploying this technology – consisting of copper cores insulated with gutta-percha (a resin from the *Isonandra Gutta* tree) and externally protected by steel wire braiding.

Accordingly Britain became preponderant in ownership; over half the world's cable network was British in 1908. Aware of the vulnerability to its communications this implied, Germany began, in 1906, constructing an alternative system based on wireless technology. The hub of this system was the powerful Nauen Transmitter Station near Berlin with, from 1911, a range of some 5,000 kilometres.[93] The receiving station was some 30 kilometres away, at Geltow near Potsdam, in order that the power of the transmitter did not overload the system.

Operated by Telefunken, a joint venture of Siemens and AEG, the German Wireless Network expanded throughout the various colonial territories. In the Pacific, the main radio station, with a range of some 1,900 kilometres, was constructed at Yap, the Pelew island being chosen because of its cable link with Tsingtau and the US. Other stations were constructed at Apia (Samoa), Nauru, Bitapaka (Rabaul, Kaiser Wilhelm's Land), Anguar and Tsingtau. All these station were able to transmit a signal from between 1,200 and 2,000 kilometres, and thus gave coverage throughout Germany's colonial sphere in the Far East.[94]

5

Tectonic Shift 2: 1902–1914
Japan and Russia, Britain and Dominion
Defence, the United States

On 12 February 1902 it was announced, simultaneously, in the United Kingdom and Japan that a treaty of alliance existed between the two states. This, the Anglo-Japanese Alliance of 1902, had actually been signed on 30 January but had not been publicly announced so that the 'Great Powers' of Germany, Russia and France could be informed.[1] These were the same powers that had, in 1896, formed the so-called Triple Intervention, or *Dreibund*, that forced Japan to give up the Liaotung Peninsula along with Port Arthur; which territory had been taken from China under the Treaty of Shimonoseki following Japanese victory in the Sino-Japanese War of 1894–95. The United States was also, though later, informed prior to the alliance being made public.

Both parties embarked on the alliance out of self-interest and as a measure to counter prospective and real Russian expansionism, which Germany and Austria-Hungary sought to divert, for obvious reasons, towards Asia, or at least had actively under Bismarck; his successors were not so astute. This in turn meant potential conflict with Britain across the Raj's northern borders, particularly in Afghanistan, and with Japan, particularly in Manchuria and Korea.

The British Admiralty, at the time under the political leadership of William Waldegrave Palmer, the 2nd Earl of Selborne, First Lord of the Admiralty 1900–05 and son-in-law of the Prime Minister, the 3rd Marquess of Salisbury, was keen on the alliance, not least for reasons of economy. Sir Michael Hicks Beach, the Chancellor of the Exchequer from June 1895 to July 1902, had to finance the Second Boer War of October 1899–May 1902, and refused extra finance for the Royal Navy, which was required in order to maintain a margin of superiority over any potential enemies. Selborne railed against financial constraints, writing in 1903:

> This is a simple question of national existence. We must have a force which is reasonably calculated to beat France and Russia and we must have something in hand against Germany. We cannot afford a three Power Standard but we must have a real margin[2] over the two Power Standard and this policy the Cabinet has definitely adopted.[3]

Russia and France had been allied since the start of 1894, a combination that Russia had entered into following the lapse of the Reinsurance Treaty with Germany in 1890. The exact terms of the Franco-Russian 'Dual Entente' were secret, but the existence of the alliance was generally known. Franco-Russian relations were cemented further by the extension of the alliance in 1899. The alliance was essentially defensive in character and directed against Germany and its co-signatories of the Triple Alliance, Austria-Hungary and Italy. It bound Russia to come to the aid of France, with all her available forces, should France be attacked by Germany, or by Italy supported by Germany, and France to aid Russia, again with all available forces should Russia be attacked by Germany, or by Austria supported by Germany. It did not bind France to come to Russia's aid in the event of an attack by another power, which was what occurred during February 1904 when Japan launched the Russo-Japanese War, the conflict lasting until September 1905.

This was perhaps fortunate for Britain, as articles two and three of the Anglo-Japanese treaty required neutrality if either signatory became involved in war with another power, but 'support' should either signatory became involved in war with more than one Power. Arthur Balfour, who was to succeed his maternal uncle, Lord Salisbury, as Prime Minister upon the latter's retirement in July 1902, had commented on the danger this feature might cause when the treaty was being considered by the Cabinet: 'we may find ourselves fighting for our existence in every part of the globe against Russia and France.'[4]

Japanese war aims were relatively straightforward; they wished to put a stop to increasing Russian influence in Manchuria that, it was felt, were a threat to Japan's interests in Korea, and to regain Port Arthur. The culminating battle of the war, in which Japan succeeded in achieving most of its objectives, was the now legendary Battle of Tsushima. This was one of the truly decisive sea battles of history, culminating as it did in the sinking or capture of almost the entire Russian Fleet, or at least those parts that had not been sunk or captured previously. With in effect the total loss of their navy the Russians could no longer hope to interdict the Japanese communications. This left them with the choice of defeating the Imperial Japanese Army in the field, something they had been consistently unable to demonstrate themselves capable of, or of accepting terms. Conversely, though the Japanese military had won battle after battle they had been unable to achieve a truly decisive land victory, hence perhaps the absence of Field Marshal Marquis (later Prince) Oyama Iwao from the roll call of Great Captains. It was these successes of Japanese arms, rather than the humbling of the Russians, which prompted the American President, Theodore Roosevelt, to intervene and offer to arbitrate.

Roosevelt's intervention was propitious as all the Great Powers, including most vitally the combatants, were keen to see an end to the conflict by the summer of 1905. The succession of defeats had clearly made the war very unpopular in Russia, which, in any event, was causing havoc economically. The Russian autocracy also feared that any prolongation would lead to revolution and the overturning of the social order. Japanese resources, in terms of manpower and material, as well as financial, were nearly exhausted. Indeed, both states were finding it problematic in raising loans in order to continue the conflict.

As one of the non-combatant powers allied to one of the warring states, the

French government greatly feared that a collapse of their ally would leave France isolated in Europe, and left to face Germany alone. A further factor involved the French banking system; this had underwritten most of the money that Russia had borrowed to wage the conflict and was becoming strained.

Britain too had an interest in the conflict being halted before one side or the other suffered irreparable damage. There was a financial aspect, inasmuch as the government had supported the loans required for Japanese to wage the war, but also because Britain, for strategic-political reasons, had become 'officially friendly' with a state, France, whose ally, Russia, was at war with Britain's ally, Japan. On 8 April 1904 Lord Lansdowne, the British Foreign Secretary had, along with Paul Cambon, the French Ambassador, signed what became known as the *Entente Cordiale*. Although ostensibly the *Entente* was about extra-European matters respecting Egypt and Morocco, the friendly relations now entered into between the two states had their genesis in the behaviour of, and worries about, Imperial Germany. These were of long standing as regards France, but fairly recent in the case of Britain; the public revealing of *Weltmacht* (literally 'world mastery') aims in 1896, and the First and Second Navy Laws, of 1898 and 1900 respectively, being factors in the equation; described as being tantamount to a declaration of 'cold war' against Britain.[5]

If we recall Lord Selborne's comments in 1903 concerning Britain's naval position ('We must have a force which is reasonably calculated to beat France and Russia and we must have something in hand against Germany') it may be adjudged just how much improved the international strategic naval situation was vis-à-vis Britain in 1905; with the Russian Fleet destroyed and France's friendly the 'something in hand against Germany' amounted to virtually the entire Royal Navy. Indeed, Tsushima totally vindicated British policy vis-à-vis Japan, inasmuch as Russia's naval threat had been annihilated decisively at no cost whatsoever to Britain.

Germany was not directly involved, but the US government, headed by the dynamic Roosevelt who was acting as his own Secretary of State, actively sought to prevent either side gaining a decisive ascendancy over the other. The United States had extensive interests in the Pacific, recently much expanded following victory in the Spanish–American War of 1898. Though the terminology would have been repugnant to Americans, it might be said that the United States had acquired an overseas empire and had begun to build a fleet to go with it. Roosevelt had quietly tried to have the conflict resolved through negotiation during 1904, but neither side was at that time amenable to such methods, believing they could gain more by continuing to fight.[6]

By 1905, as stated, the belligerents were looking for ways out, and on 31 May, four days after Tsushima, the Japanese secretly communicated with Roosevelt and sought his good offices with a view to bringing about a negotiated settlement. Tsar Nicholas II was initially unreceptive, but agreed to accept a proposal for direct negotiations with Japan if proposed by Roosevelt, who then formally extended an offer of mediation. This was accepted by both states, by Japan on 10 June and Russia on 12 June.

The peace conference took place at Portsmouth, New Hampshire, from 9 August to 5 September 1905, with Roosevelt displaying superlative diplomatic skills in the roles of chairman, conciliator and intermediary. In support of his efforts he sent telegrams to leaders in Germany, France and Britain urging them to use whatever influence they had with the parties to reach a compromise.[7] France agreed to make additional loans to Russia, but on condition that they were not used for continuing the war, while Kaiser Wilhelm encouraged Nicholas II to compromise. Britain, on the other hand, declined to intercede with Japan, and, on 12 August, while the conference was still sitting, the Anglo-Japanese Alliance was renewed. The Treaty of Portsmouth was eventually signed on 5 September 1905, and Roosevelt became, in 1906, the first American to receive the Nobel Peace Prize due to his efforts in facilitating the peace.

The 1905 Anglo-Japanese agreement contained some significant changes from the earlier, 1902, version and was therefore new, rather than a simple extension of the old. The most significant of these changes were the geographical extension, to cover British India, and the pledge of mutual assistance if either party were attacked by a single power.

The clauses in question stated it thus:

Preamble
The Governments of Great Britain and Japan, being desirous of replacing the Agreement concluded between them on the 30th of January 1902, by fresh stipulations, have agreed upon the following Articles, which have for their object:

a   The consolidation and maintenance of general peace in the regions of Eastern Asia and India;

b. The preservation of the common interests of all Powers in China by insuring the independence and integrity of the Chinese Empire and the principle of equal opportunities for the commerce and industry of all nations in China;

c. The maintenance of the territorial rights of the High Contracting Parties [viz., Britain and Japan] in the regions of Eastern Asia and of India, and the defence of their special interests in the said regions:

Article I
It is agreed that whenever, in the opinion of either Great Britain or Japan, any of the rights and interests referred to in the preamble of this Agreement [i.e., items a, b, c above] are in jeopardy, the two Governments will communicate with one another fully and frankly, and consider in common the measures which should be taken to safeguard those menaced rights or interests.

Article II
If, by reason of an unprovoked attack or aggressive action, whenever arising, on the part of any other Power or Powers, either Contracting Party should be involved in war in defence of its territorial rights or special interests mentioned in the preamble of this Agreement, the other Contracting Party will at once come to the assistance of its ally, and will conduct war in common, and make peace in mutual agreement with it.[8]

Britain had originally, in the negotiations leading up to the signing, wanted to specify that in the event of a threat to the borders of the Raj, Japan would send a certain number of troops. This did not, in any explicit form, make it into the final form, though it could have happened under the 'communications' referred to in Article 1. A change of mind took place however, one not necessarily originating in the change of administration when, in December 1905, the Conservative Balfour government fell and was replaced by the Liberal government headed by Sir Henry Campbell-Bannerman. Rather it arose from a process, largely contained within the Committee of Imperial Defence, whereby the implications of pursuing such a policy became apparent. The following memorandum, of 4 November 1905, summarises the deleterious effects that British pride would suffer if such an event were to occur:

> It is recommended that we [...] should not ask Japan to send troops to India, first, because the number of men that can be employed across the north-west frontier is limited by the means of transport and supply; and secondly, because to ask for assistance to ward off attack by a single adversary would [...] be highly detrimental, if not absolutely fatal, to our prestige throughout the Asiatic continent.[9]

This potential threat to British Imperial 'prestige' was removed on 31 August 1907, when Britain and Russia signed the Anglo-Russian Entente. Though overtly about Persia, the treaty explicitly recognised existing special interests:

> [...] each of them [Britain and Russia] has, for geographical and economic reasons, a special interest in the maintenance of peace and order in certain provinces of Persia adjoining, or in the neighbourhood of, the Russian frontier on the one hand, and the frontiers of Afghanistan and Baluchistan on the other hand [...][10]

Two months previously, on 10 June, Russia's ally France had signed an Entente with Japan, bilaterally guaranteeing an 'open door' policy vis-à-vis China and the maintenance of the status quo in, and security of, the territory in the Far East where each had 'special interests'. Paris also agreed to assist Japan with loans, the injurious financial effects of the war with Russia still being much in evidence.

A rapprochement between Russia and Japan had also taken place with the 'Secret Convention' signed at St Petersburg on 30 July 1907, whereby Russia acknowledged Japanese 'special interests' in Korea and Japan recognised Russian 'special interests' over Outer Mongolia (present day Mongolia). This convention was the first of three such over the period 1907–12 whereby the two powers defined their respective spheres of influence in, and fixed the status quo regarding, North-east Asia, including Korea, Manchuria and inner Mongolia.[11] The second of these, perhaps with an attempt at irony, was signed on 4 July 1910 and formalised a rejection of an American intervention, the scheme by Edward H. Harriman, a railway magnate, for a joint venture, concerning proposals over the railways. Article V stated:

> In order to insure the good working of their reciprocal engagements, the two High Contracting Parties will at all times frankly and loyally enter into communication

with regard to anything that concerns matters affecting in common their special interests in Manchuria.

In the event that these special interests should come to be threatened, the two High Contracting Parties will agree upon the measures to be taken with a view to common action or to the support to be accorded for the safeguarding and the defense of those interests.[12]

These various changes in international relations, combined with Japan's annexation of Korea on 22 August 1910, something that was really a formality inasmuch as Korea had been a virtual Japanese protectorate since 1905, meant that the whole basis upon which the 1905 Treaty had been structured was changed.

There was a further factor; the United States. There were several areas of friction between Japan and the US, the more rational being Japanese policy and behaviour towards China,[13] and the potential threat the Imperial Navy posed to the American position in the Philippines.[14] Under the presidency of Theodore Roosevelt an extrovert foreign and defence policy was adopted, the most enduring physical legacy of which is surely the Panama Canal. Politically, he formulated the 'Roosevelt Corollary', which stated that the United States would intervene in Caribbean affairs when 'chronic wrongdoing, or an impotence which results in a general loosening of the ties of a civilised society' by governments made it necessary, as an addition to the 'Monroe Doctrine'.[15]

One of the events providing an impetus to this updating of a long established principle was the Venezuelan Debt Crisis of 1902. This occurred when the Venezuelan government of President Cipriano Castro defaulted on large debts owed to British, Italian and German companies. In order to attempt to coerce the Venezuelans the three nations gave notice on 25 November 1902 that they would mount a 'peaceful' naval blockade of the five principal Venezuelan ports and the mouth of the Orinoco River. This began on 9 December but was hardly peaceful; three (some sources say four) Venezuelan gunboats were sunk and the fortifications at Puerto Cabello were bombarded on 15 December. These actions greatly concerned the US government, which was worried about the possibility that the European powers, particularly Germany, might take Venezuelan territory as compensation, a violation of the Monroe Doctrine. Rear Admiral Henry Clay Taylor, Chief of the Bureau of Navigation had put it thus to the President:

> Venezuela [...] could offer nothing but territory, or she could mortgage her revenue in such a way as to place herself in complete political dependence on Germany. The United States could not allow either of these, and yet Germany's right to indemnity would be incontestable. The only courses open to the United States [would be] payment of the indemnity taking such security as she can from Venezuela or war.[16]

This in many ways echoed Secretary of State John Hay's reply to the joint notice of 25 November, that, while the action was justified, the US nevertheless disapproved of European intervention. The European Powers eventually accepted that the matter could be decided by arbitration, the British agreeing on 16 December and Germany the next day, and asked Roosevelt to conduct this, though he refused to become personally involved and advised that the matter be referred to the Hague Court of Arbitration. Scholars dispute the extent to which Roosevelt pressurised, in particular, Germany to desist from direct action; the expansionist foreign policy of Bülow and Kaiser Wilhelm was regarded most suspiciously in the Venezuelan context.

Certainly he dispatched George Dewey, holder of the unique rank of Admiral of the Navy, together with a powerful fleet, to cruise off Culebra Island near Porto Rico; as Dewey later, and most circumspectly, described it: ' On October 5, 1899, my flag was hauled down from the [cruiser] *Olympia*; but I was to raise it again on the Southern drill grounds for the manoeuvres, when I had under my direction the most powerful fleet which we had ever mobilized up to that time.'[17] This fleet, eventually amounting to fifty-nine vessels including several battleships and support ships, formed a very 'big stick.' Roosevelt, speaking quietly no doubt, was later to claim that he had, verbally, informed the German Ambassador to the US on 14 December, that if Germany did not agree to settle the dispute by arbitration he would order Dewey to attack: he was 'very definitely' threatening war.[18]

This version of events is much disputed, but whether or not it is accurate the Europeans agreed to refer the matter to arbitration on 16–17 December; a decision codified in the 'Protocol between Germany and Venezuela relating to the settlement of the German claims' signed at Washington, 13 February 1903.[19]

An even bigger stick, and one of Roosevelt's best known acts, involved the creation and voyage of the Great White Fleet. As Assistant Secretary to the Navy he had, the year before the US annexed Hawaii in July 1898, instructed naval planners to develop contingency plans for fighting Japan in the Pacific; at this time however, the US Navy had no organised fleet in the Pacific.[20] He also inaugurated a campaign to modernise the Navy by constructing a fleet of the most powerful warships. The visible manifestation of the success of this campaign came with the dispatch, on 16 December 1907, of almost the entire US battlefleet from Hampton Roads, Virginia, on a circumnavigation of the globe.

The capital units of the Great White Fleet, as it came to be known, comprised sixteen battleships organised into four divisions of four ships each. The only heavy units that did not sail, apart from four coast defence ships, comprised one battleship under repair and one battleship not yet ready for deployment, though both the latter vessels joined the Fleet at a later date. The Fleet returned to Hampton Roads on 22 February 1909 having steamed some 70,000 kilometres. The object of this mighty display of power projection was several-fold, including learning the art of such matters on the part of the US Navy and, undoubtedly, a signal to Japan, which the Fleet had visited 18–25 October 1908.

Despite this show of force however, it was necessary for the US to protect its Pacific territories, particularly the Philippines, by diplomatic means also. Consequently, on 30 November 1908 American Secretary of State, Elihu Root, and the Japanese Ambassador in Washington, Takahira Kogoro, exchanged notes that came to be known as the Root–Takahira Agreement. There were five main points:

1. It is the wish of the two governments to encourage the free and peaceful development of their commerce on the Pacific Ocean.

2. The policy of both governments, uninfluenced by any aggressive tendencies, is directed to the maintenance of the existing *status quo* in the region above mentioned and to the defense of the principle of equal opportunity for commerce and industry in China.

3. They are accordingly firmly resolved reciprocally to respect the territorial possessions belonging to each other in said region.

4. They are also determined to preserve the common interests of all powers in China by supporting by all pacific means at their disposal the independence and integrity of China and the principles of equal opportunity for commerce and industry of all nations in that Empire.

5. Should any event occur threatening the *status quo* as above described or the principle of equal opportunity, as above defined, it remains for the two governments to communicate with each other, in order to arrive at an understanding as to what measures they may consider it useful to take.[21]

This Mahanian concept incarnate, the 'Mahan–Roosevelt legacy' as one authority has termed it,[22] of the big battlefleet demonstrating command of the sea was of course similar to the ideas pursued by Admiral Tirpitz and William II. Indeed, the latter had established the High Sea Fleet as a command in February 1907.[23]

According to Mahanian precept, command of the sea could only be established by keeping a fleet massed so as to be able to confront and destroy an enemy fleet. This to him was a cardinal point; if the establishment of the US Naval War College 'had produced no other result than the profound realization by naval officers of the folly of dividing the battlefleet, in peace or in war, it would by that alone have justified its existence and paid its expenses'.[24]

The implications of a US-Japanese naval conflict for Britain were then obvious, though for several reasons it was unthinkable that the United Kingdom and the United States should go to war. These included, as Roosevelt had pointed out to Mahan in 1897, the proximity and vulnerability of Canada: 'Canada' as he had stated it, 'was a hostage to British good behavior'.[25] That this was indeed the case was recognised equally by the British. An Admiralty Memorandum of February 1905 is explicit on the point:

In the event of an occurrence so much deprecated as the rupture of friendly relations with the United States, the position of Canada is one of extreme danger, and, so far as the navy is concerned, any effective assistance would be exceedingly difficult. Generally, the more carefully this problem is considered, the more tremendous do the difficulties which would confront Great Britain in a war with the United States appear. It may be hoped that that the policy of the British Government will ever be to use all possible means to avoid war.[26]

Canada might have been a guarantee of good British behaviour vis-à-vis the US, but it, and the other British Dominions in the Pacific, had concerns of their own relating to Japan, including Japanese naval expansion. The rapturous welcome given by the public to the Great White Fleet in its visits to New Zealand and Australia[27] are, it is argued by some scholars, evidence of this; America being seen as a potential ally against possible Japanese ambitions.[28] Indeed, it has been argued that Australia's Prime Minister, Alfred Deakin, to show Australia's potential enemies the might of their 'American friends', engineered the visit of the fleet.[29]

Britain's empire had evolved politically, a notable point being the extension of Dominion status to the self-governing colonies. Canada (1867), Australia (1901), New Zealand (1907), Newfoundland (1907), and the Union of South Africa (1910), formed this group, sometimes, and for obvious reasons, sometimes collectively referred to as the 'White Dominions'. The Dominions had more or less full internal control, but foreign relations and defence were still conducted through the London government, though Canada created a Department of External Affairs in 1909.

Defence, and the problems therein, of the Dominions varied greatly; Canada and Newfoundland were unique in that they were completely at the mercy of their powerful neighbour, the US, but by the same token were protected by that neighbour; the US would not have tolerated any foreign incursions into their territory. South Africa was geographically remote and possessed what were probably the most powerful military forces on its continent. Military forces capable of meeting them on a level could only have come from Europe by sea, and there was the Royal Navy to take care of that.[30]

Australia and New Zealand were a different story, and were hypothetically vulnerable to a power that could exercise power projection into the Pacific. The Royal Navy was tasked with providing maritime defence via an 1887 agreement that the, then, colonies should contribute to the Royal Navy in return for the permanent stationing of a squadron in the region.

However, with the necessity to concentrate in North European waters in order to counter the German High Seas Fleet the ability to offer a high level of naval protection became problematical.[31] It was this problem, although originally with respect more to France and Russia than Germany, which had led to the original Anglo-Japanese Alliance, but following Japan's victory over Russia in 1905, the Australasian Dominions now viewed Japanese naval power as the greatest threat. This was in contrast to the British view, as, for example enunciated by Admiral Sir John Fisher in 1906: 'Our only probable enemy is Germany. Germany keeps her *whole* Fleet always concentrated within a few hours of England. We must therefore keep a Fleet twice as powerful concentrated within a few hours of Germany.'[32]

Fisher had become First Sea Lord in October 1904 and remained in the post until the beginning of 1910, towards the end of which period the British Admiralty proposed an ingenious idea for maintaining British naval power in, particularly, the Far East and Pacific Ocean areas; the Imperial Dominions would raise and pay for the necessary forces.

There had been attempts on the part of the British government to extract larger contributions from the colonies, above all those that were self-governing, towards the cost of naval defence since the 1887 agreement. These efforts however met only with relative success; the colonial politicians knew that the British would maintain the Royal Navy as a global force in any event.[33]

What brought matters to a head were statements made in the British House of Commons on 16 March 1909 by Prime Minister Henry Asquith and First Lord – the Cabinet Minister in political charge of the Royal Navy – Reginald McKenna during the presentation of the 1909–10 naval estimates. Parliament was asked to sanction funding for three dreadnought battleships and one dreadnought cruiser (battlecruiser) to be laid down before the end of the year. However, contingent funding was also sought for another four similar vessels to be laid down no later than April 1910, unless, in the meantime, Imperial Germany agreed to negotiations limiting naval expansion. This increase in the estimates was sought because the Admiralty believed, based on intelligence reports and calculations on potential capacity, that the tempo of German dreadnought construction was increasing, to possibly encompass six units per year. It seemed, as one authority has put it, that 'for the first time since the ironclad revolution a foreign naval power had the capacity to build capital ships as fast as Great Britain'.[34] As McKenna told the House of Commons, 'we do not know, as we thought we did, the rate at which German construction is taking place'.[35]

No agreement on the limitation of capital ship production with Germany was reached, and this, together with the knowledge that Austria-Hungary and Italy were undertaking dreadnought construction, meant that parliament was asked for, and approved, the funding for the additional vessels on 26 July 1909.[36] This matter caused a great deal of domestic political controversy for the British government, and there was undoubtedly an excess of overreaction and panic surrounding the matter, but early on in the affair assistance was offered by some of the Dominions. On 22 March the Government of New Zealand offered to bear the cost of the immediate construction of one of the dreadnought battleships, as well as one of the additional vessels if necessary, an offer that was 'gratefully accepted' by the British government. The Canadian House of Commons passed a resolution on 29 March, approving 'any necessary expenditure designed to promote the speedy organisation of a Canadian naval service in co-operation with and in close relation to the Imperial Navy'. A similar offer came from Australia on 15 April, stating that 'whereas all the British Dominions ought to share in the burden of maintaining the permanent naval supremacy of the Empire, so far as Australia was concerned this object would best be best attained by the encouragement of naval development in that country'.[37]

In view of these offers, representatives of the of the four Dominions [Australia, Canada, Newfoundland and New Zealand] and the Cape Colonies (the Cape, Natal, Orange Free State and Transvaal were in the process of becoming the Union of South Africa) were, on 30 April 1909, invited 'to attend a Conference [...] to discuss the general question of the naval and military defence of the Empire, with special reference to the Canadian resolution and to the proposals from New Zealand and Australia'. There was however a change of government in Australia on 2 June, when Andrew Fisher of the Australian Labour Party was replaced by Alfred Deakin of the newly formed Commonwealth Liberal, or Fusion, Party.

This led to a further offer on 4 June; Australia would fund a dreadnought for the Royal Navy, 'or such addition to its naval strength as may be determined after consultation in London'.[38]

When the Dominion representatives arrived in London they were not expecting to undertake much more than the finalising of details regarding the offers already made. They were therefore surprised to discover that the Admiralty had formulated a quite different idea, though one of long, if somewhat secret, gestation. As the Admiralty memorandum stated it:

If the problem of Imperial naval defence were considered merely as a problem of naval strategy it would be found that the maximum output of strength for a given expenditure is obtained by the maintenance of a single navy with the concomitant unity of training and unity of command. In furtherance, then, of the simple strategical ideal the maximum of power would be obtained if all parts of the Empire contributed, according to their needs and resources, to the maintenance of the British Navy.

It has long been recognised that in defining the conditions under which the naval forces of the Empire should be developed, other considerations than those of strategy alone must be taken into account. [...]

The main duty of the forthcoming Conference as regards naval defence will be, therefore, to determine the form in which the various Dominion Governments can best participate in the burden of Imperial defence with due regard to varying political and geographical conditions. [...]

In the opinion of the Admiralty, a Dominion Government desirous of creating a navy should aim at forming a distinct fleet unit; and the smallest unit is one which, while manageable in time of peace, is capable of being used in its component parts in time of war. [...]

The fleet unit to be aimed at should, in the opinion of the Admiralty, consist of the following:

1 Armoured cruiser [of the] new 'Indomitable' class, which is of the 'Dreadnought' type.

3 Unarmoured cruisers ('Bristol' class).

6 Destroyers

3 Submarines

[and] with the necessary auxiliaries, such a depots and store ships etc.

Such a fleet unit would be capable of action not only in the defence of coasts, but also of the trade routes, and would be sufficiently powerful to deal with small hostile squadrons should such ever attempt to act in those waters. [...] [39]

This was a complete volte-face in respect of Admiralty policy, which had previously sought to restrict Dominion naval forces to those only capable of flotilla defence via small vessels such as destroyers, torpedo boats and, latterly, submarines. What was now being proposed was something approaching an early twentieth century version of the later concept of the carrier strike group, with a powerful capital ship and attendant vessels forming a balanced and powerful force capable of power projection. Some have seen a degree of cynicism in the proposal, inasmuch as operating a vessel of the size and complexity of a battlecruiser would be beyond the capacity of any Dominion navy, and thus they would be forced to lean heavily on the British Admiralty, 'giving the latter both the control and the financial backing it had always sought'.[40]

Whatever the truth in this assertion, it would have been an advantage that dissipated over time as the Dominion navy gained knowledge and experience. Certainly the concept appeared to have been one that commanded wide support within the Admiralty, as is evidenced by Fisher's statement on 10 August 1909 to the Australian delegation:

> The Admiralty, after careful consideration of the question, had arrived at the conclusion that the establishment of fleet units, as recommended in [the] Memo-randum, which could combine in time of war to form a powerful fleet, which he suggested might be called the Pacific Fleet, was the most advantageous course for the Dominion Governments to pursue. And this recommendation expressed the views not only of the present Board of Admiralty, but also the opinion of Admiral of the Fleet Sir Arthur Wilson, and of the Committee of Imperial Defence. He attached great importance to the vessel of the *Indomitable* type, as the citadel or base around which the smaller vessels of the unit could operate. Without the large vessel [...] the smaller vessels of the fleet unit would be strategically of little value, for they would not be able to deal unaided with the more powerful hostile commerce-destroyers, whereas the *Indomitable*, with her great speed and radius of action, could either catch up or avoid any vessel afloat, and her gun power would enable her to deal with any hostile vessels likely to be employed in operations against our overseas trade.[41]

These were classic Fisher arguments concerning the use of what came to be called battlecruisers and, in the context within which he put them, convincing. Not all the participants were convinced however, as Colonel J. F. G. Foxton, the Minister without Portfolio in Deakin's administration and the senior Australian delegate, was to inform his prime minister; 'no two of the Dominions appear to be able to agree upon a common line of action in regard to naval assistance to the Empire'.[42] Indeed, Australia was the only one of the Dominions to adopt the British offer, though they had sought to form a joint Australasian fleet unit with New Zealand. This attempt was however rebuffed, and the chief New Zealand delegate, Sir Joseph George Ward, the Prime Minister, was characterised as being 'very firm if not obstinate in his refusal to join us' by Foxton.[43]

According to Maurice Hankey, who had been appointed Naval Assistant Secretary to the Committee of Imperial Defence in 1908 and thus participated: '[The Conference] laid the foundations of Empire co-operation in defence. The principle was established that the defence forces of the Dominions were to be of a national character and under control of their respective governments.'[44] It was, perhaps, not quite as simple as Lord Hankey, as he had then become, remembered when writing about it nearly four decades later, for, in the main, the Admiralty proposals fell on somewhat stony ground.

The conclusions arising from the conference may be summarised from the statement that Asquith made to the House of Commons on 26 August 1909. He told parliament that South Africa, as it was in the process of becoming, was unable to submit or to approve positive proposals until the Union of South Africa was an accomplished fact.[45] A remodelling of the squadrons maintained in Far Eastern waters was considered on the basis of establishing a Pacific Fleet, to consist of three units in the East Indies, Australia and China seas. New Zealand did not wish to have her own fleet unit, but preferred to adhere to her present policy of contributing to the Royal Navy. The New Zealand offer of a battleship was to be substituted for a dreadnought cruiser, which would form part of the China Station, while Canada considered that her double seaboard rendered the provision of a fleet unit as envisaged by the Admiralty unsuitable for the present, and required a number of smaller cruisers instead. Only Australia, the House was informed, would provide and maintain her own unit of the Pacific Fleet, with some temporary assistance from Imperial funds.[46]

In other words, only two of the putative three fleet units, or four if one takes into account a potential South African contribution, were actually to come into being, and only one of these, the Australian – 'a navy within a navy' – as it has been called,[47] was not to be under direct Admiralty control. If the 'Pacific Fleet' as envisioned by Fisher was somewhat attenuated, then the Australian fleet unit, which became the nucleus of the Royal Australian Navy following the creation of that service on 10 July 1911, was nevertheless a powerful force in its own right. This was particularly so as the *Indomitable* type originally conceived as forming the core of the unit was superseded by a vessel of the newer *Indefatigable* class, as was the New Zealand contribution.

The Admiralty policy towards Dominion fleet units was not though to endure following changes to those directing matters, and there were great changes over the next three years. Admiral of the Fleet Sir Arthur Wilson, who was in accord with the concept of creating Dominion fleet units, succeeded Fisher, amid somewhat controversial circumstances,[48] as First Sea Lord in 1910, while Winston Churchill replaced McKenna in October 1911. Wilson, having reached the age of 70, was retired in November 1911 and replaced by Admiral Sir Francis Bridgeman, who was in turn replaced by Vice-Admiral Prince Louis of Battenberg a little over a year later. None of the three immediate successors to Fisher can be considered a great success in the post of First Sea Lord, particularly perhaps as McKenna's replacement had strong views of his own on every aspect of naval matters. As Strachan has remarked, this combination of frequent change in, and weak appointees to, the position of First Sea Lord led to the loss of any firm direction in the Navy's leadership.[49]

The whole concept was, in certain quarters, controversial, as exemplified by the views of Henry Page Croft MP, a leading member of the Edwardian 'Radical Right' and an ardent and reactionary Imperialist, who was later to be one of the leading Franco supporters during the Spanish Civil War.

Although the Conference was eminently satisfactory from national points of view, it was far from satisfactory from an Imperial standpoint [...] The present policy is expensive and strategically inefficient, and whereas the Mother-country must, and is ready to, take part in any war for the defence of Canada and Australia, Canada and Australia 'may' if they think fit assist the Mother-country or may remain neutral.[50]

While the views of those like Croft did not necessarily carry any weight, there being a Liberal government in office, his views concerning strategic inefficiency were echoed, and had a far more powerful advocate, in the views of Winston Churchill. On 29 January 1912 Churchill drafted a letter to Lewis Harcourt,[51] the Colonial Secretary, stating that he 'should like to have a talk with you in the near future about the Colonial Navies [sic]'. The letter continued:

I do not think anyone can doubt that the arrangements made in 1909 with Australia were not very satisfactory so far as British Naval interests were concerned. The whole principle of local Navies is, of course, thoroughly vicious, and no responsible sailor can be found who has a word say in favour of it. [...]

I do not expect that there is any chance of inducing Australia to let us have the battle cruiser *Australia* in Home waters during the next few years. I propose, therefore, to put the best face on this that we can and to aid the Australian Government to establish their complete Fleet unit as quickly as possible. The departure of these valuable modern ships, so important to our Fleet in Home waters is, of course, very unpleasant.[52] [...]

New Zealand stands in a different position. She has given her battle cruiser to the Imperial Government for service wherever desired. The existing arrangement is that the vessel shall be employed on the China Station and shall, if possible, touch at New Zealand ports on her way to the China Station. The employment of a ship like the *New Zealand* in China is not to be defended on any military grounds. She will not find her match on that side of the world unless we are to assume a rupture of the Japanese alliance and a war with that Power, in which case totally different dispositions would have to be made. On the other hand the *New Zealand* will be urgently required here at home to take part in maintaining British naval superiority in the North Sea. [...] We wish to ask the New Zealand Government to come to the assistance of the mother country by agreeing to *New Zealand* being employed in the Home Fleet during the next few years.[53]

Harcourt replied on 1 February 1912, to the effect that there were political implications contingent on the proposal to redeploy *New Zealand*, which included a 'blank refusal' from the New Zealand government to agree.[54] Churchill however had his way, and following her post-commissioning departure from Portsmouth on 8 February 1913 on a world cruise of more than 50,000 miles, during which time she remained for more than ten weeks in New Zealand waters and was inspected by nearly half a million people, the battlecruiser returned to England in November 1913. She did not return to New Zealand until 1919.[55]

It is perhaps curious that Churchill should have argued that he could find no responsible sailor who was in favour of 'local Navies', when he was to be instrumental in bringing two of the most senior such, Fisher and Wilson, back to the Admiralty following the outbreak of war in 1914.[56] Indeed, Churchill was greatly perturbed by the strategic 'unwisdom', as he was to term it, of failing to have all the major naval resources of the British Empire in the North Sea. His thoughts on the matter were encapsulated in a memorandum, undated but from the context clearly from the same period as his draft letter to Harcourt above:

> The situation in the Pacific will be absolutely regulated by the decision in the North Sea. Two or three Australian and New Zealand Dreadnoughts if brought into the line in the North Sea might turn the scale and make victory not merely certain but complete. The same two or three Dreadnoughts in Australian waters would be useless the day after the defeat of the British Navy in Home Waters. [...] |These facts may not be palatable; but the Admiralty is bound to expose the peril and military unwisdom of divided organisation, of dispersion or dissipation of forces, and of partial engagements in detail [...] and to behold and proclaim in their place the principles of unity in command and in strategic conceptions, and concentration in the decisive theatres and for the decisive events. [...]
>
> It is recognised, however, that time will be required before the true principles of naval policy are comprehended in the Dominions, and that in the interval arrangements must be made to develop, so far as is possible, their local naval establishments. The Dominions want to have their own ships under their own control, cruising in their own waters, based on their own Ports. [...]
>
> These feelings, although unrecognised by military truth, are natural. They are real facts which will govern events if the choice which is open to us in the immediate future is not one between having Australian vessels in the right strategic stations or the wrong, but between having them in the wrong or not having them at all. It is easily understood that the difficulties of enlisting the active co-operation of the Dominions in naval defence by means of ships they rarely saw, and which were observed in the great fleets of Britain at the other end of the world, are at present insuperable. Such a policy would require an effort of imagination and a gift of military intuition, which so far only New Zealand has been capable of. The Admiralty have therefore, on political grounds rather than on military or strategic grounds, co-operated to the best of their ability in the development of the Australian Fleet Unit.[57]

Churchill's strategic insights as set out indicate quite plainly that he was of the Mahanian school of thought, inasmuch as his goal was a decisive battle with the German Fleet in northern British waters. All peripheral areas, as he saw them, were then very much secondary.

It is Fisher, to a greater degree than Churchill, who has been credited with 'megalomania' as regards the strength of the Royal Navy in the North Sea,[58] but as Lambert, in particular, has pointed out in recent years, this is far too crude a judgement.[59] What the Admiralty under Fisher and McKenna had proposed in 1909, and which Churchill, and presumably Bridgeman, so vehemently opposed in 1912 was a method whereby Imperial communications, principally in the Pacific, might be safeguarded while a superior fleet could still be retained in the waters around the British Isles. As will be argued later, retaining 'two or three' battlecruisers in the Pacific would not have made intolerable inroads into the strength of Vice-Admiral Sir John Jellicoe's Grand Fleet, as it became in August 1914, and that ship type was, in fact, detached as and when required without noticeable harm. The fleet units as visualised could have combined to form a larger fleet, but the concept allowed them to work primarily as individual units, as was made clear. The potential enemy against which they might be expected to operate was patently not the Japanese Fleet. Not only was Japan a British ally in 1909, but a combination of units comprising even, say, four battlecruisers would have been an inferior force if pitted against a Japanese fleet with dreadnought battleships, as Churchill acknowledged in his memorandum.

The potential enemy that the battlecruiser-centred fleet units were conceived as deterring or countering were hostile cruisers conducting commerce-raiding. Indeed, the Australian sailor Captain William R. Creswell, later Vice-Admiral Sir William, who had attended the 1909 Conference with Foxton, stated in November 1909 that the force would be powerful enough to ensure the safety of Australia's commerce against hostile cruisers, while the possibility of these cruisers threatening ports would be 'so remote as to be hardly worth considering'.[60] It is the case that such vessels could, in 1912, have, theoretically, been ships from several nations, but realistically those in question were the East Asiatic Cruiser Squadron based at Tsingtau. Indeed, while Churchill's ability to deploy HMS *New Zealand* without reference to the New Zealand government has already been remarked upon, the fact that he was quite unable to do so, as he recognised, in the case of Australia turned out to be fortunate in the extreme for the defence of the Empire.

Defence matters generally, and the relationship between Britain and the British Empire on one hand, and Japan on the other, were to feature in the Imperial Conference of 1911 held in London; one of a series of Colonial and, after 1907, Imperial Conferences held between 1887 and 1937. These conferences were the principal means of high-level consultation between representatives from the various component parts of the British Empire, discussing, among other subjects, economic and military cooperation.

At the 1911 conference, Britain's Foreign Secretary from 1905 to 1916, Sir Edward Grey briefed the representatives of the Dominions on Anglo-Japanese relations. Grey, who had made the defence of France against German aggression the central plank of British foreign policy, consulted them on a renewal of the Anglo-Japanese alliance. The Japanese had, in January 1911, asked Britain for a renewal, and implicit renegotiation, of the 1907 treaty.[61] There were undoubtedly several factors in this approach, including the Japanese fear that the British might not renew the alliance at the end of the timescale specified in 1907.[62]

This factor was also influential as regards Sir Edward Grey:

> If the alliance were to be terminated in 1915, Japan would be left with free hands without restraint and we could not control her and her fleet might array against us in the Pacific or allied with that of some other Power. These are changes that are unpleasant to contemplate and I believe that in 1914 it will still be our policy to be in alliance with Japan.[63]

Plate 1. *Völker Europas, wahrt eure heiligsten Güter!* (Peoples of Europe, Protect your most sacred possessions!). Painted by Hermann Knackfuss. (Author's Collection)

Plate 2. A Good Friday religious procession on Saipan during German rule. (Courtesy of Micronesian Seminar)

Plate 3. A photograph of Samoan chiefs taken by Dr Kurt Boeck *circa* 1900. (Author's Collection)

Plate 4. The German cable station on Yap, constructed in 1905. (Courtesy of Micronesian Seminar)

Plate 5. This Micronesian girl poses with a German sailor. (Author's Collection)

Plate 6. Chief Samuel, pictured here, was among those taken by the Germans during their march into the interior of the island. After a summary trial, fifteen Sokehs men were sentenced to be executed by firing squad. (Courtesy of Micronesian Seminar)

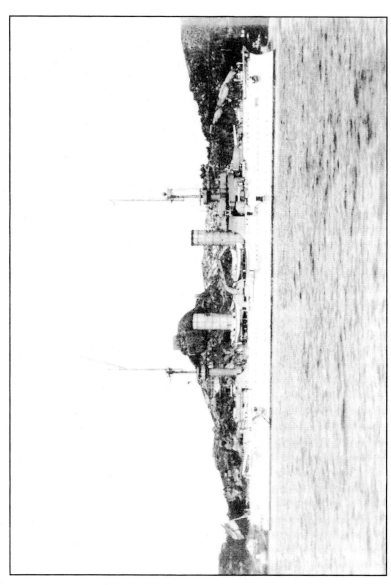

Plate 7. A view from starboard of SMS *Fürst Bismarck*, Germany's first armoured cruiser. (Author's Collection)

Plate 8. The armoured cruiser *Scharnhorst* in the floating dock at Tsingtau. (Author's Collection)

Plate 9. Japanese troops in Tsingtau following the capitulation on 7 November 1914. Note the damage to the roof of the building in the centre. (Author's Collection).

Plate 10. The remains of one of the four 280mm howitzer emplacements atop the Bismarck Hill complex. (Author's Collection)

Another factor was the Anglo-American Arbitration Treaty, proposed by the US in the autumn of 1910. This had been the brainchild of President William Howard Taft, Roosevelt's successor. As an ex-jurist, who went on to become a Supreme Court Judge, Taft was a convinced proponent of the peaceful resolution of international problems via arbitration. His State of the Union Address, on 6 December 1910, had contained references to this vis-à-vis Great Britain and France.[64]

The existence of these arrangements allowed Britain a significant get-out, for Grey negotiated a clause, Article IV, in the agreement whereby, without naming the US specifically, the renewed Anglo-Japanese Alliance would not apply to a country that had a treaty of general arbitration with either of the contracting countries.[65] On 13 July 1911 the third alliance was signed for a further 10 years, lasting until August 1923, with the unanimous approval of the Dominions.

Britain, embroiled in the naval race with Germany, saw the alliance as a bulwark ensuring the security of the Pacific Dominions and colonies, while the Japanese viewed it as a safeguard against isolation. That the existence of the alliance might exercise a restraining influence upon Japan was echoed by the public utterances of Japan's Foreign Minister, Hayashi Tadasu. He emphasised this in *The Japan Times* on 22 July 1911:

> The value and importance of the Alliance will be unchanged, nor is there any doubt of its long continuance. The only point against which Japan must guard is a wantonly aggressive policy. On the contrary, she must always adhere to a peaceful policy and endeavour to make the most of what she has gained so far, and to promote her interests and development in a manner consistent with a pacific policy. If Japan should adopt a policy of wanton aggression, the continuation of the Anglo-Japanese alliance would be out of the question.[66]

While the governments of Australia and New Zealand had supported the 1911 version of the Anglo-Japanese Alliance, and thus the existence of an alliance in general, there were elements of opinion in both countries that were at odds with this viewpoint; put simply, they feared Japanese ambitions. As one scholar has put it: 'Australians were not comforted when British officials and politicians, such as Winston Churchill, pointed to the Anglo-Japanese alliance as the protector of British interests in the Pacific. The alliance was with Australia's main perceived potential enemy.'[67]

Japanese naval expansion, though nowhere as great in scope as that of Britain and Germany, was nevertheless significant both in terms of quality and quantity. In 1906 the battleship *Satsuma* was launched, a design that pre-empted Britain's *Dreadnought*.[68] The vessel had been designed and built in Japan, though many of the components were imported from the UK, and the Japanese shipbuilding industry was increasingly becoming self-reliant and independent of foreign, particularly British, yards. Britain had constructed all Japan's major warships up to the *Satsuma* and her sister *Aki*, and Japan was to revert to British expertise only once more, when the battlecruiser *Kongo*, of extremely advanced design, was ordered from Vickers at Barrow-in-Furness in 1911.

Japanese determination to acquire a fleet capable of more than just regional power projection was of particular concern to the US, which had both commercial interests and territories in the Western Pacific to protect, particularly, in the latter category, the Philippines. Indeed, Theodore Roosevelt opined in 1907 that the archipelago formed 'our heel of Achilles. They are all that make the present situation with Japan dangerous.'[69] That the US was a likely potential enemy had been accepted by Japan since the end of the Russo-Japanese War, and, apparently for the first time, such a naval conflict was 'gamed' during the 1908 fleet manoeuvres.[70] The US Navy, on its part, had evolved a strategy for projecting its power across the ocean and fighting Japan; War Plan Orange.[71] It was not however until 'the-war-after-the-next-one' that the potential of US-Japanese conflict was to be realised.

6

War

August 1914

The causes of The Great War, as it was generally known in Britain and France until superseded by a later and a good deal greater conflict, are still the subject of much debate and inquiry, with several schools of thought having emerged.[1] It is not proposed to enter into this particular thicket here, but it can hardly be controversial to state that the origins of the conflict lay in Europe. The ostensible spark that set it off being, as Bismarck is supposed to have predicted, 'some damned silly thing in the Balkans'.[2] Whether the subsequent events were due to misjudgements and gambles, or through hardheaded calculation, is arguable. There were though several milestones along the road, if I may be forgiven for putting it so, and it as intended to highlight at least some of these.

As has already been argued, avoiding situations, whether 'damned silly', or geographically based, or neither, whereby Germany would get into a serious conflict, potential or actual, with the other European Great Powers had been the *leitmotif* of Bismarck's Chancellorship after 1871. Neither Caprivi nor Hohenlohe were desirous of foreign confrontation, though neither was wholly in control of foreign policy. Bülow, who saw himself as the 'executive tool' or 'political Chief of Staff' to the Kaiser's personal rule,[3] wanted to avoid this kind of dichotomy at the top of government. He conceived a technique for managing his volatile monarch, which involved establishing a close personal relationship with him. By thus gaining the Kaiser's trust, though his approach has been deemed 'calculating, manipulative and insincere,' he hoped to manage him in such a way as to mitigate the excesses to which he was prone.[4] Though this management was successful to a point, inasmuch as the Kaiser came to have faith in him, Bülow's management of foreign policy cannot be said to have been wholly successful. One of the most notable examples in this regard being, probably, the Tangier, or First Moroccan, Crisis of 1905–6, which backfired spectacularly and had the opposite consequences of those intended.

In provoking the crisis in March 1905 Bülow followed the strategy devised by Friedrich von Holstein, who was sure that there could be no real understanding between Britain and France and wished to torpedo the chances of one developing in order to forestall the encirclement (*Einkreisung*) of Germany. That there was a danger of encirclement was an enduring myth, especially from around the turn of the century, when 'the idea of Germany's encirclement by her neighbouring countries became a dominant paradigm'.[5] It is perhaps unsurprising to note that among the proponents of this view was the Kaiser himself, with whom, according to Asquith's retrospective view, it was 'a prime article of faith'.[6]

Holstein's objective was to end the nascent rapprochement between Britain and France, incarnated in the 1904 signing of the *Entente Cordiale*. This had delineated respective spheres of interest in colonial terms, and had established that Morocco fell into the French sphere. France accordingly began attempts to encroach on Moroccan independence. Though well short of anything that could be construed as an alliance, the *Entente* was, perhaps, indicative that another one of the pillars of Bismarckian strategy, French isolation, was being eroded.

In an effort to repair this situation a plan whereby the Kaiser, in person, was dispatched to Tangier with a pledge of support for Moroccan independence was formulated and put into action. He disembarked at Tangier with difficulty on 31 March 1905 and enunciated this support, effectively promising German support for Morocco against French intervention.

France was militarily alone at this period, due to Russian preoccupation with the war with Japan, and, well aware of this, Germany was undoubtedly threatening military action in support of her position. Indeed, tensions rose to the point where both sides began troop movements. The German strategy appeared at first to be working, to the extent that the French Foreign Minister, Théophile Delcassé, who had devised French Moroccan policy, as well as negotiated the *Entente Cordiale*, was forced to resign following domestic criticism.

That German pressure might succeed worried the British. Prime Minister Arthur Balfour, referring to himself in the third person as protocol demanded, informed the King Edward VII of the deliberations of the British Cabinet on 8 June 1905:

> Mr Balfour pointed out that Mr Delcassé's dismissal or resignation under pressure from the German Government displayed a weakness on the part of France which indicated that she could not at present be counted on as an effective force in international politics. She could no longer be trusted not to yield to threats at the critical moment of a negotiation. If Germany is really desirous of obtaining a port on the coast of Morocco, and if such a proceeding be a menace to our interests, it must be to other means than French assistance that we must look for protection.[7]

When Germany then insisted on an international conference to settle the future of Morocco, confident that France could also be isolated diplomatically, it was British policy to bolster the French position. The conference, named from its location, took place in Algeciras, Spain, and lasted from 16 January to 7 April 1906. It finally drew up a treaty dealing with the future of Morocco, known as the Act of Algeciras, but the details of the settlement, whereby France gave up control of the police, but retained effective control of Moroccan political and financial affairs, are less important than the effect that German hostility produced on the participants, with particular emphasis on the British and French.[8] As the British diplomat Eyre Crowe was to state it in his 1907 memorandum on 'British Relations with France and Germany':

When the signature of the Algeciras Act brought to a close the first chapter of the conflict respecting Morocco, the Anglo-French *entente* had acquired a different significance, from that which it had at the moment of its inception. Then there had been but a friendly settlement of particular outstanding differences, giving hope for future harmonious relations between two neighbouring countries that had got into the habit of looking at one another askance; now there had emerged an element of common resistance to outside dictation and aggression, a unity of special interests tending to develop into active co-operation against a third Power. It is essential to bear in mind that this new feature of the *entente* was the direct effect produced by Germany's effort to break it up, and that, failing the active or threatening hostility of Germany, such anti-German bias as the *entente* must be admitted to have at one time assumed, would certainly not exist at present, nor probably survive in the future.[9]

Indeed, instead of shattering the *Entente*, German bullying had the exactly opposite effect of greatly bolstering it; Britain repeatedly supported the French position at Algeciras, as did many of the other states. Germany's only consistent ally was Austria-Hungary. As Charmley so eloquently put it in relation to these and similar matters: 'Where Bismarck had played chess, Bülow and the Kaiser played poker – and badly.'[10]

Coming on top of this failure was direct and public evidence of the ill-considered judgement, to put it mildly, of the Kaiser. This followed the publication of his views in the *Daily Telegraph*, a British newspaper. Though couched in the style of an interview, a British army officer, Colonel Edward Montagu-Stuart-Wortley, had actually obtained the Kaiser's comments during, and subsequent to, Wilhelm's 1907 summer visit to his Dorset home, Highcliffe Castle.[11] The tenor of the discussions held between the two men revolved around what the Kaiser considered to be misplaced fears in Britain concerning German foreign policy and navalism.[12] Wortley wrote up his notes of the conversations to resemble an interview with Wilhelm, and sent it to him asking permission to publish it in Britain.

The Kaiser passed the draft to Bülow, asking for it to be perused, but Bülow, rather than do it himself, passed it to the Foreign Office for consideration. Despite several urgings from the officials there that he read the document, it appears that the Chancellor did not do so before returning it to the Kaiser who, in turn, sent it back to Wortley. The 'interview' saw the light of day on 28 October 1908 when published in the British *Daily Telegraph*, and caused an immediate furore internationally.

Rather than having the calming effect it was ostensibly supposed to, the interview managed to offend just about as many constituencies as was possible, both nationally and internationally. It also allowed the Kaiser to make a fool of himself; he claimed that, during what was termed the 'Black Week' of the Second Boer War in December 1899, he had received 'a letter from Queen Victoria, my revered grandmother, written in sorrow and affliction, and bearing manifest traces of the anxieties which were preying upon her mind and health'.[13] In order to alleviate these anxieties, Wilhelm alleged that, after obtaining data on the strength and position of both British and Boers from one of his officers, he worked out a plan of campaign that would see Britain victorious and sent it to the Queen. This plan, he went on, 'as a matter of curious coincidence [...] ran very much on the same lines as that which was actually adopted by Lord Roberts, and carried by him into successful operation'. The Kaiser also stated that more or less at the same time he, and he alone apparently, had rebuffed French and Russian invitations 'not only to save the Boer Republics, but also to humiliate England to the dust'.

Having claimed the credit for rescuing Britain from military disaster in South Africa, and saving her from 'humiliation' at the hands of Russia and France, Wilhelm went on to set the record straight about the construction of the German Fleet:

> Germany is a young and growing empire. [...] Her horizons stretch far away. She must be prepared for any eventualities in the Far East. Who can foresee what may take place in the Pacific in the days to come, days not so distant as some believe, but days, at any rate, for which all European Powers with Far Eastern interests ought steadily to prepare? Look at the accomplished rise of Japan; think of the possible national awakening of China; and then judge of the vast problems of the Pacific. Only those Powers which have great navies will be listened to with respect, when the future of the Pacific comes to be solved; and, if for that reason only, Germany must have a powerful fleet.

Like his 'Yellow Peril' pronouncements, expressing such sentiments was bound to cause offence to Japan in particular. Using a 'powerful fleet' for solving the 'vast problems' of the 'future of the Pacific' had the potential to sound ominous to states with interests in the Pacific. This might not only include Japan but also the US, which Germany was, on the other hand, attempting to woo.[14]

The leitmotif of the entire article however was the Kaiser's desire for peace and understanding with Britain, and how this desire was thwarted through misunderstanding and misinterpretation:

> I declared with all the emphasis at my command, in my speech at Guildhall, that my heart is set upon peace, and that it is one of my dearest wishes to live on the best of terms with England. Have I ever been false to my word? Falsehood and prevarication are alien to my nature. My actions ought to speak for themselves, but you listen not to them but to those who misinterpret and distort them. That is a personal insult which I feel and resent. To be forever misjudged, to have my repeated offers of friendship weighed and scrutinized with jealous, mistrustful eyes, taxes my patience severely. I have said time after time that I am a friend of England

While the Kaiser's comments about the Boer War might be laughable, to the political leadership and elites of Britain and the other major powers, his protestations of friendship were duplicitous to the point of derangement. What they knew that was not otherwise widely disseminated was that, on 19 July 1908, whilst the Kaiser was partaking in his annual cruise and was at Bergen, Norway, he had granted an interview to an American writer, William Bayard Hale. Speaking for some two hours, Wilhelm inveighed, most undiplomatically, against several foreign powers, mainly the British and Japanese.

Hale's account of the interview runs to several thousand words, and is in large part an incoherent rant against Japan, raising once again the question of the 'yellow peril':

> How long ago was it that I painted my picture of the yellow peril? I believe it was fifteen years ago, was it not? [...] I dare say the world smiled. The world does not smile now. The time for smiling is passed. Everybody understands what must come to pass between the East and the West, the yellow race and the white. It is imbecile folly for us to close our eyes to the inevitable, for us to neglect to prepare to meet the inevitable.
>
> All the world understands that the greatest contest in the destiny of the earth's population is at hand. The first battle has been fought. Unfortunately it was not won. Russia was fighting the white man's battle. Many did not see it then. All do now. What a pity it was not fought better! What a misfortune! Those Russians were not fit to fight this fight. What a pity it should have [fallen to] them to do it. [...] My God! I wish my battalions could have had a chance at them; we should have made short work of it.[15]

There was much more in this vein, and Britain, through its alliance with Japan, was 'a traitor to the white man's cause'. The main points of the interview were synopsised by the editor of the *New York Times*, who opined that it 'is so strong that it cannot be printed' in the paper, as follows:

> the Emperor was most bitter against England during the whole interview and that Germany was ready for war at any moment with her and the sooner it came the better. He claimed that Great Britain looked upon Germany as her enemy because it was the most dominant force on the continent of Europe and it had always been England's way to attack the strongest power. France and Russia were now out of the running [...] and she was friendly with them, so everything was directed against Germany. [...] Great Britain had been degenerating ever since the Boer War which was a war against God and for that she would be punished as all nations have been who have done wrong to a weaker Power that was in the right. He believed that a war would come, and he was aching for the fight, not for the sake of war, but as something that was unpleasant and inevitable, and the sooner the better.[16]

The motivation for giving such an interview, the publication of which was largely suppressed following great political pressure by the British, American and German governments at the highest level, is unclear.[17] Cecil suggests that it was an attempt to court favour in the US,[18] but, whether there was any rational explanation or not, the point is that its main points were known, among the senior political classes and higher echelons of society internationally, well before the publication of the *Daily Telegraph* interview. Those who had knowledge, if only partial, of the Hale interview, and next read the *Daily Telegraph* interview, could then be forgiven for concluding that the Kaiser was delusional.

Domestically, the 'Daily Telegraph Affair' as we now know it, seems to have been the catalyst for a surge of criticism of the Kaiser. A summary of German newspaper comments sent to Sir Edward Grey on 30 October 1908 gives the flavour of this:

> The publication [...] of the Emperor's interview [...] has created the greatest excitement in all sections of the German Press. The impression produced on them is on the whole a most unfavourable one. Hardly a paper, even among those which are usually more or less well disposed towards the Emperor's utterances, fails to express regret that His Majesty should have spoken as he is represented to have done, on one or other point in the interview. The *National Zeitung* [. . .] cannot refrain from pointing out that if Germany's policy during the Boer War and since then has been really so Anglophile, it would have been well for the Government to let the German people know this [...] Nor will His Majesty's references to the yellow peril be appreciated everywhere. The *Cologne Gazette* in the midst of an elaborate apology for and explanation of the Emperor's words, expresses similar regret at the references to the Far Eastern question [...]
>
> Few other German papers make any pretence of approving the Emperor's words; the *Berliner Tageblatt* takes his speech point by point and shows that His Majesty's attitude or action in every case referred to was 'mistaken'; the *Deutsche Tageszeitung* takes the opportunity to attack the Emperor vigorously for his habit of interfering in foreign policy, and the *Börsen Courier* writes [...] 'From whatever point they are viewed' [...] 'His Majesty's remarks are calculated to produce a most unfortunate effect, such as will serve to show afresh the dangerous position in which our foreign policy has been placed for the last quarter of a century, by the impossibility of reckoning with or controlling the personal interference of the Sovereign in diplomatic activity. We do not know whether Prince Bülow has ever taken the opportunity of confronting the Emperor with an 'either-or' on the subject. The present would certainly be a suitable moment for him to do so; and the nation would thank him if he could thus avert similar interference in the future.'[19]

The Kaiser was also harshly criticised in the Reichstag on 10 November 1908, indeed, domestically the affair developed into a major crisis, which focused attention on the Kaiser and his personal rule. This criticism was taken so badly by Wilhelm that it precipitated a nervous breakdown.[20] It also destroyed his confidence in Bülow, whose position became increasingly insecure.[21] The affair raised fundamental questions about the functioning of the political system, and forced the Kaiser into issuing a statement that he would in future 'respect his constitutional obligations'.[22] Coming on top of the failure at Algeciras, Mommsen argues that the German Reich suffered the severest internal crisis since its foundation.[23]

It is ironic to note that in the instance of the *Daily Telegraph* Affair at least Wilhelm had acted properly in submitting the draft of the interview to Bülow, and had not forwarded it for publication until it had been returned. The damage was done however, and if the domestic fallout was brief and resulted in no permanent alteration in the way the government worked, the international community was left wondering at the nature of that government, and the processes by which it arrived at decisions. There was also the matter of the apparently bizarre mental state of the ruler of that government.

This, combined with the bellicose and confrontational manner with which

Germany was apt to conduct foreign policy, as evidenced by the Tangier Crisis, only served to augment suspicions about the future among the other European powers. This was particularly so in the case of Britain, which also had the question of the build-up of the German Fleet to consider. Sir Edward Grey, British Foreign Secretary since December 1905,[24] was apparently optimistic as regards future relations with Germany; he put it thus to the House of Commons on 29 March 1909:

> And now as regards our future diplomatic relations with Germany, I see a wide space in which both of us may walk in peace and amity. Two things, in my opinion two extreme things, would produce conflict. One is an attempt by us to isolate Germany. [...] Another thing which would certainly produce a conflict would be the isolation of England attempted by any great continental power so as to dominate and dictate the policy of the continent. [...] But between these two extremes of isolation and domination there is a wide space in which the two nations can walk together in a perfectly friendly way.[25]

He then passed on to the so-called naval rivalry, or race, between the two powers. Grey was addressing parliament within the context of the 'Great Naval Scare', which was occasioned by the belief that Germany was building capital ships at a greater rate than had been previously thought, and so eroding British superiority.[26] This caused divisions not only between the political parties, but within the ruling party and Cabinet. Great trouble was also stirred up by the press, which, in a manner now familiar, fomented anti-German feeling among newspaper readers.

> But now I pass to [...] the relations between us with regard to naval expenditure. The German view of their program is that it is made for their own needs, and has no reference to ours, and that if we build fifty or a hundred Dreadnoughts they will not build more, but if we cease building altogether they will not build one less. We have no difficulty in hearing that view without reproach, and just as little difficulty in saying quite frankly that our own view of our naval needs is that our expenditure is, and must be, dependent upon the German, although the German is not dependent upon ours. It is essential to us that we should not fall into a position of inferiority; it is essential that we should keep a position of superiority as regards our navy. But public opinion in Germany and in the world at large increasingly measures the probable relations of England and Germany by their respective naval expenditure. An increase of naval expenditure on both sides is undoubtedly viewed by public opinion with apprehension. On the other hand, a decrease of naval expenditure will immediately produce a feeling of increased security and peace. If I was asked to name the one thing that would mostly reassure the world - or reassure Europe - with regard to the prospects of peace, I think it would be that the naval expenditure in Germany would be diminished, and that ours was following suit and being diminished also.[27]

Grey went on to propose a bilateral arrangement between Britain and Germany 'to limit or reduce naval expenditure, a comparison of naval estimates year by year in advance, to see whether the modification of the one might not lead to the modification of the other'.[28] There was to be no naval agreement limiting the build-up of fleets between the two powers, and neither, despite Bülow being replaced as

Imperial Chancellor by Theobald von Bethmann-Hollweg in July 1909, was there to be a slackening of the diplomatic tension.

Despite the fallout from the 'Daily Telegraph Affair,' the proximate cause of Bülow's resignation was domestic politics; he became embroiled in budgetary difficulties with the Reichstag. Bethmann, who was not well acquainted 'with the complicated machinery of foreign policy', appointed Alfred von Kiderlen-Wächter as Foreign Secretary.[29] The appointment of Bethmann, who was deemed by Grey to be 'moderate',[30] suggested the possibility that an accommodation might be reached. However, the Kaiser and Tirpitz remained impervious to reason in pursuit of their shipbuilding programme, thus the primary cause of tension between Britain and Germany persisted.[31] Indeed, despite his recognition of the harm that the naval rivalry was causing to German interests vis-à-vis Britain, Bethmann opined that 'A Great Power [...] must have a [...] strong fleet [...] for the general purposes of her greatness.'[32] Despite then a détente with Britain being one of the basic premises of Bethmann's foreign policy,[33] he was unable to give effect to it.

The new Chancellor's policy of détente was further obscured, and perhaps fatally damaged, by the Second Moroccan, or Agadir, Crisis, which occurred following the dispatch of a French military expedition to Fez, the Moroccan capital, on 11 May 1911 after an appeal for assistance from the ruling Sultan who was facing a rebellion.[34] Though Germany had legitimate grounds for complaining of this action, which was undertaken without consultation, Kiderlen-Wächter, saw it as an opportunity for scoring a foreign policy coup. Determined to back up diplomatic action with a touch of sabre rattling, he had the German gunboat *Panther* (1902) dispatched to Agadir to safeguard German 'interests'. He outlined his rationale in a memorandum of 3 May, before the French had moved:

> The occupation of Fez would pave the way for the absorption of Morocco by France. We should gain nothing by protesting and it would mean a moral defeat hard to bear. We must therefore look for an objective for the ensuing negotiations, which shall induce the French to compensate us. If the French, out of 'anxiety' for their compatriots, settle themselves at Fez, it is our right, too, to protect our compatriots in danger. We have large firms at Mogador and Agadir. German ships could go to those ports to protect the firms. They could remain anchored there quite peacefully – merely with the idea of preventing other Powers from intruding [...] The importance of choosing those ports, the great distance of which from the Mediterranean should make in unlikely that England would raise objections, lies in the fact that they possess a very fertile hinterland, which ought to contain important mineral wealth.[35]

Looked at dispassionately the dispatch of such an ineffectual vessel, the *Panther* was an *Iltis*-class gunboat with a top speed of some 14 knots armed with two 105mm guns and six 37mm machine guns, was a minor affair.[36] Though the diplomatic style of Kiderlen-Wächter has been characterised as being 'to stamp on his neighbour's foot and display aggrieved surprise if he received a kick in return',[37] he had the approval of the Chancellor in sending the vessel.[38] What the German

Foreign Minister wanted to extract from France was the territory known as the French Congo or French Equatorial Africa, an immense area about four times the size of France.[39] In gaining this colony he was thinking two steps ahead, inasmuch as he foresaw the advantages the possession of the territory would give Germany should the Belgian Congo ever be broken up. He clearly stated his position in a letter to Bethmann following upon the outbreak of the crisis:

The French understand that they must grant us compensation in the colonial realm. They want to keep this to a minimum, and the government will be bolstered in this by its fear of both parliament and the public sentiment generated by the Colonial Party. The French will only agree to an acceptable offer if they are firmly convinced that we are otherwise resolved to take extreme action. If we do not demonstrate this, then we will not receive, in return for our withdrawal from Morocco, the kind of compensation that a statesman could justify to the German people. This, in any case, is my conviction. We must gain all of the French Congo – it is our last opportunity to get a worthwhile piece of land in Africa without a fight. Regions in the Congo that have rubber and ivory, as nice as they may be, are of no use to us. We must go right up to the Belgian Congo so that, if it is divided up, we will take part in the partitioning. If this entity continues to exist, we will have access through it to our territories in East Africa. Any other solution would be a defeat to us, which we must be firmly resolved to avert.[40]

Perhaps thinking ahead two steps led him to neglect to ensure that the first step was achievable. In any event the German actions, in particular the 'Panther's leap to Agadir' on 1 July as it became popularly known, produced a huge reaction. In Churchill's words: 'All the alarm bells throughout Europe began immediately to quiver. France found herself in the presence of an act which could not be explained, the purpose behind which could not be measured.'[41]

On 21 July 1911 David Lloyd George delivered the annual Chancellor of the Exchequer's speech at London's Mansion House. Though normally reserved for financial matters, there was a portion of it devoted to matters of foreign policy:

[...] I believe it is essential in the highest interests, not merely of this country, but of the world, that Britain should at all hazards maintain her place and her prestige among the Great Powers of the world. Her potent influence has many a time been in the past, and may yet be in the future, invaluable to the cause of human liberty. It has more than once in the past redeemed Continental nations, who are sometimes too apt to forget that service, from overwhelming disaster and even from national extinction. I would make great sacrifices to preserve peace. I conceive that nothing would justify a disturbance of international good will except questions of the greatest national moment. But if a situation were to be forced upon us in which peace could only be preserved by the surrender of the great and beneficent position Britain has won by centuries of heroism and achievement, by allowing Britain to be treated where her interests were vitally affected as if she were of no account in the Cabinet of nations, then I say emphatically that peace at that price would be a humiliation intolerable for a great country like ours to endure.[42]

Though the speech, both in terms of authorship and intent, has been subject to some revisionist debate, contemporaneous opinion was unanimous that it was aimed squarely at Germany, particularly since Lloyd George was well known as an anti-militarist.

That the German government thought so is evident from their reaction. The German ambassador to London, Count Paul Wolff-Metternich, sought an audience with Sir Edward Grey and, this having been granted on 24 July, explained that German had no designs on Moroccan territory, did not wish to create a naval base on the Moroccan coast, and merely sought compensation from France for what was considered a breach of the Act of Algeciras. Grey asked if he could reveal this information, as it would calm the situation down, and Metternich replied that he would seek permission from his government. The next day Grey and Metternich met again, the latter with the reply from Berlin. Reasons of national prestige had now arisen; Metternich explained that if Grey were to reveal what had been communicated to him, it would appear that Germany had responded to the 'provocation' contained in Lloyd George's speech. Germany however, was prepared to use 'all means' to secure German treaty rights in Morocco.

The tenor of this meeting so shook Grey that he warned several of his colleagues that Germany might attack the British fleet at any time. In fact, despite the nature of Metternich's message, the German government was keen to avoid any escalation and was seeking a way to ease the tension. Even the Kaiser urged caution on his foreign minister, and General Franz von Wandel, the head of the General War Department of the Prussian War Ministry, revealed the disjointed nature of the German government in a diary entry of 16 August:

> In this case too, as so often before, the dispatch of our warships [...] seems to have been a matter not of carefully evaluated decision with all consequences considered, but rather of a sudden impulse. There was no understanding whatsoever of what might arise from it and of how all these possibilities were to be dealt with; the order is said to have taken shape in a few hours one afternoon, without precise knowledge of local conditions, the anchorage and the like. It is hardly surprising that we now find ourselves more or less at a loss in the face of the resulting political difficulties [...] but it is characteristic of our circumstances of government that neither the War Minister nor the Chief of the Army General Staff is in any way informed of how things stand.[43]

Metternich was given new instructions to mollify the British, which he did during a meeting with Grey on 27 July, stating that the outcome of the bilateral negotiations between France and Germany would in no way impact on British interests. Grey was also informed that the German government had no objection to these facts being reported to the British parliament. It was the Prime Minister who acquainted the House of Commons, in the most diplomatic of language, with the information that while Britain would be pleased to see a successful conclusion to the ongoing conversations between France and Germany, no British interests were involved.

Despite Asquith's emollient words the effect of the Agadir Crisis on Anglo-

German relations was profound, even though the territorial issues were settled peacefully between the two principles under the terms of the Franco-German Agreement signed on 4 November 1911, through which Germany gained New Cameroon (*Neukamerun*). This 275,000 square kilometres of ex-French territory was far less than Kiderlen-Wächter had originally sought, although it did provide a common border with the Belgian Congo.[44]

Once again German action had the effect of pushing Britain into opposition, rather than, as was Bethmann's general overriding policy, of forging a closer relationship in order to break the 'encirclement' of Germany. That this was very much still a contentious issue was exemplified by the remarks made by the Kaiser on 29 May 1908, when he made a vociferous speech to a military parade at Döberitz Barracks near Berlin. Dubbed the 'Fredericus-Rex' speech it invoked the memory of Frederick the Great and his breaking up of encircling alliances. Wilhelm denounced the contemporary conspiracy to 'encircle' Germany, and struck a warlike and threatening note – 'all this within earshot of Russian and Japanese military attachés, who were under no obligation to keep it secret'.[45] Government officials had, ever since the 'Hun Speech' of 1900, learned however to 'spin' the reporting of the Kaiser's speeches in the event of a conflict with the press over the correct wording of an address by the Kaiser, so a sanitised version was presented to the German public.[46]

The chief 'encircler' was deemed to be Britain,[47] and, despite further attempts to find an understanding, such as the visit of Lord Haldane, the Germanophile British Minister of War, in February 1912, no basis for one could be established. As a result, the British grew ever closer to France to the extent of concluding a naval agreement, albeit informal, that in the event of war the French fleet would concentrate in the Mediterranean, while the British fleet would concentrate in the North Sea.

The various crises and incidents outlined above can perhaps in retrospect be viewed as waypoints on the journey to war. They need not have been of course, but the bellicosity of German foreign policy, coupled with uncertainty as to the stability of the Kaiser, whose exact role was not easy to ascertain contemporaneously, and still remains the subject of controversy, combined to foster a distrust in Britain, particularly in the mind of the Foreign Secretary, Sir Edward Grey.

Grey served twice as Foreign Secretary, first in 1892–95 in Gladstone's final administration, and then from 1905 to 1916 in the Campbell-Bannerman and Asquith administrations. From 1906 he authorised secret 'discussions' between the General Staffs of France and Britain but kept these hidden from his Cabinet colleagues, and the full import of them even from the Prime Minister.[48] Winston Churchill, while concluding that Grey's 'Entente with France and the military and naval conversations that had taken place since 1906, had led us into a position where we had the obligations of an alliance without its advantages' also opined that the policy was, in all essentials, correct.[49] Lloyd George was less sanguine, arguing that:

During the eight years that preceded the war, the Cabinet devoted a ridiculously small percentage of its time to a consideration of foreign affairs. [...] Nothing was said about our military commitments. There was an air of 'hush hush' about every allusion to our relations with France, Russia and Germany. [...] We were made to feel that, in these matters, we were reaching our hands towards the mysteries, and that we were too young in the priesthood to presume to enter into the sanctuary reserved for the elect.[50]

A. J. P. Taylor considered that Grey 'followed a resolute line [...] but he consulted the Cabinet very little, and he informed the public hardly at all'.[51] He also argued that whilst Grey repudiated the phrase the 'Balance of Power' he was 'concerned about the European Balance in a way that no British foreign secretary had been since Palmerston'.[52] Grey later justified his policy by arguing that:

We must be free to go to the help of France as well as to stand aside [...] If there were no military plans made beforehand we should be unable to come to the assistance of France in time [...] We should in effect not have preserved our freedom to help France, but cut ourselves off from the possibility of doing so.[53]

This was, as Taylor commented, a good argument,[54] but it failed to take into account that if the arrangements were secret and non-binding they could not have the effect of deterring Germany. However, it was politically impossible for Grey to publicise his diplomacy because of the risk that it would have divided the Cabinet, the Liberal Party, and probably the country.

On 28 June 1914 the heir to the throne of Austria-Hungary, Archduke Franz Ferdinand, and his wife, Sophie, Duchess of Hohenberg, were assassinated in Sarajevo. Serbia was deemed responsible by Austria-Hungary and this 'damned silly thing in the Balkans' set in train the 'July Crisis' that led to the outbreak of war at the end of July and beginning of August.

As the crisis deepened Grey was unable to give a clear warning to Germany that, in the event of a war, Britain would fight on the side of France and Russia. Whether or not this would have made any difference remains the subject of scholarly argument. It was only after his attempts to convene a conference of all the Great Powers had failed that he warned the German Ambassador to London, Prince Lichnowsky, on 29 July, that Britain could not remain uninvolved in any general European war: 'it would not be practicable to stand aside and wait for any length of time'.[55] This warning was however contradicted by information received by the Kaiser the day before from his brother, Prince Heinrich. This was to the effect that the King-Emperor George V had told him that Britain would endeavour to stay neutral.[56] War was, by this time, probably inevitable in any case. Austria-Hungary had issued a declaration of war against Serbia on 28 July, causing Russia to order partial mobilization. This was followed by full mobilisation on 31 July. Germany declared war on Russia the next day, and on France on 3 August.

The British government had still to decide what to do, and two Cabinet meetings were held on Sunday 3 August. The last of these decided to issue an ultimatum concerning Belgian integrity, which was the issue around which the Liberal

Government and Party could, mostly, unite; two Cabinet ministers resigned, John Burns and John Morley. At 11p.m. London time on 4 August 1914 Britain declared war on Germany.

With British participation the war became a worldwide conflict, particularly since the British declaration automatically committed the dominions and colonies. This was not necessarily unpopular in the Pacific territories; the Australian Labour Party leader, the political veteran Andrew Fisher, as part of an ongoing election campaign put it thus on 31 July 1914:

> All, I am sure, will regret the critical position existing at the present time, and pray that a disastrous war may be averted. But should the worst happen after everything has been done that honour will permit, Australians will stand beside our own to help and defend her to our last man and our last shilling.[57]

Fisher's party won the subsequent election and he became Prime Minister for a third time. Australian involvement in the conflict was of vital importance to the prosecution of the conflict in the Far East against Germany; the largest and most powerful force in the area available to the British Empire was the Royal Australian Navy (RAN). At the outbreak of war the effective offensive strength of the RAN, the fleet unit as agreed at the 1909 Conference, consisted of the 1911 *Indefatigable*-class battlecruiser *Australia* (flagship), the 1912 *Chatham*-class light cruisers *Melbourne* and *Sydney*, and the 1905 *Challenger*-class light cruiser *Encounter* (the latter being an ex-Royal Navy vessel given to the RAN pending the completion of the Australian-built *Chatham*-class light cruiser *Brisbane*). There was also an obsolete 1900 *Pelorus*-class third-class protected cruiser, *Pioneer*, and three 'River'-class destroyers *Parramtatta* (1910), *Yarra* (1910) and *Warrego* (1911), together with two modern (1914) E-class submarines, *AE1* and *AE2*. This mainly modern and unquestionably powerful force was under the command of Rear-Admiral Sir George Patey RN, and was more than a match for the East Asiatic Cruiser Squadron.

Commanded since December 1912 by Vice Admiral Maximilian Graf von Spee, the core of the German force comprised the two modern armoured cruisers *Scharnhorst* (1907) and *Gneisenau* (1908). The other main fighting units of the force consisted of a quartet of light cruisers: *Dresden, Emden, Leipzig* and *Nürnberg*. This squadron, together with the, albeit sparse, infrastructure created in the German Pacific colonies made for a potent threat. As the Australian Official History has it:

> A powerful [...] fleet [...]; it had bases and coaling facilities at carefully selected points, with which it could communicate by wireless. As long as it remained [...] and could maintain communication with its bases in the islands, it was obvious that the position was one fraught with endless possibilities for Australia and New Zealand.[58]

However the presence on the Southern Pacific of the Australian flagship acted as a severe deterrent on Spee, who was to write in his diary on 18 August 1914:

'The *Australia* is my special apprehension – she alone is superior to my whole squadron.'[59]

Not in any way distinctly superior, other than in numbers, was the other major force deployed in the Pacific by the Royal Navy; the China Squadron under Vice-Admiral Sir Martyn Jerram. The main components of this force were the flagship, the armoured cruiser *Minotaur* (1906), the name ship of her class, *Hampshire* (1903), a *Devonshire*-class armoured cruiser, *Newcastle* (1910) a *Bristol*-class light cruiser, and *Yarmouth* (1911) a *Weymouth*-class light cruiser.[60] Despite this lack of superiority it was the China Squadron that had the task of dealing with the German squadron and its base in the event of war.

Knowing full well that Jerram's force as constituted was not assured of dispatching Spee's – Jerram had warned he might be unable to take on the squadron without reinforcements in 1913[61] – the Admiralty had arranged for the RAN to provide strong support in the shape of the flagship, upon which occasion Patey would hoist his flag as admiral of the Australian Squadron in the *Encounter*. The British were able to direct the disposition of *Australia*, and indeed any RAN resources, under arrangements entered into at the Imperial Conference of 1911. There it had been agreed that operational control of the RAN ships would revert to the Admiralty in time of war:

> On the receipt of a pre-arranged cablegram from the Imperial authorities, the Australian Government would place the [...] naval services of the Commonwealth directly under the control of the Admiralty. The sea-going fleet would then become a squadron of the Imperial Navy, taking orders either direct from London or from the British officer under whom they were placed.[62]

When the Admiralty's 'war warning' telegram was dispatched on 28 July 1914, Jerram was at Weihaiwei with all his vessels other than *Newcastle*, which was visiting Japan.[63] However, rather than steam directly towards Tsingtau, some 172 nautical miles away, he was directed to concentrate at Hong Kong, a further 860 miles to the south, in order to concentrate his squadron around the *Swiftsure*-class pre-dreadnought battleship *Triumph* (1903), which was refitting there.[64] This was, perhaps, an excessively cautious manoeuvre as *Triumph* was only marginally better armed, four 10in. and fourteen 7.5in. guns, than Jerram's armoured cruisers, but was a great deal slower with a maximum speed when new of some 19 knots. Jerram said later that he nearly disobeyed the order entirely, annoyed that a 'definite plan of action formed in peacetime after mature consideration' could be 'thrown to the winds by one peremptory telegram'.[65] In any event, the need to make this detour far from the object of the exercise probably allowed the light cruiser *Emden* to escape from Tsingtau and certainly, unless they parted company with the battle-ship, precluded any realistic chance of the China Squadron attempting to pursue Spee.

There are perhaps two points worth considering in relation to this episode. It may be recalled that HMS *New Zealand* had, as per Asquith's statement to the House of Commons on 26 August 1909 regarding the recently concluded Imperial Conference on Defence, been originally earmarked for the fleet unit based on China. Churchill had viewed this deployment with disfavour, disclaiming that 'The employment of a ship like the *New Zealand* in China is not to be defended on any military grounds', and had subsequently ensured that the vessel deployed to British waters in 1913. How different the course of events in 1914 might have been if Jerram had been able to deploy such an overwhelming force against the East Asiatic Cruiser Squadron and Tsingtau is unknowable. All that can be said with certainty is that it would have greatly increased the efficiency and fighting strength of the China Squadron, rather than reducing it as *Triumph* did.

The second point relates to the Admiralty orders to concentrate on the old battleship. This is in many ways a portent of similar orders to Rear-Admiral Sir Christopher Cradock, the commander of the South American Squadron later in the year. Prior to his disastrous engagement at Coronel in November, Cradock was told to keep his squadron concentrated around HMS *Canopus* (1898), another venerable pre-dreadnought, with a similar thickness of armour though larger calibre, but not necessarily longer ranged, guns than *Triumph*. It seems highly unlikely that either of these vessels, which were very slow in comparison to armoured cruisers, would have proved the slightest use in combat with Spee's much faster and almost equally well-armoured vessels had such an eventuality come to pass. Churchill seems to have had a blind spot, evident even before he became First Lord, regarding the ability of heavily gunned, though old and slow units, to deter and deal with lighter gunned, newer and faster enemy warships. His faith in *Canopus*, in respect of Cradock's command, and *Triumph*, in respect of Jerram's, reflect this in 1914, while in July 1910, he had resisted the deployment of battlecruisers in the Far East, arguing, in direct contradiction of Fisher's belief and policy, that 'older battleships or smaller cruisers could perfectly well discharge all the necessary naval duties'. He was, no doubt, disabused of this view following the Battle of Coronel.[66]

Churchill was later castigated for seeking, in the first volume of *The World Crisis*, to place the blame for the defeat at Coronel on Cradock, whom he accused of disobeying orders by engaging Spee without *Canopus*. As one reviewer of Churchill's work put it, the outcome of the Battle of Coronel 'came about partly through a lack of precision in the orders sent to Cradock and partly through an exaggeration, on Churchill's part, of the fighting and steaming capabilities of the *Canopus* [...]'. The reviewer went on to argue that the pre-dreadnought 'possessed the same armour as that of the *Good Hope*, which proved impotent against the modern 8-inch [210mm] guns of von Spee, and she carried guns which were not only of an antiquated mark (only 35 calibres), but which were quite outranged by von Spee's eights'.[67] Perhaps it is just as well that neither *Triumph* nor *Canopus* was put to the test.

Australia meanwhile had remained in Australian waters, not, as has been argued on occasion, because of a reluctance on the part of the Australian government to conform with British wishes, but because it had been discovered that Spee was not anywhere near Tsingtau but rather was 'somewhere within range of Australian wireless – i.e., not more than 1,500 miles away'.[68] Accordingly the capital ship, and attendant vessels, under the command of Patey, patrolled off New Britain from 11 to 13 August in search of the enemy cruiser squadron, before joining HMAS *Melbourne* and proceeding to New Caledonia on 21 August 1914 on missions of occupation. First these vessels, together with the French *Gueydon*-class armoured cruiser *Montcalm*, and the Royal Navy third-class cruisers HMS *Psyche*, HMS *Philomel* and HMS *Pyramus*, in 'Australia's first coalition operation'[69] escorted a New Zealand Expeditionary Force of 1,400 troops to take German Samoa, which surrendered without a fight.[70]

Following this the Australian ships formed escort to the Australian Naval and Military Expeditionary Force,[71] whose object was to take Rabaul, the seat, from 1910, of the governor of German New Guinea.[72] These expeditions had been sanctioned, indeed encouraged, by the Colonial Office in London, which had communicated with the Australian government on the matter on 6 August 1914 via the Governor-General Sir Ronald Munro-Ferguson.[73] Colonial Secretary Lewis Harcourt had stated:

> If your Ministers desire and feel themselves able to seize German wireless stations [...] we should feel that this was a great and urgent Imperial service. You will, however, realise that any territory now occupied must be at the disposal of the Imperial Government for purposes of an ultimate settlement at conclusion of the war.[74]

On 18 August a further communication was sent by Harcourt:

> In connection with the expedition against German possessions in Pacific, British flag should be hoisted in all territories occupied successfully by His Majesty's forces and suitable arrangements made for temporary administration. No formal proclamation of annexation should however be made without previous communication with His Majesty's Government.[75]

The taking of this territory, while unquestionably sanctioned by 'His Majesty's Government,' was also certainly congenial to the Australians, for Australia, or rather the precursor states,[76] had long coveted much of the territory occupied by Germany. In 1864, 1874, 1878, and 1879, New South Wales, with the cooperation of Queensland, had strongly urged that possession should be taken of the north-east coast of New Guinea, but the Imperial Government refused its consent. In 1883 the Queensland government had annexed that part of New Guinea, and adjacent islands, which fell between the 141st and 155th meridians, but again the British government demurred. It though did take action in 1884, when a British protectorate was proclaimed over the south coast of New Guinea and neighbouring islands.[77] Thus the occupations, or at least the undercurrent to them, have been classified by some as 'sub-imperialism.'[78]

Whatever the rationale behind the expeditions however, they were overwhelmingly successful through being able to apply overwhelming superiority; as Rear Admiral Patey had put it in a letter of 11 September 1914 to the Governor of German New Guinea:

I have the honour to inform you that I have arrived at Simpsonhafen [Simpson Harbour] with the intention of occupying Herbertshöhe,[79] Rabaul, and the Island of New Britain.

I will point out to Your Excellency that the force at my command is so large as to render useless any opposition on your part, and such resistance can only result in unnecessary bloodshed.[80]

Patey was not indulging in hyperbole, and, although there was some resistance and a small number of casualties on both sides, the 'Terms of Capitulation of German New Guinea' was signed on 17 September 1914.[81] It was of course the presence of HMAS *Australia* that alone rendered possible the dispatch of expeditionary forces to the German possessions in the southern Pacific, and as it turned out the lack of the battlecruiser with the China Squadron had little effect; far more formidable forces had joined the Allied cause.

The British Foreign Office had been apprised of Japan's position as regards Germany, on 3 August 1914, via a telegram from the British ambassador in Tokyo, Sir Conyngham Greene. The Japanese offered to assist Britain in the Pacific, but left it 'entirely to [the British] Government to formulate the reason for and nature of the assistance required'.[82]

Grey had, on 1 August, informed Japan via Inouye Katsunosuke, her ambassador to London, that British participation in the European war was probable, but had argued that he did not consider it 'likely' that the British would 'have to apply to Japan under our alliance'. He informed the British representative in Tokyo of his discussion the same day:

I told the Japanese Ambassador to-day that the situation in Europe was very grave. We had not yet decided what our action should be, but under certain conditions we might find it necessary to intervene. If, however, we did intervene, it would be on the side of France and Russia, and I therefore did not see that we were likely to have to apply to Japan under our alliance, or that the interests dealt with by the alliance would be involved.[83]

Grey modified this stance somewhat two days later, when he had communicated to the Japanese the view of Sir Walter Langley, an Assistant Under-Secretary of State for Foreign Affairs. The Foreign Secretary had asked Langley 'whether the present situation in any way affects the Japanese under the 1911 Agreement and whether we have anything to ask them'.[84] The reply he received set out the parameters of the issue as perceived by the Foreign Office secretariat:

The only ways in which the Japanese could be brought in would be if hostilities spread to the Far East, e.g., an attack on Hong Kong by the Germans, or if a rising in India were to take place.

There seems no reason to say anything about India, but it might be as well to warn the Japanese Government that in the event of a war with Germany there might be a possibility of an attack upon Hong Kong or Weihaiwei when we should look to them for support.

The Japanese are no doubt quite alive to this possibility, but perhaps under Article 1 of the agreement we should communicate with them.[85]

Grey obviously considered this position to be in accordance with his own views, authorising the despatch of a telegraph to Japan without further reference to him.[86] The message sent stated that 'if hostilities spread to [the] Far East, and an attack on Hong Kong or Weihaiwei were to take place, we should rely on [Japanese] support'.[87] Greene had meanwhile elicited from the Japanese Foreign Minister the official position held by Japan:

> the Imperial Government will await an intimation from His Majesty's Government as to what action they have decided to take before defining their own attitude, which will be based thereon.
>
> Japan has no interest in a European conflict, and his Excellency [Kato, the Minister for Foreign Affairs] notes what you say as to the Anglo-Japanese Alliance, but, if British interests in Eastern Asia should be placed in jeopardy – as say, for instance, by a German attack on Hong Kong or by any other aggressive act – His Majesty's Government may count upon Japan at once coming to assistance of her ally with all her strength, if called on to do so, leaving it entirely to His Majesty's Government to formulate the reason for, and nature of, the assistance required.[88]

This placing, as it seemed, of Japanese interests behind those of Britain was very much to Grey's taste as can be readily discerned from a perusal of his messages already quoted. He reinforced his appreciation of the position that he perceived Japan as adopting during a meeting he held with Inouye on 4 August 1914. Grey sent a report of the conversation to Greene in Tokyo:

> I asked the Japanese Ambassador today to thank Baron Kato most cordially for his generous offer of assistance. I told the Ambassador how much I had been impressed by the way in which Japan, during the Russo-Japanese war, demanded nothing of us under our alliance with her except what was strictly in accord with the Treaty of Alliance; indeed, he had asked almost less than at one time it seemed she might have been entitled to have from us. I had thought that a fine attitude of good faith and restraint; and now we in turn should avoid, if we could, drawing Japan into any trouble. But, should a case arise in which we needed her help, we would gladly ask for it and be grateful for it.[89]

On the same day the Foreign Secretary received from Greene a telegram containing the response to one of his earlier messages:

> Your telegram of 3rd August [(35865) No. 549.] was laid before the Cabinet this morning, and Minister for Foreign Affairs desires me to say that in the special eventualities referred to, namely: An attack on Hong Kong and Weihaiwei or a similar concrete act of aggression the Imperial Government will be ready at once to support His Majesty's Government if called upon, as explained in my telegram [(35666) No. 571]. In the hypothetical cases, such as a capture of a British merchant ship or a case involving, perhaps, a question of Chinese or Russian territorial waters,

the Imperial Government would wish to have the opportunity of considering it and consulting with His Majesty's Government before taking definite action.

Secret.

His Excellency tells me that 2nd battle fleet of four large cruisers, to which volunteer fleet may be added, is lying ready at Sasebo for immediate action if required, while a cruiser has been stationed at each of the ports of Nagasaki, Fusan, and Chemulpo to meet possible eventualities.[90]

Unless and until such eventualities materialised however, the only assistance the British government sought was, in effect, that of having the Japanese Navy act as support to the Royal Navy. This is made clear in a note sent by Grey via Greene on 5 August:

HM Government would gladly avail themselves of the proffered assistance of Japanese Government in the direction of protecting British trading vessels from German armed merchant cruisers, while British warships are locating and engaging German warships in Chinese waters [...] it would be of the very greatest assistance to HM Government if they [Japanese] would be good enough to employ some of their warships in hunting out and destroying German armed merchantmen in China. British Government realise that such action on the part of Japan will constitute declaration of war with Germany, but it is difficult to see how such a step is to be avoided.[91]

A declaration of war with Germany was, unknown to Grey it seems, very much at the forefront of Japanese political thought. Indeed, Greene had reported to him on 2 August that 'Japanese vernacular papers are now discussing the possibility of Japan being invited to support her ally in defence of her interests in the Far East. The view generally taken seems to be that Japan will gladly accept responsibility.'[92]

Indeed, the Japanese Cabinet, without waiting to be invited, accepted the responsibility at an emergency cabinet meeting on 7 August. This meeting resolved to declare war and also decided that Japan would not restrict itself to the secondary role allotted by Britain. Japan would however negotiate with Britain as to the form of its declaration of war against Germany.[93] The *Genro* and the Emperor swiftly ratified the Cabinet decision.[94] This information was sent to the Japanese ambassador to Britain on 9 August and communicated to Grey the next day:

Having once declared war, [Japan] cannot confine her actions to the destruction of [German] merchantmen alone. To attain the object common to the two allied powers, as far as Chinese waters are concerned, namely the destruction of Germany's power to damage the interests of Japan and Great Britain in Easter Asia, Japan will have to use every possible means. Besides, taking into consideration that employment of Japanese men-of-war for the purpose of destroying German armed merchantmen may be regarded as an act limited in scope and to have been necessitated by the temporary convenience of Great Britain, the Japanese Government are of the opinion that the reasons for Japan's participation in the war should be made on the broad grounds as stated in the Agreement of Alliance, and they should take such action as the development of events may dictate. [...] The

Japanese Government will therefore state in the declaration of war [...] that, as the consequences of aggressive action by Germany, the British Government finding that the general peace is threatened in Eastern Asia, and that the special interests of Great Britain are in jeopardy, have requested the support of Japan, to which she has acceded.[95]

The ambassador also made plain Japan's desire that the declaration of war should be so phrased as to convey that it had been made at Britain's request: '[The Japanese Government] also wish that Britain will [...] make a statement which will not conflict with that of [Japan].'[96]

Grey replied to this message on 11 August: 'in the absence of any present danger apparent to Hong Kong or British concessions I cannot say the special interests of Great Britain in Eastern Asia are so seriously menaced as to make it essential to appeal to the Alliance on that ground alone'.[97]

However, Grey went on to point out that:

I recognise that Japan has interests also to be considered [...] I agree therefore to a statement that the two Governments having been in communication with each other are of opinion that it is necessary for each to take action to protect the general interests contemplated by the Anglo-Japanese Alliance. It should also be stated that the action of Japan will not extend to the Pacific Ocean beyond the China Seas nor extend beyond Asiatic waters westward of the China Seas, or to any foreign territory except territory in German occupation on the continent in Eastern Asia. This is important to prevent unfounded misapprehension abroad.[98]

This was despite a reassurance received the day before that Japan had no intention of undertaking operations affecting China: 'lest a declaration of war on the part of Japan [...] give rise to the impression that extensive operations affecting China may take place [...] [Japan's actions would be limited to] the destruction of German power in these regions for which no extensive operations are required'.[99]

Even though from this distance in time it looks like mere semantics, British ambivalence had the potential to embarrass Japan as reports of an imminent declaration of war had leaked, or been leaked, into the public domain and military preparations had been undertaken. Grey's Cabinet colleague, Winston Churchill, the First Lord of the Admiralty, was, as his biographer put it, 'alarmed' when he sighted Grey's 11 August telegram.[100] He wrote immediately to Grey:

Your [...] [s]tatement [I cannot say the special interests of Great Britain in Eastern Asia are so seriously menaced as to make it essential to appeal to the Alliance on that ground alone] is not borne out by our information [...]

I must say I think you are chilling indeed to these people. I can't see any half-way house myself between having them in and keeping them out. If they are to come in, they may as well be welcomed as comrades. This last telegram is almost hostile. I am afraid I do not understand what is in your mind on this aspect – though I followed it so clearly till today. [...]

This telegram gives me a shiver. We are all in this together & I only wish to give the fullest effect & support to your main policy. But I am altogether perplexed by the line opened up by these Japanese interchanges.

You may easily give mortal offence – which will not be forgotten – we are not safe yet – by a long chalk. The storm has yet to burst.[101]

Under this pressure Grey modified his telegram, and wrote to Churchill later that day stating that he thought 'it is all right now with Japan'. Whatever the policy of the Foreign Office with respect to Japan, Churchill was keen on them becoming allies, indeed he sent a message of his own to the Japanese Minister of Marine, Admiral Yashiro Rokuro, on 13 August, welcoming him and his service as 'brothers in arms': 'On behalf of the Board of Admiralty I express the warm feeling of comradeship & pleasure with which the officers & men of the British Navy will find themselves allied in a common cause & against a common foe with the gallant & seamanlike Navy of Japan.'[102]

This message, it may be noted, was sent some five days before Japan sent any ultimatum to Germany and ten days before her declaration of war. If Churchill can be accused of jumping the gun to some extent, and being somewhat at odds with Foreign Office policy, then perhaps he may be absolved by noting that any discussion taking place in London pertaining to Japanese actions against Germany in the Pacific were academic.

Japan could see for herself the prospects that the European 'Great Powers' being at war with each other opened up, particularly recognising 'the advantages of raising Japan's status through obliterating German bases from East Asia' and the 'gains which Japan could make in the Pacific and in China, especially in Manchuria'.[103] Abe Moritaro, the head of the political bureau of the Foreign Office, had during 1912 and 1913 composed memoranda on the subject of Japanese relations with China urging a moderate approach lest Japanese intervention succeed only in uniting the Chinese and causing an anti-Japanese backlash. For being associated with political moderation Abe was assassinated.[104] Foreign Minister Makino Nobuaki took a somewhat different line, and in a memorandum composed just prior to him leaving office in April 1914 he had advocated direct intervention as the only means of protecting Japan's position in relation to China.[105] The situation, and Makino's solution to it, thereafter came within the purview of the Anglophile and new Foreign Minister Baron Kato Takaaki.

The problem with direct intervention was that it would inevitably draw in the other Great Powers, including perhaps Japan's ally, Britain, which, despite the alliance, was not necessarily overly sympathetic to Japanese attempts to broaden its influence in China.[106] This problem would be greatly mitigated of course if the powers were occupied elsewhere. The outbreak of war in Europe thus gave Japan a 'one in a million chance' both to secure her existing position and extend her economic and political influence by taking control of Germany's possessions and investments.[107] Japan's entry into the war was thus opportunist; as Inoue Kaoru, the senior member of the *Genro*, put it: 'August 1914 was a moment of "supreme opportunity" for Japan.'[108]

The prospects of territorial expansionism on the part of Japan had, naturally enough, not only exercised Grey in Britain, but was also of great concern to the US government. Indeed, Washington proposed that Germany and Japan accept the neutralisation of 'foreign settlements' (specifically treaty ports) in order to 'protect the interests of the United States in China'.[109] They were particularly concerned about the effect on trade and commerce, as well as Chinese territorial integrity, if and when Japan went to war

On 14 August Robert Lansing, the counsellor for the Department of State and an authority on international law, wrote to Secretary of State William Jennings Bryan, of the 'persistent reports and rumours [...] that Japan intends to declare war upon Germany'.[110] Recognising the motivation that existed behind the Japanese position, and their likely response to US pressure, Lansing proposed to Bryan that the United States should wait until after hostilities occurred before 'with perfect propriety' approaching 'all the belligerents simultaneously'.[111] He hoped that by adopting this method Japan would find it difficult to ignore the approach, and he also made mention of the last point of the Root–Takahira Agreement:

> Should any event occur threatening the *status quo* as above described or the principle of equal opportunity, as above defined, it remains for the two governments to communicate with each other, in order to arrive at an understanding as to what measures they may consider it useful to take.[112]

The day after Lansing had composed his note the Japanese, as he had predicted, presented their ultimatum to Germany via a note from Prime Minister Okuma Shigenobu:

> We consider it highly important and necessary in the present situation to take measures to remove the causes of all disturbance of peace in the Far East, and to safeguard general interests as contemplated in the Agreement of Alliance between Japan and Great Britain.
>
> In order to secure firm and enduring peace in Eastern Asia, the establishment of which is the aim of the said Agreement, the Imperial Japanese Government sincerely believes it to be its duty to give advice to the Imperial German Government to carry out the following two propositions:
>
> (1) Withdraw immediately from Japanese and Chinese waters the German men-o'-war and armed vessels of all kinds, and to disarm at once those which cannot be withdrawn.
>
> (2) To deliver on a date not later than September 15th, to the Imperial Japanese authorities, without condition or compensation, the entire leased territory of Kiao-chau, with a view to the eventual restoration of the same to China.
>
> The Imperial Japanese Government announces at the same time that in the event of its not receiving, by noon on August 23rd, an answer from the Imperial German Government signifying unconditional acceptance of the above advice offered by the Imperial Japanese Government, Japan will be compelled to take such action as it may deem necessary to meet the situation.[113]

At the same time as the note was delivered to Germany, Kato Takaaki, Japan's foreign minister, informed George Guthrie, the US ambassador to Japan, that 'Japan sought no territorial aggrandisement nor other selfish ends through war' and reassured the US that any action taken would not infringe upon the interests of other powers.[114] This reassurance was, perhaps, somewhat undermined when Japan totally rejected any measure that would have prevented her taking and occupying Kiautschou; Germany's attempts to retrocede the lease to China, in effect to hand back the territory, was nullified when the Japanese warned that they would not recognise any such transaction.[115] The US was also approached to accept the lease, but refused; as John Van Antwerp MacMurray, Secretary of the US Legation in Peking 1913–17, put it 'such a course would do more to provoke war than to avert war'.[116]

Bearing the above points in mind then, it appears that the message sent to Japan from the US government on 21 August vis-à-vis Kiautschou rather made a virtue out of a necessity:

> [The US] notes with satisfaction that Japan, in demanding the surrender [...] of [...] Kiautschou, does so with the purpose of restoring that territory to China [...] Should disturbances in the interior of China seem to the Japanese Government to require measures to be taken by Japan or other powers to restore order, the Imperial Japanese Government no doubt desire to consult with the American Government before deciding on a course of action [in accordance with the Root–Takahira Pact of 1908].[117]

Sir Edward Grey meanwhile had been explaining to Walter Hines Page, the US ambassador to Britain from 1913 to 1918, that the Japanese action had not been coordinated with the British. Page explained Grey's position in a message of 18 August 1914:

> Sir Edward Grey has explained to me confidentially that the Japanese government acted on their own account when they sent their ultimatum to Germany. They did not confer with the British government about it but only informed the British government after they decided to send it.[118]

If Grey, as Churchill had pointed out in his message of 11 August, was indeed cool ('chilling') towards the Japanese entry into the conflict, then the First Lord had no such inhibitions; where Grey saw potential trouble Churchill saw only potential. Shortly after Japan's formal declaration, he was badgering Grey on the subject of utilising their great naval strength on the Allied side, writing on 29 August 1914:

> Now that Austria has declared war on Japan,[119] and in view of the general situation, including the attitude of Turkey, it would seem only fitting that the Japanese Government should be sounded as to their readiness to send a battle squadron to co-operate with the Allied Powers in the Mediterranean or elsewhere. The influence and value of this powerful aid could not be overrated. It would steady and encourage Italy, and would bring nearer the situation, so greatly desired, of our being able to obtain command of the Baltic. There is reason to believe that the Japanese would take such an invitation as a compliment.[120]

Churchill was, it seems, mistaken, as no ships at all were forthcoming, never mind a battle squadron, which in the contemporary Royal Navy consisted of eight battleships. Indeed, to move forward in time somewhat, it was not until April 1917 that the Japanese Navy sent any assistance to the European Theatre with the deployment of an old protected cruiser, *Akashi*, and eight destroyers under Rear-Admiral K. Sato to the Mediterranean.[121]

To return to 1914 however, Japan wasted no time in deploying her powerful naval assets in support of her ally in the Far East. The modern battlecruiser *Kongō*[122] was immediately dispatched to patrol the sea-routes in mid ocean and three days later, on 26 August, the battlecruiser *Ibuki*[123] and second-class light cruiser *Chikuma* were ordered to Singapore, at Britain's request,[124] to provide support in the search for German commerce raiders, particularly the *Emden*.[125] While the *Chikuma* stayed in the area patrolling unsuccessfully as far south as Ceylon[126] the *Ibuki* was soon dispatched, on 18 September, back eastwards to begin the task of escorting troop convoys, carrying ANZAC contingents, from Australia and New Zealand to the Middle East.[127] In a like manner French convoys, containing contingents from French Indo-China, were also escorted.[128] The first of these voyages, ten transports from Ellington, New Zealand, was undertaken on 16 October and they were to continue throughout the war.[129]

The hunt for German commerce raiders, the original task that Sir Edward Grey had foreseen for the Japanese Navy, was not neglected however, and the battleship *Satsuma*, together with the second-class light cruisers *Yahagi* and *Hirado*, were sent to watch the shipping routes around Australia.[130] The force in the Indian Ocean was greatly reinforced during October in an effort to hunt down German forces, and it became an important command under Vice Admiral Sojiro Tochinai; ultimately employing two battlecruisers *Ibuki* and *Ikoma*,[131] three armoured cruisers, *Tokiwa*, *Yakumo*, and *Nisshin*, and three lighter cruisers, *Hirado*, *Yahagi* and *Chikuma*.[132] On 1 November 1914, in response to a British request, the Japanese Nnavy assumed temporary responsibility for all Allied naval activity in the Indian Ocean east of ninety degrees longitude and remained in command for the remainder of the month.[133]

The appearance of one such potential German raider, SMS *Geier*, at the US port of Honolulu on 15 October 1914 resulted in the dispatch of the battleship *Hizen*[134] and armoured cruiser *Asama* to intercept the vessel should she try to leave.[135] The US government prevented any such action however by interning *Geier* on 7 November, whereupon the two Japanese vessels joined the armoured cruiser *Idzumo*, which had been there since the start of hostilities, searching off the coast of South America.[136]

The Japanese also began seizing the German island colonies, and at the risk of disrupting chronological progression it is worth examining this process.

The scattered groups of German islands had been largely left unmolested, apart from operations to disrupt various strategically placed radio stations. For example, HMS *Hampshire* attacked the station at Yap on 12 August, and a party landed from HMAS *Melbourne* on 9 September similarly dealt with the installation at Nauru.[137] The occupation of the islands, though they should have been unopposed from a military point of view given the terms of capitulation signed on 17 September 1914, was prevented by a lack of available warships.

The 'guarantee' of no military resistance[138] did not however apply to Spee and the East Asiatic Cruiser Squadron, and Patey, conceiving his primary duty was to keep his assets concentrated in order to destroy this force, was unwilling to detach units for escort work. He therefore recommended that no unescorted expeditions should venture outside the relatively safe waters around New Guinea until such time as Spee had either been dealt with or at least his whereabouts were known.[139] The *Scharnhorst* and *Gneisenau* had been sighted at Apia, Samoa, on 14 September, but it was only in early October that intelligence indicated with a degree of liability that Spee was heading for the west coast of South America; consequently, no Australian military effort had been undertaken against the islands prior to this.[140]

However, the Japanese Navy in its search for Spee and other German vessels had begun, during early September, to extend its patrols further into the areas of the former German possessions. Harcourt telegraphed to Munro-Ferguson on 10 September:

> Please inform [the Australian Government] very confidentially that it is very likely that Japanese ships [...] may cruise in the Pacific round the Marianne and Caroline Islands in order to hunt down the German squadron which is believed to be in those parts and which, unless it is attacked, will prey upon British and Japanese shipping in Pacific.[141]

On 7 October a Japanese vessel visited Yap at the request of the British in order to ascertain the status of the radio station supposedly destroyed on 12 August. It found evidence that repairs had been affected, and also discovered the German survey vessel, SMS *Planet* in the vicinity.[142] The *Planet* scuttled herself to avoid capture, with the crew going ashore, but this episode led the Japanese to put forces ashore to prevent further occurrences of the kind. They communicated their thoughts on the matter to Britain on 10 October:

> [The Japanese Foreign Minister] asks whether [the] Australians propose to take Yap [...] and station a guard there, in which case [the] Japanese squadron will be instructed to hand over the place; but if not, [the] Japanese Admiralty consider it necessary in view of the strategical importance of the island, that it should be occupied by a British or Japanese force.[143]

This message was passed on to Australia on 13 October, in a telegram from Harcourt to Munro-Ferguson:

> [The] Japanese Government state that, in [the] course of searching Western Pacific islands for enemy vessels and bases, squadron called Yap on October 7th and landed marines to investigate wireless telegraph and cable stations there. They found that both had been repaired and used by Germans and since destroyed again. They have temporarily occupied it but they are ready to hand it over to an Australian force. On account of strategical importance island must be occupied by

some force. Your Ministers will remember that it was originally intended that they should send force to occupy Yap, and they will no doubt agree that it is desirable to relieve Japanese as quickly as possible of the task of holding the island. Japanese Government have therefore been informed it is intention of your Government to occupy Yap, and I am communicating with Admiralty as to provision of transport. Please ask ministers to arrange in communication with Admiral Patey details of force to be sent. It need not be large and could presumably be detached from force already in occupation of German possessions.[144]

This message was replied to on 17 October 1914 in a message from the Australian Naval Board to the Admiralty, stating that, with regard to the British request for the occupation of Yap:

Military force can now be provided from Simpsonhafen for this purpose. Vice-Admiral commanding cannot at present spare *Encounter*, also *Encounter* cannot well enter Yap or Ponape. Fully appreciate pressing importance of occupation of Yap by British force. Pending despatch of proposed expedition to make effective occupation of islands could China Squadron detach vessel [to] relieve Japanese care of Yap[?] Consider desirable to fit out small expedition with Commissioners to report on Government organisation, trade, food supplies, wireless communication, and naval requirements and to take possession Pelew, Marshall, Caroline, and Marianne islands. These islands all included in terms of surrender by Governor Simpsonhafen. Propose to mount four-inch guns in *Fantome*[145] and *Comet*[146] and send these vessels with a small supply ship carrying troops and stores also a collier round islands as soon as situation will permit. *Fantome* and *Comet* can be manned by Australian Navy. If *Pioneer* or *Encounter* available by time expedition ready and any probability of meeting superior force of enemy one or both might be attached to expedition. On account of great distance recommend arrange this cruise round islands in preference to isolated expedition to take possession of single islands.[147]

Whatever discussions and decisions the British and Australians may have been having, the situation was, on the part of the Japanese, developing its own dynamic, which was altering their perspective somewhat. Greene had communicated the changing situation as he perceived it to Grey on 12 October, explaining that Japanese public opinion, as evidenced by press reports, was moving in favour of Japan acquiring the islands for herself. Although arguing that such a proposition was 'premature', he noted that the government was being accused of subordinating Japanese interests to those of her ally. He went on:

It appears to me that it would be at once political and graceful if we offered them some signal mark of our confidence, which would vindicate their policy in the eyes of the nation and would assure us [of] their further assistance, should we require it. I submit that this object would be attained [...] [if we] refrain from requesting at the present juncture the transfer to Great Britain of any islands which Japan may occupy for strategic reasons.[148]

The requirement for 'further assistance' from Japan was very much in the mind of Churchill, who, as has been noted, viewed the Japanese Navy as, potentially, a powerful reinforcement for the Allied effort. Accordingly he was very much against in any way antagonising them, particularly by attempting to displace them from territory they already occupied. As he put it in a private letter to Harcourt of 18 October:

> We have no cruiser available for Yap at the present time and much inconvenience would be caused by changing existing arrangements. There appears to be no military reason which requires us to eject the Japanese at this juncture. I do not gather that the Australasian Governments are pressing us to act. On the contrary, it would seem that we are pressing them. The Admiralty would strongly deprecate any action towards Japan which would appear suspicious or ungracious. We are deriving benefit from their powerful and generous aid. They have intimated that their occupation is purely military and devoid of political significance and there I trust we may leave the matter for the present.[149]

This rather defensive missive is understandable if it is considered that the various missions undertaken by Japan, whether or not at the instigation of the British Admiralty, had led to a situation whereby, it could be argued, the Admiralty had been conducting something of a foreign policy of its own vis-à-vis Japan. Churchill was perhaps keen to play down the political significance of the consequences, because they were profound.

Typical of the 'powerful and generous aid' provided by the Japanese Navy was their taking, at the instigation of the British Admiralty, of the administrative centre of the Marshall Islands, Jaluit Atoll.[150] This was the site of a German coaling station, with a large reserve of the commodity, and on 22 September the Admiralty informed their Australian counterparts that a Japanese squadron would be at the atoll 'about a week later'.[151] This was in response to a report, inaccurate as it turned out, that Spee and his entire squadron, complete with colliers and store ships, were at the Marshall Islands on 15 September.[152] Germany had established a coaling station at Jaluit prior to colonising the territory, having negotiated a treaty with the indigenous population as long ago as 1878. Following the German takeover it had become the capital of the Marshall Islands protectorate, and the commercial centre of eastern Micronesia. After taking possession of Enewetak [Eniwetok] Atoll on 29 September, units of Vice- Admiral Tanin Yamaya's 1st Southern Squadron, based around the cruisers *Asama*, *Kurama* and *Tsukuba*, seized Jaluit on 3 October 1914. By the middle of the month Japan had taken possession of most of the, now, ex-German islands north of the Equator, excluding Guam which was a US possession.[153]

Nobody, least of all the Japanese, seems however to have informed either the British Foreign or Colonial Offices, the latter sending a message to Australia on 13 October urging the dispatch of the expedition to take the islands 'as soon as possible'.[154] Neither knowledge of Japanese activities, nor the sense of urgency evidenced by the British Colonial Office, seems to have been communicated to Australia; a joint naval/military conference was convened on 26 October to coordinate plans and strategy for taking the islands north of the equator. The result of this meeting was the ability to reply to another query from the British government of the next day: 'With reference to your [...] telegram dated 13 October re. Yap etc. [A] force consisting of 200 men [is] being organised to garrison [the] principal islands. Particulars as to dates, convoy, etc., will be cabled later on.'[155]

The Australian Military raised a force, known colloquially as 'The Druids' or the 'Tropical Force', more correctly, the Third Battalion of the Naval and Military Expeditionary Force. This unit contained a significant proportion of over-age men including 'a surprisingly large proportion [that] wore the ribbons of the South African War.'[156] By 13 November this force was assembled at Liverpool, New South Wales, ready to embark on a chartered vessel of the Eastern and Australian Line, and the following day instructions were issued to the expedition leader, Commander Samuel Pethebridge, who was also given the military rank of colonel on 21 November.[157] His instructions were unambiguous: 'The Government desire you to proceed with the troops being sent to occupy the islands recently held by Germany north of the equator.' They went on:

Your mission will be:

(a) To visit the various islands and possessions in the Pacific Ocean, recently held by Germany, and to be occupied by Great Britain.

(b) To place such troops in occupation as may be available, thus relieving any members of the Japanese Forces who may be now temporarily in occupation.

He was given full authority to act upon his own initiative, and the powers to command 'all officers of His Majesty's naval or military forces, together with any of His Majesty's subjects' to afford him all assistance as may lie within their power. He was however ordered not to 'take any action with regard to any matters affecting the possessions south of the equator.'[158] Having made these preparations the Australian government telegraphed Harcourt on 13 November, informing him that the expedition was nearly ready to depart: 'steamer *Eastern* with 200 troops [...] escorted by *Komet* will leave Sydney 26 November to relieve Japanese now occupying Yap and other islands north [of the] equator.'[159]

One of the islands that it was proposed to occupy was Anguar in the Palau (Pelew) archipelago.[160] Patey had advised the Admiralty against taking this territory as far back as 5 September, arguing that, while the wireless station there should be destroyed, occupying the island would involve responsibility for feeding the inhabitants. The Admiral argued that from experience and 'information received' he knew that the area was 'very short of food' and that the responsibility of 'feeding the inhabitants as well as the garrisons, will relieve the Germans of this responsibility, and become an anxiety to ourselves.'[161] He received no reply to this message, and the island was left undisturbed until 26 September when a party from HMAS *Sydney* landed and destroyed the wireless ancillary equipment, though leaving the antenna undamaged.[162]

When the possibility of taking Anguar was specifically mentioned to the British government on 21 November it brought forth a somewhat, to the Australian government, startling reply:

it would he discourteous and disadvantageous to the Japanese if we turned them out of Anguar when they are helping us in every way with their Fleet throughout [the] Pacific and in convoy[ing] Australian contingents. [The] Japanese are now erecting a wireless station on Anguar which they wish to use in connection with their Fleet movement. [...] [Australian ships are] not to call at Anguar or to interfere with its present occupation by Japan. This of course is without prejudice to permanent arrangements which will have to be made after the war when we come to settle terms of peace.[163]

Unbeknown to them Greene had informed Grey, also on 21 November, that the Japanese wished to retain Anguar, though would withdraw from Yap as previously agreed.[164] This message came as something of a surprise to the Australians, and, to his credit, the commander of the expedition, Pethebridge, sought clarification by having a direct interview with Japan's representative in the Commonwealth, Consul-General Seizaburo Shimizu. During this meeting Seizaburo referred to a statement he had seen in the press referring to the proposed occupation of the Marshall, Caroline and Marians Islands by Australia, and, from his remarks, Pethebridge concluded that a 'misunderstanding' existed over the matter.[165] He therefore asked the Defence Department to clarify with the British government exactly what places were to be occupied by his force. The cable was sent on 24 November, a mere two days before Pethebridge was scheduled to embark: 'With reference to your telegram of 13 October regarding Yap please telegraph whether whole group of Caroline, [Mariana], Marshall, and [Palau] Islands except Anguar may be occupied by Australian expedition.'[166]

This message crossed with one from Harcourt stating that the expedition 'should not proceed to any islands north of [the] equator'.[167] This volte-face by Whitehall, meant that Pethebridge's instructions issued on 14 November – 'proceed [...] to occupy the islands [...] north of the equator' – were now redundant, and the Commander was accordingly ordered to postpone his departure.[168] The change of plan had also rendered the Australian position somewhat invidious politically, and indeed a full explanation was only vouchsafed to the next Australian Prime Minister, William Hughes, in 1916.[169] Naturally enough clarification was sought from London:

> [It had been] had arranged for expedition for occupation of German islands to sail 26 November and troops already embarked. Islands mentioned in my telegram, namely, [Palau], Mariana, Caroline, and Marshall Islands, form part of German New Guinea administrative area which was included in surrender by Governor of New Guinea. Would like early and definite information as to what is now desired. Expedition will not sail pending reply.[170]

The confusion over the issue, the 'misunderstanding' discerned during the meeting between Seizaburo and Pethebridge, was, from the Japanese standpoint, cleared up completely by Foreign Minister Kato on 1 December. On that date he met Greene and passed over a *note verbale* – a formal diplomatic communication[171] – that stated Japan's position clearly:

> All the islands of Germany [...] are in the occupation of forces of [the] Imperial Navy, and [the] Imperial Government desire that none of these should be visited by Australian expeditions. The island of Yap, can, however, be excepted in view of a previous understanding respecting it, and if His Majesty's Government wish the Japanese forces will withdraw when the British forces reach [the] island.[172]

Although couched in impeccably diplomatic phraseology, this unmistakeably served notice that Japan would not be giving up any of the territory it had occupied (Yap excluded). That this occupation was to be permanent was made clear in a memorandum accompanying the note. This pointed out that while Japan accepted that its occupation of the German territory would be subject to 'final arrangements' arrived at 'when the allies come to settle terms of reference after [...] the war' it would expect Great Britain to support its claim for 'permanent' retention of the islands at that time. This support was in return for the 'very wide operations' that the Japanese Navy had been, and still was, engaging in, 'in cooperation with the British navy'.[173]

Faced with this stance on the part of Japan there was nothing that the British government could do, and accordingly the reply to the Australian query of 25 November was dispatched on 3 December. It too was unequivocal, even if also couched in most diplomatic language:

> [Palau], [Mariana], Caroline, and Marshall Islands are at present in military occupation by Japanese who are at our request engaged in policing waters Northern Pacific, we consider it most convenient for strategic reasons to allow them to remain in occupation for the present, leaving whole question of future to be settled at the end of war. We should be glad therefore if the Australian expedition would confine itself to occupation of German islands south of the equator.[174]

This telegram was followed be a personal letter, dated three days later and marked 'Private and Personal' and 'Very Secret', from Harcourt to Munro-Ferguson explaining the rationale behind the British government's thinking.

> I telegraphed to you on the 3rd that in view of the fact that the Japanese are in actual occupation of the German Pacific Islands north of the Equator, and in view of the great assistance they are rendering to us (at our request) with their fleet through the whole of the Pacific, it seemed to us here undesirable that the Australian Expedition should proceed anywhere north of the Equator at the present time. I feel that I ought to give you personally some explanation [...] but I must impress upon you that this letter is for your eye only, and under no circumstances is to be seen by anyone else.
>
> Our fleets were so fully engaged in the North Sea, Atlantic, Mediterranean, and in convoy of troops across the Indian Ocean that we could not spare enough to deal with the Pacific. We had therefore to call in Japanese aid.
>
> It has even been in contemplation (and still is) that the Japanese fleet may in the future be employed in the European theatre of war. All this has changed the character of the Japanese participation and no doubt of their eventual claims to compensation.

There is a considerable agitation in Japan against the present Govt. on the ground that they are giving much and getting nothing.

From information which reaches me I have very little doubt that it is the intention of the Japanese at the end of the war to claim for themselves all the German Islands North of the Equator. Of course we should absolutely refuse at this present time to make any admission of such a claim.

Our attitude throughout has been that all these territorial questions must be settled in the terms of peace and not before.

But it would be impossible at this moment to risk a quarrel with our Ally which would be the certain and immediate result of any attempt diplomatically to oust them now from those Islands which they are occupying more or less at the invitation of the Admiralty.

All this is a long story [...] but the moral of it is that you ought in the most gradual and diplomatic way to begin to prepare the mind of your Ministers for the possibility that at the end of the war Japan may be left in possession of the Northern Islands and we with everything south of the Equator.

I know that they won't like this, but after all the thing of most importance are those territories most contiguous to Australia, and it will be a great gain to add German New Guinea to Papua and to have the whole of the Solomon Island group under the British flag.

I fear I have set you a hard task but I am sure you will execute it with your usual skill & discretion. [...] I am writing this from my bed where I am nursing an overstrained heart, but I am getting better, and I have never missed a Cabinet since the War began![175]

The Japanese were clearly in the driving seat, as it were, in respect of terminating German possession of the various island territories, this being, as a later historian was to put it, 'a price the British Commonwealth had to pay for its inability to maintain a major fleet in the Pacific'.[176] The greatest prize however, and the one that the Japanese prepared for with the most diligence was Kiautschou, where, undoubtedly, 'Germany was engaged night and day in intensive war preparations'.[177]

7

Naval Plans and Operations 1897–1914

The Kaiser and the Tsar met at Reval (Tallinn, now capital of Estonia) from 6 to 8 August 1902, an occasion when both were impressed by a demonstration of gunnery on the part of the Russian Baltic Fleet. They and their entourages viewed this display from the flagship of a somewhat irascible admiral named Zinovi Rozhdestvenski, who took the credit for organising and supervising the demonstration.[1] The Kaiser was no doubt enthused by this display of naval strength, and on his departure signalled to the Tsar, undoubtedly to the latter's embarrassment, 'The Admiral of the Atlantic Ocean salutes the Admiral of the Pacific.'[2]

This might be considered simply as one of Wilhelm's witticisms, had he not signed himself off in a letter to the Tsar of 2 September in similar terms.[3] Contained in this communication were some flights of Imperial fancy; the Kaiser urged the Tsar to look at 'our two navies as *one* great organisation belonging to *one* great Continent whose interest it must safeguard on its shores and in distant seas. This means practically the Peace of the World.'[4] Perhaps Wilhelm had forgotten the Franco-Russian alliance of 1894. Not in an entirely dissimilar vein were his thoughts regarding Japan and China, for he cautioned Nicholas that:

> Certain symptoms in the East seems to show that Japan is becoming a rather restless customer [...] The news of the attachment of the Japanese General Yamai [...] to the Legation at Peking in order to take in hand the reorganisation of the Chinese Army [...] is very serious. [...] [This] is a future to be contemplated not without anxiety; and not impossible. In fact it is the coming into reality of the 'Yellow Peril' which I depicted some years ago, and for which engraving I was laughed at by the greater mass of the People.[5]

As far as matters naval were concerned the Kaiser was a devotee of the American theorist Rear Admiral Alfred Thayer Mahan. In 1894 he had acquired Mahan's *The Influence of Sea Power Upon History, 1660–1783* and had become a devotee; as he wrote to his friend Poultney Bigelow, the Foreign Correspondent of the *New York Herald*: 'I am just now not reading but devouring Captain Mahan's book and am trying to learn it by heart. It is a first-class book and classical on all points. It is on board all my ships and constantly quoted by my Captains and officers.'[6]

The 'Admiral of the Atlantic' was positively attempting, through the work of Tirpitz, to build a major battlefleet, and indeed was intent on keeping it concentrated. However, the German naval units in the Pacific were of a different order entirely, and in the event of war were not expected to seek out and destroy enemy warships, but rather engage in commerce raiding. Such a mode of warfare had been scrutinised by Mahan:

> Maintaining a sea-war mainly by preying upon the enemy's commerce [...] involves only the maintenance of a few swift cruisers [...] [and] possesses the specious attractions which economy always presents. The great injury done to the wealth and prosperity of the enemy is [...] undeniable; and although to some extent his merchant-ships can shelter themselves ignobly under a foreign flag while the war lasts, this *guerre de course*, as the French call it, this commerce-destroying, to use our own phrase, must, if in itself successful, greatly embarrass the foreign government and distress its people. Such a war, however, cannot stand-alone; it must be supported, to use the military phrase; unsubstantial and evanescent in itself, it cannot reach far from its base. That base must be either home ports, or else some solid outpost of the national power, on the shore or the sea; a distant dependency or a powerful fleet. Failing such support, the cruiser can only dash out hurriedly a short distance from home, and its blows, though painful, cannot be fatal.[7]

Certainly Tsingtau could be construed as a 'solid outpost' and given this point, a successful *guerre de course* might have been waged, using this 'distant dependency' as a focal point. There was of course a downside to dependence on a fixed base of operations. As one skilled practitioner in the art of war had put it over half a century previously: 'Protective harbours [...] may be likened to nets, wherein fishes seeking to escape, find themselves inextricably entangled.'[8]

Despite this disadvantage though, German naval planners regarded Britain's position as extremely weak vis-à-vis commerce warfare, given the amount of trade that could be affected. Interdiction of this traffic, from the German point of view, had many potential benefits; it could, apart from directly sinking vessels, force up insurance rates and thus erode, if not destroy, the profitability of the British merchant shipping industry. Any restriction on the conveyance of raw materials and foodstuffs would, it was considered, harm commerce and industry, and could lead to civil strife by way of food shortages and unemployment. If particularly successful it could damage, or even cripple, Britain's economy and thus place the government under such severe pressure that it would be forced to come to terms. Such was the theory.[9]

Control of the sea was not a prerequisite for commerce warfare, and individual raiders, particularly in the vastness of the Pacific Ocean, would be able to severely interdict commercial shipping simply by the threat of their presence. Hunting down these 'individual marauders' as Mahan had termed them, was, historically 'a process which even when most thoroughly planned, still resembles looking for a needle in a haystack'.[10]

Accordingly the task of the East Asiatic Cruiser Squadron, in the event of Germany becoming involved in a conflict with another power, was, primarily, to conduct *guerre de course* against the merchant marine of that state, as well as to effect the possible destruction of the enemy depots and bases. Operations against various enemies were contemplated including Great Britain, in which case Asian and Australasian merchant trade would be the target. Indeed, in 1905 the guidelines for operations in the Pacific had focused particularly on British trade, stressing the following:

> Damaging of British trade was the main goal of all operations. A secret departure into the Pacific would require the enemy to search and thereby divide his forces, creating an opportunity for success against the parts.
>
> By creating uncertainty on the main trading routes, a temporary cessation of British shipping in Asia could be achieved.
>
> If conditions were favourable, an immediate attack on enemy warships could be considered, in order to cripple British trade and to achieve superiority at sea.[11]

There was another objective. Even if the particular object of forcing the British to negotiate through the creation of economic disruption, and concomitant social unrest, were unattainable, a campaign of *guerre de course* in the Far East would nevertheless have the effect of weakening the Royal Navy in home waters. This would be achieved by necessitating the dispatch of considerable forces to protect shipping from, and hunt down, the German raiders.[12]

This facet of German strategy, of forcing the Royal Navy to dissipate its strength in the vital area of the North Sea by operating in distant waters, was, however obviously attractive it might have seemed, and still seems, somewhat flawed. That this is so may be adduced by considering what assets were detached from the Grand Fleet to deal with German vessels in other areas at the outbreak of war. These were, on the face of it, considerable. No less than three battlecruisers were sent to seek out Spee and avenge Cradock in November 1914, which still left the Grand Fleet with a marginal superiority in battleships and parity, if the hybrid SMS *Blücher* be included, in battlecruisers vis-à-vis the High Seas Fleet.[13]

This seemingly low margin came about because there was another German detached force in the Mediterranean, and this tied up two other battlecruisers, *Indefatigable* – a sister to *New Zealand* and *Australia* – and the *Invincible*-class *Indomitable*. These ships were at the eastern end of the Mediterranean Sea performing sentry duty at the entrance to the Dardanelles, following the escape of Rear Admiral Wilhelm Souchon's battlecruiser *Goeben* and light cruiser *Breslau*. The German vessels had avoided being brought to action by the Royal Navy and arrived off the Dardanelles on 10 August 1914. The British 'arrived in force on 11 August and remained on guard for the rest of the war'.[14] The Grand Fleet was then, for a brief period between November 1914 and February 1915, only slightly superior to its adversary.[15]

The Grand Fleet commander, Jellicoe, objected in vain to the weakening of his command, an objection that was, in the context he voiced it, quite valid. He was, after all, 'the only man on either side who could have lost the war in an afternoon', and had his opposite number, Admiral Friedrich von Ingenohl, taken advantage of the opportunity thus afforded, Jellicoe, the Royal Navy and indeed Britain, might well have been severely discommoded, or indeed, if Churchill's aphorism was correct, beaten. However, fighting a fleet action against the superior Grand Fleet, however marginal that fleet's superiority might have been for a brief period, was not an appealing prospect to the German Navy. German naval strategy in northern waters involved reducing that superiority by a process of attrition – through sub-fleet surface actions, where elements of the British fleet might be destroyed, and by submarine warfare. Only after the Grand Fleet had been reduced to numerical inferiority would the High Seas Fleet seek action against it. This strategy was unsuccessful, and not only was the Royal Navy able to maintain and increase the superiority of the Grand Fleet, but also to detach forces as and when required to other theatres.[16] Put simply, the margin of superiority of the British Navy over the German was simply too great for the latter's, necessarily timid, strategy of forcing dissipation of strength in distant waters to succeed to any significant extent.

Not that German strength in the Far East was insignificant. The East Asiatic Cruiser Division had been augmented over time as newer and more powerful vessels were constructed. These included the five vessels of the *Victoria Luise*-class such as the protected cruiser SMS *Hertha*, armed with two 210mm (8in.) and eight 150mm (5.9in.) guns, and with a top speed of 19 knots, that were intended for colonial service from their inception. The vessel relieved *Kaiser* in June 1899 and became the flagship of Vice Admiral Felix [later von] Bendemann, who replaced Prince Heinrich of Prussia in February the following year. Bendemann and *Hertha* took part in operations against the Taku Forts during the Boxer War, for which he received the Order of the Rising Sun from the Mikado.[17] An even more powerful vessel became squadron flagship in 1903 in the shape of Germany's first armoured cruiser *Fürst* [Prince] *Bismarck* – name ship and sole example of her class – with four 240mm (9.37in.) and twelve 150mm weapons this vessel constituted a great leap in capability. Combined with two *Victoria Luise*-class ships, *Hertha* and *Hansa* and the older *Kaiserin Augusta*, the strength of the East Asiatic Cruiser Squadron was thus steadily increased.

The potency of the squadron, as well as the need to concentrate heavy units in North European waters, were recognised by Sir John Fisher. Upon his assumption of the position of First Sea Lord in October 1904 he reorganised the way the Royal Navy was deployed by recalling from overseas stations those vessels he designated as being to old to fight and too slow to run away. His argument was cogent: 'The known intentions of our possible enemies quite preclude the hope that the ill armed unprotected second and third class cruisers, which have recently been removed from the fighting fleet, would have been of any real service as commerce protectors.'[18] The replacements for these vessels, and for the battleships of the China Station, which Fisher also recalled – following the conclusion of the Anglo-Japanese Alliance there was little justification for keeping battleships in the area – were to consist of armoured cruisers, though following Japan's defeat of Russia this programme slipped somewhat.[19]

That the East Asiatic Cruiser Squadron was a force capable of carrying out effective commerce warfare and raiding was obvious to any observer, though how it might approach this task, and what its contingency plans were was less so. All military and naval planners in every state conceive of plans to be carried out in various eventualities. The naval planners of Imperial Germany were no different in this regard and accordingly drew up plans for carrying out naval operations against several powers in the region, which were updated as circumstances dictated. German naval planning also took into account the holistic nature of maritime warfare, inasmuch as the squadron in the Pacific could have an effect on operations in the Atlantic simply by remaining in being and thus threatening. Such matters had been exemplified, though in reverse as it were, on 7 July 1898 when, during the Spanish–American War, Rear Admiral Manuel de la Cámara y Libermoore's Philippine Relief Expedition hade been recalled from its voyage to the Pacific because of the dangers of US naval operations against Spain in the eastern Atlantic.[20] As has been argued previously though, such a strategy was largely ineffective against the Royal Navy because of its superiority in ship numbers, which of course was not the case with the Spanish Navy in 1898.

There were however echoes of certain aspects of the Spanish–American conflict in a German 1903 plan to be put into practice in the event of war with the United States. This was War Case A, which was not, contemporaneously, as ludicrous, in at least some of its proposals, as it might appear to later generations. Bendemann's successor Kurt von Prittwitz und Gaffron, who had taken over command in 1902, envisaged his squadron engaging in attacks on not only US merchant shipping, but also naval bases and population centres on the US West Coast. Given the panic and political furore caused on the east coast by the possible depredations of a seven-ship Spanish squadron under Rear Admiral Pascual Cervera y Topete, which sailed from the Cape Verde Islands across the Atlantic to defend Cuba against US attack in April 1898, whereby a 'deafening clamour' had forced the US Navy to divide its fleet, such strategy apparently had much to commend it.[21]

However, attacks on the American western seaboard were not envisaged as an end in themselves, but rather auxiliary to a larger operation whereby the main body of the German Fleet would cross the Atlantic and engage in decisive battle with the US Navy in the Caribbean. This would be followed by a landing on, and occupation of, Long Island with a resulting threat to New York from the west end of this island. The attitude of the British was ignored in this appreciation, which seems a strange omission given that any German expedition could not steam anywhere without the acquiescence of the Royal Navy. This lacuna was acknowledged some three years later when it was stated that such an operation could only be mounted if Britain were an allied state; a somewhat remote contingency at the time. This fact was recognised when Vice Admiral Wilhelm Büchsel of the German Admiralty Staff had the plan downgraded to the level of a theoretical exercise.[22]

Operations against the British Empire were not confined to the naval sphere though, and there were, in the years leading up to 1914, attempts to establish what would later be termed a 'fifth column' among Germans, or those of German descent, in the Australian population. In pursuit of cultivating such sentiments, German vessels were frequent visitors to Australian ports. For example, visits by the *Bussard*-class light cruisers *Condor* and *Cormoran* to several Australian port cities in 1910 and 1912, including Adelaide, Brisbane, Hobart, Melbourne and Sydney, were considered to be serving German interests by showing the flag to those so inclined to be stirred by such displays.[23] The effectiveness of this was gauged by German naval officers established in the various port cities as part of the 'Etappe System', which was set up to compensate for the lack of German naval bases. Essentially, the job of the Etappe was to provide support for German warships in any conflict by organising and coordinating German merchant vessels beforehand. It has been termed the maritime equivalent of 'Living off the Land'.[24]

Any effort to mobilise German manpower, whether actual or potential, – and evidence has been put forward that it was more than fantasy[25] – was comprehensively thwarted upon the outbreak of war when all those identified as Germans found in Australia were interned. These totalled nearly 7,000, including the crews of merchant ships in port at the time, of whom some 4,500 were resident prior to 1914.[26] That Germans, or those of German descent, resident in states that subsequently came into conflict with Germany might constitute fifth columnists was a concern not confined to Australia. The US, a society, like Australia, essentially created by immigration, had a substantial population of German-Americans. The former US ambassador to Imperial Germany, James W. Gerard, addressed the issue, when the two states were at war, on 25 November 1917 in an address to the Ladies Aid Society:

> The Foreign Minister of Germany once said to me 'your country does not dare do anything against Germany, because we have in your country 500,000 German reservists who will rise in arms against your government if you dare to make a move against Germany'. Well, I told him that that might be so, but that we had 500,001 lampposts in this country, and that that was where the reservists would be hanging the day after they tried to rise.[27]

Pure hyperbole no doubt, and in any event, and for whatever reasons, there was little or no fifth column activity as such, though following the spectacular and massive destruction of munitions destined for the Entente powers at Black Tom railway yard in New York on 30 July 1916, 'sabotage became a national issue'.[28] This issue swiftly turned to frenzy, with a deleterious effect on the German-American community; as one noted US politician and author has put it: 'It is well that Dwight D. Eisenhower graduated from West Point in 1915; had he been younger and had the war hysteria gone on much longer, an Eisenhower might not have been admitted to the US Military Academy'.[29] It was perhaps as well for the peace of mind of many Americans that they did not know that the leader of their military effort against Germany, General of the Armies John J. 'Black Jack' Pershing, had the ancestral name of Pfoerschin.[30]

In purely naval terms German strength in East Asia and the Pacific underwent another accretion in strength in 1909 when the 'Scharnhorst'-class armoured cruiser *Scharnhorst* replaced *Fürst Bismarck* as squadron flagship. The new longer-range flagship set out on 1 April flying the flag of Vice Admiral Friedrich von Ingenohl, the new commander, and crossed paths with the outgoing commander, Vice Admiral Carl Coerper, and his flagship at Colombo. Ingenohl, later to be a commander of the High Seas Fleet, arrived at Tsingtau on 29 April and remained in command until June the following year when Vice Admiral Erich Gühler relieved him. Gühler, having been a Marine Attaché at Tokyo, had some familiarity with the region, however he had only been some six months in the position when he contracted typhus, perishing from the disease on 21 January 1911.[31] Vice Admiral Günther von Krosigk, took over and remained in the position until being in turn relieved by the most famous, and last, of the holders of the post, Vice Admiral Maximilian Graf von Spee, in December 1912.

During Krosigk's tenure there had been another significant increment in the power of the squadron when the sister ship to *Scharnhorst*, SMS *Gneisenau*, had been assigned, joining the force in March 1911. On 21 June 1911, Krosigk had reported to his superiors in Berlin that, in order to maximise the effectiveness of the force under his command, it should show itself on the most frequented Australasian trade routes. Thereafter, and in the event of a conflict, the knowledge of its general presence combined with ignorance as to its exact whereabouts would maximise its disruptive power in respect of commerce.[32] This concept was in accordance with Mahan's notion of the sea as 'a wide common, over which men may pass in all directions, but on which some well-worn paths show that controlling reasons have led them to choose certain lines of travel rather than others'.[33] The strategy was essentially sound, but would be in danger of being undermined if naval units equal or superior to the attacking force were to be encountered along those 'well-worn paths'. Such undermining took place in late 1913 however upon the arrival of HMAS *Australia*, which formed a formidable focal point for the Australian fleet. Indeed, the presence of this single vessel, due to her firepower, speed and range, completely altered the strategic options of the German Squadron, which would now have to make avoidance of an encounter with her a primary consideration.[34] The vessel was, as Spee put it 'in itself an adversary so much stronger than our squadron that we should be bound to avoid it'.[35] Had the original intention of keeping the battlecruiser *New Zealand* in East Asian waters not been departed from in 1912–13, then the difficulties facing the German squadron would have been greatly increased. In any event, and even without this adversary, Australia and New Zealand, and their trade routes, were no longer the easy targets that had previously been envisaged.

This would have been particularly so had the mercantile convoy system been introduced, though the difficulties and delays the British, in particular, had with respect to introducing convoys for merchant shipping during the Great War are well known. This was despite historical precedent; in 1798 an act, the Compulsory Convoy Act, was passed that gave the Admiralty the power to enforce convoy on all ocean-going ships. According to Mahan's analysis of the system in the Indian Ocean, 'under this systematic care the losses by capture amounted to [...] less than those by the dangers of the sea'. He went on to point out that those who neglected to adopt the system faced 'disaster' and that the convoy system 'warrants the inference that, when properly systemised and applied, it will have more success as a defensive measure than hunting for individual marauders'.[36] Perhaps the British Admiralty had not read Mahan. Nor it seems had they read the work of one of their own, for in 1907 Admiral Sir Cyprian Bridge published a short work, in which he stated: 'the strategy of commerce defence will be found in practice to be necessarily based on the convoy method, or the cruising method, or a combination of the two'. The cruising method being 'the keeping of so many cruisers on or about the trade-routes that an intending assailant is more likely to be encountered by one or more of them than to pick up prizes'. If the 'cruising method' was impractical due to the volume of warships required, then the lesson of the trooping ships was surely to hand as these were never despatched except with a powerful escort and usually in convoy.[37]

Nevertheless, despite the new factor of the Royal Australian Navy, the East Asiatic Cruiser Squadron constituted a force far too large and powerful to be treated lightly by any enemy if a conflict arose, though it would be immeasurably weakened if it were to lose the use of its 'solid outpost' of national territory, Tsingtau. Given that this was the only base proper in the entire Pacific that the squadron possessed, there being only minimally equipped anchorages and depots scattered throughout the rest of Germany's Pacific territories, it was indispensable for the pursuance of an effective *guerre de course* in the region. Without this base, the only first-class base outside of Germany, or alternatives, the squadron was, to use Churchill's later phrase, 'a cut flower in a vase, fair to see and yet bound to die'. This was acknowledged in a post-war German assessment of the naval situation: 'keeping warships abroad has proved to be a mistake in the absence of secure bases. They are bound to be inferior in number and power at all times.'[38]

One naval force that, post 1906, the German squadron was superior to was that of Wilhelm's erstwhile cousin 'the Admiral of the Pacific'. By that time of course the 'Admiral' no longer had a Pacific Fleet, the original having been destroyed or captured at Port Arthur and its replacement, more spectacularly, at the Battle of Tsushima in May 1905, where one Zinovi Rozhdestvenski had led it. The destruction of Russian naval capability had been almost total, and what remained had been re-titled the Siberian Flotilla. Based at Vladivostok, this force in 1914 was commanded by Rear Admiral Mikhail von Shulz, and consisted of two surface ships, the protected cruiser *Askold* and the light cruiser *Zhemchug*, and six submarines.[39] If there was now an 'Admiral of the Pacific' it was no longer the Tsar, but rather the Mikado.

When warnings of a possible outbreak of hostilities between Germany and Austria-Hungary on the one hand, and Russia, France and, possibly, Great Britain on the other were broadcast to the region during July 1914, Spee's command was not concentrated. The commander, together with his most powerful units, the armoured cruisers *Scharnhorst* (Flag) and *Gneisenau*, had been visiting the Japanese port city of Nagasaki, and on 28 June, in company with their collier *Titania*, they departed on a pre-arranged cruise through the German Islands. It was intended that this voyage would last some four months, by which time they should have returned to Tsingtau, where, in the meantime, Captain Karl von Müller of the *Emden* had become the senior naval officer. Spee was at Truk (Chuuk) in the Carolines on 7 July when he received news of the tense political situation pertaining in Europe following the assassination, on 28 June, of Franz Ferdinand and his wife. On 11 July he was advised that Great Britain would 'probably' be an opponent if it should lead to a general war.[40]

Von Spee sailed for Ponape (Pohnpei) in the Caroline Islands on 15 July and reached there two days later, whereupon he sent orders for the various small, weak and obsolescent vessels in the Far East (the gunboats *Iltis, Jaguar, Tiger* and *Luchs*; the river gunboats *Vaterland* and *Otter* (at Nanking) and *Tsingtau* (at Canton); and the torpedo boat *S-90*;) to concentrate at Tsingtau. The more powerful, modern units, the *Nürnberg*, a 'Königsberg'-class light cruiser, and *Leipzig*, of the 'Bremen'-class, were to join him where he was, as was the *Emden*. While awaiting developments at Pohnpei Admiral Spee received news of the rupture in relations between Serbia and Austria-Hungary, and eventually, on 1 August, the official 'Warning of War' in respect of Britain, France, and Russia. This message was passed on via radio to the German Islands, and those German vessels at large; various merchantmen and the *Geier, Planet* and *Komet*, which were in southern, waters. Over the next five days the squadron was to learn of the outbreak of war with Russia, France and, last and most fatefully of all, Great Britain.

Meanwhile, *Emden* had sailed from Tsingtau on 31 July to join Spee, and, having been informed of war with France and Russia on 2 August, promptly captured the Russian merchant vessel *Ryazan* on 4 August.[41] On 6 August, following the arrival of *Nürnberg*, the squadron left for Pagan Island in the northern Marianas, arriving 11 August, where it was joined the next day by *Emden* and the auxiliary cruisers *Yorck* and *Prinz Eitel Friedrich*. Four of eight expected supply vessels and colliers also reached the rendezvous over the next few days.

Spee had been pondering his options, as his War Diary, which survived, demonstrates:

> In case of war [...] against France, Russia, and England, without complication with Japan, war upon commerce *is* possible so long as the coal supply holds out. But – in view of the fact that it is probably intended to bring up the Australian warships – it is only possible for a short time.
>
> If Japan imposes conditions in order to avoid the moral obligation of translating into action her alliance with England, this would render impossible the plan of carrying on a cruiser-war in the waters of East Asia. For this event, therefore, I propose to follow a similar course of action to that in a war in which Japan is a direct opponent; for which [...] a withdrawal from East Asia is already intended.
>
> In the case of war [...] against England, if Japan imposes conditions, the cruiser squadron had best go with the main body to the west coast of America, because the coal supply is surest in that region, and the squadron can probably hold out longest there. To stay in the Indian Ocean, with coal supply from the Dutch Indies, is on the other hand much too uncertain.[42]

Spee's analysis demonstrates that the creation of the Royal Australian Navy, and particularly the commissioning of HMAS *Australia*, meant that Germany's strategic options in the Far East, as expressed in the various plans for waging a *guerre de course*, were now severely circumscribed. This lends weight to Billy Hughes' later justification of the Navy: 'But for the Navy, the great cities of Australia would have been reduced to ruins, coastwise shipping sunk, and communications with

Germany's Asia-Pacific Empire

the outside world cut off.'[43] Though Hughes was no doubt indulging in hyperbole, his remarks nevertheless encompass a great truth.

The entry of Japan into the conflict, even if only conditionally, was adjudged by Spee to completely negate any chance of carrying out a cruiser campaign, and, from the tone of his analysis, it was an eventuality he deems likely. This was made explicit during a conference held by Spee with his captains on 13 August, an account of which was later set down by Karl von Müller:

> The Commander-in-Chief drew attention to the threatening attitude of Japan, and to the advantage of maintaining the squadron together and concealing its whereabouts as long as possible, thereby holding a large number of enemy ships. He had decided to take the squadron to the west coast of America. When we commanding officers were asked for our opinion, I said I was afraid that the squadron would be able to do practically nothing during a long cruise in the Pacific, and questioned whether so much value should be attached to the 'fleet in being' theory. If coaling the whole squadron in East Asian, Australian and Indian waters presented too great difficulties, we might consider detaching one light cruiser to the Indian Ocean.[44]

Müller's idea met with Spee's approval and the following morning, while the admiral led the squadron east from Pagan Island, the *Emden* and collier *Markomannia* headed west to the Indian Ocean, and into naval legend.[45] It is worth giving a brief account of the cruiser war waged by Müller; during September and October *Emden* stopped and took captive sixteen British vessels, which were then sunk by gunfire or by demolition charges.[46] He also captured eight more, of varying nationalities, which he did not sink. This activity caused chaos on the trade routes and caused a huge amount of disruption to the commerce of the region. Müller seemed to have a natural aptitude for this kind of activity, resorting to ruses from days gone by in disguising his vessel.

He did not restrict himself to activities far out at sea; on 22 September the city of Madras (Chennai) was shelled. The attack began shortly after 9.30p.m. and lasted for something over 20 minutes, during which around 120–130 shells fell on and around the harbour. The most visible damage was caused to the storage tanks of the Burmah Oil Company; two were hit and set alight, burning throughout the next day, with a loss amounting to some 365,000 gallons of oil. The merchantman *Chupra*, anchored in the harbour, was also hit, but once fire began to be returned the *Emden* swiftly left the scene.[47] The psychological effects of the bombardment were greater than the physical, it being a severe blow to British prestige and the cause of several thousand of the inhabitants fleeing the city. Rumours of the ship in the vicinity of Ceylon (Sri Lanka) caused panic,[48] but possibly the greatest single coup scored during the cruise was the raid on George Town, on the north-east corner of Penang Island, on 28 October.

Müller rigged a dummy fourth stack on his vessel, so that it resembled a British cruiser, and steamed into the roads at high speed flying false colours. Once in a tactically advantageous position he, literally, showed his true colours by running up the German naval ensign. There were a number of Allied ships in the harbour, the most important probably being the Russian light cruiser *Zhemchug*. The anchored Russian warship was torpedoed from close range and subjected to a short bombardment, which broke her in two. As *Emden* made her escape back to the open sea the French destroyer *Mosquet* attempted to engage her off Muka Head, but was swiftly dispatched by the heavier metal of her opponent.[49] Once again Müller demonstrated his humanity by stopping and lowering boats in order to rescue the distressed French seamen, earning the approbation of parts of the American press:

> It was here that the chivalrous bravery of the Emden's Captain, which has been many times in evidence throughout her meteoric career, was again shown. If the French boats were coming out, every moment was of priceless value to him. Nevertheless, utterly disregarding this, he stopped, lowered boats, and picked up the survivors from the Mosquet before steaming on his way. The English here now say of him, admiringly, 'He played the game.'[50]

In terms of resources expended as against results achieved, the exploits of the *Emden* can only be viewed as a highly efficient operation of war. This of course begs the question as to what might have been achieved had Spee dispersed his entire squadron in the same way. It must not however be forgotten that one of the first targets of the British and Japanese naval forces was the German wireless system, with stations based on several of the Pacific islands. Once these had been captured or destroyed, and all of them had been within two months of the outbreak of war, then the squadron, whether taken collectively or as individual units, was effectively incommunicado. It had to rely on whatever information it might glean from various sources, or rely on guesswork.[51] It is also the case that the armoured cruisers were, because of their fuel consumption, not well suited for commerce warfare, but they might have had a role to play in terms of support as, for example, was evidenced on the mission to sever the British trans-Pacific cable at Fanning (Tabuaeran) Island on 7 September.[52]

The *Nürnberg*, despite having boiler problems,[53] accompanied by the collier *Titania*, carried out this operation; flying the French ensign the vessels gained the anchorage without exciting suspicion and landed an armed party. This swiftly captured the cable-station personnel and, over a period of about twelve hours, effectively put the station out of action by destroying the equipment. Meanwhile the *Titania* dredged up the cable and severed it.[54] When news of this exploit reached the outside world it prompted some fevered speculation. *The Times* of London, for example, published a short piece based on information obtained from Canadian naval sources. This reported that 'the object of the German cruiser *Nürnberg* in cutting the cable and taking Fanning Island is to establish a new Pacific base since the enemy has lost Samoa'.[55] Spee, however, who covered this operation with the rest of the squadron while remaining out of sight of land, had no intention of fixing himself geographically. Indeed, after ascertaining that no enemy vessels were in evidence in the area he moved on to Christmas Island and waited for the two raiders to join him.

It was during an essentially similar raid that the *Emden* came to grief. On 9

November Müller decided to raid the cable and radio station on Direction Island, one of the Cocos (Keeling) Islands. A fifty-strong landing party went ashore at about 6.30a.m. and began destroying the facilities, unaware that the presence of the *Emden* had been betrayed by a radio signal she had sent to a collier. Not only had the station at Direction Island heard this, but so had several of the transports and escorting vessels making up the first ANZAC convoy from Australia and New Zealand. Shortly afterwards the station reported by radio that there was a 'strange warship approaching' and repeated this some ten minutes later, prefixing it with the distress signal SOS. At the same time a message was sent by cable to Australia stating that a three-funnelled warship was sitting off the island and landing a party by boat.[56]

The ANZAC convoy also received this message when it was, by chance, only some fifty miles away from the island. There were three warships on escort duty, the Japanese battlecruiser *Ibuki* and the Australian light cruisers *Melbourne* (Flag) and *Sydney*. Upon receiving the signals HMAS *Melbourne* made to respond, but then delegated the duty to *Sydney* so as to remain protecting the convoy, the primary responsibility. It took about two hours for *Sydney* to reach visible distance of Direction Island, when she was spotted by lookouts in *Emden*. Müller immediately raised anchor and set out to engage the approaching vessel, abandoning the landing party.[57] It was not a contest *Emden* could win against the bigger, faster and more heavily armed *Sydney*.[58] Müller was eventually, after receiving more than 100 hits that reduced *Emden* to near impotence, forced to run his ship aground on North Keeling Island (now Pulu Keeling National Park). German losses were 131 dead and 65 wounded while Müller and the remaining crew were taken prisoner. Müller's exploits had earned him the admiration of even his enemy; he was lauded as a gallant and chivalrous opponent in *The Times*: 'If all the Germans had fought as well as the Captain of the *Emden*, the German people would not today be reviled by the world.'[59]

It is somewhat ironic that Müller became undone through the agency of a vessel that had been deployed because of fear of his depredations. The ANZAC force was only transported as an escorted convoy because of fear of German cruisers, and the Allies had known with some degree of certainty that these would not include Spee's main squadron; he had bombarded Papeete, French Tahiti, on 22 September, placing himself some 2,000 miles east of New Zealand. Therefore the danger devolved around *Emden* alone, though the *Königsberg*, thought to be off the coast of Africa, was a slighter worry.

It is fruitless to investigate 'might have beens' to any degree, but given the relative success of *Emden* one cannot avoid pondering what could have been achieved had Müller been supported. Certainly if one of the armoured cruisers had been in the vicinity it would have been the *Sydney* that came off worst, though of course even more powerful assistance was relatively near at hand in the shape of *Ibuki*. Had the whereabouts of Spee not been ascertained with some certainty, the original flagship of the convoy escort, *Minotaur*, would also have been in attendance. Against such a powerful escort the East Asiatic Cruiser Squadron would have been unlikely to prevail, so it is fanciful to suggest that the ANZAC convoy would have been threatened.

Nevertheless it is still arguable that while Müller achieved something, his erstwhile superior's voyage was a failure, as the young captain had foreseen at the meeting of 13 August at Pagan Island. Having ventured to the west coat of South America, it is true that Spee inflicted a major defeat on the Royal Navy at the Battle of Coronel on 1 November 1914, when a weaker force commanded by Rear-Admiral Sir Christopher Cradock chose to offer battle rather than, as discretion might have demanded, seek to avoid it.[60] However, despite crushing his opponents in short order, sinking Cradock's flagship, the *Drake*-class armoured cruiser *Good Hope*, and the weaker 'County'-class *Monmouth*, with all hands (1,654 officers and men), it was essentially a pyrrhic victory. All it gained was the assurance that overwhelming force would be deployed in an attempt to crush him.

With over half his ammunition expended at Coronel, Spee decided to attempt a return to Germany. We shall never know if he would have succeeded, because on 8 December, having rounded Cape Horn, he decided for reasons that are somewhat obscure to launch an attack on Port Stanley in the Falkland Islands; as Surgeon Thomas Benjamin Dixon aboard HMS *Kent* wrote: 'very kind of them to come here and save us the trouble of going round the Horn to find them'.[61] Dixon's ship was a sister of the recently sunk *Monmouth*, and was part of a 'task force' sent to the South Atlantic with the specific object of catching and destroying Spee's squadron. At the heart of this force, under Vice-Admiral Sir Frederick Doveton Sturdee, were two *Invincible*-class battlecruisers, *Invincible* (Flag) and *Inflexible*.[62] Spee of course did not know this overwhelmingly superior force was coaling at Port Stanley, and he took no precautions to establish just what might be there before approaching with his entire squadron[63] on the morning of 8 December 1914. The result was inevitable; after a general chase lasting several hours the British force caught and destroyed four of Spee's ships, only the *Dresden* escaping to survive for another three months.

We can only surmise what impulses led Spee to attempt a raid on Port Stanley, and why he failed to effectively reconnoitre before approaching. Had he sent *Dresden*, the fastest of his light cruisers, to ascertain what enemy presence was in the vicinity, whilst staying beyond visual range with the rest of his ships, the German admiral might well have avoided destruction, particularly if Sturdee had then moved his force into the Pacific. It is then possible, though improbable, that he might have succeeded in getting his squadron home to Germany, which would have been a great propaganda coup if little more. As it was Count von Spee's decision to maintain his squadron as a 'fleet in being' forfeited any chance of a large-scale and effective *guerre de course* being conducted in the Pacific, short lived though this might have been, while his actions at the Falkland Isles led to his destruction.

Strategically it is difficult to find fault with Spee's decisions. Following Japan's decision to enter the war against Germany he was pitted against insuperable odds, and the problems of fuel and ammunition precluded any prospects, beyond the short term, in terms of waging cruiser warfare against trade. It is, in any event, difficult to conceive any acceptable, realistic, alternatives. Tactically, Spee made a huge error in approaching an unreconnoitred Port Stanley and paid for it dearly. Whatever the 'might have beens' though, it was the case that within five months of the outbreak of war, the German Navy had been swept from the Pacific.

8

Kiautschou
Naval and Military Operations
22 August – 28 September 1914

The position of Kiautschou, in military and naval terms, was hopeless once Japan entered the war; geography and force disparity ensured that German retention of the territory was impossible. The German administration, under the leadership of Governor Meyer-Waldeck had little in the way of resources with which to defend the area from the military and naval power that the Japanese could deploy.

The ultimatum delivered to Germany expired on 23 August, but Meyer-Waldeck had been making preparations for a potential outbreak of hostilities against an unknown enemy or enemy combination for some time previously. He had been kept abreast of the deteriorating situation in Europe following the assassination of Archduke Franz Ferdinand in Sarajevo on 28 June. For example, on 27 July he had been warned, by a message received from his superiors in Berlin, that Austria-Hungary and Serbia had severed diplomatic relations, and that the international situation was tense. He therefore initiated precautionary measures involving the recall of outlying forces in China to the Kiautschou Territory. The principal force in this respect being the East Asiatic Marine Detachment, which, under the terms of the Boxer Protocol of 1901, constituted the German component of the foreign forces stationed in the Chinese capital and at various key points along the route to Beijing.[1] This force, with a nominal strength of four companies of infantry and supporting arms, including artillery, was thus ordered to proceed to Kiautschou from Tientsin and Beijing.[2]

Information on the deteriorating condition of European peace was confirmed on 30 July with the stark news that Austria-Hungary had declared war on Serbia on 28 July. Such an action, it was well known, was likely to involve Russian intervention, which also meant French participation if Germany backed her ally. Clearly the peace of Europe, and perhaps the world, was at grave risk, a fact underlined by German mobilisation and declaration of war against Russia on 1 August. This was followed by a declaration against France two days later. German mobilisation meant that those German citizens in the Far East were now liable for military or naval duty, and so via the various German consuls in the region, Meyer-Waldeck ordered all those liable to bear arms to travel to Kiautschou.[3]

Also making the journey to the territory was an American citizen, Alfred

McArthur Brace. Brace, who hailed from Green Bay, Wisconsin, graduated from the class of 1909 at Beloit College in the same state. He took up the post of Instructor in Rhetoric and English Literature at Pomona College, California, serving there during 1910–11; thereafter he seems to have moved to Shanghai, China and taken up journalism. Following the issue of the Japanese ultimatum to Germany, and engaged as 'a special correspondent for Reuters Agency',[4] Brace related how he 'threw a few things into my suitcase [...] and caught the first train for the north to be on hand when the trouble began.'[5]

The defences of the territory were put in a state of readiness, though these, despite earlier reports of the area 'bristling with cannon,'[6] were, in reality, not formidable regardless of enduring popular belief to the contrary.[7] The most commanding position within the city limits of Tsingtau was Bismarck Hill, from the 128-metre summit of which there were wide views over the bay, the coast and surrounding territory.[8] An underground command post was constructed there from 1899 onwards; a three-storey affair, with a further two storeys in parts, contributing a floor area totalling some 1,600 square metres. Constructed by excavation, concrete pouring and backfilling, the post was divided internally into command, storage and accommodation areas. Atop Bismarck Hill, positions were constructed for four 280mm howitzers, mounted in a line west–east, under armoured cupolas. Lower down the promontory to the north-north-east were situated two 210mm guns; the latter were for landward defence whilet the howitzers were designated as coastal defence weapons.

The most potent coastal defence installation comprised the three 150mm Skoda and two 240mm Krupp guns that formed the Hui tsch'en Huk Battery, situated on the peninsula separating Iltis and August Viktoria Bays. Mounted in Gruson turrets these weapons were proof against anything but a direct hit from an enemy heavy shell.[9] There were a total of five coastal defence batteries, with varying degrees of weaponry and types of installation (see Table 1). Sources differ somewhat as to the number and armament of the batteries dedicated to land defence, particularly as these were augmented greatly by extemporised positions once war was declared (see Table 2).

There was also a line of fortifications, known as the 'Boxer Line,' which, as the name suggests, was constructed, between 1909 and 1913, with the intention of being defensible against an irregular force.[10] Captain Bernard Smith described this as follows:

> The extent of the landward front, from the right flank on the Yellow Sea to the left flank on Kiautschou Bay is about [6.5km]. The main line of resistance consisted of five redoubts, with trenches and dug-outs of reinforced concrete. [...]
>
> The pumping plant for the town water supply was located on the north bank of the Hai po Creek, which generally covered the left of the position. It was fortified by a strong-point, and was enclosed by the main line of the entanglement. [...] The redoubts were garrisoned by 200 men, except 1 and 5 [on the shores of the Sea and the Bay respectively] which had 250 men each. The garrison of the pumping plant was about 40 men and one officer.

Forward of the redoubts by some 200 metres was a ditch around two metres in depth filled with barbed wire and similar obstacles. A sloping glacis[11] allowed an open field of fire between the works and the ditch, the scarp[12] of which was revetted with masonry. In short, the line was undoubtedly proof against any attack by unsupported infantry and the like, even though there were no arrangements for delivering flanking fire into the ditch, but was inadequate against an attacker equipped with artillery. There were several limitations as regards the repulsing of a regularly constituted attack. First, the Boxer Line was extremely close to the city of Tsingtau. Indeed the Governor's residence was only some four kilometres distant. This meant that an attacker with artillery could easily bombard, and thus render unusable, the city and port without the necessity of breaching the line.

Some eight to ten kilometres forward of the Boxer Line was a natural defensive line, the primary position of which, situated on the right flank, was Prinz-Heinrich-Berg. At around 275 metres, the summit of this dominating height gave a panoramic view of the surrounding terrain.[13] This terrain was difficult to traverse and other prominences provided obviously viable locations for the construction of defensive positions, as well as effectively canalising any advancing enemy. However, advancing the main defensive position meant lengthening it as the peninsula broadened, and in order to defend effectively a frontage of some sixteen kilometres a much larger force would have been required.

Approximately another ten kilometres to the north-west was probably the best natural position for a defensive line given contemporary military technology. Running roughly northwesterly from Laoshan Bay to Litsun (Licun) the terrain was even more rugged, with peaks rising to some 400 metres in height. There were few decent passes through the range making it ideal defensive country given a sufficient force to defend it, and there was the rub. A force equivalent to army corps strength, around 40,000 personnel together with the requisite equipment, would have, some authors have claimed, been required to properly defend this line, running as it did for some twenty kilometres, and this was beyond what was feasible both politically and economically.[14]

Maintaining such a force during peacetime would have absorbed vast resources, and the Imperial German Navy, during the period of defensive construction around Tsingtau, was desperately short of all kinds of resources, particularly financial ones. Herwig has calculated that between 1897 and 1914 naval building had added 1,040,700,000 marks to the national debt.[15] He describes the financial state of the Navy as 'horrendous' and notes that outlay had increased from 17.9 per cent of Imperial expenditure in 1901 to 23.7 per cent in 1908, occasioning the resignation of the State Secretary for the Treasury in the latter year.[16] It is true that the defences of the territory had been paid for by a Reichstag grant of seven million marks made in 1907, only some 2.5 million of which went on the land defences,[17] but the running costs would have to be paid by the Navy, and keeping the equivalent of a division, or even a corps strength unit, effectively on standby to defend a faraway territory would have been an unbearable drain on both finances and manpower.

The Imperial Navy reconciled means and ends vis-à-vis the defences of Tsingtau with a system that was however difficult to explain logically. According to Burdick there was an 'unwillingness to do much more than construct fortifications with the Chinese as the practical opponent and a hypothetical, unnamed, foe of little consequence as a possible attacker'.[18]

The 'unnamed foe' when it came to it was of massive consequence, and so it is somewhat ironic to note that on the very day the Japanese ultimatum expired, 23 August, Grand Admiral Tirpitz himself initiated the establishment of a naval unit, for use in the military context, of a size that could have provided an effective defence for Tsingtau. This was the Flanders Marine Division (MarineDivision Flandern), the initial impetus that led to the creation of which was a telegram from Tirpitz. This arose following discussions between the Army and Navy over the path that the Army was taking through Belgium. Put simply, Tirpitz wanted the capture of the Belgian and northern French ports, most importantly Ostend, before they could be destroyed or damaged by the retreating, and, as he perceived it, beaten enemy forces. Because the Army refused to countenance any such diversion, as they saw it, Tirpitz pushed for the creation of a naval force that could protect naval interests, as he, in turn, saw them.

The creation of the Division, later expanded to become a Corps, caused endless friction with the Army, which was determined that it should come under its strategic control and who had to find a quantity of personnel and equipment, drawn from the secondary reserve (*Landwehr*),[19] to create, among other units, additional infantry, an artillery section and the cavalry component. Tirpitz was successful in his quest for the creation of the force, which was officially created on 29 August, and the strength of the division in September stood at nearly 17,000 personnel with an artillery component of twelve pieces.[20] In order to find enough manpower Tirpitz had to decommission the Sixth Battle Squadron and reduce the manning of the Fifth Battle Squadron.[21] Commanded by Admiral Ludwig von Schroeder, the formation was responsible for defending the naval bases on the Belgian coast, and to prepare for the implementation of a small-scale (*Kleinkrieg*) naval war against Great Britain using submarines and destroyers. This was of course the exact opposite of the strategy that Tirpitz had advocated for many years. In any event, because of the setbacks occasioned to the German plan to conquer France in six weeks, the division found itself used as a combat unit.[22]

Such retrospective judgements are however totally unfair, and the Imperial Navy had to meet, or not, future foes with the means available to it. That they were insufficient is clear with hindsight, but it was not necessarily so clear to those at the time. Local difficulties might have been expected, as related, with the Chinese, but there were few other powers that could have brought sufficient force to bear such that the Kiautschou defences were completely inadequate. The most obvious was Britain, which maintained relatively large naval forces in the region, and had access to the Indian Army in terms of military power, though this was in reality far distant. Russia too was a potential opponent, even if, since 1905, sorely deprived of naval assets. Russia was the only European power to maintain a substantial military force in East Asia, though again it was a long way from the Kiautschou Territory and would require a major logistical effort to travel to within attacking distance. France had few naval or military assets that could be brought to bear. Moreover, when the Great War broke out in Europe none of the European powers could afford to divert substantial forces to a peripheral theatre.

The only potent potential opponents came down to the USA or Japan. The United States had a powerful, and growing navy, but only small military forces, which had been heavily engaged in the Philippines since 1898 and, according to some scholars, were still fighting there until 1913.[23] There had been occasions when the US and Germany had clashed to one degree or another. The German presence in Manila Bay in 1898 for example had caused some friction, and, dependent upon which interpretation one chooses to accept, the Venezuelan Debt Crisis of 1902–3 was perhaps very close to resulting in conflict. The conditions for actual conflict never arose however, and the United States and Imperial Germany, though general mutual suspicion and occasional tension arose from time to time, maintained generally cordial relations throughout the Roosevelt presidency.

Roosevelt did not stand for re-election in 1909 and his successor, William Howard Taft, was, as his nickname of 'Peaceful Bill' indicated, a less thrusting personality both personally and politically. Best known for 'Dollar Diplomacy' he has been described as sometimes lethargic and often unimaginative.[24] In any event, he exerted presidential power to a much lesser degree than his predecessor and was an avid proponent of arbitration as the most practicable method of settling international disputes. This approach stemmed no doubt from his legal credentials and training, a background that was to see him elevated to the Supreme Court as Chief Justice in 1921.[25]

Taft lost the 1913 election to Woodrow Wilson, thanks largely to Roosevelt splitting the anti-Wilson vote, who was, and remains, the most highly educated US President with a doctorate gained at Johns Hopkins University.[26] On 19 August 1914 Wilson declared that the US would opt for a state of neutrality in respect of what was becoming a world war.

> Every man who really loves America will act and speak in the true spirit of neutrality, which is the spirit of impartiality and fairness and friendliness to all concerned. [...] [O]ur duty as the one great nation at peace, the one people holding itself ready to play a part of impartial mediation and speak the counsels of peace and accommodation, not as a partisan, but as a friend. [...] The United States must be neutral in fact, as well as in name, during these days that are to try men's souls. We must be impartial in thought, as well as action, must put a curb upon our sentiments, as well as upon every transaction that might be construed as a preference of one party to the struggle before another.[27]

Neither 'Peaceful Bill' nor the 'Scholar-President' were men to get involved in foreign adventures, though neither was backward in enforcing the 'Roosevelt Corollary' on several occasions. As with the latter portion of the Roosevelt term of office though, there were no occasions when the foreign policy aspirations of America and Germany seriously collided. In any event, for the US to engage in operations to take Kiautschou from Germany would have meant an inevitable clash with Japan. The point being that while the US might well have had the means, it never had the motive.

The same can be said to apply to Japan, and being geographically closer the deployment of forces necessary to incommode Germany's occupation was that much easier. So while Japan always had the means it too lacked a motive, or at least the excuse to put into practice that motive, until the outbreak of war in 1914.[28] Once Japan had the necessary motivation to move on the German territories, the means were readily available. The Japanese maintained a standing army of some 19 divisions in peacetime, and this was a force that could not be resisted by any level of German defence, for whatever the strength of the those defences, the Japanese could muster superior force.

The first step taken in dispossessing Germany of her 'place in the sun' was the assembling of a naval force, named the Second Squadron, under Vice-Admiral Kato Sadakichi to enforce a maritime blockade. The squadron was built around five obsolete vessels captured during the Russo-Japanese War. Kato flew his flag in *Suwo*, which had originally been the *Peresviet*-class battleship *Pobieda*. A veteran of the Battle of the Yellow Sea, *Pobieda* had been sunk by artillery fire at Port Arthur before being salvaged and recommissioned into the Japanese Navy. Another combatant from the Yellow Sea battle was *Tango*, originally the *Petropavlovsk*-class battleship *Poltava*, and a vessel also salvaged from Port Arthur. Arguably Kato's most powerful unit, and certainly the most modern, was *Iwami*, constructed as the *Borodino*-class battleship *Orel*. *Orel* had been part of the 1st Division of the 2nd Pacific Squadron and had surrendered on the orders of Rear Admiral Nikolai Nebogatov the day after the Battle of Tsushima, the only modern battle-ship to survive on the Russian side.[29] Two more survivors of Tsushima, members of the 3rd Pacific Squadron and unfit to fight in 1905, comprised the other heavy units of Kato's command. The *Mishima* and *Okinoshima* were *Admiral Ushakov*-class coastal battleships commissioned in 1897 and 1899 as *Admiral Senyavin* and *General-Admiral Apraxin* respectively.

One more unit of somewhat similar power and vintage, to Kato's better ships at least, was later added to the blockading force in the shape of the *Swiftsure*-class battleship *Triumph*. This pre-dreadnought provided, along with the destroyer *Usk*, the British naval contingent.[30]

Kato also had four armoured cruisers; the British-constructed *Chiyoda*,[31]*Tokiwa* and *Iwate*, and the, ironically, German-built *Yakumo*. In addition there were several old lighter cruisers, including the American-constructed protected cruiser *Chitose* and the protected cruiser *Akashi*. Other notable warships were *Takachiho*, constructed in Britain and originally designated a protected cruiser but reclas-sified as a second-class coastal defence ship in 1912, and *Akitsushima* originally considered a light cruiser but similarly redesignated in 1912 and, one of the few modern vessels in the squadron, the second-class protected cruiser *Tone*. If, apart from the last mentioned, the ships of the Second Squadron were firmly rooted in the past, then an additional vessel could be said to very much represent the future; the seaplane carrier *Wakamiya Maru*, a British-built freighter, captured from Russia in 1905 and commissioned into the Japanese Navy in 1913, carrying four seaplanes.[32]

Against this large, if largely outmoded, force Captain Meyer-Waldeck had little in the way of assets. All the naval units scattered throughout East Asian waters had been recalled to Tsingtau, but even though the majority successfully complied, the resultant force was very weak. There were four *Iltis*-class gunboats; *Iltis*, *Jaguar*, *Luchs* and *Tiger*. These vessels were not designed or equipped for fighting other ships; the heaviest weapon carried being the two 105mm guns of the latter two.

Of perhaps more utility was the minelayer *Lauting*, which had a capacity of 120 mines, and the torpedo boat *S-90*, it being the original of the design that had caused a step-change in the relationship between torpedo boats and torpedo boat destroyers, known generally thereafter as just destroyers. *S-90* was designed to accompany the battlefleet to sea, and was thus larger and more substantially constructed than previous types. In reply to this danger the Royal Navy had introduced the 'River'-class destroyers, which were able to keep the sea in much tougher conditions than their predecessors, the torpedo boat destroyers, and displaced some 560 tonnes as against the *S-90*'s 315 tonnes.[33]

Augmenting this strength, if that is the correct term, was the Austro-Hungarian *Kaiser Franz Josef I*-class ram-cruiser *Kaiserin Elisabeth*. Austro-Hungarian ram-cruisers, also known as torpedo-rams, were envisaged as leading a division of warships, consisting of two light cruisers, two torpedo boat destroyers and twelve torpedo boats, in attacks on enemy battleships and heavy units. The philosophy of utilising torpedo-carrying craft to attack larger vessels came from the French *Jeune École* (Young School). Arising in the 1880s, this school of thought argued that equipping the French Navy with large numbers of torpedo-carrying vessels would nullify the overwhelming preponderance of heavy units in the British Navy. This 'strategy of the weak' was taken up by several lesser naval powers including Austria-Hungary. The British constructed one such vessel, *Polyphemus*, which was not followed up. The *Kaiser Franz Josef I*-class was quite heavily gunned as originally constructed, being armed with two 240mm guns, in turrets fore and aft, and six 150mm broadside guns in casemates, though the primary weapon was, at least initially, envisaged as the four torpedo tubes.

The ramming function was, perhaps, a hangover from the Austrian victory over Italy in the 1866 Battle of Lissa. During the engagement the deliberate ramming of the Italian battleship *Re d'Italia* by the Austrian flagship, *Ferdinand Max*, caused the total loss of the former. In 1905–6, *Kaiserin Elisabeth* and her sister ship Kaiser Franz Josef I were refitted at Pola Navy Yard, and their 240mm guns, which had proved too heavy for their mountings, replaced with modern 150mm pieces. The casemate-mounted weapons, having proved difficult to work in anything but a calm sea, were moved up to main deck level.[34]

The *Kaiserin Elisabeth*, the only naval unit deployed by Austria-Hungary in East Asia, arrived at Tsingtau on 22 July following orders from the naval command; there being nowhere else friendly to go and, with war imminent, no prospect of making the long journey home.[35] Also present, though unserviceable, were the *Bussard*-class light cruiser *Cormoran*, which had been with Diederichs during the acquisition of the Kiautschou territory, and the torpedo boat *Taku*, constructed by Germany for the Chinese Navy, but taken following the Boxer War. *Cormoran* had suffered engine failure, which was considered irreparable, and *Taku* had been severely damaged by a collision the previous year.

There were three other German warships in the theatre that were unable to obey the order to make for Tsingtau, the purpose-built *Vaterland*-class river gunboats *Vaterland*, *Tsingtau* and *Otter*. Constructed in Germany between 1899 and 1909 specifically for service on the Chinese rivers, these vessels were then broken down before reassembly and commissioning in China. They were laid up at various Chinese ports in 1914, though the crews attempted to make the overland journey to Tsingtau and several succeeded.[36]

In order to maximise his defensive position from naval attack, Meyer-Waldeck had ordered sea mines be laid in the near approaches to the territory. The day before the Japanese ultimatum expired he decided to utilise the rest of the stock around some small groups of islands lying some fifteen to twenty kilometres offshore to the south-east, during the course of which operation *Lautung* was covered by the *S-90*.

Unbeknown to the Germans, units of the British China Squadron were at sea on that day engaged in setting up a patrol line in order to intercept ships attempting to leave Tsingtau before the expiry of the ultimatum. There were four destroyers engaged in this activity during the evening of 22 August, all, coincidentally, of the 'River'-class built to counter the threat of the *S-90* torpedo boats; the *Colne*, *Jed*, *Kennet* and *Welland*. Seeing the smoke of the German torpedo boat the *Kennet*, which happened to be closest, increased to full speed and moved to engage. The *S-90* became aware of this vessel closing fast, and accordingly turned and made for Tsingtau at her full speed. The design speed of the *S-90* was 27 knots as against the 25 knots of the *Kennet*. Both vessels were around a decade old however and it would appear that the *Kennet* was in better shape, inasmuch as she was able to close on her smaller opponent. The British warship was also the more heavily armed; carrying four 110mm (12-pounder) guns in comparison to the three 77.5mm (4-pounder) weapons of *S-90*, and with her heavier metal was able to open fire first.[37]

Here then, some ten years and 20,000 kilometres from the arena that they were originally conceived as joining combat in, the torpedo boat and the [torpedo boat] destroyer finally came to blows, though in anything but the circumstances as originally envisaged. It was essentially a stern chase for the British vessel, and one that she would have won eventually given the maximum speed her opponent seemed capable of was just over 20 knots. During the chase the British vessel fired some 300 rounds, and scored no hits, while *S-90* replied with 250, and hit *Kennet* several times. Notwithstanding this, what essentially saved *S-90* was some cunning on the part of her commander, who lengthened the distance by forcing *Kennet* to avoid shallow reef water, and, ultimately, the coastal artillery of Hui tsch'en Huk battery. This began firing on *Kennet* while she was still out of range and thus gave warning of what the vessel could expect if she persisted. She did not, and turned away allowing *S-90* to escape; 'So vigorous had been the pursuit that the funnels of the *S-90* gleamed red-hot in the night.'[38] During the engagement the torpedo boat suffered no casualties, while three men were killed and six wounded, including her commander, aboard *Kennet*.[39]

With these events in mind no doubt, the next sortie by *Lauting*, carried out the following day, was afforded a more powerful escort consisting of *S-90, Jaguar* and *Kaiserin Elisabeth*; the 150mm guns of the latter being seen as powerful enough to discourage the attentions of lighter units. The operation remained unmolested by surface units and passed off successfully, but when the minelayer turned to return to port she was almost overwhelmed by a massive explosion some distance astern. The ship had clearly not hit a mine, weighing only some 580 tonnes she would have been totally destroyed by such an event, and, despite reports that a shard of steel marked with the word 'Portsmouth' was found on her deck after the explosion, indicating the presence of British ordnance,[40] the most likely explanation is that one of her recently laid mines had malfunctioned and exploded.[41] The damaged ship was able to return to port under her own steam, but required two days of repairs in the floating dock before she was fit for service again, though this was somewhat academic as, early in the morning of 27 August, Kato's squadron appeared off the coast.[42]

The Japanese came no closer than about 25 kilometres, and requested, by radio, permission for an emissary to approach Tsingtau and land. This was refused; Kato's next action was to proclaim, by radio and in English, a blockade:

> I hereby declare that on the [27 August 1914] the blockade of the whole coastline [...] of the leased territory of Kiautschou is established and will be maintained with the naval force under my command [...] the ships of friendly and neutral powers are given twenty-four hours grace to leave the blockaded area and that all measures authorised by international law [...] will be enforced [...] against all vessels which may attempt to violate the blockade.[43]

Japanese armed sailors also landed on and proceeded to occupy three small islands lying offshore, from west to east, Tschu tscha tau, Taikungtao, and Hsiakungtao , upon which they constructed signals posts and navigation lights, and began minesweeping operations.

With the announcement of a naval blockade, and the cutting of the undersea cables to Shanghai and Chefoo (Yantai) on 14 and 24 August respectively by the Singapore-based Eastern Extension Australasia & China Telegraph Company (EEA&CTC) cable ship *Patrol*, the territory was cut off from maritime and cable communication with the outside world. Radio communication was also interdicted with the network of radio stations constructed in the Pacific territories, Anguar, New Guinea, Nauru, Samoa and Yap, having been, or in imminent danger of being, captured. Communication was possible with the Telefunken station in Shanghai, but either directly or indirectly with Nauen, the powerful station near Berlin that was the core of the network, much more problematical. There was of course still the inland telegraph and the Shantung Railway, though these would come under threat if the Japanese landed military forces.

Despite their inferiority the Germans were able to strike a blow, albeit minor,

against the Second Squadron on 31 August with the assistance of the unseason-
able weather. A severe storm had blown up the previous day and raged overnight;
when the skies cleared somewhat they revealed a Japanese destroyer aground on
Lien Tau Island some ten kilometres to the south. The unfortunate vessel was
the *Asakaze-* class *Shirotaye*, which had gone, or been driven, onto the island
during the night. Other ships were undertaking a salvage attempt, but these were
dispersed by the fire of Hui tsch'en Huk battery thus allowing a foray by *Jaguar*,
which was able to destroy the beached warship by gunfire before fleeing back to
safety.[44]

The improvement in the weather was temporary, which precluded any further
naval action. It also did massive damage to the territory's infrastructure with the
swollen watercourses demolishing roads, bridges and several sections of the Shantung Railway. In respect of the latter, nature performed the work that German
engineers were preparing to carry out, since Meyer-Waldeck had ordered that
preparations be made for demolishing several railway bridges. This was in order to
prevent the Japanese capturing the railway intact, and, if they landed in the north,
using it to facilitate their operations. The weather also benefited the Japanese,
in the sense that along with the railway went the telegraph running alongside
it. From the beginning of September then Kiautschou was effectively cut off in
almost every physical sense of the word.[45]

Despite the adverse weather, a Japanese military force landed at Lungkou on
the north of Shandong Province on 2 September; the vanguard of the augmented
Japanese 18th Division commanded by Lieutenant-General Kamio Mitsuomi.
Kamio was widely experienced, seeing action during the Sino-Japanese War as
a staff officer, but does not appear to have served during the Russo-Japanese
conflict, being seconded to General Headquarters in 1905.[46] He had also been
involved in training the Chinese Army during the 1890s, and so had extensive staff
and administrative knowledge.[47] The plan followed by Kamio involved the distant
landing at Lungkou, which was some 150 kilometres away from the objective in a
straight line and probably nearer twice that taking into account the terrain. This
force would then advance in a roughly west-south-west direction across the Shandong peninsula towards Pingdu, before moving east-south-east to Tsimo (Jimo).
From there, only some eight kilometres outside the boundary of the German
territory, they would proceed through the natural defence line of the territory, as
related above, via the pass that carried the Shantung Railway. This force would
thus create a diversion, and provide cover, that would allow for further landings
in Laoshan Bay some 30–40 kilometres to the east of Tsingtau, scheduled for 18
September. An initial landing at Laoshan was ruled out because it would have
been relatively easy for the Germans to interrupt it and it was believed that mines
were sown in the bay. This cautious, one might even describe it as ultra-cautious,
approach was to characterise the entire course of the Japanese operation.[48]

One complication inherent in landing so far north, in relation to contemporary
politics and diplomacy, was that it involved decisively breaching Chinese neutrality.
China had 'in accordance with the law of nations' issued a declaration of neutrality
on 6 August. The Chinese government of Yuan desired two things; that the war

be limited to Europe, and, that if any conflict arose in China between the warring nations, the neutrality of China might be respected.[49] In both desiderata China was to be disappointed, considering that the conflict had indeed spread and Japan carried out the invasion against the will of the Chinese government, which found itself too weak to resist. That this deepened the suspicion of Japan and Japanese motives in respect of the United States counted for little or nothing.[50]

The landing at Lungkou on 2 September, carried out in weather that swiftly turned atrocious, was undertaken by components, amounting to some 8,000 personnel, of the 24th Infantry Brigade commanded by Major-General Yamada Ryuosi over an open beach. The initial party comprising an infantry battalion, with two machine guns, plus a troop of cavalry from 22nd Cavalry Regiment, and having landed safely these moved off to establish a defensive perimeter. A company of engineers then landed, and began the task of constructing piers to avoid the need for the following soldiery to wade through waist-deep water when disembarking from the light craft that ferried them from the ships. The worsening weather forced several postponements to the operation so that it was not until 7 September that the full complement of men and horses were landed, as was the Commander-in-Chief. Yamada had gone ashore on 3 September and urged the necessity of pushing ahead regardless of conditions. He ordered the cavalry to advance well ahead of the infantry and set them the object of entering and securing the town of Pingdu, some 110 kilometres distant, by 7 September, living off the country if necessary. The schedule could not be met, and it was on 10 September that the exhausted horsemen, and their equally spent mounts, which had suffered losses of around 30 per cent, finally entered Pingdu. It was, by any standards, no mean feat. Fortunately there were no German forces there to meet them.

Yamada had ordered a general advance on 4 September, and the infantry set off in the wake of the cavalry. However, upon coming ashore again on 7 September, Kamio perceived that a pause in operations was necessary in order to try and sort out the several problems, in particular the movement of food supplies to the advancing troops. Not only was there a shortage of transport carts, but the dreadful road conditions engendered by the continuing torrential rain made the roads virtually impassable and the living conditions of the advancing units intolerable. Two days, 9 and 10 September, were spent on consolidation and repair, and, by coincidence, the weather cleared somewhat on the 11th. It would now be possible to effect repairs to roads without the attempt being washed away, and the various watercourses should became fordable again, though a reduction in levels was not evident in some cases for another two days.

The cavalry at Pingdu had meanwhile pushed forward patrol units to the town of Tsimo, an advance of some forty kilometres, where a small German detachment had been encountered. This unit had swiftly withdrawn leaving the Japanese in tenuous occupation, and a call, which reached cavalry advancing from Pingdu on 13 September, was sent for reinforcements. A further detachment was rapidly dispatched followed by the entire regiment, which departed Pingdu the next day on the orders of Yamada. Tsimo was an important goal in the Japanese plan as there were, relatively, good roads from there into the German territory and then on to Tsingtau. Elements of the cavalry force reached Tsimo at noon on 14 September and took measures to secure it against a German counter move. These included sending a detachment to the town of Kiautschou, some forty kilometres to the west and on the route of the Shantung Railway. With the Japanese at Kiautschou on 17 September the railway, and adjacent telegraph, was effectively in their control. Tsingtau was now absolutely cut off by sea and land, and almost so through the ether.[51]

There remained only the air, and both sides had elements of an air component; the Japanese Navy had the *Wakamiya Maru* with her complement of four Maurice Farman floatplanes, while the Army detachment, initially consisting of three machines, deployed from an improvised airstrip near Tsimo on 21 September.[52] Japanese aviation was, as was the case in every other nation, a recent phenomenon in terms of powered aircraft. Previous interest in aeronautics had centred on the use of balloons for reconnaissance, the first Japanese military balloons were sent aloft in May 1877, and an advanced kite type was designed and constructed in 1900 and successfully used during the Russo-Japanese War. A joint committee, with army, navy and civil input, was created on 30 July 1909 to investigate and research the techniques and equipment associated with ballooning; the Provisional Military Balloon Research Association or PMBRA.

Nominated by the Japanese Army to serve on the PMBRA were two officers with the rank of captain, Tokugawa Yoshitoshi and Hino Kumazo. Both had some experience with aviation. Hino designed and constructed a pusher type monoplane with an eight-horsepower (hp) engine that he unsuccessfully, the engine was underpowered, attempted to get off the ground on 18 March 1910. Tokugawa was a member of the balloon establishment during the Russo-Japanese War. Both were sent to Europe in April 1910 to learn to fly at the Blériot Flying School at Etampes, France. Having passed the rudimentary course they purchased two aeroplanes each and had them shipped to Japan; Tokugawa obtained a Farman III and a Blériot XI-2bis in France while Hino purchased one of Hans Grade's machines and a Wright aircraft in Germany.[53]

The first flights of powered aeroplanes in Japan occurred on 19 December 1910 at Yoyogi Park in Tokyo. Tokugawa flew the Farman III, powered by a 50hp Gnome engine, for three minutes over a distance of some 3,000 metres at a height of 70 metres. Hino followed him immediately afterwards in the Grade machine, powered by a 24hp Grade engine, which flew for just over a minute and covered a distance of 1,000 metres at a height of 20 metres.

A naval member of the PMBRA, Narahara Sanji, started on designing and constructing an aeroplane, with a bamboo airframe and a 25hp engine, during March 1910. Because of the low powered engine the machine failed to lift off when this was attempted on 24 October 1910, but with a second machine, the 'Narahara Type 2' powered by a Gnome engine similar to that used in the Farman III, he managed a sixty-metre flight at an altitude of four metres on 5 May 1911. This flight, at Tokorozawa, in Saitama near Tokyo, the site of Japan's first airfield, is considered to be the first Japanese civilian flight as Narahara had left the Navy when he made it. It was also the first flight by a Japanese-manufactured aeroplane.[54]

The first military flight by a Japanese manufactured machine took place on 13 October 1911, when Tokugawa flew in a 'PMBRA Type (Kaisiki) 1' of his own design, based on the Farman III at Tokorozawa. These pioneers, while they had made astonishing progress, did not however possess the necessary research and technological resources to take Japanese aviation further.[55] Because of this the Japanese decided to import aviation technology from Europe, though the Navy established the Naval Aeronautical Research Committee in 1912 to provide facilities to test and copy foreign aircraft and train Japanese engineers in the necessary skills.[56] Via this system, the foundations of a Japanese aviation industry were being laid; in July 1913 a naval lieutenant, Nakajima Chikuhei, produced an improved version of the Farman floatplane for naval use. Nakajima Aircraft Industries, founded in 1917 after Nakajima resigned from the Navy, went on to massive success.[57]

The French were the world leaders in military aviation, with 260 aircraft in service by 1913, while the Russians had 100, Germany 48, Britain 29, Italy 26 and Japan 14. The US deployed 6.[58] It comes as no surprise then to note that during the campaign against Tsingtau all the aeroplanes deployed by both Japanese services were French. Four Maurice-Farman MF7 biplanes and one Nieuport 6M monoplane formed the Army's Provisional Air Corps, flying 86 sorties between them, while the Navy deployed one Maurice-Farman MF7 floatplane and three Henri-Farman HF7 floatplanes. The navy planes flew 49 sorties and dropped 199 bombs.[59]

A floatplane from *Wakamiya Maru* flew over Tsingtau on 5 September, causing something of a surprise to the defenders, on a reconnaissance and bombing mission, releasing three bombs that caused no harm. It was not the first aerial bombing ever; that had taken place on 1 November 1911 in what became Libya when an Italian aeroplane had dropped an explosive device on an Ottoman position.[60] It was however a total surprise to the defenders. The reconnaissance element of the mission was more useful, being able to ascertain that *Emden* was not in harbour but that there were several other warships present. It was to be the first of several visits by both Army and Navy aeroplanes, against which the Germans could offer little defence, though the fact that the defenders had their own air 'component' was to result in the first air-air combat in history. Indeed, despite the remoteness of the campaign from the main theatre, this was only one of a number of such 'firsts'.

Aviation on the German side was represented by one man and one machine; Kapitänleutnant Gunther Plüschow and his Rumpler Taube. Plüschow had served in the East Asiatic Cruiser Squadron, at the time under the command of Vice Admiral Carl Coerper, as a junior officer aboard SMS *Fürst Bismarck* in 1908. Assigned to the Naval Flying Service in autumn 1913 he arrived on 2 January 1914 at Johannisthal Air Field near Berlin to begin pilot training, and, having first taken to the air only two days previously, acquired his licence on 3 February 1914.[61] The Naval Air Service, which had been created in 1912 and divided between aeroplane and airship sections the following year, was, in 1914, something of a misnomer;

naval aviation was in a greatly underdeveloped state with sole assets consisting of two Zeppelin airships, four floatplanes and two landplanes.[62] This was largely due to Tirpitz, who, despite his later assertions that, prior to 1914, he saw the aeroplane as the weapon of the future as against the airship, was not prepared to, as he saw it, divert funds from the battlefleet in order to develop the technologies and techniques required.[63]

Having not seen it for some six years Plüschow arrived in Tsingtau by train on 13 June – an extremely long and undoubtedly tedious journey across the Siberian steppe – while two Rumpler Taube aeroplanes with 100hp engines, especially constructed for service in China, travelled by sea arriving in mid-July 1914.[64] The second machine was to be piloted by an army officer assigned to the III Naval Battalion, Lieutenant Friedrich Müllerskowski, and the arrival of the two aviators and their machines took the total 'air force' available in the territory to three men and aircraft. The third aviator was Franz Oster, a former naval officer who had settled in Tsingtau in 1899, but returned to Germany in 1911 and learned to fly. He returned to the territory in 1912, via Ceylon (Sri Lanka) complete with a Rumpler Taube equipped with a 60hp engine. During his sojourn in Ceylon he attempted a flight at Colombo Racecourse in a Blériot Monoplane on 30 December 1911 that ended in near disaster; the machine was wrecked and Oster was hurt. He nevertheless, after having returned to the territory and replaced the engine in his Taube with a 70hp Mercedes unit, made a series of flights from the Tsingtau racecourse, the first being on 9 July 1913.[65]

Plüschow and Müllerskowski took charge of reassembling the two aeroplanes delivered by sea and the former successfully made several flights from the extremely small and dangerous landing ground at the racecourse on 29 July 1914. A further two days were needed to get the second aeroplane constructed, and on the afternoon of 31 July Müllerskowski set off on his first flight. It ended in disaster; after only a few seconds in flight, and from an altitude estimated to be 50 metres, the machine lost control and plunged over a cliff onto the rocks below. Müllerskowski was seriously, though not mortally, wounded and the Taube was completely wrecked.[66]

Whether it was just bad luck or whether there were atmospheric conditions pertaining at the time that made flying problematical we cannot know, but it would seem to have been a combination of the two that afflicted Plüschow on 3 August. Having taken off successfully and flown a reconnaissance mission over the territory, his first 'important' sortie, he was experiencing difficulty in attempting to land when his engine failed and he crash landed into a small wood. He was unhurt but the Taube was badly damaged and, upon accessing the spare wings and propellers sent out with the aeroplanes, he discovered that the replacement parts had rotted away or suffered moisture induced damage during the voyage. He was fortunate that the engine, for which replacement parts could only have been extemporised with difficulty, was still serviceable and that there were skilled Chinese craftsmen available; the latter fashioned him a new composite propeller from oak. Despite this device having to be repaired after every flight, having been assembled with ordinary carpenter's glue it exhibited a disconcerting tendency to revert to its component parts under the strain of operational usage, it remained serviceable throughout the rest of the campaign.[67]

Plüschow's machine was out of action until 12 August, but on 22 August an attempt was made to augment it with Oster's aeroplane; he attempted to lift off from the racecourse in his older craft but stalled and crashed, occasioning damage necessitating several days of repair though remaining unhurt personally. Another attempt was made on 27 August with the same result, though this time the damage was more severe with the aeroplane 'completely destroyed' to such an extent that 'reconstruction was no longer viable'.[68] It seems however that Oster did not concur as the diary entry for 13 October 1914 made by the missionary Carl Johannes Voskamp, records Oster once again, and apparently finally, attempting and failing to take off, and notes that this might be due to unfavourable atmospheric conditions.[69]

Plüschow and his Taube, by default the sole representatives of German aviation, could not of course provide anything much in the way of air defence against the Japanese. Nor could they achieve a great deal in the way of keeping open communications with the world outside the Kiautschou Territory. What was possible though, within the operational capabilities of man and machine, was reconnaissance, and the clearing up somewhat of the weather on 11 September allowed an aerial sortie to take place two days later. Plüschow flew north-westwards to investigate rumours of the Japanese landing and advance, and discovered their forces in some strength at Pingdu; the marching elements of the Japanese force reached Pingdu between 11 and 14 September.[70] He also received his 'baptism of fire' from the infantry, returning with around ten bullet holes in his plane and resolving not to fly below 2,000 metres in future in order to preserve his engine and propeller.[71]

The news that Japanese forces had advanced to Pingdu in strength, despite the difficulties of terrain and weather, was disturbing to Meyer-Waldeck and the garrison; it indicated to them that the advance was progressing assuredly. In actuality it was not, and the difficulties encountered by the advance forced a reappraisal. Elements of the Japanese 23rd Infantry Brigade under Major-General Horiuchi Bunjero had followed their compatriots of 24th Brigade ashore at Lungkou, and these were now toiling along the road towards Pingdu. Because of the difficulties of following this route, and the more men and transport pushed along it then the more impassable it became, utilising it as originally envisaged threatened dislocation to timing as did the weather. The Japanese plan specified a concentration around Tsimo by 20 September, but the difficulties encountered rendered this problematical. Kamio communicated this to his superiors on 14 September and was instructed next day to halt the landing, re-embark those elements of 23rd Brigade already ashore into the troopships, and send them around the peninsula so as to effect a landing at Laoshan Bay on 18 September. By dint of prodigious efforts of extemporisation the re-embarkation was achieved in sufficient time for the landing to take place.[72]

Thus far there had been no serious fighting and infantry units of 24th Brigade had begun reinforcing the cavalry that had reached Tsimo on 14 September; the

Japanese Army was only some eight kilometres from the boundary of German territory.

On the morning of 18 September the 3rd Squadron of the 22nd Cavalry Regiment led by Captain Suida Sakama, nominally comprising 167 personnel, moved out from the town towards Liu Ting (Liuting), a village situated on the Pai-sha river, which delineated the border and was only about 32 kilometres from Tsingtau. Some days previously, on 15 September, a mounted German patrol reconnoitring the area had come into contact with Japanese advance parties, resulting in an inconclusive firefight following which the Japanese had withdrawn.[73] The squadron split up into troops as it approached the river, one of which, as it moved towards the village, encountered a forward patrol from V Company of III Naval Battalion deployed between the village and the riverbank. General firing quickly broke out and continued for some twenty minutes while the Japanese attempted to flank the German position.[74] They failed in this because the Germans withdrew in good order, and, despite the length of the engagement and the number of shots fired, there was only one fatality on either side – the Japanese squadron commander and Leutnant Gottfried von Riedesel zu Eisenbach, formerly Second Secretary at the German embassy in Beijing. Though honours were more or less even, it had been the Germans that retreated this time.[75]

Meyer-Waldeck had correctly predicted that one of the routes that the Japanese might profitably advance along was via Tsimo and Liu Ting and had ordered units thrown forward to screen the area. This position was though well in advance of the potential defensive line Laoshan Bay to Licun (Litsun). To attempt a defence of this line, or at least the several passes through the mountains the Governor had some eight companies of infantry; the four companies of III Naval Battalion plus the mounted company, and two further companies, VI and VII, formed from reservists and other Germans that had managed to make their way to Kiautschou after mobilisation on 1–2 August. VI Company was formed mainly from the civilians while VII Company contained men with greater military experience. There was also the East Asiatic Marine Detachment, which was ordered to the territory at the end of July, and complements of engineers and support troops. In command of the land front was Oberstleutnant (Lieutenant Colonel) Friedrich von Kessinger, commander of III Naval Battalion.[76]

The initial disposition of these forces, prior to the Japanese ultimatum, had been focused on manning and strengthening the Boxer Line. The five infantry works were manned and blockhouses built in the intervals between them, and communication trenches were dug and barbed wire defences laid out from coast to coast. Additional artillery batteries were constructed utilising weapons removed from the warships, and a mobile railway battery of two 88mm guns was fabricated. Some 500 landmines were also manufactured from dynamite and planted at various points ahead of the main line.[77] Following the expiration of the ultimatum it was decided to advance elements of the defence further into the territory.[78]

Before the brief action of 18 September had indicated that the route of the Japanese forces advancing from the north would almost certainly be along the line of the Shantung Railway, the possibilities of another landing had exercised the defenders. Given the nature of the terrain along the route from Liu Ting, there would be potential to mount an effective defence able to give them pause at least. However reports of Japanese shipping off Lau Schan (Laoshan) Bay to the west of Kiautschou, and the attendant prospect of a landing there, required a change of emphasis. This was put into effect on 12–13 September when units of the East Asiatic Marine Detachment, together with an artillery battery and supporting components, were shifted to positions in the Lau Schan Mountains.[79]

The Japanese landing, preceded by a bombardment of the area behind the beach, which was unnecessary as it happened, took place at Wang-ko-chuang (Wanggezhuang, Jiaonan) Bay located at the northern end of Lau Schan Bay on 18 September as scheduled. First ashore, after the preliminary parties had secured the beach, were elements of 23rd Infantry Brigade that had re-embarked at Lungkou some three days previously. There was no resistance and by noon the beachhead had been secured and spearheads thrust out to occupy strategic points. Among these was the village of Wang ko Chuang and the eastern entrance to the Duchess Elizabeth Valley (*Herzogin Elisabeth Tal*) through which the Hotung Pass (*Hotungpass*) and March Pass (*Marschpass*) allowing passage through the Laoshan mountains.[80] The pass – the names were for the eastern and western ends of the same route – traversed extremely rugged terrain and the road, really a glorified footpath, was only wide enough at certain points for two men to stand side-by-side; it was thus territory eminently suited for defence.[81]

Despite the difficulties of creating strong defensive works in the short period since being deployed there, a platoon of German troops were installed in loop-holed trenches awaiting any Japanese attempt to move through the pass.[82] Accordingly when a Japanese infantry company-sized unit approached their position, located some seven kilometres from the beachhead, they began firing. Using 'fire and movement' techniques the Japanese began to outflank the position and pin down the defenders in turn. This process lasted some three hours, from, approximately, 3p.m to 6p.m. –, before, fearing that total darkness would prevent their pressing on with the attack, the Japanese stormed the position without regard to caution. They captured the strongpoint with no loss; the Germans had taken advantage of the deterioration in visibility to abandon their position. It was a significant victory in that it secured the pass for the Japanese, meaning that the beachhead was not now liable to a counterstroke. There was further good news for the Japanese when another company sent in the direction of Tsimo, in order to establish communication with the forces there, swiftly contacted a Japanese cavalry squadron advancing in the opposite direction for the same purpose. With the link up of the two portions of the invading forces, albeit tenuous at first, the Kiautschou territory was surrounded by sea and land.[83]

During the night of 18–19 September the German platoon retraced their steps back up the pass and harassed the Japanese with rifle fire, but made no serious attempt to retake the positions that they had abandoned, before retiring to the *Mecklenburghaus*, a spa and sanatorium some seven kilometres along the pass.[84] Determined that there should be no repetition of this annoyance, the Japanese company advanced, reaching the *Mecklenburghaus* at around 5.30p.m. on 19

September, and began attacking the establishment, which comprised several buildings. As in the engagement the previous day the Germans withdrew before the enemy could come to close quarters with them, but not before firing the complex. As they retreated along the pass a twelve-metre bridge crossing a ravine was blown behind them in an attempt to impede Japanese exploitation. This action, resulting in only two wounded on the Japanese side, was the only significant exploit of the day, as, having successfully landed all the planned units, a period of consolidation was specified by Kamio, who had reached Tsimo the same day.[85] This consolidation involved the construction of landing piers at Wang-ko-chuang Bay to facilitate the landing of further personnel and equipment, and the construction of an airfield near Tsimo for the, eventual, five-aircraft complement of the Provisional Air Corps, which became operational on 21 September.[86]

The German response to the invasion was necessarily muted; they established a lookout position on Prinz-Heinrich-Berg on 22 September[87] and next day mounted a spoiling attack on a Japanese position in the Kletter Pass (*Kletterpass*) that dislodged the defenders but was not pursued.[88] Otherwise they largely drew back from the borders of the territory to the line flanked on the right by Prinz-Heinrich-Berg. This meant abandoning attempts to defend the eastern passes through the Laoshan Mountains; a decision of little consequence as Kamio did not intend to use them as the primary routes for his concentration.

Indeed, the Japanese had established divisional headquarters at Liu Ting and were building up men and supplies around that position ready for a forward move towards Litsun. In order to reach this point the troops and equipment had to travel some twenty-one kilometres from the landing area to Tsimo and then a further fourteen kilometres to Liu Ting. In order to facilitate this movement, particularly in relation to material, the construction of a Decauville Railway was undertaken.[89] The line was not used with locomotives; rather Chinese labourers manhandled the railway cars along the track. The track sections hooked together as they were laid, requiring only a relatively smooth trackbed that needed the minimum of preparation. A round trip from the beachhead to the main supply depot, soon to be located in a dry creek of the Litsun River, took four days.[90]

The Japanese were also joined by an Allied contingent dispatched by the British. This regular infantry unit, the 2nd Battalion The South Wales Borderers, was the direct counterpart of the German East Asiatic Marine Detachment, having comprised the British contingent at Tientsin under the terms of the Boxer Protocol of 1901.[91] The South Wales Borders travelled by sea, in order to avoid disputes with the Chinese government over neutrality, embarking at Tientsin on 19 September and proceeding via Weihaiwei where they took on stores. Escorted by *Triumph* and *Usk*, the 910 troops arrived at the landing place on 22 September and made arrangements to debark the following day. In command of the British contingent, which was due to be reinforced by a half-battalion (450 men) of the 36th Sikh Regiment, also stationed in China, was Brigadier-General Nathaniel Barnardiston. This 55-year-old General Officer Commanding North China, who had graduated from Staff College in 1888, had extensive experience in military-diplomatic/intelligence matters; he had occupied the post of military attaché at various European capitals and so was highly suited for conducting coalition warfare in a subordinate position.[92] That the British force was subsidiary to the Japanese, and not an independent command, had been made clear in August when the inclusion of a British military component had been decided; 'British troops are only engaged to show that England [sic] is cooperating with Japan in this enterprise.'[93] Accordingly Barnardiston became the first regular British military officer to serve under an Asian in a field command.

Upon landing, Barnardiston, obviously not cognisant with Lieutenant-General Kamio's planning and perhaps still retaining some thoughts of independence, sent an officer to reconnoitre the passes through the Laoshan Mountains. His rationale being that the British would operate on the left of the Japanese with their line of communication through the mountains to the beachhead. He was swiftly apprised of the difficulties: 'One of these roads was found to be quite unsuitable and the other only possible with a complete re-organisation of the transport, using pack mules or coolies over the worst parts of the Pass, and man-handling such carts as were necessary for use on the further side.'[94] His difficulties in this regard were alleviated when he learned on 25 September that his force was required to march, via Tsimo and Liu Ting, towards Litsun and take up a position in the centre of the Allied line. He also learned that Kamio planned to advance on 26–27 September with a view to attacking and taking the German advanced line on 29–30 September. This would enable the Japanese siege train to be brought up in order to reduce the Boxer Line fortifications.[95] The South Wales Borderers thus joined the rest of the debarked Japanese force in footslogging the *circa* thirty-five kilometres from the beachhead to Liu Ting along the only available, and extremely poor, track; it took two days to make the journey on foot.[96]

By the time the British infantry arrived at Liu Ting on 27 September, Kamio had departed on his move to Litsun. The movement had begun the day before with the Japanese 18th Division crossing the Pai-sha River in force, deploying four infantry regiments, the 46th and 55th (23rd Infantry Brigade) and the 56th and 48th (24th Infantry Brigade), arranged from east to west respectively. The 22nd Cavalry Regiment was on the right flank operating with 24th Infantry Brigade, while the 36 guns of 24th Field Artillery Regiment provided fire support to the movement.[97]

The German forces could do little to stop them, though as they advanced two naval vessels, *S-90* and *Jaguar*, moved into Kiautschou Bay and steamed north-wards in order to project enfilade fire onto the advance with their three 77.5mm and two 105mm guns respectively. To this was added that of the few field weapons possessed by the defenders, who were constantly worried that if they stood and fought the Japanese would fix them and then outflank them, particularly during the night. The Japanese progressed cautiously though steadily and by nightfall had covered some eight to ten kilometres, bringing the centre within two or three kilometres of Litsun. Several confused, but inconsequential, actions occurred through the night, leaving the 18th Division ready to resume its manoeuvres on the morning of 27 September. Meanwhile the defenders had began destroying installations prior to pulling back, the main item in this regard being the Litsun

Map 8. The Japanese Advance: September –November 1914

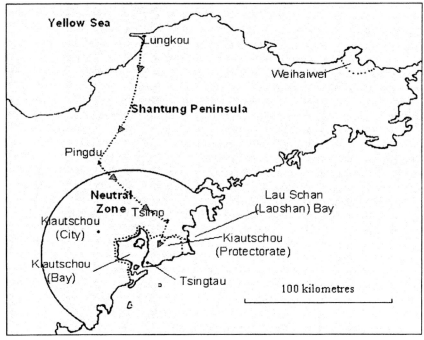

pumping station, which, utilising the nearby river, provided Tsingtau with its primary water supply.[98]

When the Allied advance resumed properly at first light on 27 September – some Japanese elements had started during darkness only to have to halt after becoming entangled with other units – the attackers discovered that the naval gunfire on their right flank had been significantly augmented. The Austro-Hungarian protected cruiser *Kaiserin Elisabeth*, despite having had two of her 150mm guns removed for land use on 24 August, had joined the two German vessels.[99] Her six remaining 150mm guns made a powerful reinforcement, and the Japanese took steps to mitigate the menace that these mobile floating batteries presented. The first attempts were revolutionary; three aircraft of the Provisional Air Corps went after them with bombs extemporised from artillery shells, thus carrying out the first ever air-sea attacks. Revolutionary they may have been, and persistent they certainly were, but they were also unsuccessful. Kamio thus directed one of the six-gun field batteries to target the ships but the land gunners had no more success.[100] Ominously for the defenders the first elements of the Japanese siege train, integrated as the 24th Artillery Brigade under Major-General Watanabe Kishinos, began to appear on the battlefield following its initial landing on 23 September.[101]

In a similar manner to their previous days' endeavours, the Japanese advance was unspectacular though certain, and likewise the defenders were only able to make limited counters through their fear of being overwhelmed by superior numbers. One advantage accruing to the defenders was that as the fighting moved closer to Tsingtau they would come within range of the fortress artillery mounted there. They also, in the observation post atop Prinz-Heinrich-Berg, had a superlative view of the battlefield. This meant they would be able to punish any large formations of Japanese, and, given that the attackers were advancing down a narrowing peninsula, then it might be reckoned that a degree of bunching was unavoidable. The Japanese answer to this potential difficulty was to take the observation post, which, in their hands, would also provide an outstanding view of Tsingtau and the defences. Accordingly, Kamio made its capture a priority and a reinforced company from the Japanese unit on the left of the German line, the 46th Infantry Regiment, together with a section from the 18th Engineer Battalion, was tasked with accomplishing this.[102]

The peak, which could only be reached after a 'long, arduous climb',[103] was accessible by at least two paths, and, astonishingly, these do not appear to have been guarded judging by the surprise occasioned to the observers by the appearance of the attackers on the morning of 28 September. The struggle for control of the post lasted several hours, the matter being settled by the appearance of attackers using the second path and appearing in the rear of the defenders. By noon, and at a cost of twenty-four men, the Japanese had stormed the position and captured most of the German personnel manning it.[104]

Japanese operations throughout 28 September involved consolidation and preparation as well as forward movement, which the Germans attempted to disrupt with artillery fire from their field guns. It might have been the presence of the first elements of 24th Artillery Brigade, which would eventually total more than 100 tubes of siege ordnance varying in calibre from 120mm to 280mm, that made itself felt with withering counter-battery fire that quickly silenced the German guns. In any event, this fire was greatly aided by the newly captured observation post on Prinz-Heinrich-Berg, which superseded to some extent the aircraft of the Provisional Air Corps in carrying out the necessary reconnaissance. The anti-ship artillery had also been reinforced, and this proceeded to direct heavy fire at *S-90*, *Jaguar* and *Kaiserin Elisabeth* when they made their appearances, at around 7.30a.m. In this instance however the ships got the better of the engagement, silencing the Japanese land batteries by about 9.30a.m. Despite this small victory the advance continued as previously, slowly but remorselessly, with the infantry making full use of the cover provided by the terrain. As they progressed the Tsingtau fortress artillery started to come into play, and both the Upper Iltis Hill and Bismarck Hill batteries fired their first shots in the half-hour from 9a.m.[105]

The Japanese were now encroaching upon the line dominated by Prinz-Heinrich-Berg, some eight to ten kilometres forward of the Boxer Line, and for the first time called in naval gunfire in support. Offshore four battleships, *Suwo*, *Tango*, *Iwami* and *Triumph*, steamed in at about 9a.m. and, with the cruiser *Tone* spotting, fired on the defences. These vessels between them deployed eight 305mm (12in., *Tango* and *Iwami*) and eight 254mm guns (10in., *Suwo* and *Triumph*) in respect of their main armament; a significant addition to the artillery already deployed ashore. The bombarding division made two runs, firing in total some 148 heavy shells. Opposed by the coastal artillery battery at Hui tsch'en Huk, which fired with increasing accuracy as the engagement progressed, the five Allied ships withdrew at around 10a.m.[106] Plüschow records that the bombardment, though impressive, did not cause much damage and that he saw to it that his aeroplane was moved into a les exposed position on the racecourse.[107]

A more significant naval operation took place at Schatsykou (Shazikou) Bay when a landing force from the armoured cruisers *Tokiwa* and *Yakumo*, took possession of the area – it had been evacuated the day previously after the German detachment there had become isolated by the advancing Japanese.[108] The bay was significant in that it offered a more direct land-line of communication than the Wang-ko-chuang–Litsun route.[109]

The German response to the advancing Japanese was as on previous days; they fought briefly then retreated. Indeed, this was the day when they moved back within the Boxer Line – the order to do so being issued at 11a.m. and the movement completed by mid-afternoon.[110] This then was their final position – they could not retreat any further and would have to fight or surrender. That they would engage in the former was certain, but that the latter was just as certain was acknowledged that evening by the scuttling of three of the disarmed gunboats – their weaponry had gone to the land defences – blockaded in the harbour; *Cormoran*, *Iltis* and *Luchs*.[111]

Since the first serious firefight on 18 September the Japanese had advanced in force some thirty-two kilometres (20 miles) while the attempts to impede them had been, of necessity, somewhat feeble. The Japanese operations had gone exactly to plan in terms of time, though had necessitated some logistical modification, as per the recall of the troops landed at Lungkou and their amphibious redeployment to Wang-ko-chuang. The Japanese rear had been secured by the seizure of the Shantung Railway by the 'Independent First battalion of Infantry' on 25 September, and the observation post atop Prinz-Heinrich-Berg was in their hands. On the same day a squadron of 22nd Cavalry Regiment took occupation of Kiautschou town, some 10 kilometres north of the northern shore of Kiautschou Bay and 40 kilometres west of Tsimo. This effectively prevented any communication with Tsingtau across the bay, and, in any event, the cavalry were now of less utility than previously. Having eschewed any attempt at storming the defences, the next operation undertaken by General Kamio and his 18th Division involved conducting a formal investment, an undertaking the Japanese Imperial Army had recent, and salutary, experience in.

9

Tsingtau
Naval and Military Operations
28 September – 7 November 1914

The Japanese Army was, in August 1914, the only modern force that had direct experience of conducting formal siege operations. This experience had been gained a decade earlier during the investment of Port Arthur, an almost isolated campaign of the Russo-Japanese War of 1904–5, by Japan's Third Army under General Nogi Maresuke. This operation had been accomplished once before by Nogi, on 21 November 1894, during the Sino-Japanese War. On that occasion, the 1st Infantry Brigade, with Nogi in command as a major-general, had successfully stormed the Chinese-held defences and taken occupation in only one day with minimal losses. His second attempt was not to be so easy, and the Third Army, initially comprising some 90,000 personnel, was engaged from 1 August 1904 to 2 January 1905, incurring massive casualties of around 55,000–60,000 in the process. Initially, Nogi had attempted to emulate his 1894 feat with attempts to penetrate the Russian-held defences by infantry assault; these were only called off on 24 August after some 16,000 men had been lost. Kamio and the Japanese Army did not intend to relearn the lesson, and, even if the defences of Tsingtau in 1914 in no way compared with those of Port Arthur in 1904, they were nevertheless treated with respect.[1]

Not only the lessons learned during the 1904–5 siege were used at Tsingtau in 1914; so were some of the key offensive weapons. In order to reduce the Port Arthur defences the Japanese had dismantled, shipped across the Yellow Sea, re-assembled, and emplaced several of their coast defence howitzers. These weapons, based on the Krupp 1892 model 280mm howitzer, had proved devastating and decisive – their use in the field had not previously been considered feasible – and once again they were removed from their normal positions around Tokyo Bay, Hiroshima, Yura and Shimonoseki and shipped to the battlefront. The deployment of such heavy ordnance, each piece weighed in at some 36 tonnes, could not though be accomplished quickly; therefore there was a lull in the advance whilst the Japanese made their preparations.

Other than awaiting the actions of their attackers, the only realistic measures the German and Austrian defenders could take was to use their artillery in an attempt to disrupt Japanese arrangements. One unrealistic measure was however attempted on the night of 2/3 October, when a 350-srong force equal

Map 9. Tsingtau: the Defences and the Siege 1914[1]

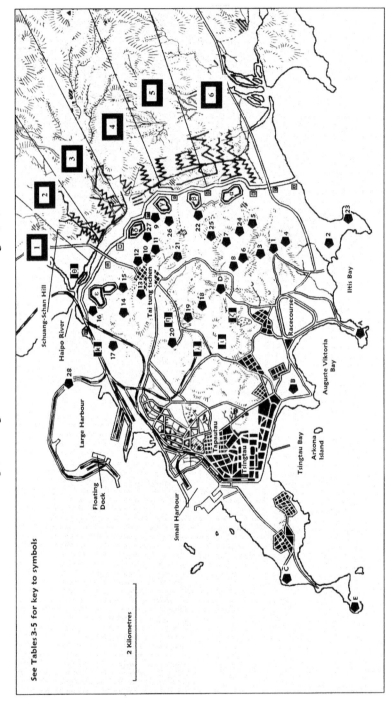

See Tables 3-5 for key to symbols

2 Kilometres

[1] This map is a synthesis derived from Kurt Aßmann, *Die Kämpfe der Kaiserlichen Marine in den deutschen Kolonien [The Struggle of the Imperial Navy in the German Colonies]* (Berlin; Mittler, 1935), and a 'Map of Tsingtau showing the Defences During the Siege' located at the UK National Archives, reference MPI 1/546/16.

Table 3
Tsingtau 1914: Coastal Artillery Batteries[1]

	Battery	Armament	Type of Mounting	Remarks
A	Hui tsch'en Huk	2x240mm	Mounted under Gruson turrets in concrete emplacements.	Ex Chinese weapons – obsolete. Manned by I Company Marine Artillery Detachment.
		3x150mm		Modern weapons mounted in turrets. Manned by I Company Marine Artillery Detachment.
B	Tsingtau	4x150 mm	Open pits.	Constructed by China pre 1897 – obsolete. Manned by IV Company Marine Artillery Detachment.
C	Hsiauniwa	4x210 mm	Under shields.	Krupp weapons removed from the Taku Forts after the Boxer War. Obsolete. Capable of land or sea service. Manned by II Company Marine Artillery Detachment.
D	Bismarck Hill	4x280 mm howitzers	Under shield in concrete emplacements with 360 degrees traverse.	Modern. Capable of land or sea service. Manned by III Company Marine Artillery Detachment. Situated atop the Bismarck Hill Command Complex.
E	Yunuisan	4x88mm Rapid Fire	Open pits	Obsolete weapons. Manned by II Company Marine Artillery Detachment.

[1] Information taken from: National Archives MPI 1/546/3 'China: Tsingtao'. A 'Point of Aim' chart, showing part of the coast and defences.' Charles B Burdick, *The Japanese Siege of Tsingtau* (Hamden, CT; Archon, 1976) pp. 21, 22, 24, 43. Kurt Assmann, *Die Kämpfe der Kaiserlichen Marine in den deutschen Kolonien* [*The Struggle of the Imperial Navy in the German Colonies*] (Berlin; Mittler, 1935) pp. 108–9. Map of Tsingtau showing the Defences During the Siege' located at the UK National Archives, reference MPI 1/546/16. Information from Dennis and Adrienne Quarmby. Captain Bernard Smith, 'The Siege of Tsingtau' in *The Coast Artillery Journal*, November-December 1934, pp. 405–419. Commander Charles B Robbins, 'German Seacoast Defences at Tsingtao, 1914' in *The Coast Defence Journal*, May 2007, pp. 85–90. Philip Sims, 'German Tsingtao Mounts Photographs' in *The Coast Defence Journal*, November 2006. For an overview of the territory and the defences see: Jork Artelt, *Tsingtau: Deutsche Stadt und Festung 1897–1914* [*Tsingtau: German city and fortress 1897–1914*] (Duesseldorf; Droste, 1984)

Table 4. Tsingtau 1914: Land Artillery Batteries[1]

	Battery	Armament	Remarks
1	Battery No 1	6x90mm	
2	Battery No 1a	2x50mm	
3	Battery No 1b	2x88mm	
4	Battery No 2	7x37mm	Maxim-Nordenfeldt 'pom-poms'
5	Battery No 2a	4x37mm	Maxim-Nordenfeldt 'pom-poms'
6	Punktkuppe	4x60mm	Removed from gunboats.
7	Lower Iltis Hill	6x120mm	
8	Upper Iltis Hill	2x105mm	On fixed mountings with shields.
9	Battery No 5[2]	4x37mm	Maxim-Nordenfeldt 'pom-poms'
10	Battery No 6	6x120mm	Field Guns.
11	Battery No 6a	2x47mm	Removed from *Kaiserin Elisabeth*.
12	Battery No 7[3]	6x90mm	Field Guns.
13	Battery No 8	2x47mm	Removed from *Kaiserin Elisabeth*.
14	Battery No 8a	2x47mm	Removed from *Kaiserin Elisabeth*.
15	Battery No 9	4x37mm	Maxim-Nordenfeldt 'pom-poms'
16	Battery No 10	4x37mm	Maxim-Nordenfeldt 'pom-poms'
17	Battery No 11[4]	6x90mm	Field Guns.
18	Battery No 12 (Lower Bismarck Hill)	2x210mm	Fixed mountings; unshielded.
19	Battery No 13	4x88mm	
20	Battery No 14 (Moltke Hill)	4x88mm	
21	Battery No 15	2x150mm	Removed from *Kaiserin Elisabeth*.
22	Howitzer Battery	3x150mm	Field Howitzers.
23	Intermediate Battery No 1	2x88mm	Field Guns.
24	Intermediate Battery No 1a	2x77mm	Field Guns.
25	Intermediate Battery No 2	2x77mm	Field Guns.
26	Intermediate Battery No 3	2x77mm	Field Guns.
27	Intermediate Battery No 3a	2x77mm	Field Guns.
28	Intermediate Battery No 4	2x88mm	Mounted on railway truck.

[1] This table is a synthesis of the details that appeared in Kurt Aßmann, *Die Kämpfe der Kaiserlichen Marine in den deutschen Kolonien [The Struggle of the Imperial Navy in the German Colonies]* (Berlin; Mittler, 1935) pp. 108–9, and, a 'Map of Tsingtau showing the Defences During the Siege' located at the UK National Archives, reference MPI 1/546/16. According to an added inscription, 'The original of this map was taken from a German artillery officer, now a prisoner of war in Hong Kong.' The shaded portions indicate batteries that were in existence prior to the outbreak of hostilities.

[2] Aßmann states that there was also a Battery No 4 equipped with 2x37mm machine guns.

[3] Aßmann divides these weapons between Batteries 7 and 7a.

[4] Aßmann divides these weapons between Batteries 11 and 11a.

Table 5. Tsingtau 1914: Defence and Other Works

α	Infantry Work 1
β	Infantry Work 2
γ	Infantry Work 3
δ	Infantry Work 4
ε	Infantry Work 5
回	Blockhouses
ζ	Bismarck Barracks
η	Moltke Barracks
θ	Water Works and Pumping Station.
ι	Diederichs Hill Signal Station
k	Oil Tanks
λ	Artillery Depot

Japanese and British Units

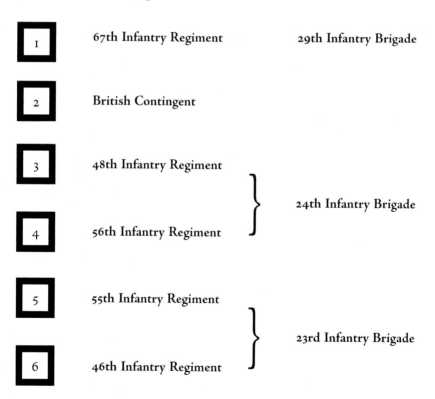

1	67th Infantry Regiment	29th Infantry Brigade
2	British Contingent	
3	48th Infantry Regiment	
4	56th Infantry Regiment	24th Infantry Brigade
5	55th Infantry Regiment	
6	46th Infantry Regiment	23rd Infantry Brigade

to three companies, mainly composed of personnel from the East Asiatic Marine Detachment, set out at 9p.m. on a foray against a Japanese position on Schuang-Schan Hill on the far left of the German front. This was pursuant to intelligence received from a reconnaissance carried out on the night of 29 September, when some twenty men had advanced from Infantry Work 5, past the pumping station and across the Haipo River, 'a small stream running over a broad bed of sand',[2] and scouted the hill. They discovered that a platoon-strength unit was deployed there, about a kilometre in advance of the Boxer Line. The manoeuvre was coordinated with artillery fire, from both land batteries, *Jaguar* and *Kaiserin Elisabeth*, which started an hour before the troops advanced. The barrage was intended to isolate the hill from the Japanese main force preventing any interference from that quarter. With one company held in reserve, the German force moved into the darkness and divided, intending to approach the target from left and right. Within twenty minutes the operation was a shambles; the members of the right-hand column lost their bearings and, in talking and using flashlights, betrayed their presence. Enemy fire from rifles and machine guns was directed at them, and misdirected friendly fire, from the 37mm Maxim-Nordenfeldt 'pom-poms' in the Infantry Work, also took a toll.

The left-hand Marine column was more careful, or had more luck, and reached the objective unobserved; there were no enemy there as they had been drawn away by the firefight to their left. However, when the German Marines drew attention to their presence, fire began to be directed towards them indicating that the position was not free of Japanese. Schuang-Schan Hill was by this time well illuminated by flares and the glare of searchlights (*scheinwerfer*) directed from within the German lines, which did not help the infiltrators who perceived themselves to be in difficulties. Accordingly the order was given to withdraw and all those that could had returned to the German lines by 01.00hrs on 3 October. Stragglers continued to appear for the next day or so, but the final account reckoned that thirty-five failed to return – a loss rate of some ten per cent for no gain.[3]

Even if one attempts to discount the inestimable benefit of hindsight, the rationale behind the foray remains elusive. It was, in all likelihood, similar to that which lay behind the 'trench-raid' attitude developing at the same time on the Western Front in France; it maintained the 'illusion of an offensive posture'.[4] When not pursued for a specific purpose, such ventures were carried out to foster 'soldierly spirit' and 'maintain morale'.[5] Just whose morale was maintained is a difficult question to answer, but it probably was not that of those who had to carry out the activity.

The aftermath of the raid convinced the defenders that their artillery was indeed the only means of carrying the war to the Japanese.[6] Spotting for this was however problematical, particularly after the loss of Prinz-Heinrich-Berg. One less than perfect option was to use the naval vessels in Kiautschou Bay, which could at least get behind the Japanese line and perhaps spot, though only from the left flank, targets of opportunity. Not only could the vessels fire upon such targets themselves, but also they could coordinate the fire of the fortress guns. *Kaiserin Elisabeth* and *S-90*, with the gunboat *Jaguar* coordinating, had undertaken just such a mission on 30 September, and it was deemed a success as the ships were able to silence several batteries that shelled them by counter-battery fire. Some intelligence was also gained, that the British contingent had joined the Japanese being an example.

Similar missions, including support for the 2 October raid, continued until 4 October, when, on that day, the Japanese made a concerted effort to destroy *Jaguar*. The attacks started at dawn with four aeroplanes unsuccessfully bombarding the vessel, followed up by a concerted artillery effort as she made her way to the Japanese flank, causing the ship, though undamaged, to retire briefly from the action and request support from the land artillery. As the German guns shelled the reported positions, the 1,031-ton *Jaguar* once again forayed into the bay, only to be once again targeted and forced to retire. Returning for the third time proved to be an error; once again a concerted effort was made to hit the 65-metre ship – this time with success. A shell hit the bow, fortunately above the waterline, creating a large hole in the ship's side and forcing an immediate withdrawal – venturing into Kiautschou Bay could clearly no longer be considered a feasible proposition.[7]

Reconnaissance duties devolved then on to the air component, represented by Plüschow and his Taube. There was also a balloon detachment consisting of two observation-balloon envelopes and the necessary ground infrastructure.[8] The German observation balloons of 1914 were known as *Drachen*, a name commonly adopted for all sausage-shaped kite-balloons, and had been developed by Parseval-Sigsfeld.[9] Adopted for use in 1893 they represented a significant investment in terms of equipment and manpower for the Tsingtau garrison, the standardised balloon section in 1914 consisting of 1 balloon (plus 1 spare envelope), 4 observers, 177 enlisted ranks, 123 horses, 12 gas wagons, 2 equipment wagons, 1 winch wagon and 1 telephone wagon.[10] The balloon had made several ascents from Tsingtau during the fighting, but the observer had been unable to see anything of value. In order to attempt to remedy this the device was moved closer to the front and another ascent made on 5 October. It was to be the last such, as the Japanese artillery immediately found its range with shrapnel shell and holed it in several places.[11] A ruse involving the spare balloon was then tried; it was sent up to draw the attackers' fire and so reveal the position of their guns. According to Alfred Brace:

> It contained a dummy looking fixedly at the landscape below through a pair of paste-board glasses. But there happened to arise a strong wind which set the balloon revolving and finally broke it loose and sent it pirouetting off over the Yellow Sea, the whole exploit, I learned afterwards, being a great puzzle to the British and Japanese observers outside.[12]

Plüschow flew reconnaissance flights every day that the weather, and his propeller, permitted, sketching the enemy positions and making detailed notes. He achieved this by setting the engine so as to maintain a safe altitude of over 2,000 metres, and then steering with his feet, the Taube had no rudder and horizontal control was achieved by warping the wings, while peering over the side of his cockpit. Photographs exist of extemporised Japanese anti-aircraft-artillery – the necessary high angle of fire achieved by dropping the long trail into a pit behind the gun – and although this was not accurate it was deemed by Plüschow to be nevertheless troublesome.[13] Where he was at his most vulnerable was on landing, and a battery of Japanese artillery was tasked specifically with destroying the Taube as it descended to the racecourse, which of course was a fixed point at a known range. Little more than good luck, and what he called 'ruses' such as shutting off the engine and swooping sharply to earth, saw him through these experiences, but remarkably both man and machine came through without serious injury.[14]

Whatever inconveniences Plüschow and the fortress artillery might inflict upon the force massing to their front, they could do nothing to prevent the landing of men and materiel at Wang-ko-chuang and Schatsykou bays, nor could they prevent the deployment of these once landed. The previous efforts by the navy in terms of mine-laying did though still pay dividends, as when the Japanese 'aircraft carrier' was badly damaged. As the report from the British Naval Attaché to Japan put it in his report of 30 November:

> [...] a few minutes after 8 a.m. [on 30 September] the 'Wakamiya Maru' struck a mine in the entrance of Lo Shan Harbour, and had to be beached to prevent her sinking; her engines were disabled owing to breaking of steam pipes, No. 3 hold full, and one man killed - fortunately no damage done to aeroplanes though it is feared that a spare engine may be injured. [...] As the Aeroplane establishment is all being moved ashore at this place this accident will not affect the efficiency of the Aeroplane Corps.[15]

Though the ship was saved, and the efficiency of the flying component was not affected, two more Japanese vessels were sunk on the same day – albeit they were only trawlers used for minesweeping and the like. The Japanese suspected that Chinese vessels in the vicinity were laying mines; accordingly they sank them.[16]

There was however nothing, in the past, the present or the immediate future, that either the Germans or the Chinese could do, or have done, about another aspect of the Japanese presence – their seizure of the Shantung Railway. Control of the line had been effectively in Japanese hands since 17 September when a detachment of cavalry had entered Kiautschou town, and on 23 September Kamio had assigned a larger unit, the Independent First Battalion of Infantry, to ensure greater control. The impetus behind this manoeuvre was not military, but rather political, and to ensure that the line remained in Japanese hands further reinforcements were despatched from Japan in the shape of the 29th Infantry Brigade under Major General Johoji Goro. The brigade, which landed on 10 October, was somewhat under strength (while its 67th Infantry Regiment comprised three battalions, the 34th Infantry Regiment had only one). Kamio directed the 67th Regiment to take up position on the right of his line, while the single battalion of 34th Regiment went to the railway.[17] The political aim behind the increased presence on the railway was, via military occupation, to utilise this primary means of communication, which was economically vital, in order to dominate the whole of Shantung Province.[18]

Kamio sought to avoid casualties among his force, and, despite the defenders belief to the contrary, was largely successful in this. The Japanese had adopted what was in certain quarters termed 'mole warfare' in front of Port Arthur, and the same technique, albeit on a greatly reduced scale, was to be put into practice before Tsingtau, as it was beginning to be, though unplanned, in Northern France.[19] Kamio's operational orders were issued on 7 October, and they harked back to 1904–5, or indeed to Marshal Vauban's seventeenth/eighteenth century fortress-warfare manuals, in their prescriptive nature. Some one to two kilometres in front of the Boxer Line the Japanese would establish an advanced investment line, digging in securely and ensuring that it was proof against any German foray. Behind this line the artillery, including the siege train under Major General Watanabe Kishinos, would deploy, and when this had been positioned, and sufficient munitions brought up, the bombardment would begin. This bombardment would be coordinated with a similar effort from the naval forces, thus Tsingtau would be caught between two fires.

The object of the combined bombardment would be the destruction of the Central Powers' artillery including, if at all possible, that mounted on naval vessels, and the reduction of the Boxer Line. Only when the Japanese artillery had begun suppressing the defences and reducing their power to intervene would the infantry advance, along saps dug for the purpose, and construct the first parallel. From there, and still under the protection of the bombardment, further saps would be advanced towards the enemy and a second parallel constructed. These trenches would be constructed so as to be at least two metres wide, well protected against enfilade fire and shell burst by following a zigzag pattern, and have overhead cover. A third parallel would then be constructed, at which time the infantry would be hard up against the enemy main positions and at a point where a breach of their line could take place and an assault launched.[20]

The prerequisite was the siege artillery, and the effort to position this was to absorb a great deal of time and effort. The time was of relatively little import and a good deal of the effort was provided by Chinese labour. The largest pieces of ordnance were the 280mm coast defence howitzers, and these were transferred, broken down into their component parts, from the beachhead via the light railway utilising several score Chinese in lieu of mechanical power. The Chinese also provided porterage for the less heavy supplies and their one-wheeled barrows, simultaneously pushed and pulled by a two-man team, proved, as might be expected from an indigenously developed device, highly efficient at moving loads weighing up to 150kg along the rudimentary roads. It is impossible to calculate how many Chinese were involved in the operations at Tsingtau, how they were recruited and paid, and their casualty rate. It is though fair to conclude that without their participation the campaign could not have progressed as expeditiously as it did.[21]

In order to gain detailed knowledge of the defences the Japanese naval and army air components were used to fly reconnaissance missions over the German positions. They also flew bombing missions, which caused little damage, and attempted to discourage their single aerial opponent from emulating them. Plüschow records that he was provided with extemporised 'bombs' made of tin boxes filled with dynamite and improvised shrapnel, but that these devices were largely ineffectual. He claimed to have hit a Japanese vessel with one, which failed to explode, and to have succeeded in killing thirty soldiers with another one that did.[22] It was during this period that the German naval flier became engaged in air-to-air combat, of a type, with the enemy aeroplanes, thus chalking up another aviation first in East Asia. Indeed, if Plüschow is to be believed, he succeeded in shooting down one of the Japanese aeroplanes with his pistol, having fired thirty shots.[23] It would appear however that even if he did engage in aerial jousting of the kind he mentions the result was not as he claimed; no Japanese aircraft were lost during the campaign. The Japanese did however do their utmost to prevent him reconnoitring their positions, as they were in the process of emplacing the siege batteries and, if the positions became known, they could expect intense efforts from the defenders to disrupt this process. Indeed, General Watanabe insisted that his batteries were emplaced during the hours of darkness, despite the inconvenience this caused, and carefully camouflaged to prevent discovery.[24]

That the threat from Plüschow, albeit indirect, was very real had been illustrated on 29 September; he had overflown an area where the British were camped and noted their tents, which were of a different pattern to the Japanese versions. This had resulted in heavy shelling, causing the camp to be moved the next day to the reverse slopes of a hill about 900 yards (1.5km) east of the former position.[25] He also posed a direct threat though perhaps of lesser import; on 10 October the Taube pilot dropped one of his homemade bombs on the British. It failed to explode, but the South Wales Borderers moved position immediately – such an option was not available to 36- tonne howitzers that required semi-permanent emplacement.[26]

The ability of the German artillery to disrupt his preparations, and the relative inability to reply – the Japanese did not wish to give away the positions of their siege batteries by using them prematurely – caused General Kamio to ask for naval support. Admiral Kato however proved reluctant to hazard his vessels by moving into waters that might contain mines, and where they could come under the fire of the coastal artillery at Hui tsch'en Huk. On 6 October, under prodding from his military counterpart, Kato did detail two battleships, *Suwo* and HMS *Triumph,* to shell the Iltis Battery but, in an effort to stay out of harm's way, the pre-dreadnoughts remained out of effective range and their bombardment fell short. The *Suwo* was sent in alone to try again on 10 October, but again did not press the matter and withdrew in the face of the perceived danger.

A more powerful effort was mounted on 14 October, with *Suwo, Tango* and *Triumph* deployed. On this occasion the *Suwo,* was detailed to engage Hui tsch'en Huk, and listed so as to improve the elevation of her guns and thus increase range. The German battery was engaged at 9a.m. from 15,750 metres and was unable to effectively reply with *Suwo* out of range. While Hui tsch'en Huk was engaged with *Suwo* the other battleships moved in closer to bombard the Iltis Battery, but the coastal artillery shifted fire onto *Tango,* which was within range. No hits were made, but the ship withdrew, while *Triumph* moved into a position to attack the battery and slightly before 10a.m. fired some 30 shells. Shortly after that time the ship prepared to move off, and as she did so a 150mm shell from Hui tsch'en Huk hit the mainmast. Little major damage was caused, the ship was ready for action again in two days, and the casualties amounted to one killed and two wounded, but it ensured that Kato would be cautious in hazarding his heavy ships again. In a like manner the bombardment caused only minor damage to the defences. The Iltis battery was not put out of action, nor was Hui tsch'en Huk, and the shells that landed on the main defence line did no major harm.[27]

On 13 October meanwhile a truce that the two sides had agreed, in order that non-combatants might be evacuated from Tsingtau, came into force. Kamio had proposed this on 4 October, but Barnardiston, who felt that he should have been consulted on the proposal, had initiated a bout of political wrangling over the matter. The answer, though not swift was thorough; the British general was informed on 12 October that he was subordinate to Kamio. Thereafter the matter progressed smoothly and the mail steamer *Tsimo*, formerly *Rauenthaler*, conveyed various civilians, neutrals and other non-combatants, to Taputou, the port of Kiautschou town, across the bay.[28]

Perhaps Barnardiston was concerned more with form than substance, because the British contingent, following orders issued by Kamio on 10 October, had taken their place in the line of investment by the 15th. This ran, more or less parallel with the Boxer Line, from Kiautschou Bay on the right to Prinz-Heinrich-Berg on the left. They had been assigned a frontage of around 550 yards (half a kilometre), and on their right, between them and Kiautschou Bay, was the recently arrived Japanese 67th Regiment. The terrain along the line was eminently suitable for an attacking force, being intersected by numerous deep ravines of clay 'excellent for protection and accommodation in dry weather'.[29] Unfortunately for the attackers though, 15 October was the date on which the heavy rain resumed, and this caused havoc in the line. The sides of the ravines collapsed, carrying away the troops' shelter, and their floors became rivers, making it impossible for the besiegers to find cover from either enemy fire or the weather. The roads and tracks turned into a morass of liquefied mud often knee-deep, preventing supplies and reinforcements from moving forward, and much equipment already in position was buried by falling earth or corroded by the waterlogged state of the ground. The troops simply had to sit it out, remaining soaked through until the downpour abated. The situation was, if anything, even more serious in the rear areas; the main supply depot had been located in a dry creek of the Litsun River, which was suddenly dry no more. Almost the entire contents, or at least all that would float, was washed into Kiautschou Bay while that which remained was submerged in mud and water. The light railway also failed, with large sections of track undermined or washed away completely. This unexpected downfall lasted two days, during which all preparations for an attack were halted.[30]

The weather moderated on 17 October and allowed the besiegers to begin sorting out their positions and equipment, a tedious and time-consuming business particularly as the German artillery continued with its harassing fire. The defenders had hatched a plan for discomfiting the enemy even further though, and as darkness descended on the evening of the 17th they put it into effect. The

388-ton *S-90*, crewed by 60 men under Leutnant Helmut Brunner, slipped out of her berth and headed for the mouth of Kiautschou Bay. Once out of the bay the turbine-powered torpedo boat destroyer would prowl around and tackle any targets of opportunity that might reveal themselves. It was, apparently, a fruitless exercise until midnight when Brunner began heading back to Kiautschou Bay, and noticed a blacked-out vessel on an opposite course. She could only be an enemy ship, so he turned to the attack and launched three 450mm (18in.) torpedoes at the target from some 500 metres. Two of the weapons struck home, the second causing a massive explosion that completely destroyed the vessel. His target turned out to be the British-built *Naniwa*-class protected cruiser *Takachiho* (1885); redesignated a second-class coastal defence ship in 1912 the 3,650-ton ship had then been converted to a minelayer. On the night of the 17 October she was carrying a large quantity of munitions and it was this ordnance that caused the massive explosion, completely destroying the ship and, aside from three survivors, 271 of her crew – the biggest single loss of life suffered by Japan during the Great War.[31]

It was, in the grand scheme of things, a relatively minor blow, but to Admiral Kato and his command it was stunning, and further compounded by a lack of knowledge regarding the whereabouts of *S-90*. Until this could be ascertained with certainty all shipping movements were suspended and sweeps conducted in search of the predator, as reconnaissance flights over Tsingtau and Kiautschou Bay were unable to ascertain the presence or otherwise of the torpedo boat with any degree of certitude. In fact, Brunner had opted not to return to his base after making the attack, reasoning that the enemy would be out in force and he would be unable to avoid detection. Plüschow records a radio message being received at 1.30a.m. on 18 October: 'Am hunted by Torpedo Boat Destroyers, return Kiautschou cut off, trying escape south and shall destroy boat if necessary.'[32]

Whether Plüschow's recollection is entirely accurate, or he was writing with the benefit of hindsight, is arguable, but in any event Brunner did indeed steer a course south along the Chinese coast and beached *S-90* before setting off on foot. The vessel was discovered two days later and a cavalry unit sent to investigate. The craft had been destroyed, but of the 60-man crew there was no sign, and it seems the Japanese found some useful paperwork in the wreck. The most useful information though was of course that *S-90* was no longer in play and naval operations could resume. They were though conducted under a much stricter regime henceforth.[33]

For the defenders the exploits of *S-90* proved morale boosting, though irrelevant to the situation in general. Indeed, though they were probably unaware of the fact, the reinforcement for the British contingent, the men of the 36th Sikhs, arrived at the beachhead on 22 October and proceeded, with difficulty given the poor state of the roads following the recent rain, to their place with Barnardiston's command - arriving on 28 October.[34] By then the Japanese were nearly ready to begin the final stages of their investment. Watanabe reckoned that he was ready to proceed with issuing his fire plan to his siege batteries on 27 October, even though the communications system was not complete. The primary artillery observation post was situated on Price-Heinrich-Berg and telephone lines, five in number for inbuilt redundancy, had to be relayed to each of the batteries and positions. This post also had radio communication with Kato's command at sea. The plan contained few surprises; the first priority was the German artillery, both that on land and at sea. When these had been dealt with the barrage would shift to the installations in the Boxer Line, and following that to the German rear areas. There would be enough ammunition for a ten-day bombardment, but it was anticipated that the process would only take seven days before the defenders were forced to capitulate. There would be no artillery registration before the main barrage commenced, and ranges would only be adjusted then. By 29 October the siege artillery was emplaced satisfactorily and all supporting services were functioning; Watanabe was ready to deliver an overwhelming weight of ordnance onto the Tsingtau defences.[35]

The Japanese Second Squadron began sending in ships to shell the city and defences again. On 25 October the battleship *Iwami* approached, though staying outside the range of Hui tsch'en Huk. By listing the ship to increase the range of her main armament, *Iwami* was able to fire some thirty 305mm (12in.) shells at Hui tsch'en Huk, Iltis Battery and Infantry Work I. The next day the vessel returned in company with *Suwo* and the two former Tsarist capital ships bombarded the same targets. On 27 October *Tango* and *Okinoshima* replaced them, and the same ships returned the next day to continue the assault. Because of the distance involved, some 14.5 kilometres (7.82 standard nautical miles) this fire was inaccurate in terms of damaging the specific installations in question, but nevertheless was destructive of the nerves of the trapped garrison. It was particularly frustrating in terms of the gunners at Hui tsch'en Huk who were unable to effectively reply.[36]

In addition to this display of naval force, Japanese air power had been much in evidence over the period, their operational activity increasing with sorties over the German lines and rear areas.

Almost every day these craft, announcing their approach by a distant humming, came overhead, glinting and shining in the sun as they sailed above the forts and city. At first they were greeted by a fusillade of shots from all parts of the garrison. Machine guns pumped bullets a hundred a minute at them and every man with a rifle handy let fire. As these bullets came raining back upon the city without any effect but to send Chinese coolies scampering under cover, it was soon realised that rifle and machine-gun fire was altogether ineffective. Then special guns were rigged and the aeroplanes were subjected to shrapnel, which seemed to come nearer to its sailing mark each day but which never brought one of the daring bird-men down. One day I saw a biplane drop down a notch after a shell had exploded directly in front of it. I looked for a volplane[37] to earth, but the aviator's loss of control was only momentary, evidently caused by the disturbance of the air. During the bombardment these craft circled over the forts like birds of prey. They were constantly dropping bombs, trying to hit the ammunition depots, the signal station, the Austrian cruiser *Kaiserin Elisabeth*, the electric light plant, and the forts. But [...] these bombs were not accurate or powerful enough to do much damage. A few Chinese were killed, a German soldier wounded, tops of houses knocked in, and holes gouged in the streets, but that was all. The bombs fell with an ominous swish as of escaping steam, and it was decidedly uncomfortable to be in the open with a Japanese aeroplane overhead. We are more or less like the ostrich who finds peace and comfort with his head in the sand: In the streets of Tsingtau I have seen a man pull the top of a jinrickisha[38] over his head on the approach of a hostile aeroplane and have noticed Chinese clustering under the top of a tree.[39]

They also managed another East Asian first on the night of 28/29 October when they bombed the defenders' positions during the hours of darkness. Attempts to keep Plüschow from effectively reconnoitring were largely successful, even though the efforts to dispose of him or his machine permanently were ineffective. However, because problems with the Taube's homemade propeller kept him grounded on occasion, and because the Japanese positions were worked on tirelessly, when he did take to the air he found the changes in the enemy arrangements – 'this tangle of trenches, zigzags and new positions' – somewhat bewildering and difficult to record accurately.[40] Precision in this regard was not assisted by the Japanese fliers' attempts to shoot him down or otherwise obstruct him.

The artillery coordinating position on Prinz-Heinrich-Berg reported itself ready for action on 29 October and Kato sent four battleships in to continue the naval bombardment while acting under its direction. Between 9.30a.m. and 4.30p.m. *Suwo, Tango, Okinoshima* and *Triumph* bombarded the Tsingtau defences, adjusting their aim according to the feedback received from the observation position via radio. They withdrew after discharging some 197 projectiles from their fifteen main guns, following which the gunboat SMS *Tiger*, was scuttled during the hours of darkness.[41]

Plüschow managed to get airborne on the morning of 30 October and was able to over-fly the Japanese positions before the enemy air force could rise to deter him. He was able to report the large scale and advanced preparations of the besieging force, information that the defence used to direct its artillery fire. This was repaid when Kato's bombarding division returned at 9a.m. to resume their previous day's work. Despite the communication channel working perfectly, and the absence of effective return fire from Hui tsch'en Huk – the ships had established the maximum range of this battery was 14.13 kilometres and accordingly stayed just beyond its reach – the firing of 240 heavy shells again did little damage.[42]

Saturday 31 October was, as the defenders knew well, the birthday of the Japanese Emperor and by way of celebration Kamio's command undertook a brief ceremony before, at about 6a.m., Watanabe gave the order for the siege train to begin firing, or, as one of the correspondents of *The Times* put it: 'daylight saw the royal salute being fired with live shell at Tsingtau'.[43] There were, roughly, 23 Japanese artillery tubes per kilometre of front, a density that was comparable to that attained during the initial stages of the war on the Western Front, though soon to be dwarfed as artillery assumed the dominant role in positional warfare.[44] The land-based artillery was augmented, from about 9p.m., by the naval contribution as Kato once again sent his heavy ships into action.

The combined barrage soon silenced any German return fire because, even though they had refrained from pre-registering their siege batteries, the Japanese knew where the fixed defensive positions were and shortly found their range; fire was also brought to bear on any targets of opportunity. The German batteries were suppressed less by direct hits than by their positions being submerged in debris from near misses. This was to prove of some importance for the defenders were able in several cases to return their weapons to service, largely due to the relative antiquity and thus lack of sophistication of much of the ordnance, without the need for extensive repairs.[45] Indeed, despite the crushing superiority enjoyed by the attackers, the defensive fire was to continue to some degree throughout the day and into the night. The most obvious sign of the effects of the bombardment, at least to those observing from a distance, were the huge plumes of smoke caused by hits on the oil storage tanks adjacent to the Large Harbour. Two of these, owned by the Asiatic Petroleum Company – the first Royal Dutch/Shell joint venture – and Standard Oil respectively, had been set afire early on and their contents in turn caused other fires as they flowed around the installations, these proving beyond the capacity of the local fire-brigade to control.[46]

There were independent observers of the operations at this stage; correspondents from various journals and foreign military observers had arrived in the theatre in late October. Though the Japanese were intensely secretive they could not conceal the fact of their bombardment or the plainly visible results.

> The thunder of the great guns broke suddenly upon that stillness which only dawn knows, and their discharges flashed readily on the darkling slopes. The Japanese shooting, it is related, displayed remarkable accuracy, some of the first projectiles bursting upon the enormous oil tanks of the Standard Oil Company and the Asiatic Petroleum Company. A blaze roared skywards, and for many hours the heavens were darkened by an immense cloud of black petroleum smoke which hung like a pall over the town. Shells passing over these fires drew up columns of flame to a great height. Chinese coolies could be seen running before the spreading and burning oil. Fires broke out also on the wharves of the outer harbour.[47]

Many of the Japanese shells, no doubt due to the lack of pre-registration, were over-range and landed in Tapautau and Tsingtau, though the former received the worst of it. It has been estimated that at least hundred Chinese were killed during this period and a deliberate targeting exercise carried out later in the day on the urban areas.[48] The bombardment continued with varying levels of frequency throughout the daylight hours of 31 October, and at nightfall the Japanese gunners switched to shrapnel – by bursting shrapnel shell over the defenders' positions they made it difficult, if not impossible, for repairs to be carried out. Such fire also covered the forward movement of the Japanese engineers as they extended their saps towards the Boxer Line and began constructing the second parallel some 300 metres in advance of the advanced investment line.[49]

At daylight on 1 November the high-explosive barrage resumed, again concentrating primarily on the German artillery positions though many of these were now out of action. The secondary targets were the defences in the Boxer Line,

Table 6. Japanese Army Order of Battle – November 1914[1]

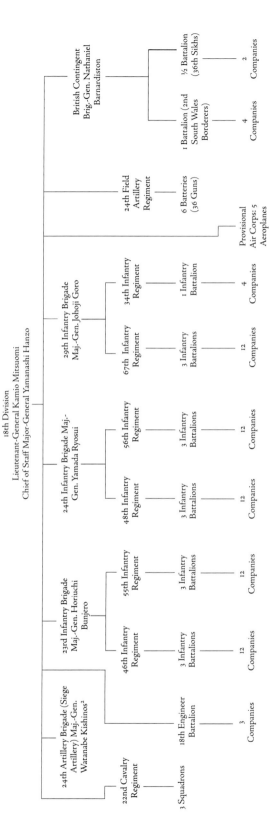

18th Division
Lieutenant-General Kamio Mitsuomi
Chief of Staff Major-General Yamanashi Hanzo

- 24th Artillery Brigade (Siege Artillery) Maj.-Gen. Watanabe Kishinos[2]
- 22nd Cavalry Regiment — 3 Squadrons
- 18th Engineer Battalion — 3 Companies
- 23rd Infantry Brigade Maj.-Gen. Horiuchi Bunjero
  - 46th Infantry Regiment — 3 Infantry Battalions — 12 Companies
  - 55th Infantry Regiment — 3 Infantry Battalions — 12 Companies
- 24th Infantry Brigade Maj.-Gen. Yamada Ryosui
  - 48th Infantry Regiment — 3 Infantry Battalions — 12 Companies
  - 56th Infantry Regiment — 3 Infantry Battalions — 12 Companies
- 29th Infantry Brigade Maj.-Gen. Johoji Goro
  - 67th Infantry Regiment — 3 Infantry Battalions — 12 Companies
  - 34th Infantry Regiment — 1 Infantry Battalion — 4 Companies
- Provisional Air Corps: 5 Aeroplanes
- 24th Field Artillery Regiment — 6 Batteries (36 Guns)
- British Contingent Brig.-Gen. Nathaniel Barnardiston
  - 1 Battalion (2nd South Wales Borderers) — 4 Companies
  - ½ Battalion (36th Sikhs) — 2 Companies

1 Not including non-combat units such as Pioneers, Medical Services etc., or the 'Independent First battalion of Infantry' under Major Kanazawa, which occupied the Shantung Railroad from 25 September 1914.

2 Included in this complement were detachments from the heavy artillery regiments that formed the coastal defences around strategic points on the Japanese main islands. These included elements from the Yokosuka Regiment, usually found protecting Tokyo Bay, and the Tadanoumi Regiment from Hiroshima, as well as units that, as a rule, defended Yura and Shimonoseki. Watanabe thus disposed of an immensely powerful unit with over 100 tubes ranging in calibre from 120mm to the 280mm of the coastal artillery pieces. See: Spencer C Tucker, *The Great War 1914–18* (Bloomington IN; Indiana University Press, 1999) p. 196; Katsuji Inahara, *The Japan Year Book* (Tokyo: The Foreign Affairs Association of Japan, 1933) pp. 235–7; Gōtarō Ogawa and Yasuma Takata, *Conscription System in Japan* (Oxford: Oxford University Press, 1921) p. 131.

particularly the infantry works and the extemporised defences between them. The ferro-concrete works withstood the bombardment without any serious damage, and, though they were scarred and badly battered externally, none of the projectiles penetrated any vital interior position. The communication trenches and other intermediate field-works were however obliterated and this, together with the destruction of much of the telephone system, isolated the personnel manning the works, both from each other and from the command further back. The targeting of the signal station further hindered communication of every kind, and with the bringing down of the radio antenna even one-way communication from the outside world was terminated.[50]

After nightfall the sappers returned to their task of advancing the siege works while infantry patrols went forward to reconnoitre and probe the defences. One such probe crossed the Haipo River and a four-man party entered the ditch near Infantry Work 4, which was under the command of Captain von Stranz, and began cutting the wire.[51] They remained undetected for some time, indicating the lack of awareness of the defenders who remained within the work, but were eventually heard and forced to retire, with the loss of one man, after machine-gun fire was directed at them. A second patrol took their place a little later and, under the very noses of the defence, completed the wire-cutting task before they too were detected. The defenders conceived that an assault in strength was under way and called down artillery fire in support from Iltis Battery and moved a reserve formation made up of naval personnel, whose ships had been scuttled, towards the front. The Japanese patrol withdrew, leaving the defenders under the erroneous impression that they had defeated a serious attempt at breaching the line, rather than, as was the case, an opportunistic foray. However, what the probe had revealed to the attackers was that the defenders were remaining largely inside the concrete works, leaving the gaps between them vulnerable to infiltration. This was confirmed by the experiences of a separate patrol that reconnoitred near Infantry Work 3; the knowledge gained being of some value to the Japanese.[52]

Apart from repelling the Japanese attack, as they thought, the defenders spent the night of 1–2 November destroying further equipment that might be of use to the besiegers. Chief among this was *Kaiserin Elisabeth*; shortly after midnight, having fired off her remaining ammunition in the general direction of the Japanese, the vessel was moved into deep water in Kiautschou Bay and scuttled. Explosive charges extemporised from torpedo warheads ensured that the ship was beyond salvage even if the wreck was located. The Austro-Hungarian cruiser was only one of several vessels scuttled that night, including the floating dock, which was seen to have disappeared the next morning. Only the gunboat *Jaguar* remained afloat at sunrise at which point the rapid rate of advance of the attackers, up to the edge of the Haipo River between Kiautschou Bay and the area in front of Infantry Work 3, was revealed to the Germans.[53]

Revealed to the Japanese, by their action during the hours of darkness, was the precise position of the Iltis Battery and this was promptly targeted and put out of action by counter-battery fire. The remorseless battering by the siege train also resumed, and the German inability to respond effectively due to the accuracy of Japanese return fire began to be exacerbated by a shortage of ammunition.[54] The Japanese bombardment, though intense, was perhaps not as destructive as it could have been. What seems to have mitigated the effect to some extent was the high rate of dud shells. One press correspondent that entered Tsingtau after the end of operations noted the proliferation of 'giant shells, some three feet long and a foot in diameter, [that] were lying about on side-walk and street still unexploded'.[55] Burdick, working from contemporary German estimates, calculates that between ten and twenty-five per cent of the Japanese ordnance failed to explode. This shortcoming, being attributable to faulty manufacture, played a major role in sparing the defenders a worse ordeal than they had to endure anyway.[56]

Also sparing the defenders to some extent on 2 November was the onset of rain, which affected the assailants more than the defence to the extent as the attackers' diggings became waterlogged and collapsed in some cases. Further alleviation was attributable to the withdrawal from service of the 280mm howitzers, as the temporary emplacements could not stand the strain of their immense recoil and rendered firing both dangerous and inaccurate.[57] The remainder of the siege train concentrated its fire on the Boxer Line, particularly in an attempt to destroy the wire and obstacles in the trench and thus mitigate the need to resort to manual methods with their inevitable human cost. The power station was also targeted, with the result that the chimney was brought down in the evening, thus rendering the city dependent on primitive forms of lighting.[58]

The days 3 and 4 November saw further progress in the advancement of the siege works and continuing bombardment, though useful targets for this were now at a premium as little of the defences remained other than the concrete infantry works. The defenders had begun destroying their batteries on 2 November as they ran out of ammunition, and in any event returning the Japanese fire was a hazardous business due to the rapidity and accuracy of the response. The lack of defensive fire allowed some reorganisation of the siege artillery and several of the batteries were moved forward and swiftly re-emplaced with the minimum of disruption.

On the far right of the Japanese line the sappers attached to 67th Infantry Regiment had advanced their works to within a short distance of the Haipo River, and thus close to the city's water pumping station situated on the eastern bank. The decision was taken by 29th Infantry Brigade to attempt to take the station on the evening of 4 November and a company-sized unit, comprising infantry and engineers, was assembled. The engineers cut through the defensive wire with Bangalore torpedoes[59] allowing the infantry to surround the station, while a box artillery barrage cut the installation off from any attempted relief. The small garrison in the station, some twenty-one strong, quickly surrendered leaving Tsingtau without a mains water supply and thus reliant on the several wells within the city.[60]

Elsewhere along the line the nocturnal 'mole warfare' techniques advanced the saps and trenches ever nearer to the ditch fronting the infantry works in order to construct the third parallel – the final assault line. This progressed everywhere apart from the British sector of front, immediately to the left of the 67th

Infantry Regiment, where enemy fire prevented the final approach being made. As Barnardison reported:

> On 5 November I was ordered to prepare a Third Position of attack on the left bank of the river. This line was to a great extent enfiladed on both flanks by No. 1 and 2 Redoubts, especially the latter, from which annoying machine-gun fire was experienced. The bed of the river [...] had also to be crossed, and in doing so the working parties of the 2nd Battalion South Wales Borderers suffered somewhat severely, losing 8 non-commissioned officers and men killed and 24 wounded. The 36th Sikhs had only slight losses. Notwithstanding this a good deal of work was done, especially on the right flank. I considered it my duty to represent to the Japanese Commander-in-Chief the untenable nature, for permanent occupation, of the portion of the Third Position in my front, but received a reply that it was necessary for it to be held in order to fit in with the general scheme of assault.[61]

Though most diplomatically phrased, it is possible to distinguish in the final sentence of this quotation a hint of asperity in the relations between the allies. Indeed, though suppressed for political reasons at the time, the British military contribution did not impress the Japanese in any way, shape or form. Reports from the front revealed the perception that the British were reluctant to get involved in the fighting and 'hard to trust'. More brutal opinions had it that they were no more than 'baggage' and 'decoration' on the battlefield. The nature of these observations filtered through to the Japanese press, one report stating that: 'Only when nothing happened were British soldiers wonderful and it was like taking a lady on a trip. However, such a lady can be a burden and lead to total disaster for a force when the enemy appears.'[62]

Daylight on 5 November saw three Japanese aeroplanes overfly the German positions dropping not explosive devices, as might have been expected, but rather bundles of leaflets carrying a message from the besiegers:

> To the Respected Officers and Men of the Fortress.
> It would act against the will of God as well as humanity if one were to destroy the still useful weapons, ships, and other structures without tactical justification and only because of the envious view that they might fall into the hands of the enemy.
> Although we are certain in the belief that, in the case of the chivalrous officers and men, they would not put into effect such thoughtlessness, we nevertheless would like to emphasise the above as our point of view.[63]

On the face of it this message seemed to clearly indicate that the besiegers, perceiving that they would shortly be in occupation of the city, desired that as much of it be preserved as was possible. If so, they adopted a rather contradictory attitude inasmuch as shortly after dispensing it a naval barrage, delivered by *Mishima*, *Tango*, *Okinoshina* and *Iwami* from Hai hsi Bay to the west of Cape Jäschke, was directed onto the urban area of Tsingtau. Backed by the land batteries, this bombardment caused great damage to the city, though one shot, apparently misaimed, struck one of the 240mm gun positions at Hui tsch'en Huk, destroying the gun and killing seven of the crew. Without a mains water supply the possibility of fire-fighting in Tsingtau was greatly reduced and several buildings were burned down, though because of the relative spaciousness of the city fires did not jump easily from building to building and so there was no major conflagration. Tapautau, the Chinese quarter, was not constructed on such generous proportions, though the relatively smaller size of the dwellings and their less robust structural strength meant they collapsed rather than burned, and it too was spared an inferno.[64]

Because the German artillery was now virtually silent the sapping work continued during daylight hours without fear of interruption, and the third parallel was completed during the day close up to the defensive ditch. Unable to effectively counter these moves the defenders, also ignoring the Japanese plea as contained in their airdropped leaflets, began putting their coastal artillery batteries out of action, which in any event, other than Hui tsch'en Huk, had proved mostly ineffective. It was clear to all that the end was not far off, and only the ferro-concrete infantry works remained as anything like effective defensive positions, though a report from one to Meyer-Waldeck 'reflected the universal condition':

> The entire work is shot to pieces, a hill of fragments, without any defences. The entire trench system is knocked out; the redoubt still holds together, but everything else, including the explosives storage room, is destroyed. Only a single observation post is in use. I shall hold the redoubt as long as possible.[65]

Given the impossibility of offering effective resistance to the besiegers, Meyer-Waldeck was under no illusions as to the length of time left to the defence. Evidence for this may be adduced from his ordering Plüschow to make a getaway attempt the following day. He was to carry away papers relating to the course of the siege and several symbolic items such as the fastenings from the flagpole, as well as private letters from members of the garrison.[66]

The attackers saw the elusive Taube take to the air the next morning, and, according to Plüschow himself, make a last circuit of Tsingtau before setting off southwards. Though the Japanese artillery made what was to turn out to be their final efforts to shoot him down, hostile aircraft did not follow him and he made good his escape towards neutral China, eventually reaching Tientsin where he was reunited with the crew of *S-90*. As he left his ground crew destroyed any remaining equipment, but his place over the city was soon taken by the Japanese aeroplanes which sortied in force, dropping numerous bombs onto the defenders' positions, as a less than effective adjunct to the efforts of the artillery. As the bombardment from land and air went on the Japanese infantry began to move into their final assault positions in the third parallel. The British however, still troubled by the fire from the German machine guns, only occupied their sector with a thin outpost line. The Governor, noting the proximity of the attackers and expecting an imminent assault, ordered a general alert for the afternoon.[67]

General Kamio now had all his infantry where he wanted them, with the exception of the British contingent, and all his equipment in place. His orders for the night of 6/7 November did not however call for a general assault, but rather stipulated small scale, though aggressive, probing of the Boxer Line to test for weak spots, together with the usual artillery barrage. He emphasised flexibility and the exploitation of success. As darkness fell the sappers dug forward from the third parallel and broke into the ditch, allowing direct access without the need to leave the entrenchments. Wire that had remained intact following the previous attention of the artillery was cut or covered, allowing more or less unrestricted access within the ditch, and patrols moved across it and out onto the German side as darkness fell. At around 11p.m. a firefight broke out around Infantry Work 4 as a patrol from 56th Infantry Regiment attempted to infiltrate the line by bypassing the work. The defenders were more alert than they had been on 1 November and sallied out to meet them. Eventually, after about one hour of fighting, the Japanese retreated, and called down an artillery barrage onto the defenders for their pains.[68]

More or less concurrently, Infantry Work 3, under the command of Captain Lancelle, was the object of similar tactics. A company-sized unit under Lieutenant Nakamura Jekizo, again from 56th Infantry Regiment, crossed the ditch around midnight and were able to creep around the work undetected and surround it. The entrance to the work was open and the patrol loosed a heavy fire at, and into, it, effectively trapping the defenders inside. Another Japanese company arrived on the scene shortly afterwards and, within about half an hour of the beginning of the engagement, Lancelle surrendered the work complete with its complement of about 200 men. It had been, in Burdick's words, 'ridiculously easy'.[69]

There was now a large gap in the centre of the Boxer Line, and word quickly got to Meyer-Waldeck who ordered his reserves to counter-attack under cover of a German barrage. While such a move was theoretically sound, it was, practically, almost impossible. There was simply not enough artillery left to provide an effective bombardment, and precious little manpower, particularly in comparison with that available to the attackers, to seal the breach. The effort was made, but the counter- attackers, including a contingent of Austro-Hungarian sailors landed from *Kaiserin Elisabeth*, were simply too weak to throw back the rapidly reinforcing Japanese; Kamio too had received rapid word of the success of the assault on the 'Central Fort' as they came to term it.[70]

The Boxer Line, being a linear defence, was vulnerable to being 'rolled up' from the flanks once breached at a given point. The Japanese having made the breach now proceeded to widen it by moving against Infantry Works 2 and 4 on either side. Both works held out for some hours, assisted by the gunboat *Jaguar*, the last Central Powers warship afloat, which fired away her remaining ordnance in support. The outcome however could be in no doubt and both works surrendered after some three hours of resistance. The Boxer Line was now useless, for with no defence in depth the penetration meant the route to Tsingtau was now as good as wide open. The Japanese infantry surged through the gap and began a general advance on Tsingtau and various strategic points, such as the Iltis and Bismarck hills with their four key artillery batteries. The two batteries on the former fought the attackers for a time before surrendering, whereas the artillerymen on the latter, having fired away the last of their ammunition, set charges to destroy their six guns and vacated the position at around 5a.m. This final destruction of land-based artillery had its counterpart on the water; *Jaguar,* after attempting to repulse the infantry attack, had been scuttled in Kiautschou Bay.[71]

At 6a.m. Meyer-Waldeck held a meeting at his headquarters in the Bismarck Hill Command Post where the latest information was assimilated. There was no real option, leaving aside the fanatical 'fight to the last man and last bullet' scenario, and Meyer-Waldeck was no fanatic. Brace put it thus:

> If the governor had permitted the unequal struggle to go on his men would have lasted only a few hours longer. It would be an Alamo, and the name of the German garrison would be heralded throughout history as the heroic band of whites who stood against the yellow invasion until the last man. On the other hand the governor had with him a large part of the German commercial community of the Far East which Germany had built up with such painstaking care.[72]

The Governor ordered the white flag hoisted on the signal station and over the German positions and composed a message to General Kamio:

> Since my defensive measures are exhausted I am now ready to enter into surrender negotiations for the now open city. [...] I request you to appoint plenipotentiaries to the discussions, as well as to set time and place for the meeting of the respective plenipotentiaries. [...] [73]

The carrier of this message was Major Georg von Kayser, adjutant to Meyer-Waldeck's Chief of Staff, naval Captain Ludwig Saxer – the latter being the Governor's appointee as German plenipotentiary. Despite Barnardiston's contention that all firing ceased at 7a.m.[74] Kayser had difficulty getting through the lines in safety, but he was eventually allowed to proceed under his flag of truce to the village of Tungwutschiatsun, some four kilometres behind the Japanese front line, more or less opposite to Infantry Work 3. It was agreed that a general armistice would come into play immediately, and that formal negotiations for the capitulation would begin that afternoon at 4p.m. in Moltke Barracks.[75]

The Japanese had meanwhile advanced into the area between the Boxer Line and the city, as had their ally – though the latter had seen no fighting. As Barnardiston was to state it:' [At] about [07:30hrs] I received orders to advance, and, the enemy along the whole of our front having then retired, I marched into Tsingtau.'[76] It is then ironic to note that probably the last casualties of the campaign, at least caused by direct enemy action, were two British soldiers who thought that all fighting had ceased and left cover. They were hit by an artillery shell; fighting went on for some time in areas difficult to communicate with, particularly Infantry Works 1 and 5, which, being largely peripheral to the Allied advance, were not seriously assaulted and did not capitulate until reached by German staff officers.[77]

The meeting of the plenipotentiaries, Kamio being represented by his Chief of Staff, Major General Yamanashi Hanzo, was largely a formality, as the Japanese were in a position to dictate terms as they pleased. The terms were presented to the Germans, led by Saxer, at the 4p.m. meeting and an adjournment then took place for him to consider the document setting them out. It was, in all essentials, very simple; The Kiautschou Protectorate would formally transfer to Japan on 10 November. German military and naval personnel would become prisoners of war, while all equipment, of which there was to be no further destruction, would become Japanese property.

The plenipotentiaries reconvened at 7p.m. General Yamanashi had largely taken up this somewhat lengthy interval with a visit to the city at Captain Saxer's request, the latter being concerned about the possible depredations of the Japanese soldiery. The Chief of Staff promptly ordered all the troops out of the urban area and set up a demarcation line some two to three kilometres outside, which they were forbidden to pass. The only qualification of the terms proposed by Saxer was that the German officers be allowed to retain their swords, which was refused on the grounds that Yamanashi did not posses the authority to accede to the request.[78] The parties then signed; General Yamanashi for the Japanese Army, Commander Takakashi for the Navy and naval Captain Saxer for the German administration. Brigadier-General Barnardiston was neither consulted as to the terms nor asked to attend the meetings, and the sole British officer present, Lieutenant-Colonel Everard Calthrop, was there by virtue of his being the liaison officer attached to 18th Division.[79]

General Kamio's conquest marked the end of the German territorial presence in East Asia and the Pacific. The naval presence was also drawing to a close; *Emden* was destroyed on 9 November and Count von Spee, having revealed himself to be at the very periphery of the theatre with his defeat of Cradock on 1 November, was to meet superior force on 8 December in another ocean.

Kamio had shown himself to be a prudent and professional commander of an effective and well-trained corps-sized expeditionary force. The campaign against Germany's Kiautschou territory had been conducted throughout with competence. There had never been any doubt as to the outcome, and the numbers finally involved, some 60,000 on the Japanese side as against something over 4,000 on the German and Austrian, clearly demonstrate the scale of the disparity in forces. The losses, to both sides were small; Japanese losses amounted to 415 dead and 1,451 wounded, a rate of about three per cent, while Barnardiston's command of some 950 lost 13 dead and 61 wounded, nearly eight per cent. German (and Austrian) losses were one hundred per cent as they were all taken prisoner, but the battlefield casualties amounted to 199 dead and 294 wounded, which equates roughly to ten per cent of the total.[80]

The capture of Tsingtau left the Japanese with 4,592 German and Austro-Hungarian prisoners of war, many of them reservists and somewhat advanced in years.[81] These were shipped to Japan and incarcerated in various prisoner-of-war 'camps' throughout Japan; these places of imprisonment, comprising temples, former barracks and other non-purpose built structures, were ill adapted for the purpose and unsuited to Europeans unused to the cold winter weather. Though the conditions under which the prisoners were held was undoubtedly unpleasant, there appears to have been little or none of the brutality that was associated with those in Japanese captivity later in the century. Indeed the Japanese authorities allowed the power representing German interest, the United States, to send officials on an inspection tour of the camps in 1916 following a barrage of complaints from the Germans.[82]

The US official that conducted this tour of inspection was a young diplomat of impeccable breeding and background who was to later go on to somewhat greater fame; Benjamin Sumner Welles.[83] Welles, accompanied by a Japanese-speaking companion, Joseph W. Ballantine, set out on 29 February 1916 for a two-week tour of ten of the camps. He found that the conditions varied from camp to camp, and in his final report of some 120 pages, dated 21 March 1916, he detailed his findings at each of the ten sites visited. Four, he adjudged, had sub-standard regimes including, for example, the commandant at the camp, an ex-army barracks, located outside the town of Kurume, on the island of Kyushu, who allowed his men to strike the prisoners for minor offences. Welles was pleased to note, while on a return visit to the sites at the end of 1916, that the commandants of the four camps in question had been replaced.[84]

The campaign threw up few novel elements, perhaps the most original being the use made of air power on the Japanese side. It was the most intensive use of aircraft up to that time, with several firsts as has been related, and predated the beginnings of the integration of aircraft into battle for reconnaissance purposes.[85] Indeed, Kamio had gone further, and used aeroplanes for what would later be termed strike missions, though with little success, and in attempts to shoot down enemy aircraft, as represented by the sole example on the German side.

With the fall of the territory the various outside observers began to depart. Brace's description of his leave-taking is somewhat poignant:

> When I left Tsingtau it was on the back of a hardy Mongol pony, for the Germans had put their railway out of commission by blowing up the bridges. The cutting north wind was chasing the dry leaves around the Moltke Barracks where the Japanese had established staff headquarters. [...] Everywhere the country was gouged with the great holes and gashes of shells. [...] Then we went through the maze of Japanese trenches. One last glance at the little city [...] With its roofs of red-tile and many gables Tsingtau was still, in appearance at least, the Little Germany Across the Sea. But already the Japanese had begun to rename the streets and hills.[86]

As one Japanese writer put it (in translation): 'Sei-To has fallen under the gallant leadership of Lieutenant-General Kamio Mitsuomi.'[87] Indeed, the change of sovereignty had begat a change of name for Tsingtau itself. It became, in its Romanised English version, Sei-Tö.[88] These types of actions were not of the kind that suggested the restoration of the territory to China would be likely in the short term.

IO

Aftermath

Though driven entirely from the Pacific during 1914, the Imperial German Navy was to return over two years later in the shape of the commerce raiders SMS *Wolf* and *Seeadler*. The former vessel was a converted merchantman, armed with six 150mm guns, one 105mm gun, four torpedo tubes and some 460 mines, that sailed from Kiel on 30 November 1916 under Commander Karl August Nerger. Evading the British blockade, Nerger was able to steam to the South Atlantic and then into the Indian Ocean and the waters off Australia and New Zealand. *Wolf* carried some 8,000 tonnes of coal giving her a cruising range of over 50,000 kilometres at eight knots – her maximum speed being eleven knots. Also carried aboard the vessel was an FF (*Friedrichshafen Flugzeugbau*) 33 seaplane, christened *Wölfchen*, to be used for reconnaissance. SMS *Wolf* returned to the Austian Adritic port of Pola on 24 February 1918, having completed a voyage of around 100,000 kilometres lasting some 452 days, during which some 30 plus merchantmen of various nation had been accounted for, whether sunk by her mines or taken directly, including the Japanese freighter *Hitachi Maru*, captured on 26 September and sunk on 7 November 1917. It was an incredible achievement, and Kaiser Wilhelm II decorated Commander Nerger with the Prussian Pour le Mérite.[1]

The second raider to reach the Pacific in 1917, SMS *Seeadler* was, on the face of it, an anachronism, being a fully rigged three-masted windjammer – a steel-hulled, cargo- carrying, sailing ship. Constructed on Clydeside by Robert Duncan & Company of Port Glasgow in 1888 as *Pass of Balmaha*, the name coming from an area on the east side of Loch Lomond, the vessel was captured by Germany on 3 August 1915 and taken to Cuxhaven. The impetus behind the idea to refit the vessel for *guerre de course* came from the extreme difficulty German ships faced of accessing coal supplies. A sailing vessel would be spared this problem, and so *Seeadler*, as she became, was fitted with an auxiliary diesel engine and a main armament of two 105mm guns. Her captain was Count Felix von Luckner, chosen for the position because he was one of the few officers in the Imperial Navy with experience of large sailing ships. *Seeadler* left port on 21 December 1916 under a Norwegian flag and successfully traversed the North Sea blockade. Her first victim was captured and sunk on 9 January 1917; there were to be eleven more such occurrences – though the last of them, on 21 March, was released after capture – before Luckner entered the Pacific via Cape Horn on 18 April.

The *Seeadler* sailed north-westerly and was off Christmas Island (Kiritimati) by early June when Luckner learned that the US had declared war on Imperial

Germany on 6 April 1917. American shipping thus became fair game, though between 14 June and 8 July only three US vessels were taken. In order to attempt to find fresh food to combat signs of beriberi (thiamine deficiency) in the crew, Luckner sailed to Mopelia (Maupelia, Maupi-haa) in the Leeward (Society) Islands, anchoring outside the entrance to the lagoon on 31 July. It was there, after sailing some 65,000 kilometres, that *Seeadler* met her doom on 2 August; not through enemy action but rather by grounding on the reef. This was caused, depending on which source is believed, by a tidal wave, a gale, or negligence.[2]

The fact that there were only two raiders whose exploits are worth recounting, albeit briefly, underlines the untroubled nature of maritime trade in East Asia and the Pacific after late 1914. It is also the case that during the Great War it became obvious that the best weapon for carrying out commerce warfare was not the surface ship, but the submarine. Indeed, such were the depredations eventually inflicted by this weapons system that Britain, a nation that in 1914 possessed the largest navy ever seen and around half of the entire world's merchant tonnage, was, some two years later, in grave danger of being starved, both in the literal sense and in terms of vital resources. Admiral Sir John Jellicoe, having given up command of the Grand Fleet to Admiral Sir David Beatty, became First Sea Lord in November 1916 and warned that the German submarine campaign was in danger of winning the war for Germany. There was, he argued:

> a serious danger that our losses in merchant ships, combined with the losses in neutral merchant ships, may, by the early summer of 1917, have such a serious effect upon the import of food and other necessaries into the Allied countries as to force us into accepting peace terms which the military position on the Continent would not justify, and which would fall short of our desires.[3]

The *guerre de course* by submarine was confined, in the main, to the Atlantic; there were no German submarines in the Pacific, and no possibilities of deployment because there were no bases. That the naval forces of Imperial Germany were unable to operate in any effective way in the Pacific – the auxiliary cruisers were of nuisance value only – can be attributed in the main to the intervention of Japan.

Without the Imperial Japanese Navy the task of clearing the theatre would have fallen to the British and Australians, who might have been hard pressed to spare the resources, but undoubtedly could have done if necessity dictated. As has been already noted, the Royal Navy during late 1914 and early 1915 had six battlecruisers deployed on duties away from the Grand Fleet, which, though occasioning protests from Jellicoe, did not lead to adverse consequences.

What might have led to such consequences would have been the removal of battleships, whether through remote deployment or attrition via enemy action – the latter being the main plank of German strategy. The strategy of attrition failed and, since Germany deployed no battleships outside North European waters, any attempt at which would have been strategically unsound, to put it mildly, and in any case logistically impossible, there was no necessity for Britain to detach similar vessels for duty away from the Grand Fleet. Indeed it might even be argued that the Grand Fleet, in its insatiable thirst for numbers, was assigned vessels that were unsuitable for service should it realise what many considered its *raison d'être* - action with the High Seas Fleet. The best example of this is perhaps the fate of the three armoured cruisers lost at Jutland, a battle in which they should have had no place.[4] In short, in order for the Royal Navy to achieve and maintain a preponderance of force in what was perceived as the main theatre, the North Sea, Japanese intervention was not indispensable.

As has been argued, the type of warship that was essential in the North Sea was the battleship. This was not the category that would have been suitable for tackling the East Asiatic Cruiser Squadron. Cruisers of various types were required for that duty, including battlecruisers best of all, and it will be recalled that the presence in the Pacific of *Australia* alone had a significant deterrent effect upon Spee, who eventually met his doom via two others of the variety. Battlecruisers however were also deemed of great importance for service with the Grand Fleet, and perhaps only in retrospect can it be clearly perceived that doctrine regarding their tactical employment with the fleet was flawed – the Royal Navy lost three, to Germany's one, during the thirteen-hour Jutland battle. Whether or not the Grand Fleet would have been severely depleted by the detachment of a portion of its battlecruiser strength, and whether the High Seas Fleet could have taken advantage of this, cannot be known for sure. However, given that the five fast battleships of the *Queen Elizabeth*-class were commissioned between 1915 and 1916 [5] with only a 2.5–3 knot designed speed deficit in comparison with the *Lion*-class battlecruisers,[6] and could thus fulfil the battlecruiser role if necessary, the answer is probably not. Indeed, at Jutland the Grand Fleet deployed 28 battleships and 9 battlecruisers as against 16 and 5 respectively for the High Seas Fleet. Four of the British battleships comprised *Queen Elizabeth*-class super-dreadnoughts organised in the 5th Battle Squadron, which, to reinforce the point, was attached to the Battlecruiser Fleet under Beatty to make up for unavailable ships.

Even without 5th Battle Squadron Jellicoe still had a superiority of one entire battle squadron of eight battleships, and counting the four *Queen Elizabeth*s as battlecruisers gave an identical advantage in that ship type; 13 to 5. It follows therefore that if, say, four battlecruisers had been deployed away from the Grand Fleet then while the total British preponderance in capital ships would have been reduced, there would still have been nearly twice as many British battlecruisers, or ships that could fulfil the battlecruiser function, as there were German present at Jutland.

Of course, redeployment was not as simple as merely having the numbers available; there are logistical issues to consider, not the least of which is fuel. All the Royal Navy's battlecruisers up until *Repulse* and *Renown*, both commissioned in 1916, were coal fired. In order to achieve optimum performance from their warships, the British Admiralty required high-grade coal, specifically Welsh Steam Coal, often referred to as 'Admiralty Coal'. Deep mined in the Rhondda Valley area of South Wales the Grand Fleet based at Scapa Flow had a vast appetite for this product, the entire output of which, during the Great War, was purchased by the Admiralty.

Fuelling the fleet involved a massive industrial infrastructure: 'The total number of special trains run from South Wales with Admiralty coal between 27 August 1914 and 31 December 1918 was 13,631. Taking an average of forty wagons per train this was equal to 545,240 wagons.' These 'Jellicoe Specials' as they were known, hauled their loads from the heads of the valleys in South Wales all the way up to Thurso in North Scotland. There the coal was transhipped into colliers, before being sent to the fleet at Scapa and again transferred to the individual ships. Coaling a ship was an onerous task, dirty, backbreaking and loathed by the crew-members that had to complete it at regular intervals, and a battlecruiser consumed huge quantities if steaming at speed.[7]

The Royal Navy kept large stocks of Welsh coal in the East Asia region, some 300,000 tonnes at Hong Kong for example, and fortunately, as transporting coal from the Rhondda to the Pacific in sufficient quantities during wartime would have been an immensely difficult task, there were deposits of equal quality coal to be found in the Antipodes, specifically New Zealand's 'Westport Coal'. This, it had been established in 1900, would fulfil British and imperial naval requirements during both peace and war; in the latter case a supply equal to some 500,000 tonnes per year being required.[8] This was a factor of some importance, as inferior coal had a significant effect on performance; with Australian coal sourced at Newcastle, New South Wales, the top speed of the battlecruiser *Australia* was reduced by some five knots.[9]

Base facilities for a division of battlecruisers were also available, in the shape of King's Graving (Dry) Dock at Keppel harbour in Singapore. Opened on 26 August 1911 by the Governor, Sir Arthur Young, and fully functional by 1913, King's Dock, at some 267 by 28 metres and able to accommodate vessels up to 10 metres in draught, was the largest such facility in the Far East. For smaller vessels there were four other graving docks: Keppel Harbour No. 1 and No. 2 Docks, of 120 and 141 metres length, and draughts of 4.4 and 5 metres respectively, and the Victoria Dock and the Albert Dock, of 147 and 151 metres, and draughts of 5.7 and 6 metres respectively.[10] All classes of British battlecruiser, up to the *Renown*-class of 1916, would then have been able to fit into the King's Dock, though HMS *Tiger* would have been a tight fit.[11] Even the *Queen Elizabeth*-class fast battleships would just have fitted, though not the *Revenge* class, as they were the first to be fitted with anti-torpedo bulges.[12]

As Hector Bywater put it in 1927 in relation to the dock; it would 'take any cruiser and any unbulged battleship in the navy.'[13] MacIntyre makes the point that damaged capital ships could draw a great deal more draught than normal, 13 metres or so, and that King's Dock would not be able to accommodate them in such circumstances.[14] While undoubtedly true, this point is rendered of less importance in the current context, inasmuch as the damage likely to be sustained by British battlecruisers in a battle with the East Asiatic Cruiser Squadron would have been limited in comparison to combat against other capital ships.

It can be argued then that, both in terms of residual superiority in northern European waters and logistics in Pacific waters, it would have been possible for the Royal Navy to have on medium-term deployment at least four battlecruisers to hunt down the German Squadron in 1914. Provided that lighter cruisers, including the armoured cruisers that had no real place with the Grand Fleet and such French and Russian units as were available, could have supplemented these, then it follows that the role taken by the Japanese Navy was not strictly essential to clearing the Pacific. Vice Admiral Spee, as has already been related, was in agreement on this point:

> In case of war [...] against France, Russia, and England, without complication with Japan, war upon commerce *is* possible so long as the coal supply holds out. But – in view of the fact that it is probably intended to bring up the Australian warships – it is only possible for a short time.[15]

How much shorter if the 'Australian warships' were four times as many? There is no definitive answer to that of course, and it is probably safe to conclude that, without the Japanese Navy, Spee would have had a much less difficult time, and might not have been forced to evacuate the Pacific as early as he did. It is though legitimate to argue that, without Japanese intervention, Britain and British Dominion forces, together with whatever assistance could be provided by French and Russian assets in the region, could have coped with German naval forces in East Asia and the Pacific.

Where Japanese intervention was of much greater importance was in relation to Kiautschou. It would have been extremely difficult, though not impossible, for the British to have blockaded the territory and conducted the various other operations needed to contain the East Asiatic Cruiser Squadron simultaneously. It would have been even more problematical to have invaded Kiautschou and taken Tsingtau. The Japanese, unencumbered elsewhere, were able to devote large resources in both military and naval terms to its reduction, and these resources could not have been matched by any combination of Britain and her allies. In order to militarily neutralise the German base early in the war, Japanese intervention was then probably essential.

This intervention has not always been perceived in that light however, and no less an authority than Arthur Marder has argued that:

> The Royal Navy had little reason to be grateful to the Japanese in the First World War. Japan refused to send any ships to fight Germany until 1917, when a destroyer flotilla was sent to the Mediterranean, and made hay in the Far East while the British were committed in Europe, as through the seizure of German-occupied Tsingtau and German islands in the Pacific – the Marshalls, Marianas, Carolines, and Palau.[16]

It is self evident that Japan did send ships to fight Germany before 1917 and by so doing freed the Royal Navy from the requirement. It follows that the ability to achieve the Royal Navy's desiderata, of almost overwhelming numerical superiority in the North European theatre, was thus facilitated by Japanese actions.

The second point made by Marder in terms of 'making hay' has some force, considering that in political-strategic terms Japan had made vast gains for minimal cost through declaring war on Germany in August 1914. Indeed, it was evident almost from the outset that the Japanese presence was not intended to be limited in either time or space. In respect of Kiautschou, evidence for this may be adduced by noting that, under the mantle of 'military necessity', the Japanese Imperial Army had taken over control of the Shantung Railway during the operations against Germany. At the capitulation this control had lengthened to include Tsinan, a distance of nearly 400 kilometres, and had broadened to accommodate the Poshan mines.[17] That the occupation was, from the Japanese perspective, less limited than might have been implied by the phrase 'eventual restoration [...] to China' used in the ultimatum of 15 August, was evidenced by the response to a Chinese point that the 'war zone' might be abolished, made on 25 November 1914. The Japanese reply was curt: 'Our military authorities desire no change in the status of the war zone for the time being.' Upon further pursuing the subject, on 2 December, China received much the same response; the invocation of 'military necessity'.[18]

Further indication of Japanese intentions was evidenced by Foreign Minister Kato's clarification of the matter in the Japanese Parliament on 8 December. The matter was published in the Japanese press as a question and answer session:

Questions:
(a) Whether Kiautschou will be returned to China?
(b) Whether the Imperial Government of Japan were pledged to China, or to any other Power, in the matter of the final disposition of Kiautschou?
(c) Whether the clause in the ultimatum [to Germany] referring to the final restitution of Kiautschou to China did not bind the action of Japan?

Baron Kato's Replies
(a) the question regarding Kiautschou was, at present, unanswerable.
(b) Japan had never committed herself to any foreign Power on this point.
(c) The purpose of the ultimatum to Germany was to take Kiautschou from Germany and so to restore peace in the Orient. Restitution after a campaign was not thought of and was not referred in the ultimatum.[19]

That Japan did not have a benevolent attitude towards China was reemphasised on 18 January 1915 when the Japanese presented China with a secret ultimatum in a note outlining what became known as the 'Twenty-One Demands'. These would, if acceded to in total, have 'reduced China to vassalage'.[20] The Chinese leaked details of the demands to the press and international community, provoking an outburst of nationalism in China and the disapprobation of President Woodrow Wilson and the US government. This remonstration, accompanied by similar protests from Britain, succeeded, in part, in toning down the demands, which had become 'requests' by 21 March.[21]

Bruce Elleman has recently demonstrated that the issue of the 'Twenty-One Demands' vis-à-vis Chinese domestic politics was far from straightforward;[22] what is more clear cut is the suspicion of Japanese motives and ambitions in respect of China and Chinese territory engendered in the American body politic by Japanese behaviour. Conversely, Japan felt resentment at what they saw as US intervention in an essentially bilateral matter.[23] Consequently, the issue delineated Japanese-US differences over China, and though it was not always at the forefront it was a matter that was not to be finally settled until August 1945.

It was similar with regard to the Pacific islands; the possession of the formerly German island territory north of the equator advanced Japan's naval perimeter by several thousand kilometres and provided the opportunity for anchorages well outside home waters. This was of particular concern to the US Navy, as it afforded the Japanese Navy a flank position on the line of communication between the continental United States and American territory in the western Pacific, primarily the Philippines. That these territories were held under a League of Nations Mandate that precluded fortification was of little consequence to the US, as the Japanese kept the islands veiled in secrecy and generally denied all access to foreigners.[24]

Japan had of course no intention of giving up or otherwise vacating the islands she had occupied in 1914. The same could be said to apply to Australia and New Zealand in respect of the territories they had acquired. Indeed, Germany had been forced to relinquish any claim to the former colonies under the terms of the Treaty of Versailles, whereby the defeated state renounced all overseas territories under Articles 118–158, which dealt with German Rights and Interests Outside Germany. For example, Article 119 stated that 'Germany renounces in favour of the Principal Allied and Associated Powers all her rights and titles over her oversea possessions.' Not only did Germany lose her 'rights' over these territories, but German national residents there had their residency rights removed: Article 122 stated:

The Government exercising authority over such territories may make such provisions as it thinks fit with reference to the repatriation from them of German nationals and to the conditions upon which German subjects of European origin shall, or shall not, be allowed to reside, hold property, trade or exercise a profession in them.[25]

Protests concerning the terms dealing with colonial matters, among many others, were effectively dismissed in a letter of May 1919:

the Allied and Associated Powers are satisfied that the native inhabitants of the German colonies are strongly opposed to being again brought under Germany's sway, and the record of German rule, the traditions of the German Government and the use to which these colonies were put as bases from which to prey upon the commerce of the world, make it impossible for the Allied and Associated Powers to return them to Germany, or to entrust to her the responsibility for the training and education of their inhabitants.[26]

The phrase about preying on commerce can only refer to the Pacific Islands, but German colonial rule as a whole tended to be judged by what occurred in her African colonies, particularly in what is now Namibia:

There is a tendency on the part of the public to judge Germany's fitness for colonial responsibilities by her record in South-West Africa. This is indeed a grisly record, and one which, if it stood alone, could earn only one verdict, namely permanent disqualification from sovereignty over native peoples.[27]

Such sentiments were however very much retrospective, and there is no evidence that Germany was regarded as an especially immoral or brutal colonial power before 1914, unlike, for example, Belgium vis-à-vis the Congo. Unjust retrospective judgement or not, there was not the slightest chance of the government of the Weimar Republic being in a realistic position to attempt any recovery of former German territory. Despite this, a section of the population, especially those who had personally suffered from the loss of the colonies, kept the issue in the public arena via propaganda campaigns. Perhaps unsurprisingly the hypocritical nature of the post-war judgement on Germany's ex-colonies gave rise to denouncements of the so-called 'colonial guilt lie' – as with the similar but more widespread outrage concerning the 'war guilt lie' – and it was often pointed out that all the colonial powers had, at some point, been guilty of excesses.[28]

During the 1925 Locarno negotiations, the Allied Powers recanted somewhat on their allegations of colonial guilt, and 'Germany's moral right to colonial mandates' was, obliquely at least, conceded.[29] As Prime Minister Stanley Baldwin told the House of Commons on 6 July 1926:

> The question of Colonial mandates is not dealt with in the Locarno Agreement at all. On the other hand [...] it was indicated to the German delegation at Locarno verbally that Germany, when a member of the League [of Nations], would be a possible candidate for Colonial mandates like all other members. It is incorrect, however, to suggest that any promise or undertaking was given to the German Government.[30]

In fact Germany was never to recover any of her former colonies, nor gain any mandated territory under the auspices of the League. Even Adolf Hitler, who had made noises concerning colonial matters – 'Germany has by no means abandoned her colonial efforts [...] Germany required colonies imperatively as any other power'[31] – failed to convert talk into any kind of action. In terms of the Pacific territories in particular, it would have been of little moment if he had. They had, because of their mid-ocean location, become a significant factor in respect of the potential 'frontier' between Japan and the USA.

In the event of conflict with Japan the US Navy planned to project its sea power across the Pacific, relieve American forces at Guam and the Philippines, and then wage a decisive battle close to the Japanese home islands – the famous War Plan Orange. The Japanese plan to counter this strategy involved weakening the advancing fleet as it progressed by the use of submarine and aircraft attack, so that when the decisive battle occurred the Japanese fleet would be the stronger and thus the likely victor. Both navies were then in thrall to the Mahanian objective of the decisive battle.[32]

In order to reduce the threat these flank positions posed to the naval thrust of their war plan it would be necessary to neutralise them, which would be a task entrusted to the US Marine Corps. Accordingly, Major General John A. Lejeune, the commandant (commanding officer) of the Corps in 1920, tasked a Marine Corps staff officer, Major Earl H. Ellis, 'reputed to be the most brilliant planner in the Corps,'[33] with studying the problem. Ellis' conclusions were embodied in

Operation Plan 712, Advanced Base Operations in Micronesia, which was endorsed by Lejeune in July 1921 as the basis for future training and wartime mobilisation planning in the Marine Corps.[34]

Ellis succinctly described the problem:

> In order to impose our will upon Japan, it will be necessary for us to project our fleet and land forces across the Pacific and wage war in Japanese waters. To effect this requires that we have sufficient bases to support the fleet, both during its projection and afterwards. As the matter stands at present, we cannot count upon the use of any bases west of Hawaii except those which we may seize from the enemy after the opening of hostilities. Moreover, the continued occupation of the Marshall, Caroline and Pelew Islands by the Japanese [...] invests them with a series of emergency bases flanking any line of communications across the Pacific throughout a distance of 2300 miles. The reduction and occupation of these islands and the establishment of the necessary bases therein, as a preliminary phase of the hostilities, is practically imperative.[35]

Japan, had been granted legal jurisdiction over the islands she had occupied in 1914 by way of League of Nations Class C Mandates. These arrangements had arisen form consideration of the question of how to dispose of the ex-European possessions of the vanquished powers, which had been addressed at Versailles in 1919. The result was the Mandate system, whereby one or more of the victorious powers was made responsible for a given former-enemy territory, ostensibly under the auspices of the League. There were three classes of League Mandates. A 'Class A Mandate' was for those territories that were considered ready to receive independence within the foreseeable future, and were parts of the former Ottoman Empire: Iraq, Palestine, and Transjordan (Britain); Lebanon and Syria (France). Those territories where the possibility of independence was unlikely within the foreseeable future formed 'Class B Mandates'. They were all in Africa: Cameroon and Togoland (Britain and France); Tanganyika (Britain); and Ruanda-Urundi (Belgium). A 'Class C Mandate' was for those territories where any degree of independence or self-rule was considered effectively impossible. Such a mandate authorised the holder to administer the mandated territory under its own laws, but not to construct fortifications upon it. Former German colonies in this class, other than those occupied by Japan, were: New Guinea (Australia); Nauru (Australia, New Zealand and Britain); Western Samoa (New Zealand); and South-West Africa (South Africa).[36]

As the agency that had effected their capture, it was the Imperial Japanese Navy that administered the formerly German Pacific islands until, following the inception of the mandate system, it withdrew in favour of the Nan'yō-chō, a civilian administration, in 1920. The seat of government was established at Koror in Palau with district headquarters at Yap, Saipan, Chuuk, Pohnpei, Kosrae and Jaluit. Under the administration of the Nan'yō-chō, the Japanese, in contradistinction to the former rulers, set about administering their mandate with a strength of purpose and attention to detail that, it has been claimed, was unrivalled elsewhere in the Pacific.[37] An indigenous, though Japanese-led, police force was formed, while bureaucrats supervised a large number of infrastructural improvements, in areas such as health and sanitation, fisheries, agriculture, and harbour and road construction.[38]

One feature of colonial rule that did not change however, was the explicit exploitation; to the Japanese, no less than to the Germans and before them the Spanish, the indigenous Micronesians were expected to serve the needs of their masters.[39] It should however be noted that the rule exercised by Australia, New Zealand and Britain over their mandated territory was hardly such as to allow them any feelings of moral superiority. Indeed, one of the few scholars to scrutinise the matter has painted a vivid picture of the abuses of power – corporal and capital punishments, murder, rape, and plundering – that were perpetrated in New Guinea in particular. New Zealand's occupation of formerly German Samoa also comes in for severe criticism and the British, in relation to Nauru, are also heavily censured.[40]

Despite the apparent demilitarisation of the islands, the Japanese Navy maintained a strong interest in the area and did indeed derive great advantage from possession, though the systematic militarisation of them did not begin until 1937.[41] Indeed, by 1941 work had advanced on several of the islands, Saipan in the Marianas, Truk, Ponape and the Palau Islands in the Carolines and Kwajalein, Wotje, Jaluit and Maloelap in the Marshalls, enough to warrant their inclusion in Admiral Yamamoto Isoruku's 'Combined Fleet Secret Operation Order No. 1' of 5 November. This document formed the blueprint for the offensive phase of the war against the US. Truk in particular became an important base for Japan's Combined Fleet.[42]

It was not only the United States that was rendered more vulnerable and disadvantaged by the extension of Japanese power; Australia, New Zealand and, by extension, Britain perceived themselves threatened too. Put bluntly, the Japanese Navy possessed capabilities far in excess of those of the East Asiatic Cruiser Squadron of 1914. While HMAS *Australia* had been a deterrent to that squadron, a single capital ship was no such thing to the Japanese fleet. Since the Royal Navy was responsible for the maritime defence of the Empire, it followed that it, or the Royal Australian Navy, or both, would have to be greatly reinforced in order to provide an effective defence in the event of a war with Japan.

This was not seen as either likely or imminent immediately following the end of the Great War; on 15 August 1919 the British government adopted the 'Ten Year Rule' whereby military and naval plans and estimates should be drafted 'on the assumption that the British Empire would not be engaged in any great war during the next ten years'.[43] Despite this there were matters requiring rather urgent attention. The 'Two Power Standard' with a 'real margin' over and above it, as enunciated in 1903, was now nothing more than a fond memory.[44] Indeed, on 20 August 1916 the Naval Appropriations Act 1916 had been signed in Washington. This Act committed $313,384,212 towards creating 156 new ships, including ten battleships and six battlecruisers, for the US Navy, with construction beginning over the next three years and completed by 1921.[45]

Among the vessels planned and started were the six battleships of the *South*

Dakota-class: *South Dakota, Indiana, Montana, North Carolina, Iowa* and *Massa-chusetts*. These ships, which should not be confused with the class of the same name constructed in the late 1930s, were to displace some 40,000 tonnes and carry twelve 16in. (406mm) guns in four triple turrets. The battlecruisers laid down were six capital ships of the *Lexington*-class: *Lexington, Constellation, Saratoga, Ranger, Constitution* and *United States*. Designed to be 10 knots faster than the battleships, with a design speed of slightly over 33 knots, they also displaced some 40,000 tonnes, but carried less armour and armament, with a main battery of eight 16in. (406mm) guns.

There were several and varied factors that influenced the successful passage of this legislation, including the Battle of Jutland, which reaffirmed the capital ship as the final arbiter of naval power. The impetus for the programme came from President Woodrow Wilson, who had, somewhat euphemistically, dubbed it a programme of 'preparedness'. Whatever it was called it amounted to a massive challenge to the previously supreme Royal Navy; indeed on 2 February 1916 during an address at St Louis, the President had told his audience, to 'overwhelming applause', that he desired the US Navy 'to be incomparably the greatest navy in the world'.[46]

The accession of the US to a position of naval pre-eminence was further indicated in 1918 when, on 15 October, Wilson approved a further three-year construction programme. It virtually replicated that of 1916 inasmuch as another ten battleships and a further six battlecruisers were mooted as well as some 140 smaller warships.[47] The choices facing Britain with regard to this potential onslaught were stark. In order to achieve even a 'One Power Standard' of equality with the US, Britain would have to embark on an arms race, and one moreover from a greatly inferior position. Almost the entire capital ship strength of the Royal Navy in 1918 was coal burning, and so faced obsolescence. One alternative was to drop to second position in world naval power, and, with Japan also constructing new tonnage, perhaps to third position in the Pacific – or even globally.

Japan became engaged in what became known as the '8:8' Programme, constructing eight battleships and eight battlecruisers, and suffering 'the greatest financial difficulties' in so doing.[48] Indeed the programme was extensive; four 30-knot battlecruisers of the *Amagi*-class: *Akagi, Amagi, Atago* and *Takao*, of some 42,000 tonnes displacement, were budgeted for in 1918–19. The planned battleship construction envisaged two 40,000-tonne ships of the *Kaga/Toso* class – *Kaga* and *Toso*. Also planned were four *Kii*-class, ships, the first two, *Kii* and *Owari*, displacing around 42,000 tonnes, were scheduled to be laid down in 1922 and 1923 respectively. All these capital ships were to have had main batteries of ten 16in. (416mm) guns in twin turrets.

If nothing were done to remedy this situation, the British Empire, particularly in the Pacific, would become a hostage to the 'unlikely indulgence of others'.[49] Keenly aware of their potential vulnerability now that Japan had displaced Germany, the Australian government, in 1919, requested Admiral of the Fleet Lord Jellicoe to survey the situation.[50] Jellicoe's *Report on the Naval Mission to the Commonwealth* was submitted to the Governor-General in August 1919; one of its recommendations was that a naval presence of two battle squadrons – eight battleships and eight battlecruisers – plus their necessary support, including four aircraft carriers, was required to satisfy the requirements of a permanent presence. Jellicoe also concluded that Japan posed a serious potential threat to British interests in the Far East.[51]

Arthur Balfour was later, in 1922, to characterise British options as being a choice between 'naval peril and financial peril'.[52] Jellicoe's scheme was deemed unviable, though in an attempt to avert the first of Balfour's 'perils' the British seemed prepared to court the second; in March 1921 funds were authorised to begin four new battlecruisers.[53] The designs, provisionally entitled 'G3-type battlecruisers', were for huge vessels of nearly 50,000 tonnes mounting nine 16in. (406mm) guns in three turrets as main armament and capable of over 30 knots. A class of similarly configured battleships, mounting nine 18in. (457mm) guns and capable of 23.5 knots, were also mooted.[54]

If Jellicoe's solution to the potential difficulty with Japan was rejected, his conclusion that there was a problem was accepted. The Admiralty subsequently compiled a War Memorandum, the main feature of which, in the absence of a permanent naval presence, was a strategy to dispatch a powerful fleet from North European and Mediterranean waters to the Far East as and when required. However, because there was no base with sufficient facilities to accommodate a fleet of capital ships, both proposed and existing (once they had been fitted with anti-torpedo bulges), one would have to be constructed. The decision was taken to build this at Singapore, and so the strategy of projecting naval power halfway around the world became known as the 'Singapore Strategy'.[55]

Unlike many of the capital ships, whether afloat or only on the drawing boards and slipways of Britain, Japan and the United States, the Singapore Naval Base, and the associated strategy, was to survive the Naval Conference held at Washington, DC from November 1921 to March 1922 at the instigation of the US government. The USA was probably the only one of the three naval powers that could have, in financial terms, afforded the level of fleet expansion that was in progress post World War I, and then only with severe difficulty. There were however political costs that some American politicians were reluctant to pay; the US Congress, prompted in part by a 'popular revolt against navalism', began to press for the limitation of naval armaments.[56] This met with a degree of presidential approval; the Republican Warren G. Harding had replaced Wilson on 4 March 1921 and had indicated that he was receptive to international cooperation on matters of disarmament.[57] Harding wanted to reduce the size and influence of the US government, massively expanded during wartime, and, logically, chose members of his Cabinet from men of a similar mind.

Harding's Secretary of the Treasury was the banker and industrialist Andrew W. Mellon, who argued soon after taking office in 1921 that 'In the absence of drastic cuts in military and naval expenditures there is almost no prospect [...] of any substantial available surplus even in fiscal [year] 1922.'[58] The government's debts could only be paid by spending less money on armaments or by raising taxes, and Mellon was a proponent of the philosophy of low taxes; 'the greatest tax cutter until Ronald Reagan'.[59] In a similar manner to the 40th President, Mellon was a proponent of the 'trickle down theory' in respect of wealth, but unlike him was not an advocate of exempting defence from government budgetary cuts.

Diplomatically, there was another strand of US thinking that came into play respecting the Anglo-Japanese Alliance. The existence of the Alliance aroused deep suspicions within the US naval planning fraternity. While it was accepted that if a conflict should arise with Japan, Britain would be unlikely to become involved against the US, the reverse did not apply; if Britain and the US should clash then Britain was almost certain to ask Japan to join in on her side. While it was no doubt accepted that the original intent of it was very different, after 1918 the Alliance was viewed as being anti-American.[60]

The Washington Conference was seen as a method whereby these various problem areas might be resolved. A set of proposals was formulated, which would be put to the Conference by the US Secretary of State, Charles Evans Hughes, a distinguished lawyer.[61] Delegates from nine nations with interests in the East Asia and Pacific regions attended, representing the United States, Britain, Japan, France, Italy, Belgium, The Netherlands, Portugal and China. On 6 February 1922, the first five states concluded an agreement on limiting the size of their navies; the Naval Armaments Treaty. This agreed a ten-year naval holiday during which no new capital ships (ships over 10,000 tons with guns larger than 203mm/8in.) were to be built. The ratio of existing capital ships between the five powers, it was agreed, would be 5–5–3–1.67–1.67. This meant that Britain and America were each allowed 525,000 tons, Japan 315,000, and France and Italy 175,000 each. Total tonnage of aircraft carriers was restricted and a maximum size fixed for capital ships, aircraft carriers, and cruisers. If Singapore survived, few other schemes to build or fortify bases in the Pacific did likewise; the signatory powers agreed not to fortify their possessions in the region.

In terms of capital ships, the new allowances meant not only the cancellation of new construction, such as the four battleships of Japan's *Kaga* and *Kii* classes and battlecruisers of the *Amagi* class already laid down, and the battlecruisers of the US *Lexington* class and the British 'G3' type, but also the scrapping of significant existing tonnage.[62] In total the US plan consisted of proposals to scrap fifteen of its own existing battleships and another fifteen planned. The British were requested to scrap or not build twenty-three vessels, while Japan was asked to sacrifice seventeen existing or putative capital ships.[63] Britain's Admiral of the Fleet Lord Beatty, who had taken over command of the Grand Fleet from Jellicoe in 1916 and shepherded the High Seas Fleet into internment at Scapa Flow some two years later, was at the conference in his position as First Sea Lord. He is said to have physically staggered upon hearing the list of capital ships that it was proposed Britain should scrap, among which was counted HMAS *Australia*.[64]

US diplomacy at the conference was assisted in no small measure by having detailed inside information on the Japanese negotiating position. This information was provided to Hughes by MI-8, more famously known as the 'Black Chamber', the cryptanalysis organisation headed by the eccentric Herbert O. Yardley. The 'Black Chamber' had broken the Japanese diplomatic cipher used by the Japanese delegation to communicate with Tokyo; Hughes thus knew the Japanese position each day before beginning negotiations.[65]

Other significant outcomes of the Washington Conference were the dissolution of the Anglo-Japanese Alliance and the return of Kiautschou to China, a treaty being signed by both powers on 4 February 1922.[66] However, despite the treaty, it became evident that the Japanese would not, in fact, respect Chinese territorial integrity – that the policy as outlined by Kato in 1914 would continue in some shape or other. The incident often cited as the decisive one in this regard began at Jinan (Tsinan) the capital of Shandong Province on 3 May 1928. Japanese troops had been sent to support forces opposed to the Kuomintang under General Chiang Kai-shek, which had launched the 'Northern Expedition' in 1926 in an attempt to defeat 'warlordism' and unite the country under Chiang. The Japanese reoccupied Tsingtau and once again took territory along the Shantung Railway. They also took Jinan, where fighting broke out between them and the Kuomintang forces and continued for two days.

The incident is often seen as a major turning point in Sino-Japanese relations and the beginning of Japanese military expansionism in China.[67] The incident was, as one scholar has put it, 'an ominous close to a decade that had opened with the promise of international cooperation and non-intervention in China's domestic affairs'.[68]

Indeed, in terms of resolving the various Great Power issues in the Far East/ Pacific context, the outcome of the Great War was inconclusive. The removal of Germany from the area, indeed the elimination of Germany from the ranks of the Great Powers, particularly in the naval sense, did little in terms of providing greater security for the other powers in the region. This was particularly so for the British Empire in relation to the defence of her territories and dominions. New Great Powers had arisen in the shape of Japan and the US, and the dismantling of the Anglo-Japanese Alliance meant that the British Empire now had to provide the means to defend herself.

Unable to construct and maintain a dedicated fleet sufficient to do so, the Singapore Strategy was evolved, whereby the European- based fleet would be enabled to deploy effectively to the Far East should the need arise. The purpose of the deployment was to defend Imperial 'main interests', defined as trade and territorial integrity.[69] It was calculated that some 23 per cent of the total trade of the British Empire and 60 per cent of Australia's trade passed through the Indian Ocean; a figure vital to the existence of Australia.[70] That severe disturbance to this trade was more likely from Japan in any future conflict, than it had been from Germany in a previous one, was obvious: 'The "Emden" alone was able to seriously dislocate British trade in the Indian Ocean at the commencement of the last war, although she had no base and no support of any sort. [...] How much greater, therefore, would be the effect of 20 "Emdens"?'[71]

When the British Empire and Commonwealth did become embroiled with Japan in the Far East it was with a foe that deployed forces considerably more powerful than the equivalent of '20 Emdens' and with more far-reaching intentions than the disruption of trade. Whether or not the Singapore Strategy was, in Admiral Sir Herbert Richmond's retrospective words, based on an 'illusion that a Two-Hemisphere Empire could be defended by a One-Hemisphere Navy'[72] is not a matter it is proposed to go into here in any depth. Suffice to say it failed for a variety of reasons. Among these, in naval terms, was the detention of the majority of the British Fleet in European waters. This was because there were two main theatres of war, one in Europe and one in the Far East, and the European theatre took precedence. There were simply not enough resources to dispute command of the sea with Japan as well as maintain a powerful enough navy to defend British interests in Europe. This problem had been foreseen. For example, the controversial ex-Royal Naval Commander Russell Grenfell published his contribution to the 'Next War' series, edited by Basil Liddell Hart, in 1938. His logic was persuasive:

> If we send the fleet to the Far East in sufficient strength to dispute the command at sea with the Japanese, what must that strength be? The Japanese capital ships now number nine. In the last war a fifty per cent, superiority in capital ships was deemed barely sufficient to ensure our command at sea against the Germans. If we reduce that necessary superiority to as low as thirty per cent, for our Far Eastern force, we should need to send out at the very least twelve capital ships. Two of our fifteen capital ships being under reconstruction, this means that at the moment the whole of our capital ship fleet but one would have to proceed eastward. With the bulk of the fleet 10,000 miles from Europe and only one battleship left to deal with, would it not be a terrible temptation to Italy with four battleships and Germany with three pocket ones to try to get the better of us while our main strength was occupied elsewhere [?] [...].[73]

That the Imperial Japanese Navy had become, in terms of technology and tactics, very much superior to the Royal Navy was not, in 1938, generally known, and if it had been it would not have been admitted. What actually happened when Japan began hostilities is well known. Rather than a fleet, a small unbalanced force of two capital ships, Force Z, was dispatched, and this proved fatally vulnerable to attack from land-based (naval) aircraft and was swiftly destroyed. In military terms the Singapore Base, which was useless without a fleet in any event, proved vulnerable to land attack from the north.

The inability of the British Empire to reconcile ends with means meant that large portions of it in the Far East had their territorial integrity decisively breached. That Australia and New Zealand were, at least in terms of their mainland territory, untouched other than by air raids was due to the involvement of the other Great Power in the Pacific, the US. The Japanese–American struggle in the Pacific during 1942–45 involved many of the former German territories; for example, from early 1942 Rabaul became the the headquarters for the Japanese Southeastern Fleet, the 11th Air Fleet and the 8th Area Army, with a combined deployment of some 94,000 personnel.[74] Mention has already been made of the fleet headquarters at Truk in the Carolines, which became, in addition, an advanced

Combined Fleet Headquarters.[75] Ultimately, one of the most significant events in human history took place on Tinian Island in the Marianas, at *circa* 0245 on 6 August 1945, when a B-29 bomber named *Enola Gay* took off; the target being Hiroshima.

On 30 October 1918, Winston S. Churchill is said to have remarked that the end of the Great War saw 'a drizzle of Empires falling through the air'.[76] He was referring to the capitulation of the Ottoman Empire and the imminence of the Austro-Hungarian Empire following suit. The German Empire of Kaiser Wilhelm II was not long to survive, and, if one counts Russia as an imperial power, it was the fourth such polity to collapse since 1917. In the current context the end of World War II was to see the destruction of the Japanese Empire, and it registered the beginning of the end for the style of imperialism that had pertained until then. In terms of the Far East, the British Empire was able to reassert itself and reoccupy the territories taken by Japan – and vis-à-vis the French and Dutch Empires the same process was applicable – but not for long.[77]

British prestige had been destroyed by the failure of the Singapore Strategy, and even when the Royal Navy was able to deploy a fleet to the Pacific, nearly at the end of the war, it was subsidiary to the US Navy in every sense.[78] There is perhaps some irony in noting that, with its main base at Sydney, Australia, Task Force 57, as it was designated when operating under the control of the US fleet, used Seeadler Harbour (Port Seeadler), 'one of the best fleet anchorages in the South Pacific,'[79] at Manus Island as its advanced base.[80] Manus, the largest of the Admiralty Islands in the Bismarck Archipelago, was a former German territory.

However, if the formal empires of France, the Netherlands and Britain did not dissolve as drizzle falling through the air, they were certainly melting away. For Britain the most notable sign of the decline of empire was the loss of the 'Jewel in the Crown',[81] occurring when the British Raj on the Indian subcontinent was dissolved in August 1947. The Great Powers had been replaced by two superpowers, and, post 1945, it became ridiculous for Australia and New Zealand to expect that Britain could, or should, be responsible for their defence.

The reality of British abilities in terms of power projection was reflected in the Security Treaty agreed between Australia, New Zealand and the United States of America (ANZUS) on 1 September 1951. The ANZUS Treaty, as it became known, excluded Britain, much to the discomfiture of the British government. Winston S Churchill, who had become Prime Minister again in October 1951, told his Cabinet he 'greatly regretted the Australian acquiescence in the attempt of the United States to usurp our special position in relation to Australia and New Zealand.'[82] Churchill, who had first entered British political life in the reign of Queen Victoria, was of course famously zealous about the British Empire.[83] He was though undoubtedly representing the feelings of many in the party which he led in deprecating any notion of dilution to the principles of imperialism.[84]

None other than Kaiser Wilhelm II had predicted this situation several decades previously, though for the wrong reasons. In one of the few instances where he got things, more or less, right he opined that the visit of the Great White Fleet to

Australia and New Zealand in 1908 presaged a defensive alignment, at the cost of
the British connection, between the three states:

> When self-interest comes in at the door, sentimental patriotism flies out of the
> window. Do you know why Australia and New Zealand invited Mr [Theodore]
> Roosevelt to send the American [Great White] fleet to their shores? [...] That
> invitation was for the express purpose of serving notice of the government of
> [Britain] that those colonies understand they have in the United States a friend
> who understands the white man's duty better then the 'mother country' seems to
> understand it.[85]

While it is probably the case that German colonialism in the Far East was neither
better nor worse than that imposed by various other powers, it is difficult to
escape the conclusion that colonialism per se was a practice that had nothing but
pernicious effects on those subject to it. Foreign interference in Chinese affairs
ceased on 1 October 1949 when Mao proclaimed the People's Republic, but
for many of the peoples of the Pacific Islands, independence took even longer.
For example, the ex-German portion of Samoa only attained independence
from New Zealand in 1962, while Papua New Guinea, comprising the former
German territories of Kaiser Wilhelm's Land and the Bismarck Archipelago
with the British/Australian territory of Papua, became an independent state
only in 1975. The island of Nauru, now the Republic of Nauru and the world's
smallest island nation, became independent in 1968 after being a joint British,
Australian and New Zealand trusteeship from 1947.

The position of the German Pacific island territories that were taken by Japan
in 1914 is more complex. Following Japanese defeat in 1945 many of the various
islands and island groups were administered by the US as part of the United
Nations 'Trust Territory of the Pacific Islands'. These have now evolved into a
number of polities, though with some link to, and in many cases dependence on,
the United States.

The Federated States of Micronesia (FSM) consist of 607 islands extending
across the Caroline Islands archipelago, organised into four groups: Yap, Chuuk
(Truk), Pohnpei (Ponape) and Kosrae. The FSM achieved independence in 1986,
though the federation is a part of the Compact of Free Association with the US
under the auspices of which Washington is responsible for defence and provides
aid and other services.

The Palau Islands became the Republic of Palau after deciding in 1979 not to
join the FSM, and are also, since 1994, part of the Compact of Free Association.
The Republic of the Marshal Islands (RMI) also joined the Compact of Free
Association in 1986, while the Northern Mariana Islands decided in the 1970s not
to seek independence, but instead to forge closer links with the US.[86]

It is however apparent that the colonial legacy lives on long after the phenomenon itself has vanished. Edward Gibbon argued as long ago as 1764 that 'the
history of empires is that of the miseries of humankind'[87] and this, in terms of
the Pacific Islanders, is reinforced to this day. As one of them, Dr Ana Maui
Taufe'ulungaki, put it in 2004:

The history of colonialism for many Pacific peoples and their cultures was one of subjugation and subservience and the swift and sure erosion of the values and the relationships that bound communities together.[88]

And that should be the last word for sure.

Notes to the Text

Chapter 1, pp. 1–16

1. Sir John Robert Seeley, *The Expansion of England: Two Courses of Lectures* (Boston: Little, Brown, 1883). Quoted in Elleke Boehmer, *Empire Writing: An Anthology of Colonial Literature 1870–1918* (Oxford: Oxford University Press, 1998) p. 74.

2. Hans Lothar von Schweinitz, *Briefwechsel des Botschafters* [Exchange of letters of Ambassador] *General von Schweinitz* (Berlin : Reimar Hobbing, 1928) p. 193.

3. Sir Frederick Ponsonby (ed.), *Letters of the Empress Frederick* (London: Macmillan, 1929) p. 195.

4. Four Kingdoms [Bavaria, Prussia, Saxony, Württemberg], six Grand Duchies [Baden, Hesse, Mecklenburg-Schwerin, Mecklenburg-Strelitz, Oldenburg, Saxe-Weimar-Eisenach], five Duchies [Anhalt, Brunswick-Lüneburg, Saxe-Altenburg, Saxe-Coburg and Gotha, Saxe-Meiningen], seven Principalities [Lippe, Reuss-Gera, Reuss-Greiz, Schaumburg-Lippe, Schwarzburg-Rudolstadt, Schwarzburg-Sondershausen, Waldeck-Pyrmont] and three city Republics [Bremen, Hamburg, Lübeck]. All these polities were 'disparate in size, constitutional development, religion, social structure, economy and historical origin.' David Schoenbaum, *Zabern 1913: Consensus Politics in Imperial Germany* (London: George Allen & Unwin, 1982) p. 29.

5. Richard William Mackey, *The Zabern Affair 1913–1914* (New York: University Press of America, 1991) p. 29.

6. Quoted in V. R. Berghahn, *Germany and the Approach of War in 1914*, 2nd edn (London: Palgrave Macmillan, 1993) p. 20.

7. Guenther Roth, *The Social Democrats in Imperial Germany: A Study in Working-Class Isolation and National Integration* (Totowa, NJ: Bedminster Press, 1963) p. 59.

8. Schoenbaum, p. 29.

9. H. W. Koch, *A History of Prussia* (London: Longman, 1978) p. 245.

10. Schoenbaum, p. 60.

11. Robert B. Kane, *Disobedience and Conspiracy in the German Army, 1918–1945* (Jefferson, NC: McFarland, 2002) p. 38 n82.

12. Otto Fürst [Prince] von Bismarck *Die Gesammelten Werke* [The Collected Works] 15 vols (Berlin: Stollberg, 1924–35) VIII, p. 646.

13. Matthew S. Seligmann, *Rivalry in Southern Africa, 1893–99: The Transformation of German Colonial Policy* (London: Palgrave Macmillan, 1998) p. 137.

14. Wilhelm II, Emperor of Germany, 1888–1918 (trans. Thomas R. Ybarra), *The Kaiser's Memoirs* (New York; Harper & Brothers, 1922) p. 7

15. A. J. P. Taylor opined that 'The League of the Three Emperors was 'a fair weather system. Though designed to prevent an Austro-Russian conflict in the Balkans, in fact it worked only so long as there was no conflict.' A. J. P. Taylor, *The Struggle for Mastery in Europe 1848–1915* (Oxford; Oxford University Press, 1954) p. 304.

16. Wilhelm II, p. 9.

17. S. S. Mackenzie, *Rabaul: The Australians at Rabaul: The Capture and Administration of The German Possessions in the Southern Pacific*, 10th edn (Sydney, NSW: Angus & Robertson, 1941),Vol. X of C. E. W. Bean (ed.), *The Official History of Australia in the War of 1914–1918*, 12 vols various edns (Sydney, NSW: Angus & Robertson, 1941) p. 7.

18. Mackenzie, p. 22.

19. Gordon A Craig, *Germany 1866–1945* (Oxford: Oxford University Press, 1988) p. 119.

20. Craig, p. 119. See also: Arne Perras, *Carl Peters and German Imperialism 1856–1918: A Political Biography* (Oxford: Clarendon Press, 2004).

21. E. A. Jacob, *Deutsche Kolonialpolitik in Dokumenten: Gedanken und Gestalten der letzten fünfzig Jahre* [German Colonial Politics in Documents: Thoughts and Patterns from the Last Fifty Years] (Leipzig: Dieterich, 1938) pp. 85–7.

22. Judith A. Bennett, 'Holland, Britain, and Germany in Melanesia', in K. R. Howe, Robert C. Kiste and Brij V. Lal (eds) *Tides of History: The Pacific Islands in the Twentieth Century* (Honolulu: University of Hawaii Press, 1994) p. 53. The reference to 'the dead' is on account of the mortality rate among the labourers shipped there to work the plantations. Some forty per cent of them are reckoned to have perished. Robert J. Foster, *Social Reproduction and History in Melanesia: Mortuary Ritual, Gift Exchange, and Custom in the Tanga Islands* (Cambridge: Cambridge University Press, 1995) p. 42.

23. Steven Roger Fischer, *A History of the Pacific Islands* (London: Palgrave Macmillan, 2002) p. 165.

24. For an account of the matter see Bernard O'Reilly, *Life of Leo XIII from an Authentic Memoir Furnished by His Order: Written with the Encouragement, Approbation and Blessing of His Holiness the Pope* (Sydney: Oceanic Publishing, 1887) pp. 537–54.

25. The International Court of Justice, *Case Concerning Certain Phosphate Lands in Nauru (Nauru v. Australia)* Vol. 1, *Application: Memorial of Nauru* (New York: United Nations Publications, 2003) p. 33.

26. Gerd Hardach, 'Defining Separate Spheres: German Rule and Colonial Law in Micronesia', in Herman J. Hiery and John M MacKenzie (eds.), *European Impact and Pacific Influence: British and German Policy in the Pacific Islands and the Indigenous Response* (London: I. B. Tauris 1997) p. 235. W. O. Henderson, *Studies in German Colonial History* (London: Frank Cass, 1962) p. 26.

27. For example, in relation to Herbert Bismarck: 'the policy pursued was always Bismarck's own; there is nothing to show that he [Herbert] took any share in determining the ends that German policy was designed to achieve [...] He differs from other statesmen in that he was never carrying out a policy of his own. What he did [...] with enormous success was to act as an instrument of his father, almost as an extension of his father's personality', William Osgood Aydelotte, *Bismarck and British Colonial Policy: The Problem of South West Africa 1883–1885* (Philadelphia: University of Pennsylvania Press, 1937) p. 162.

28. Wilhelm II, p. 35.

29. Wilhelm II, p. 2.

30. 9 March – 15 June.

31. Alan Palmer, *The Kaiser: Warlord of the Second Reich* (London: Weidenfeld & Nicolson, 1978) p. 34.

32. Bismarck, Vol. XV, pp. 455–6.

33. Quoted in Palmer, p. 54.
34. James W. Gerard, *Face to Face with Kaiserism* (London: Hodder & Stoughton, 1918) pp. 4–5.
35. Gerard, p. 4.
36. Winston S. Churchill, *Great Contemporaries* (London: Odhams Press, 1949) pp. 27–8.
37. Craig, p. 225.
38. W. B. Ober, 'Obstetrical events that shaped Western European history', *Yale Journal of Biology and Medicine* 65 (May–June 1992), pp. 208–9.
39. Willem-Alexander van't Padje, 'The "Malet Incident," October 1895: A Prelude to the Kaiser's "Kruger Telegram" in the Context of the Anglo-German Imperialist Rivalry', in Geoff Eley and James Retallack (eds), *German Modernities, Imperialism, and the Meanings of Reform, 1890–1930: Essays for Hartmut Pogge von Strandmann* (Oxford: Berghahn, 2003) p. 138.
40. Quoted in: John C. G. Röhl (trans. Sheila de Bellaigue), *Wilhelm II: The Kaiser's Personal Monarchy, 1888–1900* (Cambridge: Cambridge University Press, 2004) p. 305.
41. David H. Olivier, *German Naval Strategy, 1856–1888: Forerunners of Tirpitz* (London: Frank Cass, 2004) p. 130.
42. Lawrence Sondhaus, *Naval Warfare, 1815–1914* (London: Routledge, 2001) pp. 146–7.
43. Olivier, p. 175.
44. Röhl, *Personal Monarchy*, p. 321.
45. Bernard Heller, *Dawn or Dusk?* (New York: Bookman's, 1961) p. 34
46. Garrett Epps, *Democracy Reborn: The Fourteenth Amendment and the Fight for Equal Rights in Post-Civil War America* (New York: Henry Holt, 2006) p. 265.
47. Helga Hughes, *Germany's Regional Recipes: Foods, Festivals, Folklore* (Iowa City, IA; Penfield, 2002) p. 34.
48. Hermann Lutz (trans. E. W. Dickes), *Lord Grey and the World War* (London: Allen & Unwin, 1928) p. 35.
49. Martin Kitchen, *A History of Modern Germany 1800–2000* (Oxford: Blackwell, 2006) p. 184.
50. Konrad Hugo Jarausch and Michael Geyer, *Shattered Past: Reconstructing German Histories* (Princeton, NJ: Princeton University Press, 2003) p. 242.
51. Katherine A. Lerman, 'Some Basic Statistics for Germany, 1815–1918', in Mary Fulbrook (ed.), *German History since 1800* (London: Arnold, 1997) p. 216.
52. John C. G. Röhl, *Germany Without Bismarck: The Crisis of Government in the Second Reich, 1890–1900* (Berkeley: University of California Press, 1967) p. 25.
53. Das Staatsarchiv (trans. Adam Blauhut), *Sammlung der offiziellen Aktenstücke zur Geschichte der Gegenwart* [Collection of Official Documents Relating to Contemporary History] (Leipzig: Duncker & Humblot, 1891) Vol. 51, p. 151.
54. Helmuth Stoecker, *German Imperialism in Africa: From the Beginnings until the Second World War* (London: Hurst, 1986) p. 101. Richard J. Evans, *The Coming of the Third Reich* (New York; Penguin, 2004) p. 30.
55. Mildred S. Wertheimer, *The Pan-German League, 1890–1914* (New York: Columbia University Press, 1923), p. 31. See also: Ed Feuchtwanger *Imperial Germany 1850–1918* (London: Routledge, 2001) p. 117.

56. For an account of the construction and history of the canal see Wilhelm Otto Lampe 'The Kiel Canal', in Renate Platzoder and Philomene Verlaan (eds), *The Baltic Sea: New Developments in National Policies and International Cooperation* (The Hague: Kluwer Law International, 1996) pp. 133–42.

57. Das Staatsarchiv (trans. Adam Blauhut), *Sammlung der offiziellen Aktenstücke zur Geschichte der Gegenwart* [Collection of Official Documents Relating to Contemporary History] (Leipzig; Duncker & Humblot, 1891) Vol. 51, p. 151.

58. Only the lower Zambezi is navigable for a distance of some 650km from the Indian Ocean. The 'Strip' itself contains difficult terrain, it is intersected by the Cubango–Okavango and Cuando–Linyati–Chobe rivers and contains large areas of swamp, making it impassable during certain seasons. It has been mooted as a possible attempt to acquire a route across southern Africa. See Ieuan L. Griffiths 'African Land and Access Corridors', in Dick Hodder, Sarah J. Lloyd and Keith McLachlan (Eds.), *Land Locked States of Africa and Asia* (London: Frank Cass, 1998) p. 73.

59. For an authoritative account of the 'Chancellor Crisis' of 1894 see Röhl, *Germany Without Bismarck*, pp. 110–17.

60. Martin Kitchen, *A History of Modern Germany, 1800–2000* (Malden, MA; Blackwell, 2006) p. 185.

61. Paul Kennedy, *The Rise and Fall of the Great Powers: Economic Change and Military Conflict from 1500–2000* (New York; Random House, 1987) p. 214.

62. Modris Eksteins, *Rites of Spring: The Great War and the Birth of the Modern Age* (Boston: Houghton Mifflin, 1989) p. 86.

63. See for example, Iikura Akira 'The "Yellow Peril" and its Influence on Japanese-German Relations', in Christian W. Spang and Rolf-Harald Wippich (eds), *Japanese-German Relations, 1895–1945: War, Diplomacy and Public Opinion* (London: Routledge, 2006) p. 80.

64. S. C. M. Paine *The Sino-Japanese War of 1894–1895: Perceptions, Power, and Primacy* (Cambridge: Cambridge University Press, 2002) p. 3.

65. An archipelago off the western coast of Formosa (now Taiwan) consisting of 64 small islands covering an area of some 80km.

66. For an account of the conflict see Paine.

67. Richard Rubinger, 'Education in Meiji Japan', in Wm. Theodore de Bary, Carol Gluck, Donald Keene (eds), *Sources of Japanese Tradition*, 2 vols, 2nd edn (Columbia University Press, 2003) Vol. II, p. 86.

68. Frank W. Ikle, 'The Triple Intervention: Japan's Lesson in the Diplomacy of Imperialism', *Monumenta Nipponica* 22, no. 1–2 (1967) p. 125.

69. Ian Nish, *Collected Writings* (London; Routledge Curzon, 2001) Part 1, p. 188.

70. Journal Entry of 11 September 1895. Friedrich Curtius (ed.) *Memoirs of Prince Chlodwig of Hohenlohe Schillingsfuerst*, trans. George W. Chrystal, 2 vols (London: William Heinemann, 1906). Vol. II, p. 463.

71. W. G. Beasley *Japanese Imperialism 1894–1945* (Cary, NC: Oxford University Press, 1991) p. 59.

72. Nish, *Collected Writings*, p. 188.

73. Prince Bernhard von Bülow (trans. Marie A. Lewenz), *Imperial Germany*, 3rd impression (London: Cassell 1914) pp. 43–4.

74. Schwarzenstein to Bülow, 19 June 1907. E. T. S. Dugdale (ed. and trans.) German Diplomatic Documents, 1871–1914. Vol. III, 'The Growing Antagonism, 1898–1910' (New York: Harper & Brothers, 1930), p. 13.

75. Schwarzenstein to Bülow, 19 June 1907. Dugdale, p. 13.

76. Paine, p. 288.

77. 'Imperial Rescript', *The Japan Weekly Mail* (Yokohama) 18 May 1895, p. 565.

78. Mutsu Munemitsu (ed. and trans. Gordon Mark Berger) *Kenkenroku: A Diplomatic Record of the Sino-Japanese War, 1894–95*, repr. edn (Tokyo: University of Tokyo Press, 1995) p. 250. Aside from the protagonists, those most affected, at least on the commercial front, by the Sino-Japanese War were the British. British involvement in China was of long standing and almost entirely trade-based. It has been argued that Britain, India and China were structurally linked to one another in a trade triangle that, until the 1860s, was one of the most important components of the world economy. It is rather shocking to modern sensibilities to realise that this trade was to a large extent based on the supply of a narcotic substance; opium. Some 30 per cent of the total exports from India to China in 1868 were of opium, and by 1880 this had risen to nearly 40 per cent; some 4,800 tonnes. Thereafter the trade declined to around 3,000 tonnes per annum, a level maintained until 1905. Such was the degree of domination exercised by Britain in terms of commerce that the Inspector General of the Chinese Maritime Customs Service was British. The longest holder of this post, from 1863 to 1908, was an Irishman, Sir Robert Hart, and the higher levels of the service were filled predominantly by British personnel. Such an arrangement was tolerated by China because it guaranteed a reliable source of revenue, and was internationally acceptable because of the implied safeguards for foreign capital investment. For a study of the opium trade see Gregory Blue, 'Opium for China: the British Connection', in Timothy Brook and Bob Tadashi Wakabayashi, *Opium Regimes: China, Britain, and Japan, 1839–1952* (Collingdale, PA: Diane, 2000). For a somewhat hagiographic account of Hart's life and career see the work by his niece: Juliet Bredon, *Sir Robert Hart: The Romance of a Great Career* (London: Hutchinson, 1909). Hart's papers are at Queen's University, Belfast.

79. Matthew Jefferies, *Imperial Culture in Germany, 1871–1918* (New York: Palgrave Macmillan, 2003) **p. 63.** Barbara W. Tuchman, *The Zimmerman Telegram* (New York: Viking Press, 1956) pp. 25–6. John C. G. Röhl (trans. Terence F. Cole), *The Kaiser and his Court: Wilhelm II and the Government of Germany* (Cambridge; NY: Cambridge University Press, 1994) p. 203. Lamar Cecil, *Wilhelm II: Emperor and Exile, 1900–1941* (Chapel Hill: University of North Carolina Press, 1996) p. 38.

80. Iikura Akira 'The "Yellow Peril" and its Influence on Japanese-German Relations', in Christian W. Spang and Rolf-Harald Wippich (eds) *Japanese-German Relations, 1895–1945: War, Diplomacy and Public Opinion* (London: Routledge, 2006) p. 81.

81. Iikura, p. 81.

Chapter 2, pp. 17–30

1. Terrell D. Gottschall, *By Order of the Kaiser: Otto von Diederichs and the Rise of the Imperial German Navy 1865–1902* (Annapolis MD; Naval Institute Press, 2003) p. 134.

2. Grand Admiral von Tirpitz, *My Memoirs* (London: Hurst & Blackett, 1919) 2 vols, Vol. I, p. 70.

3. Tirpitz, p. 73.

4. Tirpitz, p. 93.

5. Gottschall, p. 136.

6. Walter Nuhn, *Kolonialpolitik und Marine: Die Rolle der Kaiserlichen Marine bei der Gründung und Sicherung des deutschen Kolonialreiches 1884–1914* [Colonial Policy and the Navy: The Role of the Imperial Navy in the Establishment and Protection of the German Colonial Empire 1884–1914] (Bonn; Bernard & Graefe, 2003) p. 132.

7. Gottschall, p. 104.

8. The accolade is taken from an invitation by the Gesellschaft für Erdkunde zu Berlin (Geographical Society of Berlin) to attend an International Symposium in Honour of Ferdinand von Richthofen. Held at the Humboldt-Universität between 6 and 8 October 2005, this event commemorated the 100th anniversary of his death.

9. Arvo Vercamer, 'German Military Mission to China 1927–1938', article on website; consulted on 31 August 2006, www.feldgrau.com/articles.php?ID=11.

10. Gottschall, p. 146.

11. Tirpitz, p. 75.

12. Joseph W. Esherick, *The Origins of the Boxer Uprising* (Berkley: University of California Press, 1987) p. 81.

13. George Steinmetz, '"The Devil's Handwriting": Precolonial Discourse, Ethnographic Acuity, and Cross-Identification in German Colonialism', Comparative Studies in Society and History 45/1 (January 2003) p. 26.

14. Lanzin Xiang, *The Origins of the Boxer War* (London: Routledge Curzon, 2002) p. 67.

15. Steinmetz, p. 26.

16. For an account of this incident and the context within which it took place see Esherick, pp. 123–35.

17. Kaiser Wilhelm to the Foreign Office 6 November 1897. Quoted in John C. G. Röhl (trans. Sheila de Bellaigue) *Wilhelm II: The Kaiser's Personal Monarchy, 1888–1900* (Cambridge: Cambridge University Press 2004) p. 955.

18. The Kaiser to Diederichs, telegram 7 November 1897. Quoted in Röhl, *Personal Monarchy*, p. 955.

19. Diederichs to Knorr, 8 November 1897. Quoted in Gottschall, p. 157.

20. Gottschall, p. 157.

21. Quoted in Röhl, *Personal Monarchy*, p. 956.

22. Extract from the Kaiser to Bernhard von Bülow, telegram 7 November 1897. E. T. S. Dugdale (ed. and trans.) German Diplomatic Documents, 1871–1914. Volume III, The Growing Antagonism, 1898–1910 (New York: Harper & Brothers, 1930) p. 14.

23. Extract from the Kaiser to Bernhard von Bülow, telegram 7 November 1897. Dugdale, p. 14.

24. Quoted in Röhl, *Personal Monarchy*, p. 956

25. The Kaiser to Bernhard von Bülow, telegram 7 November 1897. Dugdale, p. 14.

26. Extract from the Kaiser to Bernhard von Bülow, telegram 7 November 1897. Dugdale, p. 14.

27. Ibid.

28. http://peterhof.ru.

29. Mikhail Muraviev was Russia's Foreign Minister from 1896 until his death in 1900.

30. Count Witte (ed. A. Yarmolinsky), *The Memoirs of Count Witte* (London: William Heinemann, 1921) p. 410.

31. Rotenhan to the Kaiser, 10 November 1897. Dugdale, p. 14.

32. Holstein to Hohenlohe, 9 November 1897. Quoted in Röhl, *Personal Monarchy*, p. 957.

33. Hohenlohe to Rotenham, 10 November 1897. Quoted in Röhl, *Personal Monarchy*, p. 957.

34. Rotenhan to Bülow, 11 November 1897. Quoted in Röhl, *Personal Monarchy*, p. 957.

35. Captain Bernard Smith, 'The Siege of Tsingtau', The Coast Artillery Journal, November–December 1934, p. 405.

36. Information taken from Qingdaoshan Hill Battery Fort Educational Base. This area was visited by Dennis and Adrienne Quarmby in 2006, and I am extremely grateful to them for sharing it with me, and for allowing me to use several photographs they took while there.

37. Gottschall, p. 160.

38. Feng Djen Djang, *The Diplomatic Relations Between China and Germany since 1898* (Shanghai: Commercial Press, 1936) p. 45.

39. Röhl, *Personal Monarchy*, p. 957. For Tirpitz's 'cold feet' on the matter, which he omitted to mention in his memoirs, see Jonathan Steinberg, *Tirpitz and the Birth of the German Battle Fleet: Yesterday's Deterrent* (London: Macdonald, 1968) pp. 155–6.

40. Koester to Diederichs, 13 November 1897. Quoted in Gottschall, p. 160.

41. Diederichs to Koester, 14 November 1897. Quoted in Gottschall, p. 160.

42. Knorr to Diederichs, 15 November 1897. Quoted in Gottschall, p. 160.

43. Memo of 15 November 1897. Quoted in Röhl, *Personal Monarchy*, p. 958.

44. The 'Triple Intervention'.

45. Journal Entry of 11 September 1895. Friedrich Curtius (ed.), *Memoirs of Prince Chlodwig of Hohenlohe Schillingsfürst*, trans. George W. Chrystal, 2 vols (London: William Heinemann, 1906) Vol. II, p. 463.

46. Hohenlohe to Count Hatzfeldt, 16 November 1897. Dugdale, p. 14.

47. Hohenlohe to the Kaiser, 18 November 1897. Quoted in Röhl, *Personal Monarchy*, p. 958.

48. Marginal annotation by the Kaiser in Hohenlohe to the Kaiser, 18 November 1897. Quoted in Röhl, *Personal Monarchy*, p. 958.

49. Steinberg, p. 172.

50. Kaiser Wilhelm to the Foreign Office, 24 November 1897. Quoted in Röhl, *Personal Monarchy*, pp. 958–9.

51. The Second Division was to consist of: the protected cruiser Kaiserin Augusta (1892), name ship of her class; the Gefion-class light cruiser Gefion (1893); the central battery ironclad Deutschland (1874), sister ship to Kaiser); and Cormoran, which was already on station.

52. Feng Djen Djang, *The Diplomatic Relations Between China and Germany since 1898* (Shanghai; Commercial Press, 1936) p. 50.

53. Kaiser Wilhelm to Hohenlohe, 26 November 1897. Quoted in Röhl, *Personal Monarchy*, p. 958.

54. Diary entry, 29 November. Quoted in Röhl, *Personal Monarchy*, p. 958.

55. Feng, p. 91.

56. King Frederick William of Prussia had constituted the first Naval Battalion in 1852 from the Marinierkorps, a body that had itself been created in 1850 as an organic naval replacement for army troops assigned to naval duties. The Battalion had been increased to five companies in 1869 and then six companies in 1871. In 1889 it was divided to form I and II Naval Battalions.

57. C. Hugüenin, Oberleutnant im III. See-Bataillon, Geschichte Des III. See-Bataillons (Tsingtaü: Adolf Haupt, 1912) [C. Hugüenin, First Lieutenant III Naval Battalion, History of the III Naval Battalion (Tsingtaü; Adolf Haupt, 1912)] p. 15.

58. Kaiser Wilhelm, speech of 15 December 1897. Quoted in Röhl, *Personal Monarchy*, p. 960.

59. The Times (London), 17 December 1897.

60. 1 commander (Major Kopka von Lossow)
    5 company commanders
    14 lieutenants
    2 physicians
    1 paymaster
    2 assistant paymasters
    3 armourers
    1,117 NCOs and men
    1 second lieutenant (Marine Artillery).
    1 pioneer section
    1 field telegraphic section
    1 military hospital together with personnel.
    See Hugüenin, p. 13.

61. Feng, p. 70. Taken from *Handbuch far das Schutzgebiet Kiautschou* (this book contains all the Imperial decrees, edicts and laws for the German Protectorate of Kiautschou, compiled by F. W. Mohr, formerly assistant interpreter of the Kiautschou government).

62. Gottschall, p. 176.

63. Feng, p. 70.

64. German Historical Institute, Washington, DC. German History in Documents and Images (GHDI), http://germanhistorydocs.ghi-dc.org, Wilhelmine 'Germany and the First World War, 1890–1918. An "Unequal Treaty": Lease Agreement between China and the German Empire' (6 March 1898).

65. German Historical Institute, Washington, DC. German History in Documents and Images (GHDI), http://germanhistorydocs.ghi-dc.org Wilhelmine 'Germany and the First World War, 1890–1918'.

66. Eyre Crowe, 'Memorandum on the Present State of British Relations with France and Germany' (1 January 1907), in G. P. Gooch and H. W. V. Temperly (eds), *British Documents on the Origins of the War, 1898–1914*, 11 vols (London: HM Stationery Office, 1926–1938), Vol. III, *The Testing of the Entente 1904–6*, Appendix A.

Chapter 3, pp. 31–48

1. John W. Steinberg, Bruce W. Menning, David Schimmelpenninck Van Der Oye *et al.* (eds), *The Russo-Japanese War in Global Perspective: World War Zero* (Leiden: Brill Academic Publishers, 2005) pp. 31–2.

2. Hong Kong Island had been a British Crown Colony since 1843, and the southern portion of the Kowloon Peninsula had been added to this in 1860 following the Second Opium War. On 1 July 1898 a further 740 square kilometres, the 'New Territories', was leased for 99 years.

3. Clarence B. Davis and Robert J. Gowen, 'The British at Weihaiwei: A Case Study in the Irrationality of Empire', *The Historian* 63, 22 September 2000, p. 88.

4. 'Convention between Great Britain and China, respecting Wei-hai Wei, Signed at Peking, 1 July 1898', in *British and Foreign State Papers, 1897–1898*, Vol. 90 (London: HMSO, 1901) pp. 16–17.

5. Immanuel C. Y. Hsu, *The Rise of Modern China*, 6th edn (New York: Oxford University Press, 1999) p. 381. See Lanxin Xiang, *The Origins of the Boxer War: A Multinational Study* (London: Routledge Curzon, 2003) pp. 79–104 for a detailed explanation of Italy's 'Theatrical Performance' in its attempts to carve out a chunk of Chinese territory.

6. Herbert H. Gowen, *An Outline History of China*, 2 vols (Boston; Sherman, French & Co., 1913) Vol. II, p. 158. An 1886 graduate of St Augustine's College, Canterbury, England, Gowen was much involved in missionary work before becoming rector of Seattle's Protestant Episcopal Trinity Church in 1897. The possessor of a formidable intellect, Gowen was trained in classical Arabic, Sanskrit, and Hebrew and taught himself Chinese and Japanese; he was therefore well placed to become the first, and for many years the only, professor in the Department of Oriental Studies at the University of Washington state in 1909. From then until he retired in 1944 he taught the history and literature of China, Japan, India, and the Near East, as well as Sanskrit, Arabic, Hebrew, and the history of religion. He was alleged to have read a book a day, and students and faculty members remember seeing him stroll across the campus, head down reading, pockets sagging with the weight of still more books to be read. Gowen continued his learning habits until the day of his death in 1960 at the age of 96, http://www.washington.edu/newsroom/tour/lib_quad.html.

7. George Steinmetz, '"The Devil's Handwriting": Precolonial Discourse, Ethnographic Acuity, and Cross-Identification in German Colonialism', *Comparative Studies in Society and History* 45/1 (January 2003) pp. 6–7.

8. Steinmetz, pp. 6–7.

9. Ibid.

10. See Wolfgang U. Eckart, *Medizin und Kolonialimperialismus: Deutschland 1884–1945* [Medicine and Colonial Imperialism: Germany 1884–1945] (Vienna: Ferdinand Schoeningh, 1997).

11. Lord Charles Beresford *The Break-Up of China: With an Account of Its Present Commerce, Currency, Waterways, Armies, Railways, Politics, and Future Prospects* (New York; Harper & Brothers, 1900) p. 73.

12. Beresford, p. 75.

13. Arthur Judson Brown, *New Forces in Old China: An Inevitable Awakening*, 2nd edn (New York; F. H. Revell, 1904) p. 176.

14. Brown, p. 176.
15. Brown, pp. 177–8.
16. Brown, p. 178.
17. Brown, p. 177.
18. Ibid.
19. F. H. King, *Farmers of Forty Centuries: Organic Farming in China, Korea and Japan* (Madison, WI; F.H. King, 1911) p. 217. This work is now available online at http://www.soilandhealth.org/01aglibrary/010122king/ffc10.html .
20. King, p. 217.
21. King, pp. 217–18.
22. P. Sprigade and M. Moisel (eds), *Deutscher Kolonialatlas mit Jahrbuch: Herausgegeben auf Veranlassung der Deutschen Kolonialgesellschaft* [German Colonial Atlas with Year-book] (Berlin: Ernst Vohsen, 1918) p.30.
23. Beresford, p. 310.
24. Pukou lies across the Chang Jiang (Yangtze River) from Nanjing (Nanking). The Nanjing–Shanghai Railway was linked with the Tientsin–Pukow line by train ferry, whereby travellers crossed the river between Nanjing and Pukou.
25. Hsu, p. 435.
26. For an account of the area and China's natural resources in general, see Geo. G. Chisholm, 'The Resources and Means of Communication of China', The Geographical Journal 12/5 (November 1898) pp. 500–19.
27. P. Sprigade and M. Moisel (eds), 'Rückblick auf die Entwicklung Ostasiens im Jahre 1904', in *Deutscher Kolonialatlas mit Jahrbuch* (Berlin: Ernst Vohsen, 1905) p. 22.
28. Sprigade and Moisel (1905) p. 23.
29. P. Sprigade and M. Moisel (eds) 'Rückblick auf die Entwicklung Ostasiens im Jahre 1904' in *Deutscher Kolonialatlas mit Jahrbuch* (Berlin; Ernst Vohsen, 1909) p. 35.
30. Werner Abelshauser, Wolfgang von Hippel, Jeffrey Allan Johnson and Raymond G. Stokes, *German Industry and Global Enterprise: BASF: The History of a Company* (Cambridge: Cambridge University Press, 2003) p.140.
31. More accurately, there were two cartels formed by the six dominant German companies. BASF, Bayer, and Hoechst formed one, while Agfa, Cassella, and Kalle made up the other. These six, together with another two, Ter Meer and Greisham, formed a single, more integrated group in 1916, and eventually merged formally in 1925, to form *Interessen Gemeinschaft Farbenindustrie Aktiengesellschaf,* or the, post-World War II, infamous I. G. Farben.
32. Augustin M. Prentiss, *Chemicals in War: A Treatise in Chemical Warfar* (New York: McGraw-Hill, 1937) p. xvi.
33. See Joseph Borkin, *The Crime and Punishment of IG Farben* (London: Andre Deutsch, 1979).
34. See Chang Kia-ngau *China's Struggle for Railroad Development* (New York: The John Day Company, 1943).
35. Prince Heinrich to Kaiser Wilhelm, 11 July 1898. Quoted in Bernhard von Bülow (trans. F A Voight) *Memoirs of Prince von Bülow: From Secretary of State to Imperial Chancellor 1897–1903* (Boston; Little, Brown, 1931) p. 240.
36. Sprigade and Moisel (1909) p. 35.

37. *Deutscher Kolonial-Atlas mit Jahrbuch* [Atlas German Colonies with Yearbook], edited by the Deutsche Kolonialgesellschaft [German Colonial Society] (Berlin 1907), p.27

38. None of Germany's colonies appealed as investment opportunities for German capitalists, who, by 1914, had put only some 3.8 per cent of a total overseas investment amounting to 25 billion Marks into the various territories. Holger H. Herwig, '*Luxury*' *Fleet: The German Imperial Navy 1888–1918* (London: George Allen & Unwin, 1980) p. 107

39. John E. Schrecker, *Imperialism and Chinese Nationalism: Germany in Shantung* (Cambridge MA; Harvard University Press, 1971) pp. 21–5; Herwig, '*Luxury*' *Fleet*, p. 105.

40. See Wolfgang Bauer, 'Tsingtao's Trade and Economy from the Japanese Occupation in 1914, until the End of the 1920s', *The Asiatic Society of Japan Bulletin* No. 1, January 1996.

41. Herwig, '*Luxury*' *Fleet*, p. 105.

42. http://www.tsingtaobeer.com/index.htm.

43. Thomas Schoonover, *Uncle Sam's War of 1898 and the Origins of Globalization* (Lexington: University Press of Kentucky, 2003) p. 46.

44. Fred D. Cavinder, *Amazing Tales from Indiana* (Indianapolis: Indiana University Press, 1990) pp. 20–1.

45. Yongling Lu and Ruth Hayhoe, 'Chinese Higher Learning: the Transition Process from Classical Knowledge Patterns to Modern Disciplines, 1860–1910', in Christopher Charle, Jürgen Schriewer and Peter Wagner (eds) *Transitional Intellectual Networks: Forms of Academic Knowledge and the Search for Cultural Identities* (Frankfurt: Campus, 2004) p. 284.

46. *The Chinese Recorder*, 28 March 1897, pp. 111–16. The Protestant missionary community in China published *The Chinese Recorder* on a monthly basis from the 1860s until 1941. While it provided information about individual missionaries and mission activities, it also featured articles on China's people, history, and culture.

47. W. A. P. Martin, *The Awakening of China* (New York: Doubleday, Page, 1907) p. 30.

48. Benjamin A. Elman, *A Cultural History of Civil Examinations in Late Imperial China* (Berkeley: University of California Press, 2000) p. 589.

49. Ichisada Miyazaki (trans. Conrad Schirokauer), *China's Examination Hell: The Civil Service Examinations of Imperial China* (New Haven, CT: Yale University Press, 1976) p. 14.

50. Michael R. Godley, *The Mandarin-Capitalists from Nanyang: Overseas Chinese Enterprise in the Modernisation of China 1893–1911* (Cambridge: Cambridge University Press, 2002) p. 86.

51. Kenneth Lieberthal, *Governing China: From Revolution Through Reform* (New York: Norton, 1995) p. 23.

52. Lieberthal, p. 24.

53. Michael Dillon, *China: A Historical and Cultural Dictionary* (London: Curzon Press, 1998) p. 169.

54. Yang Xiao, 'Liang Qichai's Political and Social Philosophy', in Chung-Yin Cheng and Nicholas Bunnin, *Contemporary Chinese Philosophy* (Malden, MA: Blackwell, 2002) p. 17.

55. For an account of the Dowager Empress see Marina Warner, *The Dragon Empress: The Life and Times of Tz'u-hsi, Empress Dowager of China, 1835–1908* (New York: Macmillan, 1972).

56. Yang Xiao 'Liang Qichai's Political and Social Philosophy', in Chung-Yin Cheng and Bunnin, *Contemporary Chinese Philosophy*, p. 18.

57. W. Scott Morton and Charlton M. Lewis, *China: Its History and Culture*, 4th edn (New York; McGraw-Hill, 2005) p. 171. Lanxin Xiang, p. 22.

58. Yang, p. 18.

59. Quoted in Lanxin Xiang, p. 112. Also in Hosea Ballou Morse, *The International Relations of the Chinese Empire: The Period of Subjection 1894–1911* (London: Longmans, Green, 1918) pp. 175–6.

60. Lanxin Xiang, p. 112.

61. Mike Davis, *Late Victorian Holocausts: El Niño Famines and the Making of the Third World* (New York: Verso Books, 2002) p. 448.

62. Joseph W. Esherick, *The Origins of the Boxer Uprising* (Berkeley: University of California Press, 1987) p. 1

63. Esherick, pp. 188–9.

64. Annika Mombauer, 'Wilhelm, Waldersee, and the Boxer Rebellion', in Annika Mombauer and Wilhelm Deist (eds), *The Kaiser: New Research on Wilhelm II's Role in Imperial Germany* (Cambridge: Cambridge University Press, 2003) p. 92.

65. Manfred Franz Bömeke, Roger Chickering and Stig Förster, *Anticipating Total War: The German and American Experiences, 1871–1914* (Cambridge; Cambridge University Press, 1999) p. 462.

66. For an account of Waldersee's relationship with Wilhelm see John C. G. Röhl, *Young Wilhelm: The Kaiser's Early Life, 1859–1888* (Cambridge: Cambridge University Press, 1998) pp. 490–507. Wilhelm's closeness to Waldersee has also been attributed to the person of Waldersee's American- born wife, the former Mary Esther Lee of New York, Countess Waldersee was some twenty-one years senior to Wilhelm, and while this does not of itself rule out the possibility of a relationship there is no evidence to support the contention. See Alson J. Smith, *A View of the Spree: The Extraordinary Career of the American Grocer's Daughter Who Became a 'Sanctified Pompadour'* (New York: John Day, 1962).

67. Mombauer, 'Wilhelm, Waldersee, and the Boxer Rebellion', pp. 93, 108.

68. Wilhelm Schroeder (ed.) (trans. Richard S. Levy), *Das persönliche Regiment: Reden und sonstige öffentliche Äusserungen Wilhelms II* [*The Personal Regime: Speeches and Public Expressions of Wilhelm II*] (Munich: Birk, 1912) pp. 40–2.

69. The troop strength of the various nationalities has been computed as follows: Japanese 8,000, Russians 4,800, British (mainly Indian) 3,000, Americans 2,100, French (mainly from French Indo-China) 800, Austrian 58, and Italian 53. See Hosea Ballou Morse, *The International Relations of the Chinese Empire: Volume 3. The Period of Subjection 1894–1911* (Elibron Classics, 2001) p. 262.

70. David Steele, *Lord Salisbury: A Political Biography* (London: Routledge, 2005) p. 337.

71. Bömeke, Chickering and Förster, *Anticipating Total War: The German and American Experiences, 1871–1914* , p. 462.

72. Not just the Imperial capital was affected, but 'virtually every town and city of Zhili

province.' See James Louis Hevia, *English Lessons: The Pedagogy of Imperialism in Nineteenth-Century China* (Durham, NC: Duke University Press, 2003) pp. 210–11.

73. Mark Levene, *Genocide in the Age of the Nation State* (New York: I. B. Tauris, 2005) p. 263.

74. Levene, p. 264.

75. William J. Duiker, *Cultures in Collision: The Boxer Rebellion* (San Rafael, CA; Presidio Press, 1978) p. 186.

76. Isabel V. Hull, *Absolute Destruction: Military Culture and the Practices of War in Imperial Germany* (Ithaca, NY; Cornell University Press, 2004) p. 148

77. Dr Smith is credited with having convinced President Theodore Roosevelt that a large part of the indemnity for the Boxer Rebellion should be returned to China for the education of Chinese students in the US. Obituary in *Time Magazine* Monday, 12 Sept. 1932.

78. Arthur H. Smith, *China in Convulsion*, 2 vols (New York: F. H. Revell, 1901) Vol. II, p. 716.

79. Thomas F. Millard, 'Punishment and Revenge in China', *Scribner's Magazine* 29 (February 1901) p. 187.

80. E. J. Dillon, 'The Chinese Wolf and the European Lamb', *Contemporary Review* 79 (May 1901) pp. 1–31.

81. J. Martin Miller, *China: The Yellow Peril at War With the World* (no place: no publisher, 1900) p. 448.

82. Miller, p. 455.

83. Hull, p. 148

84. E. Baron Binder-Krieglstein, *Die Kämpfe des Deutschen Expeditionskorps in China und ihre militärischen Lehren* (Berlin: E. S. Mittler, 1902) pp. 144, 265, 202–4.

85. Röhl, *Young Wilhelm*, p. 115.

86. Mark Cocker, *Rivers of Blood, Rivers of Gold: Europe's Conquest of Indigenous Peoples* (New York: Grove Press, 2001) p. 327.

87. Mahmood Mamdani, *When Victims Become Killers: Colonialism, Nativism, and the Genocide in Rwanda* (Princeton, NJ: Princeton University Press, 2002) p. 12.

88. For an account of the atrocities see Mark Levene, *Genocide in the Age of the Nation State: Volume II: The Rise of the West and Coming Genocide* (New York: I. B. Tauris, 2005) pp. 234–5.

89. Levene, p. 236.

90. Mamdani, *When Victims Become Killers*, p. 11.

91. The Uhehe was the area where the Hehe people, the Wahehe, lived.

92. Quoted in: Jan-Bart Gewald, 'Colonial Warfare: Hehe and World War One, the Wars besides Maji Maji in South-Western Tanzania' (ASC Working Paper 63/2005) [A working paper first presented at the symposium, 'The Maji Maji War 1905–1907: Colonial Conflict, National History and Local Memory', held at the Wissenschaftskolleg zu Berlin, 30 March – 1 April 2005] p. 11.

93. Jan-Bart Gewald, 'Learning to Wage and Win Wars in Africa: A Provisional History of German Military Activity in Congo, Tanzania, China and Namibia.' (ASC Working Paper 60/2005) [A working paper presented at the conference 'Genocides: Forms, Causes and Consequences' held in Berlin 13 – 15 January 2005] p. 24.

94. Quoted in Gewald, 'Learning to Wage and Win Wars in Africa', p. 25.

95. Kurd Schwabe, *Dienst und Kriegsführung in den Kolonien und auf überseeischen Expeditionen* [Service and war guidance in the colonies and on overseas expeditions] (Berlin: E. S. Mittler, 1903). Quoted in: Gewald, 'Learning to Wage and Win Wars in Africa', p. 27.

96. George Steinmetz, 'From "Native Policy" to Exterminationism: German Southwest Africa, 1904, in Comparative Perspective', in Paper 30, *Theory and Research in Comparative Social Analysis*, Department of Sociology, UCLA (Los Angeles: University of California, 2005) p. 17. n. 34. Pakenham however states that Trotha made a reputation for himself 'as a man of iron' during the Chinese campaign. Thomas Pakenham, *The Scramble for Africa* (London: Abacus, 1992) p. 610.

97. Quoted in Gewald, 'Learning to Wage and Win Wars in Africa', p. 27.

98. Gail Hershatter, *Dangerous Pleasures: Prostitution and Modernity in Twentieth-Century Shanghai*, reprint edn (Berkeley, CA; University of California Press, 1999) pp. 461–2, n. 127.

99. Röhl, *Young Wilhelm*, p. 114.

100. Mombauer, 'Wilhelm, Waldersee, and the Boxer Rebellion', pp. 114–17.

101. Hsu, pp. 394–5.

102. Esherick, pp. 188–9.

103. George Steinmetz, 'Precoloniality and Colonial Subjectivity: Ethnographic Discourse and native Policy in German Overseas Imperialism, 1780s–1914', in Diane E. Davis (ed.), *Political Power and Social Theory*, Vol. 15 (Oxford: Elsevier Science, 2002) p. 144.

104. Ibid.

105. T. G. Otte, '"The Baghdad Railway of the Far East": the Tientsin-Yangtze Railway and Anglo-German Relations, 1898–1911', in T. G. Otte and Keith Neilson, *Railways and International Politics: Paths of Empire, 1848–1945* (Abingdon, UK: Routledge, 2006) pp. 122–3.

106. Herwig, 'Luxury' Fleet, p. 105.

107. Compiled from statistics in W. O. Henderson, 'Germany's Trade with Her Colonies, 1884–1914', *Economic History Review* 9/ 1 (November 1938) p. 15.

108. A Phillip Jones, *Britain's Search for Chinese Cooperation in the First World War* (New York: Garland, 1986) p. 80.

109. Joseph Walton, *China and the Present Crisis: With Notes on a Visit to Japan and Korea* (London; Sampson Low, Marston, 1900) p. 93.

110. During his 1898 visit, Lord Charles Beresford noticed that the regulations concerning the sale of land were a long way from being laissez faire. As he put it: 'The Government owns the land. If it is bought by private individuals or firms, all sales by auction or otherwise have to be registered. Six per cent is charged on the assessed value of the land, and it is to be reassessed every twenty-five years for the above tax. If the land is sold at a profit at any time, one-third of that profit is to go to the Government. The Government claims the right, as a safeguard against fraud, to take over any piece of land themselves at the price stated by the seller and purchaser to be the selling price.' Beresford, *The Break-Up of China*, p. 74. The issue of land and the taxation thereof is discussed in: V. G. Peterson and Tseng Hsiao, 'Kiao-chau', in Robert V. Andelson (ed.), *Land-Value Taxation Around the World* (Malden, MA; Blackwell, 2000) pp. 365–8.

111. Steinmetz, 'Precoloniality and Colonial Subjectivity', p. 144.

112. Steinmetz, '"The Devil's Handwriting"', p 7.

113. Ibid., p. 10.

114. Hermann Joseph Hiery, *The Neglected War: The German South Pacific and the Influence of World War I* (Honolulu: University of Hawai'i Press, 1995) pp. 2–3. See also the review of this work by James M. Vincent in the *Micronesian Journal of the Humanities and Social Sciences* 2/1–2 (December 2003) (Albury, NSW; Letao Publishing, 2003) p. 59.

115. Volker R. Berghahn, *Imperial Germany, 1871–1918: Economy, Society, Culture and Politics* (Oxford; Berghahn Books, 2005) p. 46.

116. Carl Dahlhaus, *Nineteenth-Century Music* (Berkeley: California University Press, 1989) p. 183.

117. Luiz von Liliencron, *Die Deutsche Marine: Unter Zugrundelegung des neuen Flottengesetzes* [The German Navy: Using the New Fleet Law] (Berlin: E. S. Mittler, 1899).

118. Hew Strachan, *The Outbreak of the First World War* (Oxford: Oxford University Press, 2004) p. 15.

119. Charles B. Burdick, *The Japanese Siege of Tsingtau* (Hamden CT; Archon, 1976) p. 18.

120. P. Sprigade and M. Moisel (eds), 'Rückblick auf die Entwicklung Ostasiens im Jahre 1904' in *Deutscher Kolonialatlas mit Jahrbuch* (Berlin: Ernst Vohsen, 1914) p. 43; P. Sprigade and M. Moisel (eds), 'Rückblick auf die Entwicklung Ostasiens im Jahre 1904', in *Deutscher Kolonialatlas mit Jahrbuch* (Berlin: Ernst Vohsen, 1914) p. 41; P. Sprigade and M. Moisel (eds), 'Rückblick auf die Entwicklung Ostasiens im Jahre 1904', in *Deutscher Kolonialatlas mit Jahrbuch* (Berlin: Ernst Vohsen, 1911) p. 38.

121. For accounts of the role of the New Army and its political role see Edmund S. K. Fung, *The Military Dimension of the Chinese Revolution: The New Army and Its Role in the Revolution of 1911* (Vancouver: University of British Columbia Press, 1980); Edward L. Dreyer, China at War, 1901–1949 (London: Longman, 1995); Stephen R. MacKinnon, *Power and Politics in Late Imperial China: Yuan Shi-kai in Beijing and Tianjin, 1901–1908* (Berkeley, CA; University of California Press, 1980).

122. See Marie-Claire Bergere (trans. Janet Lloyd), *Sun Yat-sen* (Stanford, CA; Stanford University Press, 1998).

123. The life of Pu Yi formed the subject of the *The Last Emperor*, the multiple Academy Award-winning 1987 motion picture directed by Bernardo Bertolucci. Pu Yi was briefly restored to the Chinese throne in 1917, and was ruler and Emperor of the Japanese puppet-state of Manchuko from 1932 to 1945. He later, after undergoing a lengthy period of 're-education', became a member of the Chinese People's Political Consultative Conference under communist rule, serving until his death in 1967. For accounts of his life see Aisin-Gioro Pu Yi (trans. W. J. F. Jenner), *From Emperor to Citizen: The Autobiography of Aisin-Gioro Pu Yi* (Peking: Foreign Languages Press, 1964); Arnold C Brackman, *The Last Emperor* (New York: Charles Scribner's Sons, 1975); Edward Behr, *The Last Emperor* (New York: Bantam Books, 1987); Raymond Lamont-Brown, *Tutor to the Dragon Emperor: The Life of Sir Reginald Fleming Johnston at the Court of the Last Emperor* (Stroud, UK; Sutton, 1999).

124. John E. Schrecker, *The Chinese Revolution in Historical Perspective* (Westport, CT: Greenwood Press, 1991) p. 178.

125. For accounts of the Chinese Revolution of 1911 see Harold Z. Schriffin *Sun Yat-sen*

and the Origins of the Chinese Revolution (Berkeley, CA: University of California Press, 1970); Jingchun Liang, *The Chinese Revolution of 1911* (Jamaica, NY: St John's University Press, 1972); Chan Lau Kit-Ching, *Anglo-Chinese Diplomacy in the Careers of Sir John Jordan and Yüan Shih-kai 1906–1920* (Hong Kong: Hong Kong University Press, 1978) pp. 30–76; Kenji Shimada, *Pioneer of the Chinese Revolution: Zhang Binglin and Confucianism* (Stanford, CA; Stanford University Press, 1990); Linda Pomerantz-Zhang, *Wu Tingfang (1842–1922): Reform and Modernization in Modern Chinese History* (Hong Kong: Hong Kong University Press, 1992).

126. Ross Terrill, *The New Chinese Empire* (Sydney, NSW; University of NSW Press, 2003) pp. 97–8; Paul John Bailey, *China in the Twentieth Century* (Oxford: Blackwell, 2001) pp. 70–2; Peter Zarrow, *China in War and Revolution, 1895–1949* (London; Routledge, 2005) p. 79.

127. For an account of the emergence of the warlord tendency see Edward A. McCord, *The Power of the Gun: The Emergence of Modern Chinese Warlordism* (Berkeley: University of California Press, 1993).

128. W. G. Beasley, *Japanese Imperialism 1894–1945* (Oxford: Oxford University Press, 1987) pp. 107–9.

129. Noriko Kawamura, *Turbulence in the Pacific: Japanese-US Relations During World War I* (Westport, CT; Praeger, 2000) p. 12.

Chapter 4, pp. 49–66

1. Quoted in: David F. Trask, *The War with Spain in 1898* (New York: Simon & Schuster, 1981) p. 96.

2. Quoted in: Stuart Creighton Miller, *Benevolent Assimilation: The American Conquest of the Philippines, 1899–1903* (New Haven, CT: Yale University Press, 1982) p. 37.

3. Kyle Roy Ward, *In the Shadow of Glory: The Thirteenth Minnesota in the Spanish-American and Philippine-American Wars, 1898–1899* (St Cloud, MN; North Star, 2000) p. 9.

4. Sharon Delmendo, *The Star-Entangled Banner: One Hundred Years of America in the Philippines* (New Brunswick, NJ; Rutgers University Press, 2004) p. 45.

5. Terrell D. Gottschall, *By Order of the Kaiser: Otto von Diederichs and the Rise of the Imperial German Navy 1865–1902* (Annapolis MD; Naval Institute Press, 2003) p. 187.

6. Gottschall, p. 189–94.

7. Total British naval forces deployed in Manila Bay consisted of one armoured and two light cruisers, plus six gunboats. France sent one armoured and one protected cruiser, plus the obsolete barbette ship *Bayard*, while four protected cruisers represented the Imperial Japanese Navy. Even Austria-Hungary sent along a sloop. Not all of these vessels, including the German contingent, were always present at any one time. See Gottschall, p. 196.

8. See, for example: Thomas A. Bailey, 'Dewey and the Germans at Manila Bay', The American Historical Review 45/1 (October 1939) pp. 59–81.

9. George Dewey, *Autobiography of George Dewey: Admiral of the Navy* (New York: Scribner, 1913) p. 258.

10. The 'Eastern Extension Telegraph Company' had refused the Americans the use of their apparatus, stating 'contractual' reasons. Having been refused permission, Dewey

cut the cable and took one end aboard ship, intending to make use of it without the shore-based office. The Spanish government however exercised its rights under the contract it had, and embargoed Dewey's messages at the Hong Kong end. Dewey therefore had to send his messages to Hong Kong via ship for onward transmission. See Severo Gómez Núñez, *The Spanish American War: Blockades and Coast Defense* (Washington, DC: Government Printing Office, 1899) p. 57; Gottschall, p. 189.

11. Bernhard von Bülow (trans. F. A. Voight), *Memoirs of Prince von Bülow: From Secretary of State to Imperial Chancellor 1897–1903* (Boston: Little, Brown, 1931) p. 481.

12. Bülow to Wilhelm II, 14 May 1898. Quoted in Nancy Mitchell, *The Danger of Dreams: German and American Imperialism in Latin America* (Chapel Hill: University of North Carolina Press, 1999) p. 27.

13. Bülow to Kruger, 18 May 1898; Mitchell, p. 27.

14. Knorr to Diederichs, 2 June 1898. Quoted in Gottschall, p. 190.

15. Gottschall, p. 193.

16. Gottschall, p. 195.

17. Signed by Austria, France, Great Britain, Prussia, Russia, Sardinia and Turkey following the Crimean War. See Gómez Núñez, p. 19.

18. Douglas Owen, *Declaration of War: a Survey of the Position of Belligerents and Neutrals with Relative Considerations of Shipping and Marine Insurance during War* (London: Stevens & Sons, 1889) p. 27.

19. Elbert Jay Benton, *International Law and Diplomacy of the Spanish-American War* (Baltimore: John Hopkins, 1898) pp. 130–1.

20. Coleman Phillipson, *International Law and the Great War* (London: T. Fisher Unwin, 1915) p. 351. Letters of marque were traditionally issued to private ships of war or privateers.

21. Murat Halstead, *Life and Achievements of Admiral Dewey from Montpelier* [Vermont] *to Manila* (Chicago: Dominion, 1899) p. 217.

22. The British were extremely concerned that any prolongation of the conflict could lead to it spreading across the Atlantic. See John L. Offner, *An Unwanted War: The Diplomacy of the United States and Spain Over Cuba, 1895–1898* (Chapel Hill; University of North Carolina Press, 1992) pp. 195–6.

23. Ibid.

24. Lawrence Sondhaus, *Naval Warfare, 1815–1914* (London: Routledge, 2001) pp. 175–6. Donald H. Dyal, Brian B. Carpenter and Mark A. Thomas, *Historical Dictionary of the Spanish-American War* (Westport, CT: Greenwood Press, 1996) p. 256.

25. Offner, p. 237.

26. Sebastian Balfour, *The End of the Spanish Empire, 1898–1923* (Oxford: Clarendon, 1997) p. 46. For the full text of the Protocol see Offner, pp. 237–8.

27. Albert A. Nofi, *The Spanish-American War: 1898* (Conshohocken, PA; Combined Books, 1996) pp. 289–90.

28. http://avalon.law.yale.edu/19th_century/sp1898.asp.

29. On 21 November 1899 McKinley had an interview with a group of clergymen and missionaries at the White House, which no doubt accounts for the frequent religious references. In the notes written up by one of the attendees, the accuracy of which

was confirmed by others that were present, McKinley had this to say concerning the decision to annexe the Philippines:

I have been criticized a good deal about the Philippines, but don't deserve it. The truth is I didn't want the Philippines, and when they came to us, as a gift from the gods, I did not know what to do with them. When the Spanish War broke out Dewey was at Hong Kong, and I ordered him to go to Manila and to capture or destroy the Spanish fleet, and he had to; because, if defeated, he had no place to refit on that side of the globe, and if the Dons were victorious they would likely cross the Pacific and ravage our Oregon and California coasts. And so he had to destroy the Spanish fleet, and did it! But that was as far as I thought then.

When next I realized that the Philippines had dropped into our laps, I confess I did not know what to do with them. I sought counsel from all sides – Democrats as well as Republicans – but got little help. I thought first we would take only Manila; then Luzon; then other islands, perhaps, also.

I walked the floor of the White House night after night until midnight; and I am not ashamed to tell you, gentlemen, that I went down on my knees and prayed to Almighty God for light and guidance more than one night. And one night late it came to me this way – I don't know how it was, but it came:

(1) That we could not give them back to Spain – that would be cowardly and dishonourable;

(2) That we could not turn them over to France or Germany, our commercial rivals in the Orient – that would be bad business and discreditable;

(3) That we could not leave them to themselves – they were unfit for self government, and they would soon have anarchy and misrule worse then Spain's was; and

(4) That there was nothing left for us to do but to take them all, and to educate the Filipinos, and uplift and civilize and Christianize them and by God's grace do the very best we could by them, as our fellow men for whom Christ also died.

And then I went to bed and went to sleep, and slept soundly, and the next morning I sent for the chief engineer of the War Department (our map-maker), and I told him to put the Philippines on the map of the United States (pointing to a large map on the wall of his office), and there they are and there they will stay while I am President!

Quoted in Charles S. Olcott, *The Life of William McKinley*, 2 vols (Boston: Houghton Mifflin, 1916) Vol. II, pp. 110–11. See also: Daniel B. Schirmer and Stephen Rosskamm Shalom (eds), *The Philippines Reader: A History of Colonialism, Neocolonialism, Dictatorship, and Resistance* (Boston: South End Press, 1987) pp. 22–3.

30. Offner, pp. 195–6.
31. Bülow, *Memoirs*, p. 256.
32. Balfour, pp. 46–7.
33. Robert F. Rogers *Destiny's Landfall: A History of Guam* (Honolulu: University of Hawaii Press, 1995) p. 112.
34. Manfred Jonas, *The United States and Germany: A Diplomatic History* (Chapel Hill: University of North Carolina Press, 1992) pp. 60–2
35. José María Jover, *Política, diplomacia y humanismo popular: Estudios sobre la vida española en el siglo XIX* (Madrid: Turner, 1976) p. 136.
36. President McKinley's State of the Union Address to the Senate and House of Representatives, 5 December 1899, http://www.thisnation.com/library/sotu/1899wm.html.

37. Bülow, *Memoirs*, p. 384.

38. Dirk H. R. Spennemann, *Centenary of German Annexation of the Carolines* (2000), http://marshall.csu.edu.au/Marshalls/html/german/Annex.html.

39. John C. G Röhl (trans. Sheila de Bellaigue) *Wilhelm II: The Kaiser's Personal Monarchy, 1888–1900* (Cambridge: Cambridge University Press, 2004) p. 964.

40. Lord Odo Russell (Ambassador to Berlin) to Lord Granville (Foreign Secetary), 11 February 1873. Quoted in Lord Edmond Fitzmaurice, *The Life of Granville George Leveson Gower, Second Earl Granville 1815–1891*, 2 vols (London; Longmans Green, 1905) p. 337.

41. Alessandro Duranti, *A Companion to Linguistic Anthropology* (Malden, MA; Blackwell, 2004) p. 97.

42. David L. Hanlon, *Remaking Micronesia: Discourses over Development in a Pacific Territory, 1944–1982* (Honolulu: University of Hawai'i Press, 1998) p. 1.

43. Major Earl H. Ellis USMC, *Advanced Base Operations in Micronesia* [Fleet Marine Force Reference Publication (FMFRP) 12–46. Department of the Navy – Headquarters US Marine Corps] (Washington, DC; US Government Printing Office, 1992) p. 31.

44. Gerd Hardach, 'Defining Separate Spheres: German Rule and Colonial Law in Micronesia', in Herman J. Hiery and John M. MacKenzie (eds), *European Impact and Pacific Influence: British and German Policy in the Pacific Islands and the Indigenous Response* (London: I. B. Tauris, 1997) p. 235.

45. Hermann Joseph Hiery, *The Neglected War: The German South Pacific and the Influence of World War I* (Honolulu; University of Hawaii Press, 1995) p. 12.

46. Hardach, p. 235.

47. Hiery, p. 2.

48. Hardach, p. 234.

49. Ibid.

50. Bülow, *Memoirs*, p. 331.

51. See Robert Louis Stevenson, *A Footnote to History: Eight Years of Trouble in Samoa* (New York; Charles Scribner's Sons, 1892); Robert Louis Stevenson, *Vailima Letters: Being Correspondence Addressed by Robert Louis Stevenson to Sidney Colvin. November 1890–October 1894* (London: Methuen, 1895).

52. For information on Samoa see Lowell D. Holmes (ed.), *Samoan Islands Bibliography* (Wichita, KS, Poly Concepts, 1984).

53. President McKinley's State of the Union Address to the Senate and House of Representatives, 5 December 1899, http://www.thisnation.com/library/sotu/1899wm.html.

54. See Paul M. Kennedy, *The Samoan Tangle: A Study in Anglo-German-American Relations, 1878–1900* (New York; Barnes & Noble, 1974).

55. Tirpitz to Bülow, 11 October 1899. E. T. S. Dugdale (ed. and trans.), *German Diplomatic Documents, 1871–1914*, Volume III, *The Growing Antagonism, 1898–1910* (New York: Harper & Brothers, 1930) pp. 42–73.

56. Ima C. Barlow, *The Agadir Crisis* (Hamden, CT: Archon Books, 1971); Victor Julius Ngoh, *History of Cameroon Since 1800* (Limbé, Cameroon: Presbook, 1996).

57. Alan Palmer, *The Kaiser: Warlord of the Second Reich* (London; Weidenfield & Nicolson, 1978) p. 104. For the exclusion of the normal state apparatus from Walder-

see's expedition see Annika Mombauer, 'Wilhelm, Waldersee, and the Boxer Rebellion', in Annika Mombauer and Wilhelm Deist (eds), *The Kaiser: New Research on Wilhelm II's Role in Imperial Germany* (Cambridge: Cambridge University Press, 2003) p. III.

58. Norman Rich, *Friedrich von Holstein: Politics and Diplomacy in the Era of Bismarck and William II*, 2 vols (Cambridge: Cambridge University Press, 1965) Vol. II, p. 501.

59. William Young, *German Diplomatic Relations 1871–1945: The Wilhelmstrasse and the Formulation of Foreign Policy* (New York; iUniverse, 2006) p. 90; Palmer, *The Kaiser*, p. 104.

60. Hiery, pp. 20–1.

61. P. Sprigade and M. Moisel (eds) *Deutscher Kolonialatlas mit Jahrbuch* (Berlin: Ernst Vohsen, 1914) p. 37.

62. Sprigade and Moisel (1914), p. 37.

63. P Sprigade and M Moisel (eds) 'Rückblick auf die Entwicklung Ostasiens im Jahre 1904', in *Deutscher Kolonialatlas mit Jahrbuch* (Berlin: Ernst Vohsen, 1905) p. 22.

64. Sprigade and Moisel (1914) p. 12.

65. Ibid., p. 37

66. Sprigade and Moisel (1905) p. 23.

67. W. E. Mosse, *The German-Jewish Economic Elite, 1820–1935: A Socio-Cultural Profile* (Oxford: Clarendon Press, 1989) p. 270–1. For a biography of Dernburg see Werner Schiefel, *Bernhard Dernburg 1865–1937: Kolonialpolitiker und Bankier im wilhelmischen Deutschland* (Zurich; Atlantis, 1974).

68. J. K. Noyes, *Colonial Space: Spatiality in the Discourse of German South West Africa 1884–1915* (Reading, UK; Harwood, 1992) p. 130.

69. Mark Levene, *The Rise of the West and the Coming of Genocide*, 4 vols, Vol. II *Genocide in the Age of the Nation State* (London: I. B. Tauris, 2005) p. 265.

70. Hardach, p. 235.

71. Sprigade and Moisel (1914), p. 38.

72. Ibid., p. 12.

73. Ibid., p. 38.

74. Hardach, p. 104.

75. Rögnvaldur Hannesson, *Investing for Sustainability: The Management of Mineral Wealth* (Boston, MA: Kluwer, 2001) p. 48. See also: A. F. Ellis, *Mid Pacific Outposts* (Auckland, NZ; Brown & Stuart, 1946).

76. Hardach, p. 252.

77. Hardach, p. 104.

78. Compiled from statistics in W. O. Henderson, 'Germany's Trade with Her Colonies, 1884–1914', *Economic History Review* 9/1 (November 1938) p. 15.

79. Hardach, p. 236.

80. Sprigade and Moisel (1905) p. 22.

81. Sprigade and Moisel (1914) p. 12.

82. Sprigade and Moisel (1914) p. 39.

83. For an account of these matters see Damon Salesa, 'Samoa's Half-Castes and Some Frontiers of Comparison', in Ann Laura Stoler, *Haunted by Empire: Geographies of*

Intimacy in North American History (Durham, NC: Duke University Press, 2006) pp. 71–94.

84. Henderson, pp. 2–3.

85. Hiery, pp. 2–3.

86. Assenka Oksiloff, *Picturing the Primitive: Visual Culture, Ethnography, and Early German Cinema* (New York: Palgrave, 2001) p. 74.

87. J. A. C., Gray *Amerika Samoa* (Annapolis, MD: US Naval Institute, 1960) p. 158.

88. George Steinmetz, 'From "Native Policy" to Exterminationism: German Southwest Africa, 1904, in Comparative Perspective', in Paper 30, *Theory and Research in Comparative Social Analysis*, Department of Sociology, UCLA (Los Angeles; University of California, 2005) p. 35.

89. Hardach, p. 247.

90. For an account of the struggle see Francis X. Hezel, *Strangers in Their Own Land: A Century of Colonial Rule in the Caroline and Marshall Islands* (Honolulu: University of Hawaii Press, 1995) pp. 137–46.

91. For accounts of the affair, see Peter Sack, 'The "Ponape Rebellion" and the Phantomisation of History', *Journal de la Société des océanistes* 104/1(1997), pp. 23–38, and Howard Rice, *The Fire of Komwonlaid Cape: The Story of Sokehs Rebellion* (Pohnpei, FSM: Division of Historic Preservation & Cultural Affairs, 1998).

92. See Hiery; Kapitän Leutnant Gartzke, *Der Aufstand in Ponape und seine Niederwerfung durch S. M. Schiffe "Emden", "Nürnberg", "Cormoran", "Planet"* [The Rebellion on Ponape and its Suppression by SMS *Emden, Nürnberg, Cormoran* and *Planet*] Nach amtlichen Berichten zusammengestellt von Kapitän Leutnant Gartzke [From the Official Reports of Lieutenant Captain Gartzke] (Berlin: Marine Rundschau, 1911); Malama Meleisea, Donald Denoon, Karen L. Nero, Jocelyn Linnekin and Stewart Firth, The *Cambridge History of the Pacific Islanders* (Cambridge: Cambridge University Press, 1997). For some excellent photographs see http://www.micsem.org/photos/sokehs/intro.htm.

93. James Wood, *History of International Broadcasting*, 2 vols (London: Peregrinus, 1992) Vol. I, p. 56–7.

94. Roger Cullis, 'Technological Roulette –A Multidisciplinary Study of the Dynamics of Innovation' (University of London Ph.D. Thesis, 1986) p. 257. For accounts of the German radio system see Erdmann Thiele (ed.), *Telefunken nach 100 Jahren: Das Erbe einer deutschen Weltmarke* [Telefunken at 100 Years: The Legacy of a Global Brand] (Berlin: Nicolai, 2003); Michael Friedewald, 'The Beginnings of Radio Communication in Germany, 1897–1918', *Journal of Radio Studies* 7/2 (2000) pp. 441–63. See also: Paul Kennedy, 'Imperial Cable Communications and Strategy, 1870–1914', in Paul Kennedy (ed.), *The War Plans of the Great Powers, 1880–1914* (London: Allen & Unwin, 1979).

Chapter 5, pp. 67–84

1. For a comprehensive account of the how the alliance came into being from the Japanese perspective see Tatsuji Takeuchi, *War and Diplomacy in the Japanese Empire* (Chicago: Allen & Unwin, 1936) Chapter 11.

2. The margin was later defined as being a 10 per cent superiority over the combined strength of the next two strongest navies

3.   D. G. Boyce (ed.), *The Crisis of British Power: The Imperial and Naval Papers of the Second Earl of Selborne, 1895–1910* (London: The Historians' Press, 1990) pp. 154–5, http://www.manorhouse.clara.net/book3/chapter1.htm#_ftn53.

4.   Balfour to Lansdowne, 12 December 1901 in the Balfour Papers at the British Library; Add MSS 49727.

5.   Holger H. Herwig, *'Luxury Fleet': The Imperial German Navy, 1888–1918* (London: George Allen and Unwin, 1980) p. 43.

6.   Raymond A. Esthus, *Theodore Roosevelt and Japan* (Seattle: University of Washington Press, 1966).

7.   http://process.portsmouthpeacetreaty.org/process/index.html.

8.   http://www.firstworldwar.com/source/anglojapanesealliance1902.htm.

9.   CID 38/10/79 Memorandum by the General Staff, 4 November 1905.

10. Great Britain, Parliamentary Papers, London, 1908, Vol. 125, Cmd. 3750.

11. For an analysis of these matters see Ernest Batson Price, *The Russo-Japanese Treaties of 1907–1916 Concerning Manchuria and Mongolia* (Baltimore: The John Hopkins Press, 1933).

12. Ibid., pp. 113–14.

13. According to Mahan, writing in 1910, America had 'two principle and permanent external policies: the Monroe Doctrine and the Open Door', Alfred Thayer Mahan to Philip Andrews, 24 September 1910. Robert Seager II and Doris Maguire (eds), *Letters and Papers of Alfred Thayer Mahan*, 3 vols (Annapolis, MD: US Naval Institute Press, 1975) Vol. III, p. 353.

14. Theodore Roosevelt had written to Senator Henry Cabot Lodge on 21 September 1897, arguing that if the US fought Spain,'we would have the [Japanese] on our backs'. Elting E. Morison (ed.), *The Letters of Theodore Roosevelt*, 8 vols (Cambridge, MA; Harvard University Press, 1951–1954) Vol. I, p. 607.

15. An inversion of the Doctrine, from being reactive to active. Theodore Roosevelt, *Addresses and State Papers: Including the European Addresses*, Executive Edition, 8 vols (New York: Collier & Son, 1910) Vol. III, pp. 176–7.

16. Quoted in: Edmund Morris, "A Matter of Extreme Urgency": Theodore Roosevelt, Wilhelm II, and the Venezuela Crisis of 1902', *Naval War College Review* 55/2 (Spring 2002) p. 3.

17. George Dewey, *Autobiography of George Dewey: Admiral of the Navy* (New York: Charles Scribner's Sons, 1913) p. 290.

18. Quoted in: Morris, p. 8.

19. The Italian and British governments signed identical agreements. 'Germany, Great Britain, Italy, Venezuela et al.', *American Journal of International Law* 2/4 (October 1908) pp. 902–3. For accounts of Roosevelt and the Venezuelan affair see Brian S. McBeth *Gunboats, Corruption, and Claims: Foreign Intervention in Venezuela, 1899–1908* (Westport, CT; Greenwood, 2001); Nancy Mitchell,'The Height of the German Challenge: The Venezuela Blockade, 1902–03', *Diplomatic History* 20/2 (Spring 1996) pp. 185–209; Howard C. Hill, *Roosevelt and the Caribbean* (New York: Russell & Russell, 1965); Dana G. Munro, *Intervention and Dollar Diplomacy in the Caribbean, 1900–1921* (Princeton, NJ: Princeton University Press, 1964); Dexter Perkins, *The Monroe Doctrine 1867–1907* (Baltimore: Johns Hopkins, 1937); and Chester Lloyd Jones, *The Caribbean Since 1900* (New York: Prentice Hall, 1936).

20. William Braisted, *The United States Navy in the Pacific 1897–1909* (Austin: University of Texas Press, 1958) p. 4.

21. For the text of the agreement see www.usd.edu/~sbucklin/primary/roottakahira. htm. For a discussion on the background and context see Choi Jeong-soo, 'The Russo-Japanese War and the Root-Takahira Agreement', *International Journal of Korean History* 7 (February 2005) pp. 133–63.

22. Richard W. Turk, *The Ambiguous Relationship: Theodore Roosevelt and Alfred Thayer Mahan* (Westport, CT.; Greenwood Press, 1987) p. 4.

23. Holger H. Herwig, *'Luxury Fleet': The Imperial German Navy, 1888–1918* (London: George Allen & Unwin, 1980) p. 45.

24. Alfred Thayer Mahan, *Naval Strategy Compared and Contrasted with the Principles and Practice of Military Operations on Land: Lectures Delivered at US Naval War College, Newport, R.I., between the years 1887 and 1911.* Reprinted facsimile of the 1911 edn (Oxford: Greenwood Press, 1975) p. 6.

25. Theodore Roosevelt to Captain Alfred Thayer Mahan, 3 May 1897. Morison, pp. 685–6. Mahan had himself echoed this sentiment in an undated letter (June 1910) to the *Daily Mail* newspaper, pointing out the 'military check [...] the interests of Canada impose upon Great Britain.' Seager II and Maguire, *Letters and Papers of Alfred Thayer Mahan*, Vol. III, p. 342–3.

26. Admiralty Memorandum of February 1905. Quoted in Phillips Payson O'Brien, *British and American Naval Power: Politics and Policy, 1900–1936* (Westport, CT; Praeger, 1998) p. 28.

27. Auckland, New Zealand, 9–15 August 1908; Sydney, Australia, 20–28 August 1908; Melbourne, Australia 29 August–5 September 1908; Albany, Australia, 11–18 September 1908.

28. A. Trotter, 'Friend to Foe? New Zealand and Japan: 1900–1937', in Roger Peren (ed.), *Japan and New Zealand: 150 Years* (Palmerston North: New Zealand Centre for Japanese Studies, Massey University, on behalf of the Ministry of Foreign Affairs, Tokyo, in association with the Historical Branch, Dept. of Internal Affairs, Wellington, 1999) pp. 70–1.

29. E. M. Andrews, *The Anzac Illusion: Anglo-Australian relations during World War I*, reprint edn (Cambridge: Cambridge University Press, 1994) p. 21.

30. For an account of all these matters see Lionel Curtis, *The Problem of the Commonwealth* (London; Macmillan, 1916).

31. 'In the Navy Bills of 1898 and 1900 augmented by Supplementary Bills in 1906, 1908 and 1912, the Reich proposed to create a modern battle fleet of 41 battleships, 20 large cruisers and 40 light cruisers.' Herwig, *'Luxury Fleet'*, p. 1.

32. Quoted in ibid.

33. Richard H. Gimblett, 'Reassessing the Dreadnought Crisis of 1909 and the Origins of the Royal Canadian Navy', *The Northern Mariner/Le Marin du nord* 4/1 (January 1994) p. 36.

34. Peter Padfield, *The Great Naval Race: Anglo-German Naval Rivalry, 1900–1914* (Edinburgh: Birlinn, 2005) p. 201.

35. W. D. Hancock (ed.), *English Historical Documents* (London: Eyre & Spottiswoode, 1977) p. 414.

36. Hancock, p. 422.

37. Reginald McKenna, Imperial Conference on Defence: Admiralty Memorandum of 20 July 1909. National Archives CAB 37/100/98. This memorandum formed the basis of the British position at the subsequent conference.

38. McKenna Memorandum.

39. Ibid.

40. M. D. Tunnicliffe, 'The Fleet We Never Had', *Canadian Naval Review* 2/1 (Spring 2006) p. 17.

41. 'Notes of the Proceedings of a Conference at the Admiralty On Tuesday, 10th August 1909, between Representatives of the Admiralty and of the Government of the Commonwealth of Australia to Consider a Scheme for the Establishment of an Australian Navy', *Imperial Conference: Proceedings* Vol. I. National Archives CAB 18/12A.

42. J. F. G. Foxton to Alfred Deakin, 13 August 1909. National Library of Australia, MS 1540, Papers of Alfred Deakin, 1804–1973, Item 15/3705–12: Foxton, J. F. G., Colonel to Alfred Deakin, pp. 3–4.

43. J. F. G. Foxton to Alfred Deakin, 13 August 1909, p. 1.

44. Lord Hankey, *Diplomacy by Conference: Studies in Public Affairs 1920–1946* (London: Ernest Benn, 1946) p. 152.

45. The Union came into being on 31 May 1910.

46. *Hansard*, House of Commons, 26 August 1909, Vol. 9 cc2311–3.

47. Jeffrey Grey, *A Military History of Australia* (Cambridge: Cambridge University Press, 1999) p. 72.

48. Nicholas A. Lambert, *Sir John Fisher's Naval Revolution* (Columbia: University of South Carolina, 1999) pp. 199–203.

49. Hew Strachan, *The First World War, Volume 1: To Arms* (Oxford: Oxford University Press, 2003) p. 380. For accounts of the relevant holders of the position of First Sea Lord, see Nicholas A. Lambert, 'Admiral Sir Arthur Knyvett-Wilson, VC (1910–1911)'; Nicholas A. Lambert, 'Admiral Sir Francis Bridgeman-Bridgeman (1911–1912); and John B. Hattendorf, 'Admiral Prince Louis of Battenberg (1912–1914), in Malcolm H. Murfett (ed.), *First Sea Lords: From Fisher to Mountbatten* (Westport CT: Praeger, 1995) pp. 35–91.

50. Henry Page Croft, *The Path of Empire* (London: John Murray, 1912) pp. 65–6.

51. Harcourt was Secretary of State for the Colonies from November 1910 until May 1915. He was elevated to the peerage as the 1st Viscount Harcourt in 1917.

52. HMAS *Australia* was launched from the Clydeside yard of John Brown on 25 October 1911, but did not sail under her own steam until February 1913. Following sea trials she was commissioned into the Royal Australian Navy on 21 June 1913. See David Stevens, 'HMAS *Australia*: a Ship for a Nation', in David Stevens and John Reeve (eds), *The Navy and the Nation: The Influence of the Navy on Modern Australia* (Crows Nest, NSW: Allen & Unwin, 2005) pp. 172–3. HMS *New Zealand* was launched from the yard of the Fairfield Shipbuilding and Engineering Company, also on the Clyde, on 11 July 1911. She was commissioned into the Royal Navy on 23 November 1912. See S. D. Waters, *The Royal New Zealand Navy* (Wellington: Department of Internal Affairs, 1956) pp. 541–2.

53. Draft of letter from W. S. Churchill to Lewis Harcourt, 29 January 1912, Randolph

S. Churchill, *Winston S. Churchill: Young Statesman 1901–1914*, Companion Volume
II, Part 3, 1911–1914 (London: Heinemann, 1969) pp. 1507–8.

54. Letter from Lewis Harcourt to W. S. Churchill, 1 February 1912, Churchill, *Winston
S. Churchill: Young Statesman*, Companion Volume II, Part 3, 1911–1914, p. 1511.

55. Waters, pp. 542–3.

56. Fisher was to return as First Sea Lord and Wilson as an unofficial special adviser. See
Barry D. Hunt, *Sailor-Scholar: Admiral Sir Herbert Richmond 1871–1946* (Waterloo,
ON; Wilfrid Laurier University Press, 1982) p. 44.

57. Undated memorandum by W. S. Churchill, Churchill, *Winston S. Churchill: Young
Statesman*, Companion Volume II, Part 3, 1911–1914, pp. 1512–13.

58. Arthur J. Marder, *From the Dreadnought to Scapa Flow: The Royal Navy in the Fisher
Era*, 5 vols Vol. I, *The Road to War 1904–1914* (New York: Oxford University Press,
1961) p. 87.

59. For example, see Nicholas A. Lambert, 'Admiral Sir John Fisher and the Concept
of Flotilla Defence, 1904–1909', *Journal of Military History* 59/4 (October 1995) pp.
639–60. Also: Lambert, *Sir John Fisher's Naval Revolution*.

60. William Creswell, 'Captain Creswell's Views on Result of Imperial Conference, 16
November 1909', in G. L. Macandie, *The Genesis of the Royal Australian Navy: A
Compilation* (Sydney, NSW; Government Printer, 1949) p. 252.

61. MacDonald to Grey, 5 April 1911. G. P. Gooch and H. W. V. Temperly (eds), *British
Documents on the Origins of the War, 1898–1914*, 11 Volumes (London: HM Stationery
Office, 1926–38). Vol. VIII, no. 417.

62. Ian Nish et al., *Anglo-Japanese Relations 1892–1925*, 6 vols (London: Palgrave
Macmillan, 2003) Vol. VI, p. 47.

63. Nish et al., p. 51.

64. For an account of this process see Sir Thomas Barclay, *New Methods of Adjusting
International Disputes and the Future* (London: Constable, 1917), particularly Appendix
VII.

65. In fact the US Senate refused to pass the Anglo-American arbitration treaty,
rendering inoperative Article IV of the Alliance. This meant that in certain circumstances Britain might be bound to enter a war against the US. This potential difficulty
was overcome by the negotiation of the Peace Commission Treaty, signed by the
British Ambassador, Sir Cecil Spring-Rice, and the US Secretary of State, William
Jennings Bryan, on 15 September 1914. This stipulated that all disputes which could
not be settled by diplomacy should be referred for investigation and report to an
International Commission, and that the two powers would not declare war while the
investigation was ongoing and before the report was submitted. The British notified
the Japanese that it would consider this treaty as a general arbitration agreement,
thus bringing back into force Article IV. There appears to have been no objection
from Japan. See Raymond Leslie Buell, *The Washington Conference: A Dissertation
presented to the Faculty of Princeton University in Candidacy for the Degree of Doctor of
Philosophy* (New York: D. Appleteon, 1922) pp. 125–6; Peter Lowe, *Great Britain and
Japan 1911–1915: A Study of British Far Eastern Policy* (London: Macmillan, 1969) p.
53.

66. A. M. Pooley (ed.), *The Secret Memoirs of Count Tadasu Hayashi* (New York and
London: G. P. Putnam's sons, 1915) p.17.

67. Andrews, *The Anzac Illusion*, p. 22.

68. 'Laid down before Dreadnought and intended to carry 12-inch [305mm] guns, she should have been completed as the world's first all-big-gun battleship. However there were not enough Armstrong 1904 pattern 12-inch guns available, and 10-inch [254mm] guns had to be substituted for all but four of the weapons. Thus, it was that future all-big gun battleships were to be called "dreadnoughts", and not "satsumas".' Bernard Ireland, *Jane's Battleships of the 20th Century* (New York: HarperCollins, 1996). The USS *South Carolina*, laid down in December 1906, might also have pre-empted Dreadnought.

69. Warren I. Cohen (ed.), *The Cambridge History of American Foreign Relations*, 4 vols, Vol. II, Walter LaFeber, *The American Search for Opportunity, 1865–1913* (Cambridge: Cambridge University Press, 1993) p. 207.

70. Ian Gow, *Military Intervention in Pre-War Japanese Politics: Admiral Kato Kanji and the 'Washington System'* (London: Routledge, 2004) pp. 70–1.

71. Edward S. Miller, *War Plan Orange: The U.S. Strategy to Defeat Japan, 1897–1945* (Annapolis, MD; US Naval Institute Press, 2007).

Chapter 6, pp. 85–116

1. The best short piece on these various perspectives and arguments is, arguably, the first chapter of: Hew Strachan, *The First World War, Volume One: To Arms* (Oxford: Oxford University Press, 2003).

2. The evidence that Bismarck actually said this is at several removes, and seems to originate in a speech made by Winston S. Churchill in the House of Commons on 16 August 1945. According to Churchill: 'I remember that a fortnight or so before the last war, the Kaiser's friend Herr Ballin, the great shipping magnate, told me that he had heard Bismarck say towards the end of his life, If there is ever another war in Europe, it will come out of some damned silly thing in the Balkans.' Churchill was thus recalling a second-hand remark made to him some 31 years previously, which was itself a recollection of a comment made around 17 years before that. Robert Rhodes James (ed.), *Winston S. Churchill: His Complete Speeches, 1897–1963*, 8 vols (New York; Chelsea House Publishers, 1974) Vol. VII *1943–1949*, p. 7214.

3. Katharine Anne Lerman, *The Chancellor as Courtier: Bernhard von Bülow and the Governance of Germany, 1900–1909* (Cambridge: Cambridge University Press, 1990) p. 23.

4. Lerman, p. 94.

5. Jörn Leonhard, 'Construction and Perception of National Images: Germany and Britain, 1870–1914', in Daniel Gallimore and Dimitrina Mihaylova (eds): '"The Fatal Circle": Nationalism and Ethnic Identity Into the 21st Century', *The Linacre Journal: Number 4* (Oxford: Linacre College, 2000) p. 57.

6. Herbert Henry Asquith, *The Genesis of the War* (New York: George H. Doran, 1923) p. 54.

7. Balfour to the King, 8 June 1905. Quoted in: Jason Tomes, *Balfour and Foreign Policy: The International Thought of a Conservative Statesman* (Cambridge: Cambridge University Press, 2002) p. 135.

8. For accounts of the Tangier Crisis and Algeciras Conference see Eugene N. Anderson,

The First Moroccan Crisis, 1904–1906 (Chicago: University of Chicago Press, 1930); Helmuth Stoecker and Helmut Nimschowski, 'Morocco 1898–1914' in Helmuth Stoecker (ed.), *German Imperialism in Africa: From the Beginnings Until the Second World War*, trans. Bernd Zöllner (London: Hurst, 1986) pp. 230–49; Christopher Andrew, *Theophile Delcassé and the Making of the Entente Cordiale: A Reappraisal of French Foreign Policy, 1898–1905* (London: Macmillan, 1968); Jeffrey W. Taliaferro, *Balancing Risks: Great Power Intervention in the Periphery* (Ithaca NY; Cornell University Press, 2004) pp. 55–94.

9. Eyre Crowe, 'Memorandum on the Present State of British Relations with France and Germany' (1 January 1907), in G. P. Gooch and H. W. V. Temperly (eds.), *British Documents on the Origins of the War, 1898–1914*, 11 vols (London: HM Stationery Office, 1926–1938) Vol. 3, *The Testing of the Entente 1904–6*, (Appendix A) p. 402.

10. John Charmley, *Splendid Isolation? Britain and the Balance of Power 1874–1914* (London: Hodder & Stoughton, 1999) p. 250.

11. For an account of the life of Wortley see Robert Franklin, *The Fringes of History: The Life and Times of Edward Stuart Wortley* (Christchurch, UK; Natula, 2003).

12. Peter Winzen, *Das Kaiserreich am Abgrund: Die Daily-Telegraph-Affaere und das Hale-Interview von 1908* [The Empire at the Abyss: The *Daily-Telegraph* Affair and the Hale-Interview of 1908] (Stuttgart: Franz Steiner, 2002) pp. 98–101. The rest of this section, except where otherwise stated, is based on Winzen.

13. The text of the interview is reproduced in: Louis L. Snyder (Ed.), *Documents of German History* (New Brunswick NJ: Rutgers University Press, 1958) pp. 296–300. It may also be found at various sites on the Internet.

14. See for example 'A Futile Courtship: The Kaiser and Theodore Roosevelt', Chapter 3 of Manfred Jonas, *The United States and Japan: A Diplomatic History* (Ithaca, NY: Cornell University Press, 1984) pp. 65–94.

15. Winzen, pp. 344–5.

16. Winzen, p. 343.

17. Reinhard R. Doerries, 'From Neutrality to War: Woodrow Wilson and the German Challenge', in William N. Tilchin and Charles E. Neu (eds), *Artists of Power: Theodore Roosevelt, Woodrow Wilson, and Their Enduring Impact on US Foreign Policy* (Westport, CT; Praeger, 2006) p. 119. Winzen suggests that its publication could have led to a military conflagration. Winzen, p. 8.

18. Lamar Cecil, *Wilhelm II: Emperor and Exile, 1900–1941* (Chapel Hill: University of North Carolina Press, 1996) p. 141.

19. Telegram from John Francis Charles, 7th Count de Salis-Soglio, Britain's Berlin chargé d'affaires 1906–1911, to Sir Edward Grey, 30 October 1908. Quoted in: Winzen, pp. 137–9.

20. Cecil, p. 139.

21. Lerman, p. 221.

22. Sheri Berman, *The Social Democratic Moment: Ideas and Politics in the Making of Interwar Europe* (Cambridge, MA; Harvard University Press, 1998) p. 125.

23. Wolfgang J. Mommsen (trans. Michael S. Steinberg) *Max Weber and German Politics, 1890–1920* (Chicago: University of Chicago Press, 1984) p. 147.

24. At which time Arthur Balfour, the leader of the Conservative Party, had resigned as Prime Minister and a minority government under Henry Campbell-Bannerman, the

Liberal Party leader, had been formed. The subsequent General Election in January–February 1906, saw the Conservatives destroyed as an electoral force, with only 133 MPs plus 24 Liberal Unionists on whom they could rely on for support. The Liberals by contrast took 400 seats and could count on the support of a further 83 Irish Nationalist MPs and 29 members elected under the aegis of the new Labour Representation Committee (LRC).

25. British *Parliamentary Debates*, 29 March 1909, cols 52ff.

26. There is a vast literature on the matter, including: Peter Padfield, *The Great Naval Race: Anglo-German Naval Rivalry 1900–1914* (Edinburgh: Birlinn, 2004); Winston S. Churchill, *The World Crisis 1911–1918*, Vol. I (New York: Charles Scribner's Sons, 1928); Robert K. Massie, *Dreadnought: Britain, Germany and the Coming of the Great War* (New York: Random House, 1991).

27. British *Parliamentary Debates*, 29 March 1909, cols 52ff.

28. Ibid.

29. William Young, *German Diplomatic Relations 1871–1945: The Wilhelmstrasse and the Formulation of Foreign Policy* (Lincoln, NE; IUniverse, 2006) p. 103.

30. David Reynolds, *Britannia Overruled: British Policy and World Power in the Twentieth Century* (Harlow, UK: Pearson, 2000) p. 79.

31. John Lowe, *The Great Powers, Imperialism, and the German Problem 1865–1925* (London: Routledge, 1994) p.197.

32. Konrad H. Jarausch, *The Enigmatic Chancellor: Bethmann Hollweg and the Hubris of Imperial Germany* (New Haven, CT; Yale University Press, 1973) pp. 141–2.

33. Annika Mombauer, *Helmuth von Moltke and the Origins of the First World War* (Cambridge; Cambridge University Press, 2001) p. 219.

34. For a detailed study of the affair see Geoffrey Barraclough, *From Agadir to Armageddon: Anatomy of a Crisis* (New York: Holmes & Meier, 1982). Also: Ima C. Barlow, *The Agadir Crisis* (Hamden, CT; Archon Books, 1971).

35. Memorandum by Kiderlen-Wächter, 3 May 1911, in E. T. S. Dugdale (ed. and trans.) *German Diplomatic Documents, 1871–1914*, Vol. IV *The Descent to the Abyss, 1911–14* (London: Methuen, 1931) pp. 2–4.

36. Interestingly, the *Panther* had form in this area, having actually fired her guns at forts during the Venezuelan Debt Crisis of 1902–3. Thus it might be said that this minor vessel almost caused war to break out on both sides of the Atlantic at different times.

37. Edward Crankshaw, *The Fall of the House of Hapsburg* (New York: Viking, 1963) p. 369.

38. Jarausch, p. 126.

39. Roughly the area of the present-day Republic of the Congo, Gabon, Chad and the Central African Republic.

40. Ernst Jäckh (ed.), *Kiderlen-Wächter, der Staatsmann und Mensch: Briefwechsel und Nachlass* [Kiderlen-Wächter, the Statesman and the Man: Correspondence and Private Papers] 2 vols (Stuttgart: Deutsche Verlags-Anstalt, 1924) Vol. II, p. 128.

41. Winston S. Churchill, *The World Crisis 1911–1918*, 2 vol. edn (London: Odhams, 1938) Vol. I, p. 42.

42. *The Times*, 22 July 1911.

43. Quoted in: David G. Hermann, *The Arming of Europe and the Making of the First World War* (Princeton, NJ; Princeton University Press, 1996) pp. 159–60.

44. Helmuth Stoecker, 'Cameroon 1906–1914', in Helmuth Stoecker (ed.) (trans. Bernd Zöllner), *German Imperialism in Africa: From the Beginnings until the Second World War* (London: Hurst, 1986) p. 173. A minor domestic casualty of the affair was the Colonial Secretary, Friedrich Lindequist, who had replaced Dernburg in 1910. Believing that Kiderlen had misled him, and aghast at the way the business ended, he resigned. Woodruff D. Smith, *The Ideological Origins of Nazi Imperialism* (Cary, NC; Oxford University Press USA, 1989) p. 137.

45. J. A. Spender, *Fifty Years of Europe: A Study in Pre-War Documents* (London: Cassell, 1933) p. 275. See also: Lerman, *The Chancellor as Courtier: Bernhard von Bülow*, p. 211.

46. Bernd Sösemann, 'Forms and Effects of Public Self-Display in Wilhelmine Germany', in Annika Mombauer and Wilhelm Deist, *The Kaiser: New Research on Wilhelm II's Role in Imperial Germany* (Cambridge: Cambridge University Press, 2003) p. 49, n. 42.

47. Jörn Leonhard, 'Construction and Perception of National Images: Germany and Britain, 1870–1914', in Daniel Gallimore and Dimitrina Mihaylova (eds), 'The "Fatal Circle": Nationalism and Ethnic Identity Into the 21st Century', *The Linacre Journal: Number 4* (Oxford; Linacre College, 2000) p. 57.

48. John Charmley, *Splendid Isolation? Britain and the Balance of Power 1874–1914* (London: Hodder & Stoughton, 1999) p. 325.

49. Churchill, *The World Crisis*, Vol. I, pp. 164–5.

50. David Lloyd George, *War Memoirs*, 2 vol. edn (London: Odhams, 1938) Vol. I, pp. 27–8.

51. A. J. P. Taylor, *The Struggle for Mastery in Europe 1848–1915* (Oxford: Oxford University Press, 1954) pp. 436–7.

52. Taylor, p. 437.

53. Viscount Grey of Falloden, *Twenty-Five Years: 1892–1916*, 2 vols (London: Hodder & Stoughton, 1925) Vol. I, p. 75.

54. Taylor, p. 438.

55. Sneh Mahajan, *British Foreign Policy 1874–1914: The Role of India* (London: Routledge, 2002) p. 190.

56. Scott D. Sagan, '1914 Revisited: Allies, Offense, and Instability', in Michael E. Brown, Owen R. Coté Jr, Sean M. Lynn-Jones and Steven E. Miller (eds), *Offense, Defense, and War* (Cambridge, MA; The MIT Press, 2004) p. 174.

57. Neville Meaney, *Australia and the World: A Documentary History from the 1870s to the 1970s* (Melbourne: Longman Cheshire, 1985) p.217.

58. S. S. Mackenzie, *Rabaul: The Australians at Rabaul; The Capture and Administration of The German Possessions in the Southern Pacific*, 10th edn (Sydney, NSW: Angus & Robertson, 1941), Vol. X of C. E. W. Bean (ed.), *The Official History of Australia in the War of 1914–1918*, 12 vols various edns (Sydney, NSW; Angus and Robertson, 1941) p. 5, http://www.awm.gov.au/histories/volume.asp?conflict=1

59. Anon., 'Before Gallipoli – Australian Operations in 1914', *Semaphore: Newsletter of the Sea Power Centre, Australia*, Issue 7 (August 2003) p. 1.

60. The 'armoured' cruiser became a feasible concept only in 1897 when a new hardening

process, developed by Germany's Krupp, allowed vessels that had formerly been designated as 'protected' cruisers, having a protective deck covering the machinery and other vitals, to be fitted with side armour. This type of armour was designed to withstand penetration from 6in. shell while not greatly adding to the displacement, dimensions, or cost of the vessels. In the context of the British Royal Navy, the first armoured cruisers formed the *Cressy*-class of 1899–1901 and the design culminated in the *Minotaur*-class of three ships constructed 1904–5. The 'Minotaurs' were large, 490 feet long and displacing 14,600 tons, powerful, four 9.2in. and ten 7.5in. guns, and fast, 23 knots. As a type they were eclipsed by the battlecruiser. For a detailed discussion of the type see William Hovgaard, *Modern History of Warships* (New York: Spon & Chamberlain, 1920).

61. Peter Overlack, 'The Force of Circumstance: Graf Spee's Options for the East Asian Cruiser Squadron in 1914', Journal of Military History 60/4 (October 1996) p. 660.

62. Arthur W. Jose, *The Royal Australian Navy 1914–1918*, 9th edn (Sydney, NSW; Angus & Robertson, 1941) Vol. IX of C. E. W. Bean (ed.), *The Official History of Australia in the War of 1914–1918*, 12 vols, various edns (Sydney, NSW: Angus & Robertson, 1941) p. 7.

63. Jose, *The RAN*, p. 17.

64. Ian Nish, *Collected Writings* (London: Routledge Curzon, 2001) Part I, p. 170.

65. Jerram's entire letter is reproduced in Nish, *Collected Writings*, pp. 167–8.

66. Nicholas Lambert, 'Economy or Empire? The Fleet Unit Concept and the Quest for Collective Security in the Pacific, 1909–1914', in Keith Neilson (ed.), *Far-flung Lines: Studies in Imperial Defence in Honour of Donald Mackenzie Schurman* (London; Frank Cass, 1997) p. 68.

67. Edward Breck, review of The World Crisis by Winston S. Churchill in American Historical Review,. 29/1 (October 1923) p. 139.

68. Jose, p. 5.

69. *Semaphore: Newsletter of The Sea Power Centre Australia*, Issue 10, September 2004.

70. This territory consisted of the islands of Savaii, Upolu, Apolimo, and Manono.

71. 'six companies of the Royal Australian Naval Reserve, a battalion of infantry at war strength (1,023 strong), two machine-gun sections, a signalling section, and a detachment of the Australian Army Medical Corps. The naval reservists were drawn from Queensland, New South Wales, Victoria, and South Australia; but, in view of the imperious necessity for rapid organisation, the infantry battalion, the machine-gun and signalling sections, and the medical complement were enlisted in New South Wales. The unit was under the military command of Colonel William Homes.' From: Mackenzie, pp. 23–4.

72. The protectorate of German New Guinea consisted of: Kaiser-Wilhelmsland, the Bismarck Archipelago, the German Solomon Islands (Buka, Bougainville and several smaller islands), the Carolines, Palau, the Marianas (except for Guam), the Marshall Islands, and Nauru.

73. Sir Ronald Craufurd Munro-Ferguson (created 1st Viscount Novar in 1920) was the sixth Governor-General of Australia, and the most politically active holder of the post. The outbreak of war in 1914 caused an acute crisis in Australian government as parliament had been dissolved and the government was in caretaker mode. Given also that contemporary Australian politicians were inexperienced in foreign affairs,

Munro-Ferguson, who reckoned he had both the constitutional authority and the confidence, took an extremely active role, which included becoming the conduit of communication between the Australian and British governments. See Chris Cunneen, *King's Men: Australia's Governors-General from Hopetoun to Isaacs* (Sydney: Allen & Unwin Australia, 1984) and David Torrance, *The Scottish Secretaries* (Edinburgh: Birlinn, 2006).

74. Mackenzie, *Rabaul*, pp. 5–6.

75. Mackenzie, p. 6.

76. It was only on 1 January 1901, that federation of the individual colonies was achieved, and the Commonwealth of Australia came into being as a British Dominion.

77. Mackenzie, p. 2.

78. See, for example, Hew Strachan, *The First World War* (London: Viking, 2004) p. 71. The term 'sub-imperialism' was coined by the Marxist writer Ruy Mauro Marini: '"sub-imperialism" is a small-scale parody of the high imperialism of the late 19th century'. Jay Lewis, 'Imperialism Yesterday and Today', *Workers' Liberty*, Issue 63 (July 2000). Available at http://archive.workersliberty.org/wlmags/wl63/imp-yt1.htm.

79. Herbertshöhe was the site of the landing by Australian troops on the morning of 11 September 1914. Only 25 personnel were landed initially but reinforcements consisting of four companies of infantry, a machine-gun section, and a 12-pounder gun were landed later that day, http://www.awm.gov.au/units/place_2439.asp.

80. Mackenzie, pp. 51–2.

81. Mackenzie, pp. 82–5.

82. Quoted in Grey to Greene, 11 August 1914. In Martin Gilbert, *Winston S. Churchill: Companion Volume III, Part 1 July 1914–April 1915* (Boston: Houghton Mifflin, 1973) pp. 28–9.

83. Grey to Greene, 1 August 1914. Gooch and Temperly, Vol. XI *The Outbreak of War: Foreign Office Documents June 28th–August 4th, 1914* (35371) No. 436.

84. Note by Sir Walter Langley (wrongly attributed to Sir William Tyrrell) dated 3 August 1914. Gooch Temperley, Vol. XI (35865) No. 534. See also Lowe, p. 180.

85. Ibid.

86. Ibid.

87. Grey to Greene, 3 August 1914. Gooch and Temperley, Vol. XI (35865) No. 549.

88. Greene to Grey, 4 August 1914. Gooch and Temperley, Vol. XI (35666) No. 571.

89. Grey to Greene, 4 August 1914. Gooch and Temperley, Vol. XI (36531) No. 641.

90. Greene to Grey, 4 August 1914. Gooch and Temperley, Vol. XI (35937) No. 637.

91. Gooch and Temperley, Vol. X, Part II: *The Last Years of Peace* (London: HMSO, 1938) Appendix II p. 823. Also quoted in Nish, *Collected Writings*, pp. 176–7.

92. Greene to Grey, 2 August 1914. Gooch and Temperley, Vol. XI (35445) No. 499.

93. Nish, *Collected Writings*, p. 177.

94. The Genro, *Genrō* were an extra-constitutional group composed of specific Japanese elder statesmen. Their function was to serve as informal, learned, advisers to the emperor.

95. Communicated by Inouye 10 August 1914. Quoted in Lowe, p. 185.

96. Nish, *Collected Writings*, p. 178.

97. Grey to Greene, 11 August 1914. In Gilbert, *Winston S. Churchill: Companion Volume III, Part 1 July 1914–April 1915*, pp. 28–9.

98. Nish, *Collected Writings*, p. 180.

99. Ibid., p. 178.

100. Martin Gilbert, *The Challenge of War: Winston S. Churchill 1914–1916* (London: Minerva, 1990) p. 42.

101. Churchill to Grey, 11 August 1914. Gilbert, *Companion Volume III, Part 1*, p. 30.

102. Gilbert, *Companion Volume III, Part 1*, p. 30.

103. Ian Nish, *Japanese Foreign Policy 1869–1942* (London: Routledge & Kegan Paul, 1977) pp. 94–5.

104. Barbara J. Brooks, 'Peopling the Japanese Empire: The Koreans in Manchuria and the Rhetoric of Inclusion', in Sharon A. Minichiello (ed.), *Japan's Competing Modernities: Issues in Culture and Democracy, 1900–1930* (Honolulu: University of Hawaii Press, 1998) p. 36. Assassination was an occupational hazard for Japanese politicians and others thought to be too 'moderate' until after the end of World War II. See Ozaki Yukio (trans. Fujiko Hara), *The Autobiography of Ozaki Yukio: The Struggle for Constitutional Government in Japan* (Princeton, NJ: Princeton University Press, 2001).

105. W. G. Beasley, *Japanese Imperialism 1894–1945* (Oxford: Oxford University Press, 1987) pp. 108–9. For biographical details of Makino see Peter Wetzler, *Hirohito and War: Imperial Tradition and Military Decision Making in Prewar Japan* (Honolulu: University of Hawaii Press, 1998) pp. 142–3.

106. Beasley, p. 108.

107. Noriko Kawamura, *Turbulence in the Pacific: Japanese-US Relations During World War I* (Westport, CT; Praeger, 2000) p. 12.

108. Quoted in Nish, *Collected Writings*, p. 193.

109. Lansing to Bryan, 7 August 1914. *Papers Relating to the Foreign Policy of the United States: The Lansing Papers, 1914–1920*, 2 vols (Washington, DC: Government Printing Office , 1939–40) Vol. I, p, 2.

110. Lansing to Bryan, 7 August 1914. *Lansing Papers*, Vol. I, pp. 3–4.

111. Lansing to Bryan, 7 August 1914. *Lansing Papers*, Vol. I, p. 4.

112. http://www.usd.edu/~sbucklin/primary/roottakahira.htm.

113. http://www.firstworldwar.com/source/tsingtau_okuma.htm.

114. Kajima Morinosuke, *The Diplomacy of Japan, 1894–1922*, 3 vols (Tokyo: Kajima Institute of Peace, 1976) Vol. III, p. 55.

115. MacMurray to Bryan, 20 August 1914, *Foreign Relations of the United States: 1914 (World War Supplement)*, (Washington, DC: Government Printing Office, 1928) pp. 173–4.

116. MacMurray to Bryan, 20 August 1914, *Foreign Relations*, p. 174.

117. Nish, *Collected Writings*, p. 185.

118. Page to Bryan, 18 August 1914, SD 763.72/508. Quoted in Charles B. Burdick, *The Japanese Siege of Tsingtau* (Hamden, CT; Archon, 1976) p. 224.

119. Austria-Hungary declared war on Japan on 25 August 1914.

120. Churchill to Grey, 29 August 1914. In Gilbert, *Companion Volume III, Part 1*, p. 65.

121. For an authoritative account of this deployment see David Evans and Mark Peattie,

Kaigun: Strategy, Tactics, and Technology in the Imperial Japanese Navy, 1887–1941 (Washington, DC: US Naval Institute, 1997).

122. Launched in 1912 *Kongō* was the last major Japanese warship to be built abroad, being built by Vickers in the UK, and the world's first to be armed with 14in. main guns.

123. Launched in 1907 with a main armamemt of four 305mm (12in.) guns as a first-class heavy cruiser, this vessel and her sister *Kurama* were reclassified as battlecruisers in 1912.

124. Grey to Greene, 6 August 1914. Quoted in Gilbert, *The Challenge of War: Winston S. Churchill 1914–1916*, p. 202.

125. 'Operations – Japanese Navy in the Indian and Pacific Oceans during War 1914–1918', Office of Naval Intelligence, Record Group 45, Subject File 1911–1927, WA-5 Japan, box 703, folder 10, NND 913005, p. 98.

126. 'Japanese Naval Activities during European War', 11 December 1918; Office of Naval Intelligence, Record Group 38.4.3 Communications with Naval Attachés, U-4-B, 11083, National Archives, Washington, DC, p. 11.

127. C. E. W. Bean, *The Story of Anzac: The First Phase*, 11th edn (Sydney, NSW: Angus & Robertson, 1941) Vol. I of C. E. W. Bean (ed.), *The Official History of Australia in the War of 1914–1918*, 12 vols, various edns (Sydney, NSW: Angus & Robertson, 1941) p. 90.

128. 'Operations – Japanese Navy in the Indian and Pacific Oceans during War 1914–1918', Office of Naval Intelligence, Record Group 45, Subject File 1911–1927, WA-5 Japan, box 703, folder 10, NND 913005, p. 38.

129. Ibid., pp. 55–8; Bean, p. 94.

130. 'Official Report of Japanese Naval Activities during the War', 11 December 1918, translation of official statement issued by Japanese Navy Department on 8 December 1918; Office of Naval Intelligence, Record Group 38.4.3 Communications with Naval Attaches, U-4-B, 11083, National Archives, Washington, D.C. p. 7.

131. Launched as a first-class heavy cruiser of the *Tsukuba* class in 1906 and reclassified as a battlecruiser in 1912.

132. 'Official Report of Japanese Naval Activities during the War', 11 December 1918, translation of official statement issued by Japanese Navy Department on 8 December 1918; Office of Naval Intelligence, Record Group 38.4.3 Communications with Naval Attaches, U-4-B, 11083, National Archives, Washington, DC, p. 6.

133. 'Operations – Japanese Navy in the Indian and Pacific Oceans during War 1914–1918', Office of Naval Intelligence, Record Group 45, Subject File 1911–1927, WA-5 Japan, box 703, folder 10, NND 913005, p. 13. Timothy D. Saxon, 'Anglo-Japanese Naval Cooperation, 1914–1918', *Naval War College Review* 53/1 (Winter 2000).

134. The ex-Russian pre-dreadnought *Retvizan*, sunk at Port Arthur in 1904 but subsequently raised and commissioned in the Japanese fleet.

135. A member of the *Bussard*-class of unprotected steel-hulled light cruisers (main armament eight 105mm rapid-firers), SMS Geier was launched at the Imperial Dockyard, Wilhelmshaven, on 18 October 1894. Designed for extended overseas duties the vessels had a large coal capacity and could be rigged for sail in order to expand their endurance. When World War I broke out, the *Geier* was in Indonesian waters en route to patrol Germany's island possessions in the Central and South Pacific Ocean, designated the 'Australia Station' by the German Navy. The warship travelled to German

colonial possessions in the Bismarck Archipelago and then to the Marshall Islands in an unsuccessful attempt to join with Spee. The *Geier* then attempted to operate against British and Japanese shipping in the central Pacific, but engine problems compelled her to enter Honolulu, Hawaii, on 15 October 1914. Interned by the US government *Geier* was, following American entry into World War I, commissioned in the US Navy on 15 September 1917 as USS *Schurz*. The vessel was lost on 19 June 1918 after being rammed by the merchant ship SS *Florida* off the coast of North Carolina. A sister ship, SMS *Cormoran*, was at Tsingtau when war broke out. See Timothy P. Mulligan, *M2089: Selected German Documents from the Records of the Naval Records Collection of The Office Of Naval Records And Library, 1897–1917* (Washington, DC: National Archives and Records Administration, 2006) p. 3.

136. 'Operations – Japanese Navy in the Indian and Pacific Oceans during War 1914–1918', Office of Naval Intelligence, Record Group 45, Subject File 1911–1927, WA-5 Japan, box 703, folder 10, NND 913005, p. 9.

137. Mackenzie, p. 148.

138. Mackenzie, p. 150.

139. Mackenzie, pp. 148–9.

140. Bean, p. 90.

141. Harcourt to Munro-Ferguson, 10 September 1914, FO 371/2017. Quoted in Lowe, p. 201.

142. SMS *Planet*, and her sister *Möwe* (scuttled at Dar-es-Salem, German East Africa [now Tanzania] on 9 August 1914), launched 1905 and 1907 respectively, were scientific survey ships displacing some 650 tonnes apiece. Each had a nominal crew of just over a hundred officers and men, and they were very lightly armed. The *Planet* was raised and refloated by the Japanese in 1916. These vessels carried out some significant scientific work. See for example Reichs-Marine-Amt, *Forschungsergebnisse S.M.S. 'Planet' 1906/7, Band 1: Reisebeschreibung* (Berlin: Karl Sigismund, 1909)

143. Greene to Grey, 10 October 1914, FO 371/2017. Quoted in Lowe, p. 201.

144. Mackenzie, p. 149.

145. HMS *Fantome* was constructed for the Royal Navy Survey Service. Launched in 1901 she displaced 1,070 tonnes and was designated a sloop. She arrived in Australian waters in 1907 to continue the Barrier Reef survey begun in 1905. Rearmed with three 12-pounder guns, she was manned by and commissioned into the Royal Australian Navy as HMAS *Fantome* on 27 November 1914.

146. Built by Bremer Vulcan in 1911 as a yacht for the Governor of German New Guinea, *Komet* was captured by HMAS *Nusa* (another ex-German vessel commandeered into the Australian Navy) on 11 October 1914 at Talasea on the Willaumez Peninsula, now part of Papua New Guinea. Designated a sloop, she was armed with three 4in guns and renamed HMAS *Una*. Somewhat astonishingly the vessel survived until 1955, being renamed *Akuna* following the Great War, as the pilot boat for the Port Phillip Sea Pilot organisation, which provides pilotage services to the ports of Melbourne, Geelong, and Westernport. See http://www.ppsp.com.au/history/history.aspx

147. Mackenzie, pp. 150–1.

148. Greene to Grey, 12 October 1914, FO 371/2017. Quoted in Lowe, p. 202.

149. Churchill to Harcourt, 18 October 1914. Harcourt Papers, Colonial Office 1910–15, Box 6. Quoted in Lowe, p. 204.

150. Ernest Scott, *Australia During The War*, 7th edn (Sydney, NSW: Angus & Robertson, 1941) Vol. XI of C. E. W. Bean (ed.), *The Official History of Australia in the War of 1914–1918*, 12 vols, various edns (Sydney, NSW; Angus & Robertson, 1941) p. 163.

151. Jose, p. 129.

152. Jose, p. 104.

153. Oliver A. Gillespie, *Official History of New Zealand in the Second World War 1939–45: The Pacific* (Wellington, Dept. of Internal Affairs: War History Branch, 1952) p. 2.

154. Lowe, p. 202.

155. Mackenzie, p. 153.

156. Ibid.

157. http://www.adb.online.anu.edu.au/biogs/A110216b.htm.

158. Mackenzie, pp. 155–6.

159. Mackenzie, p. 157.

160. Anguar (or Ngeaur) is now a part of the island nation of Palau. It is also known as 'Monkey Island' because of its population of feral macaques, which were released during German occupation.

161. Jose, p. 72.

162. Jose, p. 101.

163. Mackenzie, pp. 157–8.

164. Green to Grey, 21 November 1914, FO 371/2018. Quoted in Lowe, p. 202.

165. Mackenzie, p. 158.

166. Ibid.

167. Harcourt to Munro-Ferguson, 24 November 1914. *British Documents on Foreign Affairs: Reports and Papers from the Foreign Office Confidential Print, Series E, Asia, 1914–1939*, Part II, *From the First to the Second World War* (Frederick, MD; University Publications of America, 1991) p. 136; Jose, p. 136.

168. Mackenzie, p. 159.

169. William Morris 'Billy' Hughes, Attorney-General in the Australian Labour government of 1914–15, became Prime Minister in October 1915. Hughes was born in London of Welsh parents and, partially at least, raised in Llandudno, North Wales. He thus had somewhat more in common with David Lloyd George than merely being a political maverick. During a visit to London in early 1916 he spoke at length with Sir Edward Grey and various other Foreign Office dignitaries concerning the position vis-à-vis Japan and the German Islands. Hughes was told that acquiescence to Japanese occupation was determined by the degree of assistance sought by the Allies (Japan was to send naval forces to the Mediterranean early in the following year), and that the prospect of getting the Japanese to disgorge their conquests after the war would raise great resentment. When asked if he objected to such a situation he is reported to have replied 'I am confronted with a fait accompli and can do nothing.' See Scott, *Australia During The War*, Vol. XI of Bean, *The Official History of Australia in the War of 1914–1918*, p. 765. See also Brian Carroll, *Australia's Prime Ministers: From Barton to Howard* (Stanmore, NSW: Cassell Australia, 1978).

170. Munro-Ferguson to Harcourt, 25 November 1914. Quoted in Mackenzie, p. 150.

171. See, for example, the *US Department of State Foreign Affairs Handbook Volume 5*

Handbook 1 – Correspondence for an explanation the various statuses of diplomatic communications, http://www.state.gov/documents/organization/89308.pdf.

172. Greene to Grey, 1 December 1914, FO 371/ 2018. Quoted in Lowe, p. 206.

173. Ibid.

174. Harcourt to Munro-Ferguson, 3 December 1914. Quoted in Mackenzie, p. 150.

175. Harcourt to Munro-Ferguson (Private and Personal, Very Secret), 6 December 1914. National Library of Australia, Papers of Ronald Craufurd Munro Ferguson, 1912–1935. MS 696.

176. Gillespie, *Official History of New Zealand in the Second World War*, p. 3.

177. Kajima Morinosuke, *The Diplomacy of Japan*, p. 30.

Chapter 7, pp. 117–130

1. Constantine Pleshakov, *The Tsar's Last Armada: The Epic Voyage to the Battle of Tsushima* (New York: Perseus Books Group, 2003) pp. 52–3.

2. Aleksandr Solzhenitsyn, *August 1914: The Red Wheel*, 3rd printing (New York; Farrar, Straus & Giroux, 2000) p. 718. Emil Ludwig, trans. by Ethel Colburn Mayne, *Wilhelm Hohenzollern: The Last of the Kaisers* [1925] (Whitefish, MT; Kessinger Publishing, 2003) pp. 327–8.

3. Kaiser Wilhelm II to Tsar Nicholas II, 2 September 1902. The 'Willy-Nicky Letters', http://www.lib.byu.edu/~rdh/wwi/1914m/willnick/wilnickc.htm.

4. Kaiser Wilhelm II to Tsar Nicholas II, 2 September 1902.

5. Ibid.

6. The Kaiser to Poultney Bigelow, 26 May 1894. Quoted in Carroll Storrs Alden and Ralph Earle, *Makers of Naval Tradition* (London: Ginn and Company, 1925) p. 243. See also John C. G. Röhl (trans. Sheila de Bellaigue), *Wilhelm II: The Kaiser's Personal Monarchy, 1888–1900* (Cambridge; Cambridge University Press, 2004) p. 1003.

7. Alfred Thayer Mahan, *The Influence of Sea Power Upon History, 1660–1783* [1890] (Boston, MA; Adamant Media Corporation, 2002) p. 132.

8. The 10th Earl of Dundonald [the then Vice Admiral, Thomas, Lord Cochrane], Letter to *The Times*, 29 November 1845. Quoted in Charles Stephenson, *The Admiral's Secret Weapon: Lord Dundonald and the Origins of Chemical Warfare* (Woodbridge, UK; Boydell Press, 2006) p. 37.

9. Peter Overlack, 'The Force of Circumstance: Graf Spee's Options for the East Asian Cruiser Squadron in 1914', *Journal of Military History* 60/4 (October 1996) pp. 657–8.

10. Alfred Thayer Mahan, *The Influence of Sea Power upon the French Revolution and Empire, 1793–1812*, 2 vols [1892] (Boston, MA; Adamant Media Corporation, 2002) Vol. II, p. 217.

11. Overlack, 'The Force of Circumstance', p. 659.

12. Jurgen Tampke (ed.), *Ruthless Warfare: German Military Planning and Surveillance in the Australia-New Zealand region before the Great War* (Canberra: Southern Highlands Publishers, 1998) pp. 69–70.

13. Hew Strachan, *The First World War*, Vol. I, *To Arms* (Oxford: Oxford University Press, 2003) pp. 428, 475.

14. Geoffrey Miller, *Superior Force: The Conspiracy Behind the Escape of Goeben and*

Breslau (Hull, UK; Hull University Press, 1996) p. 1, http://www.manorhouse.clara. net/book1/index.htm.

15. David French, 'The Royal Navy and the Defence of the British Empire, 1914–1918', in Keith Neilson and Elizabeth Jane Errington (eds), *Navies and Global Defense: Theories and Strategy* (Westport, CT: Praeger, 1995) p. 118.

16. French, pp. 118–19.

17. See http://web.genealogie.free.fr/Les_militaires/1GM/Allemagne/Marine/Admiral/ B.htm for a brief resume of Bendemann's career. The Certificate conferring the Order of the Rising Sun can be found in the British Library; Ref. Or.14819.

18. Fisher to Balfour, undated. Quoted in: Nicholas Lambert, 'Economy or Empire? The Fleet Unit Concept and the Quest for Collective Security in the Pacific, 1909–1914', in Keith Neilson (ed.), *Far-flung Lines: Studies in Imperial Defence in Honour of Donald Mackenzie Schurman* (London: Frank Cass, 1997) p. 58. See also: Nicholas Lambert, *Sir John Fisher's Naval Revolution* (Columbia: University of South Carolina Press, 1999) pp. 86–7.

19. Lambert, 'Economy or Empire?' p. 57.

20. Lawrence Sondhaus, *Naval Warfare, 1815–1914* (London: Routledge, 2001) pp. 175–6; Donald H. Dyal, Brian B. Carpenter and Mark A. Thomas, *Historical Dictionary of the Spanish-American War* (Westport, CT: Greenwood Press, 1996) p. 256.

21. Albert A. Nofi, *The Spanish-American War: 1898* (Conshohocken, PA: Combined Books, 1996) pp. 80–2.

22. See Holger H. Herwig, *Politics of Frustration: The United States in German Naval Planning, 1889–1941* (Boston: Little, Brown, 976) p. 90; John A. S. Grenville and George B. Young, *Politics, Strategy, and Diplomacy: Studies in Foreign Policy, 1873–1917* (New Haven, CT: Yale University Press, 1966) pp. 306–7. The German Bundesarchiv-Militärarchiv (Federal Military Archive), at Freiburg contains correspondence between the principals and updates of versions of the Pacific War Plans, in BA/MA Reichs-Marine 5/v 5955.This was utilised by Peter Overlack for 'German War Plans in the Pacific, 1900–1914', *The Historian* 60/3 (1998) pp. 579–93. Available at: http://findarticles.com/p/articles/mi_hb3498/is_199803/ai_n8291670.

23. Tampke, *Ruthless Warfare*, p. 113.

24. Tobias R. Philbin, *The Lure of Neptune: German-Soviet Naval Collaboration and Ambitions, 1919–1941* (Columbia: University of South Carolina Press, 1994) pp. 81–2. Etape comes from the French word for a stage, stopping place or a day's march.

25. Tampke, p. 28.

26. See Gerhard Fischer, *Enemy Aliens: Internment and the Homefront Experience in Australia, 1914–1920* (Brisbane: University of Queensland Press, 1989).

27. Will Brownell and Richard N. Billings, *So Close to Greatness: A Biography of William C Bullitt* (New York: Macmillan, 1987) p. 55; Lauran Paine, *Britain's Intelligence Service* (London: Hale, 1979) p. 86, http://www.firstworldwar.com/audio/loyalty.htm.

28. Daniel Patrick Moynihan, *Secrecy: The American Experience* (New Haven, CT; Yale University Press, 1999) p. 102. For an account of the Black Tom incident see Jules Witcover, *Sabotage at Black Tom: Imperial Germany's Secret War in America, 1914–1917* (Chapel Hill, NC; Algonquin, 1989).

29. Moynihan, p. 106.

30. Thomas Sowell, *Ethnic America: A History* (New York; Basic Books, 1981) p. 65.

Among other Americans of German ancestry who went on to render great naval and military services for their country might be numbered Admiral Chester Nimitz and General Carl Spaatz. Kevin P. Phillips, *The Cousins' Wars: Religion, Politics, and the Triumph of Anglo-America* (New York: Basic Books, 1999) p. 596.

31. Klaus-Volker Giessler, *Die Institution des Marineattachés im Kaiserreich* [The Institution of the Imperial Marine Attachés] (Boppard am Rhein: Boldt, 1976) p. 311.

32. Peter Overlack, 'German Commerce Warfare Planning for the Asia-Pacific Region before World War I' available at http://www.geocities.com/peteroverlack/page2.htm.

33. Mahan, *Influence of Sea Power upon History*, p. 25.

34. Tampke, p. 191.

35. Tom Frame, *No Pleasure Cruise: The Story of the Royal Australian Navy* (Crows Nest, NSW: Allen & Unwin, 2005) p. 103.

36. Mahan, *French Revolution and Empire*. Vol. II, p. 217.

37. Admiral Sir Cyprian Bridge, *The Art of Naval Warfare: Introductory Observations* (London; Smith, Elder and Co., 1907) pp. 144–5.

38. Tampke, p. 194.

39. For the Russian Navy in the Great War see René Greger, *Die Russische Flotte im Ersten Weltkrieg 1914–1917* (München: J. F. Lehmanns, 1970) published in English as *The Russian Fleet 1914–1917* (Shepperton, UK: Ian Allan, 1973).

40. There are a huge number of works detailing the fate of Spee and the Cruiser Squadron. One of the best is undoubtedly that by Keith Yates: Keith Yates, *Graf Spee's Raiders: Challenge to the Royal Navy 1914–1915* (Annapolis, MD: Naval Institute Press, 1995).

41. This prize was sent to Tsingtau, where it was armed with the weaponry from the laid up and unrepairable gunboat *Cormoran* for use as an auxiliary cruiser. Rechristened *Cormoran II*, she met with no success.

42. Dated only 'the end of July'. Quoted in Arthur W. Jose, *The Royal Australian Navy 1914–1918*, 9th edn (Sydney, NSW: Angus and Robertson, 1941) Vol. IX of C. E. W. Bean (Ed.), *The Official History of Australia in the War of 1914–1918*, 12 vols, various edns (Sydney, NSW: Angus & Robertson, 1941) pp. 26–7.

43. The Australian Centre For Maritime Studies, Submission To The 'Inquiry Into Australia's Maritime Strategy', 4 November 2002, p. 10, http://www.tamilnation.org/intframe/indian_ocean/australia_centre_for_maritime_studies.pdf.

44. Geoffrey Bennett, *Naval Battles of the First World War*, rev. edn (London: Penguin, 2002) p. 40.

45. There have been several excellent accounts of the adventures of the *Emden*. One of the best, and certainly the most accessible, is by Dan Van der Vat, *The Last Corsair: The Story of the Emden*, rev. edn (Edinburgh: Birlinn, 2001). Other works include R. K. Lochner (trans. Thea and Harry Lindauer), *The Last-Gentleman-Of-War: The Raider Exploits of the Cruiser Emden* (Annapolis, MD; Naval Institute Press, 1988) and Hugo von Waldeyer-Hartz, *Der Kreuzerkrieg 1914–1918: das Kreuzergeschwader, Emden, Königsberg, Karlsruhe, die Hilfskreuzer* (Oldenburg: Gerhard Stalling, 1931).

46. According to *Merchant Shipping (Losses)* House of Commons Paper 199, 1919 (London: HMSO, 1919) the following British vessels were captured and sunk by *Emden*: *Indus*, 10 September; *Lovat*, 11 September; *Killin*, 13 September; *Diplomat*, 13 September; *Trabboch*, 14 September; *Clan Matheson*, 14 September; *King Lud*,

25 September; *Tymeric*, 25 September; *Buresk*, 27 September; *Ribera*, 27 September; *Foyle*, 27 September; *Clan Grant*, 16 October; *Benmohr*, 16 October; *Ponrabbel*, 16 October; *Troilus*, 18 October; *Chilkana*, 19 October. To these may be added: *Pontoporus* (Greek) 9 September, captured with a cargo of British coal and impressed; *Kabinga* (British) 12 September, captured with neutral cargo and released; *Loredano* (Italian) 13 September, stopped and released; *Gryfevale* (British) 26 September, captured and released with captured crewmen from previous prizes; *St Egbert* (British) 18 October, captured and released with captured crewmen from previous prizes. See also Van der Vat.

47. On the east wall of the High Court at Parry's Corner, at the intersection of North Beach Road and NSC (Netaji Subhas Chandra) Bose Road, Madras (Chennai) there is a plaque commemorating the shelling. Every 22 September there is a gathering at this site, not to remember the shelling, but rather to commemorate Dr Champaka-raman Pillai, a committed anti-imperialist. He is credited with coining the phrase 'Jai Hind' meaning 'Victory for India' which became a nationalist mantra. At the start of the Great War Dr Pillai was in Switzerland, though he shortly moved to Berlin where, with German encouragement, he became a founder member of the Indian Independence Committee. It is said that Champakaraman Pillai was aboard the *Emden* when she raided the city and even helped direct fire onto specific targets. He returned to Germany after the war and was supposedly murdered by the Nazis in 1934. His wife, following Independence, returned his ashes to India. He is today remembered in India as a great Freedom Fighter. See *The Hindu*, Monday, 1 October 2001 and 19 November 2001, http://www.hinduonnet.com/ and also Sadhu Prof. V. Rangarajan and R. Vivekanandan, *The Saga of Patriotism: Revolutionaries in India's Freedom Struggle* (Bangalore: Sister Nivedita Academy, 2004).

48. The panic resulted in the arrest of a game ranger at what is today Ruhunu (Yala) National Park in Sri Lanka. The ranger, H. H. Engelbrecht, was taken prisoner by the British during the 1899–1902 Boer War but was not returned to South Africa on account of his refusal to swear allegiance to the British monarchy. He became the first ranger of the forerunner to the National Park, the game sanctuary, in 1908. He was accused, an accusation completely without foundation, of supplying meat to the *Emden* in 1914 and incarcerated until after the war, http://padayatra.org/yala.htm.

49. John Ashley Hall, *The Law of Naval Warfare*, rev. and enlarged edn (London: Chapman & Hall, 1921) p. 85.

50. *New York Times*, 29 October 1914.

51. Overlack, 'The Force of Circumstance', p. 680.

52. The Trans-Pacific cable, linking Vancouver to New Zealand and Australia via Norfolk Island, Fiji and Fanning Island, had been completed in 1902.

53. Jose, *The RAN*, p. 29.

54. Jose, p. 560.

55. *The Times*, 10 September 1914, p. 7.

56. Jose, p. 181.

57. The adventures of the abandoned landing party constitute a story straight out of the British *Boy's Own Paper* (1879–1967). Finding themselves marooned the 50 Germans commandeered the *Ayesha*, a small three-masted schooner, and made for the neutral territory of Padang, on Sumatra, in the Dutch East Indies. There they rendezvoused with a German merchantman that took them to Ottoman territory on the Red Sea.

A nightmare land journey then began, and eventually most of them made it to safety and eventually back home to Germany and a heroes' welcome. See Van der Vat; also, Hellmuth von Mücke, *The Emden-Ayesha Adventure: German Raiders in the South Seas and Beyond, 1914* (Annapolis, MD; Naval Institute Press, 2000).

58. HMAS *Sydney*: 4,900 tonnes; 26 knots; eight 152mm (6in.) guns; 475 men. SMS *Emden*: 3,052 tonnes; 23 knots; ten 105mm (4.1in.) guns; 311 men.

59. Quoted in Martin Gilbert, *The First World War: A Complete History* (New York: Henry Holt, 1994) p. 110.

60. See, for example, Geoffrey Bennett, *Coronel and the Falklands* [1962], rev. edn (Edinburgh: Birlinn, 2001). Barrie Pitt, *Coronel and Falklands: Two Great Naval Battles of the First World War* [1960] (London: Cassell, 2004).

61. T. B. Dixon, *The Enemy Fought Splendidly* (Poole, UK: Blandford Press, 1983) p. 26.

62. The other ships were the cruisers *Caernarvon, Cornwall, Glasgow* and *Bristol*.

63. *Scharnhorst, Gneisenau, Nürnberg, Leipzig* and *Dresden*.

Chapter 8, pp. 131–152

1. Immanuel C. Y. Hsu, *The Rise of Modern China*, 6th edn (New York: Oxford University Press, 1999) pp. 394–5.

2. Albert Röhr, *Handbuch der deutschen Marinegeschichte* [Manual of German Naval History] (Oldenburg: Gerhard Stalling, 1963) p. 130.

3. Charles B. Burdick, *The Japanese Siege of Tsingtau* (Hamden, CT: Archon, 1976) p. 30.

4. The *Los Angeles Times*, 31 August 1914. I am grateful to the following people and organisations for their assistance in tracing information and material relating to Alfred M. Brace: Sam Markham, Assistant Archivist at Associated Press, Katie Morgan, Beloit College Archives Summer Manager, and, in particular, Carrie Marsh, Special Collections Librarian at the Honnold/Mudd Library, Claremont, California, who very kindly supplied me with some important documentation.

5. Alfred M. Brace, 'With the Germans in Tsingtau: an Eye Witness Account of the Capture of Germany's Colony in China', *The World's Work: A History of Our Time*, Vol. 29, November 1914–April 1915 (New York: Doubleday, Page & Co., 1915) p. 634.

6. Arthur Judson Brown, *New Forces in Old China: An Inevitable Awakening*, 2nd edn (New York: F. H. Revell, 1904) p. 176.

7. For example: 'Germany's large expenditure upon fortified works in Kiautschou is exciting considerable interest, amounting, in certain quarters, to suspicion and anxiety concerning the ulterior designs of this country in the Far East.' *International Herald Tribune*, 17 May 1905.

8. The sources for this description of the defences, unless otherwise stated, are: Kurt Assmann, *Die Kämpfe der Kaiserlichen Marine in den deutschen Kolonien* [The Struggle of the Imperial Navy in the German Colonies] (Berlin: Mittler, 1935) pp. 108–9. This work gives a breakdown of the artillery positions, both permanent and extemporized. A 'Map of Tsingtau showing the Defences During the Siege' located at the UK National Archives, reference MPI 1/546/16. According to an added inscription, 'The original of this map was taken from a German artillery officer, now a prisoner of war in Hong Kong.' It details the positions of the various batteries and, in general, is in accord with Assmann's work. Information taken from photographs of plaques

mounted at Qingdaoshan Hill Battery Fort Educational Base, formerly the Bismarck Hill complex, which was visited by Dennis and Adrienne Quarmby in 2006. Captain Bernard Smith, 'The Siege of Tsingtau', *Coast Artillery Journal*, November–December 1934, pp. 405–19. Captain Smith made a 'detailed reconnaissance' of the area *circa* 1929 and discovered that there had been 'comparatively small damage to the works after 72 days of siege and lapse of some fifteen years'. Commander Charles B. Robbins, 'German Seacoast Defences at Tsingtao, 1914', in *Coast Defence Journal*, May 2007, pp. 85–90. Commander Robbins analyses an earlier article by Philip Sims, 'German Tsingtao Mounts Photographs', in *Coast Defence Journal*, November 2006 – which had attempted to identify photographs of the defences taken by US sailors during the 1920s. As he put it: 'The pictures are prints in scrap books without dates or captions, so which batteries are shown in the pictures is a subject of educated guesswork.'

9.   Gruson chilled cast-iron armour was invented at the works of Hermann Gruson, at Magdeburg-Buckau, in 1868. It was extremely hard and thus difficult to penetrate, though more vulnerable to fracture. A potential rival to the giant Krupp corporation, Gruson's company was taken over by Krupp in 1893. See Julius von Schütz (trans. Hubert Herbert Grenfell), *Gruson's Chilled Cast-Iron Armour* (London: Whitehead, Morris & Lowe, 1887).

10.   Tirpitz refers to the line of defences as the 'so-called Boxer protection' and the 'Boxer line'. Since it does not seem to have been called anything else I have followed his usage. Grand Admiral von Tirpitz, *My Memoirs* (London: Hurst & Blacket, 1919) 2 vols, Vol. I, pp. 79, 89.

11.   An artificial slope, usually of earth, in front of fortifications and constructed so as to deprive any assailant of cover and keep them under fire.

12.   In the terminology of the science of fortification the scarp is, from the point of view of the defenders, the inner side of the ditch. The opposite side is termed the counter-scarp.

13.   *Journal of the United States Artillery* (Fort Monroe, VA; Coast Artillery School Press, 1916) p. 127.

14.   Walter von Schoen, *Auf Vorposten für Deutschland: Unsere Kolonien im Weltkrieg* [On Germany's Outposts: Our Colonies in the World War] (Berlin: Ullstein, 1935) p. 28. Gunther Plüschow, *Die Abenteuer des Fliegers von Tsingtau: Meine Erlebnisse in drei Erdteilen* [The Adventures of the Tsingtau Flier: My Experiences in Three Continents] (Berlin; Ullstein, 1916) p. 47.

15.   Holger H. Herwig *'Luxury' Fleet: the Imperial German Navy, 1888–1918* (London: George Allen & Unwin, 1980) p. 61.

16.   Herwig, p. 63.

17.   Burdick, p. 23.

18.   Burdick, p. 202, n. 11.

19.   Often made up of men in their thirties and forties; the upper age limit for service being forty-five. See Norman Stone, *The Eastern Front 1914–1917* (New York: Charles Scribner's Sons, 1975) p. 55.

20.   Tirpitz's opposite number politically, Winston S. Churchill, was the prime mover behind the creation of a British equivalent, the Royal Naval Division. See Douglas Jerrold, *The Royal Naval Division* (London: Hutchinson, 1923).

21.   This was no real loss; the 5th Battle Squadron comprised the five pre-dreadnoughts of

the *Kaiser Friedrich III*-class; *Kaiser Friedrich III, Kaiser Wilhelm II, Kaiser Wilhelm der Grosse, Kaiser Karl der Grosse*, and *Kaiser Barbarossa*. Laid down between 1895 and 1898, and armed principally with four 240mm and fifteen 150mm they were obsolete in 1914 and unfit for operations against the Grand Fleet. Of even less utility were the vessels of the 6th Battle Squadron. This unit consisted of eight coastal defence battleships of the *Siegfried-* and *Odin-* (modified *Siegfried*) classes: *Siegfried, Beowulf, Frithjof, Heimdall, Hildebrand, Hagen, Odin*, and *Agir*. Laid down between 1889 and 1895 their main armament consisted of three 240mm guns with eight 88mm as secondary armament.

22. Mark D. Karau, *'Wielding the Dagger': The MarineKorps Flandern and the German War Effort, 1914–1918* (London: Praeger, 2000) pp. 7–15. See also: Alex Deseyne, *De Kust Bezet 1914–1918* [The Coast Occupied 1914–1918] (Nieuwpoortsesteenweg, Belgium; Provincial Domain of Raversijde, 2007).

23. H. W. Brands, *Bound to Empire: The United States and the Philippines* (Oxford: Oxford University Press, 1992) p.46.

24. Walter LaFeber, *The Cambridge History of American Foreign Relations*, 4 vols, Vol. II *The American Search for Opportunity* (Cambridge: Cambridge University Press, 1993) p. 210.

25. For views on Taft's Presidency see David H. Burton, *William Howard Taft, Confident Peacemaker* (Philadelphia: Saint Joseph's University Press, 2004); Michael L. Bromley, *William Howard Taft and the First Motoring Presidency, 1909–1913* (Jefferson, NC: McFarland, 2003); Paolo E. Coletta, *The Presidency of William Howard Taft* (Lawrence: University Press of Kansas, 1973).

26. James D. Startt, *Woodrow Wilson and the Press: Prelude to the Presidency* (New York: Palgrave Macmillan, 2004) p. 1.

27. Woodrow Wilson, *Message to Congress*, 63rd Congress, 2d Session, Senate Doc. No. 566 (Washington, DC: Government Printing Office 1914) pp. 3–4. Available from: http://net.lib.byu.edu/~rdh7/wwi/1914/wilsonneut.html. Biographical works on Wilson include: Mario R Di Nunzio (ed.), Woodrow Wilson: Essential Writings and Speeches of a Scholar-President (New York: New York University Press, 2006); Kendrick A. Clements, *The Presidency of Woodrow Wilson: American Presidency Series* (Lawrence: University Press of Kansas, 1992); Arthur Walworth, *Woodrow Wilson*, 2 vols (New York: Longmans, Green, 1958); and Arthur S. Link, *Woodrow Wilson and the Progressive Era, 1910–1917* (New York: Harper, 1954).

28. For an account of the relationship between the two states see Ian Nish, *Collected Writings* (London: Routledge Curzon, 2001) Part 1, pp. 188–203.

29. Nebogatov's flagship, *Tsar Nicholas I*, a *Tsar Alexander II*-class battleship commissioned in 1891, was also captured after Tsushima. Recommissioned as *Iki* she was used as a gunnery training ship and not deployed with Kato.

30. Because they were unsure of the whereabouts of Spee and his squadron, Kato's command initially included three modern heavy units: the battleships *Settsu* (1912) and *Kawachi* (1912) and the 'semi-dreadnought' *Satsuma* (1910). These were detached when it was ascertained that Spee was not in the vicinity.

31. This vessel should probably be classed as a light cruiser.

32. On board was a young sub-lieutenant named Onishi Takijiro. During the Second World War he founded the Kamikaze Corps. Walter J. Boyne, *Clash of Wings: World War II in The Air* (New York; Simon & Schuster, 1994) pp. 94–5

33. See David Lyon, *The First Destroyers* (London; Caxton Editions, 2001).

34. See Arne Røksund, *The Jeune Ecole: The Strategy of the Weak* (Leiden, Netherlands: Brill, 2007); Erwin F. Sieche, 'The Kaiser Franz Joseph I Class Torpedo-rams of the Austro-Hungarian Navy', in *Warship 1995* (London: Conway Maritime Press, 1995); Lawrence Sondhaus, *The Naval Policy of Austria-Hungary 1867–1918: Navalism, Industrial Development and the Politics of Dualism* (West Lafayette, IN; Purdue University Press, 1994).

35. Burdick, p. 28.

36. Burdick, pp. 38–9.

37. The primary armament of *S-90* consisted of three torpedo tubes; the *Kennet* had two.

38. Brace, p. 634.

39. British reports of the engagement are in the National Archives ADM 137 'Admiralty: Historical Section: Records used for Official History, First World War.' An account utilising these sources, as well as German documents, can be found in: Burdick, pp. 65–7, p. 216, nn. 15–16.

40. The 'finding' of the piece of steel is described in Burdick, p. 67.

41. For a description of British attitudes towards, and equipment for, minelaying see Peter F. Halvorsen, 'The Royal Navy and Mine Warfare, 1868–1914', *The Journal of Strategic Studies* 27/4 (December 2004) pp. 685–707.

42. Minus the British contingent, which did not join until 12 September.

43. National Archives, FO 228/2306. Quoted in Burdick, p. 218.

44. Burdick, p. 74.

45. For an account of the storm and its damaging effects see Burdick, pp. 74–5.

46. Kamio's service record can be viewed at: http://imperialarmy.hp.infoseek.co.jp/index.html. See also: Spencer C. Tucker (ed.) *Who's Who in Twentieth Century Warfare* (London: Routledge, 2001) p. 162.

47. Sterling Seagrave, *Dragon Lady: The Life and Legend of the Last Empress of China*, reprint edn (London: Vintage, 1993) p. 507.

48. Copies of the campaign plans are in the National Archives, WO 106/668 'Japanese and Chinese maps and literature relating to operations at Tsingtau', and these, together with Japanese documents, form the basis of Burdick's work on the subject. See Burdick, pp. 58–127.

49. Gilbert Reid, 'The Neutrality of China', Yale Law Journal 25/2 (December 1915) p. 122.

50. Noriko Kawamura, *Turbulence in the Pacific: Japanese-US Relations during World War I* (Westport, CT: Praeger, 2000) p. 18.

51. Burdick, p. 105.

52. Burdick, p. 104.

53. Hans Grade was an engineer and a German aviation pioneer. On 28 October 1908, at Magdeburg, he successfully conducted the first powered flight in Germany in an aeroplane of his own construction. On 30 October 1909 he won a 40,000 mark prize for being the first German to fly an indigenously constructed and powered aeroplane in a 'figure of eight' around two marker posts set one kilometre apart. For details on Grade's life and achievements see Ruth Glatzer, *Panorama einer Metropole: Das Wilhelminische Berlin* (Berlin: Siedler, 1997) p. 258; Niels Klussmann and Arnim Malik, *Lexikon der Luftfahrt* (Berlin: Springer, 2004) p. 320; Hans Fabian, 'Aero-

nautical Research comes into being during the Time of Empire', in E. H. Hirschel, H. Prem and G. Madelung, *Aeronautical Research in Germany: From Lilienthal Until Today* (Berlin: Springer, 2004) pp. 38–40.

54. Lila Sumino, 'L'Avion: l'Envol du Japon', in *Asia: Journal collégien et lycéen d'établissements français de la zone Asie-Pacifique*, No. 2 (December 2006) p. 4.

55. For the story of early Japanese aviation see Shinji Suzuki and Masako Sakai, 'History of Early Aviation in Japan', a paper [AIAA 2005–118] presented to the 43rd AIAA [American Institute of Aeronautics and Astronautics] Aerospace Sciences Meeting and Exhibit 10–13 January 2005, Reno, Nevada.

56. Richard J. Samuels, *'Rich Nation, Strong Army': National Security and the Technological Transformation of Japan* (Ithaca, NY: Cornell University Press, 1994) p. 109.

57. Stéphane Nicolaou, *Flying Boats and Seaplanes: A History from 1905* (Osceola, WI: MBI, 1998) p. 48.

58. Tom D. Crouch, *Wings: A History of Aviation from Kites to the Space Age* (New York: W. W. Norton, 2003) pp. 137–8.

59. James Davilla and Arthur Soltan, *French Aircraft of The First World War* (Stratford CT: Flying Machines Press, 1997) p. 218.

60. At the time of the conclusion of the Italo-Turkish (or Italo-Ottoman) War in October 1912 the Italians had carried out 127 sorties and dropped 330 bombs. See Paul Hoffman, *Wings of Madness: Alberto Santos-Dumont and the Invention of Flight* (New York: Theia Press, 2003) pp. 292–3.

61. Gunther Plüschow, *Die Abenteuer des Fliegers von Tsingtau: Meine Erlebnisse in drei Erdteilen* [The Adventures of the Tsingtau Flier: My Experiences in Three Continents] (Berlin: Ullstein, 1916) pp. 3–4.

62. John Killen, *The Luftwaffe: A History* (Barnsley, UK: Pen & Sword, 2003) p. 8.

63. Grand Admiral von Tirpitz, *My Memoirs* (London: Hurst & Blacket, 1919) 2 vols, Vol. I, p. 139.

64. Plüschow, pp. 10, 20.

65. For a biographical account of Franz Oster see Wilhelm Matzat, 'Franz Oster (1869–1933) – der erste Flieger von Tsingtau' [Franz Oster (1869–1933) – The First Tsingtau Flier] available online at: http://www.tsingtau.info/index.html?geschichte/oster1.htm. For the Ceylon crash see the 'Air Traffic Control Sri Lanka' website at: http://atcsl.tripod.com/1911_1949.htm.

66. Plüschow, pp. 26–8.

67. Plüschow, pp. 38–40.

68. *Flugzeug vollständig zertrümmert. Wiederaufbau lohnt sich nicht mehr.* Gunther Plüschow; diary entry for 27 August 1914. Quoted in Matzat, 'Franz Oster (1869–1933)'.

69. See Carl Johannes Voskamp, *Aus dem belagerten Tsingtau* (Berlin: Society of Evangelical Missions, 1915) p. 60. Also: Matzat, 'Franz Oster (1869–1933)'.

70. Burdick, pp. 93–4.

71. Plüschow, p. 49.

72. Burdick, pp. 88–9.

73. Burdick, p. 97.

74. The Japanese cavalry, like that of European nations, was trained and equipped to fight

dismounted when necessary. Edward A. Altham, *The Principles of War Historically Illustrated* (London: Macmillan, 1914) p. 83.

75. Waldemar Vollerthun, *Der Kampf um Tsingtau: eine Episode aus dem Weltkrieg 1914/1918 nach Tagebuchblättern* [The Battle for Tsingtau: an Episode from the World War of 1914–18 from the Pages of a Diary] (Leipzig: Hirzel, 1920) p. 98; Burdick, p. 90; H. G. W. Woodhead and H. T. M. Bell, *The China Year Book* (Shanghai: North China Daily News & Herald, 1914) p. 623, http://homepage3.nifty.com/akagaki/cyuui3.html

76. Burdick, pp. 44–5.

77. Ibid., pp. 46–8.

78. Ibid., pp. 61–2.

79. Ibid., p. 96.

80. Otto von Gottberg, *Die Helden von Tsingtau* (Berlin: Ullstein, 1915) p. 147.

81. Burdick, p. 100.

82. These, and similar, works, although hastily constructed would appear to have been robust. James R Lilley, the US Ambassador to the People's Republic of China 1989–91, spent his early childhood (he was born in 1924) in Tsingtau, and, later, he recalled exploring the 'old German forts' dug into the hillsides in 'Laoshan Mountain'. This must have been in the late 1920s or early 1930s. See James R Lilley with Jeffrey Lilley, *China Hands: Nine Decades of Adventure, Espionage, and Diplomacy in Asia* (New York: PublicAffairs, 2004) p. 12.

83. Burdick, pp. 100–2.

84. The Mecklenburghaus opened on 1 September 1904 and was named in honour of the president of the German Colonial Society, Duke Johann Albrecht zu Mecklenburg. See Deutsche Kolonialgesellschaft [German Colonial Society] (eds), *Deutscher Kolonial-Atlas mit Jahrbuch* [German Colonial Atlas and Yearbook] (Berlin: Deutsche Kolonialgesellschaft, 1905) p. 22.

85. Burdick, pp. 102–3.

86. James Davilla and Arthur Soltan, *French Aircraft of the First World War* (Stratford, CT: Flying Machines Press, 1997) p. 218; Burdick, p. 104.

87. Burdick, p. 98.

88. Burdick, pp. 104–5.

89. A 'Decauville Railway' was a 600mm (1/8in. less than 2ft) narrow-gauge light railway line made up of easily portable pre-assembled sections. The inventor was French farmer Paul Decauville, who conceived the idea after visiting the narrow gauge Rheilffordd Ffestiniog (Ffestiniog Railway) between Blaenau Ffestiniog and Porthmadog in North Wales. He originally devised it as a means of improving access to his land, but realised that it could be adapted for other purposes. He formed a company to produce track and rolling stock in 1875. The French Army adopted the system in 1888 and it had become standardised equipment for the militaries of several countries by 1914. See 'Portable Railways', *Scientific American Supplement No. 446*, New York, 19 July 1884; Pascal Ory, *1889 La Mémoire des siècles: L'Expo universelle* (Paris: Editions Complexe, 1989) p. 119; Ffestiniog Railway Company, *Rheilffordd Ffestiniog Guide Book* (Porthmadog, Wales: Ffestiniog Railway Company, 1997); Jim Harter, *World Railways of the Nineteenth Century: A Pictorial History in Victorian Engravings* (Baltimore, MD; John Hopkins University Press, 2005) p. 141.

90. Burdick, pp. 109, 147, 231 n. 42

91. For a Great War history of the regiment see C. T. Atkinson, *The History of the South Wales Borderers 1914–1918* [1931] (Uckfield, UK; Naval & Military Press, 2002).

92. John Albert White, *Transition to Global Rivalry: Alliance Diplomacy and the Quadruple Entente, 1895–1907* (Cambridge: Cambridge University Press, 2002) p. 181. Details of Barnardiston's career and his papers are located at the Liddell Hart Centre for Military Archives at King's College London, Reference code: GB99 KCLMA Barnardiston.

93. Lord Kitchener (Secretary of State for War) to General Officer Commanding (GOC) North China, 21 August 1914. Quoted in Burdick, p. 82.

94. As well as 970 personnel, Barnardiston commanded 240 Chinese labourers with 98 wagons as well as 200 pack-mules. See UK National Archives ADM 137/35.

95. Barnardiston to The War Office, 9 October 1914. WO 106/667 'Operations at Tsing Tau: Reports by Brig.-Gen N. W. Barnardiston MVO.' Also printed in the *Supplement to the London Gazette* of 30 May 1916. Attached to Barnardiston's command as liaison officer was Lieutenant-Colonel Everard Ferguson Calthrop of the Royal Artillery. Calthrop was one of the 'Language Officers' attached to the British Legation in Tokyo, a scheme initiated in September 1903 so that British military personnel could learn to communicate with their new ally. See Sebastian Dobson (Introduction), *The Russo-Japanese War: Reports from Officers Attached to the Japanese Forces in the Field*, 5 vols, reprint edn with an introduction by Sebastian Dobson (Bristol, UK: Ganesha Publishing, 2000) Vol. I, pp. v–lxii. Calthrop's notes on his attachment are in WO 106/661 'Japanese participation in North China (Tsing Tau): Original Transcripts.'

96. In so doing, Barnardiston became the first British general to set foot on German territory during the Great War. Burdick, p. 111.

97. Burdick, pp. 113–14.

98. Ibid., pp. 114–18.

99. Ibid., pp. 68, 71. *Kaiserin Elisabeth* also equipped three land batteries (see Table 2) by disembarking six of her fourteen 47mm quick-firing guns.

100. Ibid., p. 118.

101. Spencer C. Tucker, *The Great War 1914–18* (Bloomington: Indiana University Press, 1999) p. 196; Burdick, p. 234, n. 73.

102. Burdick, p. 124.

103. Ibid., p. 23.

104. Ibid., p. 124.

105. Ibid., p. 121.

106. Ibid., p. 122.

107. Plüschow. pp. 52–53.

108. 'Until several years after World War I, Japan had no separate permanent naval landing organization corresponding to the U.S. Marine Corps. Instead, naval landing parties were organized temporarily from fleet personnel for a particular mission and were returned to their ships at its conclusion. This practice was made possible by the fact that every naval recruit was given training in land warfare concurrently with training in seamanship. The results of such training, together with any special skills [...] were noted on the seaman's service record to serve as a basis for his inclusion in a landing party. Normally, the fleet commander designated certain ships to furnish personnel

for the landing party. This practice, however, depleted their crews and lowered their efficiency for naval action. Therefore, in the late 1920s Japan began to experiment with more permanent units known as Special Naval Landing Forces (*Rikusentai*).' *Handbook on Japanese Military Forces: War Department Technical Manual TM-E 30–480* (Washington, DC: War Department, 1944) p. 76.

109. G. Nash and G. Gipps, 'Narrative of the Events in Connection with the Siege, Blockade, and Reduction of the Fortress of Tsingtau', in ADM 137/35; Burdick, p. 231, n. 42.

110. Burdick, p. 123.

111. Plüschow, p. 54; Burdick, pp. 125–6, 235, n. 87.

Chapter 9, pp. 153–176

1. There is a massive canon of work concerning the Russo-Japanese War in general and the Siege of Port Arthur in particular. I have used the following in the main: B. W. Norregaard, *The Great Siege: The Investment and Fall of Port Arthur* (London: Methuen, 1906); Lt. Gen. N. A. Tretyakov, *My Experiences at Nan-Shan and Port Arthur with the Fifth East Siberian Rifles* (London: Hugh Rees, 1911); Reginald Hargreaves, *Red Sun Rising* (London: Weidenfeld & Nicolson, 1962); Richard Connaughton, *The War of the Rising Sun and Tumbling Bear*, paperback edn (London: Routledge. 1991).

2. Barnardiston to War Office, 10 November 1914. 'Operations at Tsing Tau: Reports by Brig.-Gen. N. W. Barnardiston MVO', WO 106/667. Also printed in the *Supplement to the London Gazette* of 30 May 1916. Available at: http://www.1914–1918.net/barnardistons_first_despatch.htm.

3. Otto von Gottberg, *Die Helden von Tsingtau* (Berlin: Ullstein, 1915) p. 127; Charles B. Burdick, *The Japanese Siege of Tsingtau* (Hamden, CT; Archon, 1976) pp. 134–6. According to Brace the Japanese sent a full list of those they had captured to the defenders by wireless. Alfred M. Brace, 'With the Germans in Tsingtau: an Eye Witness Account of the Capture of Germany's Colony in China', in *The World's Work: A History of Our Time* Vol. XXIX, November 1914–April 1915 (New York: Doubleday, Page & Co., 1915) p. 640.

4. John Ellis, *Eye-Deep in Hell: Trench Warfare in World War I* (Baltimore: Johns Hopkins University Press, 1976) p. 76.

5. Nikolas Gardner, *Trial by Fire: Command and the British Expeditionary Force in 1914* (Westport, CT; Praeger, 2003) p. 95.

6. The form the German artillery operation would take had been decided at a war council presided over by Meyer-Waldeck on 28 September. Burdick, *Japanese Siege of Tsingtau*, pp. 128–9.

7. Burdick, pp. 130–1.

8. Gunther Plüschow, *Die Abenteuer des Fliegers von Tsingtau: Meine Erlebnisse in drei Erdteilen* [The Adventures of the Tsingtau Flier: My Experiences in Three Continents] (Berlin: Ullstein, 1916) p. 43.

9. E. F. Young, 'Tethered Balloons – Present and Future', a paper [AIAA-1968-941] presented to the Aerodynamic Deceleration Systems Conference of the AIAA [American Institute of Aeronautics and Astronautics], 23–25 September 1968, El Centro, California, p. 1.

10. Ian Sumner, *German Air Forces 1914–18* (Oxford: Osprey, 2005) p. 29.
11. Brace, p. 637; Burdick, pp. 131–2.
12. Brace, p. 637.
13. Plüschow, pp. 57–9.
14. Plüschow, pp. 59–61.
15. ADM 137/35. Attachment to report dated 30 November 1914.
16. Burdick, p. 241, n. 45.
17. Burdick, p. 145.
18. For Japan's occupation of the railway and the political impetus behind it, see Madeleine Chi, *China Diplomacy 1914–1918* (Cambridge, MA: Harvard University Press, 1970) pp. 14–25; John T. Pratt, *War and Politics in China* (London; Jonathan Cape, 1943) p. 178.
19. For 'mole warfare' at Port Arthur see Chapter XXX of: E. K. Nozhin, A. B. Lindsay (trans.) and E. J. Swinton (ed.), *The Truth about Port Arthur* (London; John Murray, 1908) pp. 206–21.
20. Burdick, pp. 140–1.
21. Chinese citizens were also used by the Germans, and not only for carrying out the donkey-work. Tsingtau had a contingent of Chinese police, and some of these, prior to the Japanese closing up with the defences, were sent into enemy-held territory in civilian guise in order to collect intelligence. Such missions were dangerous in the extreme – the Japanese had no hesitation in shooting those they thought might be spies – and, while such men were undoubtedly brave, the effort was, in all likelihood, unproductive. Burdick, pp. 133–4, 138–9.
22. Plüschow p. 68.
23. Plüschow p. 70.
24. Burdick. p. 242, n. 58.
25. Barnardiston to War Office, 9 October 1914.
26. Burdick, pp. 142, 239, n. 33.
27. Ibid., pp. 144–5, 151–2.
28. Ibid., pp. 142–3.
29. Barnardiston to War Office, 29 October 1914.
30. Ibid.; Burdick, pp. 146–7.
31. Burdick, pp. 152–3. The name *Takachiho* means 'sacred place in Japan'.
32. Plüschow, p. 78.
33. Burdick, pp. 153, 244, nn. 75–9.
34. Ibid., pp. 148–9, 160.
35. Ibid., pp. 139, 158–9.
36. Ibid., pp. 161, 246, nn. 15–16.
37. Glide with the engine off.
38. Usually spelt *jinrikisha*, a rickshaw.
39. Brace, p. 637.
40. Plüschow, p. 80.
41. Burdick, p. 162.

42. Burdick, pp. 161, 246, n. 17.

43. Correspondents of 'The Times', *The Times History of the War*, Vol. II (London: The Times, 1915) p. 119.

44. During the Battle of the Somme in 1916 the British deployed 54 artillery tubes per kilometre. A record at the time, though soon surpassed. See B. H. Liddell Hart, *History of the First World War* (London: Pan Books, 1972) p. 234.

45. Burdick, p. 165; Plüschow, p. 83.

46. Burdick, p. 165; Brace, p. 638. For information on the Asiatic Petroleum Company see Charles van der Leeuw, *Oil and Gas in the Caucasus and Caspian: A History* (Richmond, UK; Curzon Press, 2000) p. 80.

47. A. N. Hilditch, 'The Capture of Tsingtau (Nov. 7) Japan Expels Germany from the Far East', in Charles F. Horne (ed.) *Source Records of World War I*, 7 vols, Vol. II, *1914 – The Red Dawning of 'Der Tag'* (New York: Edwin Mellen Press, 1997) p. 402.

48. Burdick, pp. 165, 247, n. 29; Hilditch, p. 402.

49. Burdick, pp. 166–7.

50. Burdick, pp. 168–9.

51. Sources differ as to who was in command of the various Infantry Works during the bombardment. I have chosen to follow Kurt Assmann, *Die Kämpfe der Kaiserlichen Marine in den deutschen Kolonien* [The Struggle of the Imperial Navy in the German Colonies] (Berlin: Mittler, 1935), part I of which deals with the Tsingtau campaign. A career naval officer, Assmann rose to flag rank and was, during World War II, head of the Kriegsmarine's Historical Office. He wrote widely after 1945, including *Deutsche Schicksalsjahre* [Germany's Fateful Years] (Wiesbaden: Brockhaus, 1950), and *Deutsche Seestrategie in zwei Weltkriegen* [German Naval Strategy in Two World Wars] (Heidelberg: Vowinckel, 1957).

52. Burdick, pp. 170–1, 249, n. 46.

53. Burdick, pp. 170–1; Hilditch, p. 403.

54. Burdick, pp. 170–1.

55. Jefferson Jones, *The Fall of Tsingtau, With a Study of Japan's Ambitions in China* (Boston: Houghton Mifflin, 1915). Portions relating to the siege and fall of Tsingtau are available online at: http://www.greatwardifferent.com/Great_War/Tsing_Tao/Japanese_Orient_01.htm. Jones, who was the Staff Correspondent of *The Minneapolis Journal* and *Japan Advertiser*, had this work added to the UK's proscribed list during the Great War. His study of Japan's ambitions in China was considered to be hostile to Japan, and Britain had no wish to antagonise a valuable ally. For the banning of the book see Peter Fryer, *Private Case-Public Scandal* (London: Secker & Warburg, 1966) pp. 139–40.

56. Burdick, p. 248, n. 41.

57. Ibid., pp. 172, 249, n. 53.

58. Ibid., p. 172.

59. Major R. L. McClintock, Royal Engineers, who was at the time attached to the Madras Sappers and Miners, a unit of the Indian Army based at Bangalore, invented the original Bangalore Torpedo in 1912. It consisted of lengths of explosive-filled metal tubing that could be attached end to end to the requisite length. These were then pushed through barbed-wire entanglements and detonated, the resultant explosion

cutting a channel through the wire. Major-General W. Porter, *The* History of the Corps of Royal Engineers, Vol. II (London: Longmans, Green, 1952) p. 67. Also see the Royal Engineers Museum website: http://www.remuseum.org.uk/corpshistory/rem_corps_part13.htm.

60. Burdick, pp. 172–3.

61. Barnardiston to War Office, 10 November 1914.

62. Yoichi Hirama, 'The Anglo-Japanese Alliance and the First World War', in Ian Gow, Yoichi Hirama and John Chapman (eds), *History of Anglo-Japanese Relations, 1600–2000 Volume III: The Military Dimension* (Basingstoke, UK: Palgrave Macmillan, 2003) p. 51. FO 371/3816 – Japan. Code 23 / Code W23 File 86–4026. Document 345 'Abstracts of Newspapers'.

63. Quoted in Burdick, p. 174.

64. Hilditch, p. 403; Burdick, p. 174.

65. Quoted in Burdick, p. 175.

66. Plüschow, pp. 95–6; Isot Plüschow and Gunther Plüschow, *Deutscher Seemann und Flieger* [German Sailor and Flier] (Berlin: Ullstein, 1933) p. 171.

67. Burdick, p. 176; Barnardiston to War Office, 10 November 1914.

68. Burdick, pp. 176–7.

69. Burdick, pp. 178, 251, n. 68; Assmann, p. 112.

70. Nakamura Jekizo (trans. J. A. Irons), 'Assault on the Central Fort, Tsingtao Campaign, 1914'. Report in the US Army Military Research Collection at US Army Military History Institute, Carlisle Barracks, PA.

71. Burdick, pp. 180, 251, n. 71.

72. Brace, p. 639.

73. Quoted in Assmann, p. 90; quoted in translation in Burdick, p. 181.

74. Barnardiston to War Office, 10 November 1914.

75. Burdick, p. 181.

76. Barnardiston to War Office, 10 November 1914.

77. Burdick, p. 182.

78. This was granted by order of the Japanese Emperor on 9 November.

79. Burdick, pp. 185–6; WO 106/661 'Japanese participation in North China (Tsing Tau): Original Transcripts'.

80. Burdick, p. 194.

81. Charles B. Burdick and Ursula Moessner, *The German Prisoners-of-War in Japan, 1914–1920* (Lanham, MD; University Press of America, 1984) p. 67.

82. Burdick and Moessner, pp. 9–11.

83. Welles, the grand-nephew of Senator Charles Sumner, whose wife had, apparently dallied with Holstein in 1866–67, went on to have a glittering career in the US diplomatic service, thanks to his closeness to Franklin D. Roosevelt. He reached the rank of Assistant Secretary of State, but his affinity with the President 'made his diplomatic role often more important than that of Secretary [of State] [Cordell] Hull'. Justus D. Doenecke, 'The United States and the European War, 1939–1941: A Historiographical Review', in Michael J. Hogan (ed.), *Paths to Power: The Historiography of American Foreign Relations to 1941* (Cambridge: Cambridge University Press, 2000) p. 250.

84. Benjamin Welles, *Sumner Welles: FDR's Global Strategist, a Biography* (New York: St Martin's Press, 1997) pp. 45–7. There is an excellent German-language website devoted to the German POWs and their incarceration: http://www.tsingtau.info/index.html?lager/gefangenenlager.htm.

85. Prior to the Western Front Battle of Neuve Chapelle, 10–13 March 1915, the then General Sir Douglas Haig commanding First Army told the then brevet Lieutenant-Colonel Hugh Trenchard commanding 1st Wing, Royal Flying Corps: 'If you can't fly because of the weather, I shall probably put off the attack.' Rebecca Grant, 'Trenchard at the Creation', *Air Force Magazine* 87/2 (February 2004) p. 78.

86. Brace, p. 640.

87. Shinji Ishii, 'The Fall of Sei-Tö (Tsing-Tao) and its Aftermath' in *Asian Review: Journal of the Royal Society for India, Pakistan, and Ceylon*, Nos. 13–16. January – May 1915. p. 17.

88. Using the Nippon-shiki Rōmaji system. See J. Marshall Unger, *Literacy and Script Reform in Occupation Japan* (New York: Oxford University Press, 1996) p. 147.

Chapter 10

1. William Lowell Putnam, *The Kaiser's Merchant Ships in World War I* (Jefferson, NC: McFarland, 2001) pp. 210–15; Roy Alexander, *The Cruise of the Raider 'Wolf'* (London: Cape, 1939); Blaine Pardoe, *The Cruise of the Sea Eagle: The Amazing True Story of Imperial Germany's Gentleman Pirate* (Augusta, GA; Lyons Press, 2005) pp. 201–3; Karl August Nerger, *SMS Wolf* (Berlin: Scherl, 1918).

2. The tale does not end there as von Luckner and five of his crew took one of the ship's boats on an epic journey to the Fijian island of Wakaya, a voyage of some 3,700 km, where, on 21 September, they were captured and made prisoners of war. In a story that almost parallels that of the Emden's landing party, the Germans remaining on Mopelia managed to capture a French sailing ship that called at the island, the Lutece, and set off for South America under the command of first officer Leutnant Kling. Meanwhile one of the stranded American prisoners, Captain Smith, took to the sea in another open boat, accompanied by three seamen, and sailed the 1,600 kilometres to Pago Pago in American Samoa. They arrived on 4 October and the rescue of those remaining marooned on Mopelia was arranged. Kling and his companions however were wrecked off Easter Island, though all survived and were interned by Chile for the duration of the war. Luckner, together with some of his compatriots, made a daring escape from his prison camp on Motuihe Island, off New Zealand, on 13 December and attempted, after seizing a flat-bottomed boat, to get to the Kermadec Islands, some 1,000 kilometres north-east of New Zealand. They were recaptured on 21 December 1917 and remained prisoners until 1919. James N. Bade, *Von Luckner: A Reassessment. Count Felix von Luckner in New Zealand and the South Pacific. 1917–1919 and 1938* (Frankfurt: Peter Lang, 2004); Graf Luckner, *Seeteufels Weltfahrt: Alte und neue Abenteuer* (Gütersloh: Bertelsmann, 1953); Robin Bromby, *German Raiders of the South Seas* (Sydney: Doubleday, 1985); Pardoe, *The Cruise of the Sea Eagle*; J. A. C. Gray, *Amerika Samoa* (New York: Arno Press, 1980) p. 189.

3. Henry Newbolt, *History of the Great War Based on Official Documents by Direction of the Historical Section of the Committee of Imperial Defence*, Vol. IV *Naval Operations* (London: Longmans, Green, 1928) p. 323.

4. John Keegan, *The Price of Admiralty: The Evolution of Naval Warfare* (New York: Viking, 1989) p. 180.

5. Queen Elizabeth (January 1915), Warspite (March 1915), Barham (October 1915), Valiant (February 1916) and Malaya (February 1916). The last named was paid for by the Federated Malay States, hence her name.

6. Lion (June 1912), Princess Royal (November 1912), and Queen Mary (August 1913).

7. R. H. Walters, *The Economic and Business History of the South Wales Steam Coal Industry, 1840–1914* (New York: Arno Press, 1977) p. 337; D. S. M. Barrie, *A Regional History of the Railways of Great Britain*: Vol. XII South Wales (Newton Abbot, UK; David & Charles, 1980) p. 254; Peter Herring, *Yesterday's Railways: Recollections of an Age of Steam and the Golden Age of Railways* (Newton Abbot, UK; David & Charles, 2002) p. 230. For the South Wales coal industry see M. J. Daunton, *Coal Metropolis: Cardiff 1870–1914* (Leicester, UK; Leicester University Press, 1977). See also: Jon Tetsuro Sumida, 'British Naval Operational Logistics, 1914–1918', *Journal of Military History* 57/3 (Lexington VA; Virginia Military Institute, 1993) pp. 447–80.

8. John Bach, *The Australia Station: A History of the Royal Navy in the South West Pacific, 1821–1913* (Kensington, NSW; New South Wales University Press, 1986) p. 220.

9. Nicholas Lambert, 'Economy or Empire? The Fleet Unit Concept and the Quest for Collective Security in the Pacific, 1909–1914', in Keith Neilson (ed.), *Far-flung Lines: Studies in Imperial Defence in Honour of Donald Mackenzie Schurman* (London: Frank Cass, 1997) pp. 57, 77, n. 23.

10. W. G. Huff, *The Economic Growth of Singapore: Trade and Development in the Twentieth Century* (Cambridge UK; Cambridge University Press, 1994) pp. 245–6; Gretchen Liu, *Singapore – A Pictorial History 1819–2000* (Abingdon, UK; Routledge, 2001) p. 107.

11. Invincible class 172.8m x 23.9m x 7.6m draught; Indefatigable class 180m x 24.4m x 8m draught; Lion class 214m x 27.1m x 8.5m draught; Tiger 214.6m x 27.6m x 8.7m draught; Renown class 240 m x 30 m x 8.94 m draught; Hood (1920) 262.3m x 31.7m x 10.1m draught.

12. Queen Elizabeth class 195.3m x 27.6m x 9.5m draught; Revenge class [Revenge (1916); Royal Sovereign (1916); Royal Oak (1916); Resolution (1916); Ramillies (1917)] 190m x 31.1m x 8.5m draught. For an account of the evolution of anti-torpedo bulges see D. K. Brown, *The Grand Fleet: Warship Design and Development 1906–1922* (Annapolis, MD; Naval Institute Press, 1999).

13. Hector C. Bywater, *Navies and Nations: A Review of Naval Developments since the Great War* (London: Constable 1927) p. 94. 'Bulges' or 'Blisters' were retrofitted to most capital ships after the Great War as protection against underwater attack. These added to the beam of the vessel.

14. W. David MacIntyre, *The Rise and Fall of the Singapore Naval Base* (Hamden CT: Archon, 1979) p. 10.

15. Dated only 'the end of July'. Quoted in Arthur W. Jose, *The Royal Australian Navy 1914–1918*, 9th Edition (Sydney, NSW; Angus & Robertson, 1941) Vol. IX of C. E. W. Bean (ed.), *The Official History of Australia in the War of 1914–1918*, 12 vols, various edns (Sydney, NSW: Angus & Robertson, 1941) pp. 26–7.

16. Arthur J. Marder, *Old Enemies, New Friends: The Royal Navy and the Imperial Japanese Navy* (Oxford: Clarendon Press, 1981) p. 5.

17. Thomas F. LaFargue, *China and the World War* (Palo Alto, CA: Stanford University Press, 1937) pp 23–4.

18. Kajima Morinosuke, *The Diplomacy of Japan, 1894–1922*, 3 vols (Tokyo: The Kajima Institute of International Peace, 1976) Vol. III [The First World War, Paris Peace Conference, Washington Conference] pp. 164–6.

19. Thomas F. Millard, *Our Eastern Question* (New York: Century, 1916) p. 121.

20. Benjamin Welles, *Sumner Welles: FDR's Global Strategist* (New York: St Martin's Press, 1997) p. 32.

21. Kendrick A. Clements, *The Presidency of Woodrow Wilson: American Presidency Series* (Lawrence: University Press of Kansas, 1992) p. 109.

22. Bruce A. Elleman, *Wilson and China: A Revised History of the Shandong Question* (Armonk, NY; Sharpe, 2002) pp. 15–21.

23. Noriko Kawamura, *Turbulence in the Pacific: Japanese-US Relations during World War I* (Westport, CT: Praeger, 2000) p. 57.

24. Dirk Anthony Ballendorf, 'Earl Hancock Ellis: A Marine in Micronesia', *Micronesian Journal Of the Humanities And Social Sciences* 1/1–2 (December 2002) pp. 9, 11.

25. Treaty of Versailles, 28 June 1919, http://www.firstworldwar.com/source/versailles.htm.

26. Georges Clemenceau's Letter of Reply to the Objections of the German Peace Delegation, May 1919, http://www.firstworldwar.com/source/parispeaceconf_germanprotest2.htm

27. C. H. Rodwell, review of 'The German Colonial Claim by L. S. Amery', International Affairs (Royal Institute of International Affairs 1931–1939) 18/5 (September–October 1939) p. 693. On 14 August 2004, Heidemarie Wieczorek-Zeul, the German Minister for Development and Economic Cooperation, officially apologised for German behaviour at a ceremony to mark the 100th anniversary of the Hereros' 1904 uprising. Her words were unequivocal: 'A century ago, the oppressors – blinded by colonialist fervour – became agents of violence, discrimination, racism and annihilation in Germany's name. The atrocities committed at that time would today be termed genocide – and nowadays a General von Trotha would be prosecuted and convicted. We Germans accept our historical and moral responsibility and the guilt incurred by Germans at that time.' Andrew Meldrum, 'German Minister says Sorry for Genocide in Namibia', *The Guardian*, 16 August 2004.

28. W. O. Henderson, *Studies in German Colonial History* (London: Routledge, 1962) p. xii.

29. A. Edho Ekoko, 'The British Attitude towards Germany's Colonial Irredentism in Africa in the Inter-War Years', *Journal of Contemporary History* 14/2 (April 1979) pp. 287–307; Mary E. Townsend, 'The German Colonies and the Third Reich', *Political Science Quarterly* 53/2 (June 1938) p. 187.

30. *Hansard*, House of Commons, 6 July 1926, Vol. 197, cc. 1874–5

31. Townsend, p. 194.

32. A. T. Mahan, *Naval Strategy* (London: Sampson Low, Marston & Co., 1911) p. 199.

33. Anne Cipriano Venzon, *From Whaleboats to Amphibious Warfare: Lt. Gen. 'Howling Mad' Smith and the US Marine Corps* (Westport, CT; Praeger, 2003) p. 50.

34. Allan R. Millett, 'Assault From the Sea: The Development of Amphibious Warfare

between the Wars – the American, British, and Japanese Experiences', in Williamson Murray and Allan R. Millett (eds), *Military Innovation in the Interwar Period* (Cambridge: Cambridge University Press, 1996) p. 72.

35. Major Earl H. Ellis USMC, *Advanced Base Operations in Micronesia* [Fleet Marine Force Reference Publication (FMFRP) 12–46. Department of the Navy – Headquarters US Marine Corps] (Washington, DC; US Government Printing Office, 1992) p. 29. Earl H. 'Pete' Ellis is a fascinating, larger than life, character who served in the Philippines during the insurrection and was later stationed at Guam before serving under General Pershing in France. Having set out the issues in Advanced Base Operations in Micronesia he then visited the area to gather detailed information. Ellis perished under what were considered mysterious circumstances while at Koror in the Pelews on 12 May 1923. However, recent scholarship has revealed that his death was from illness, he was an alcoholic, rather than Japanese intervention. For details of his life and untimely death see Dirk Anthony Ballendorf, 'Earl Hancock Ellis: A Marine in Micronesia,' *Micronesian Journal of the Humanities and Social Sciences* 1/1–2 (December 2002), pp. 9–17.

36. See Quincy Wright, *Mandates Under the League of Nations* (Chicago : University of Chicago, 1930); Pitman B. Potter, 'Origin of the System of Mandates under the League of Nations,' *American Political Science Review* 16/4 (November 1922), pp. 563–83.

37. Mark R. Peattie, *Nan'yō: The Rise and Fall of the Japanese in Micronesia, 1885–1945* (Honolulu; University of Hawaii Press, 1988) p. 68.

38. Peattie, p. 73.

39. Peattie, p. 75. See also Francis X. Hezel, *Strangers in their Own Land: A Century of Colonial Rule in the Caroline and Marshall Islands* (Honolulu: University of Hawaii Press, 1995).

40. See Hermann Joseph Hiery, *The Neglected War: The German South Pacific and the Influence of World War I* (Honolulu: University of Hawaii Press, 1995); Hermann Joseph Hiery. *Das Deutsche Reich in der Sudsee (1900–1921): Eine Anndherung an die Erfahrun: gen verschiedener Kulturen* [*The German Empire in the South Seas (1900–1921): An Approach to the Experiences of Different Cultures*] (Göttingen: Vandenhoeck & Ruprecht, 1995).

41. Hezel, Strangers in their Own Land, p. 215.

42. Samuel Eliot Morison, *History of United States Naval Operations in World War II*, Vol. 7 *Aleutians, Gilberts and Marshalls, June 1942–April 1944* [1951] (Urbana: University of Illinois Press, 2002) pp. 66, 70.

43. Ian Hamill, *Strategic Illusion: The Singapore Strategy and the Defence of Australia and New Zealand, 1919–1942* (Singapore: Singapore University Press, 1981) p. 42.

44. D. G. Boyce (ed.), *The Crisis of British Power: The Imperial and Naval Papers of the Second Earl of Selborne, 1895–1910* (London: The Historians' Press, 1990) pp. 154–5.

45. Josephus Daniels, *Annual Report of the Secretary of the Navy, 1916* (Washington, DC: Government Printing Office, 1916).

46. Arthur S. Link (ed.), *The Papers of Woodrow Wilson*, 69 vols (Princeton, NJ: Princeton University Press, 1966–1994) January–May, 1916, Vol. 36, p. 120.

47. Kenneth J. Hagan, *This People's Navy: The Making of American Sea Power* (New York: Free Press, 1991) p. 273.

48. Ian Nish, *Japanese Foreign Policy, 1869–1942* (London: Routledge & Keegan Paul, 1977) p. 290.

49. G. A. H. Gordon, 'The British Navy, 1918–1945', in Keith Neilson and Elizabeth Jane Errington (eds.), *Navies and Global Defence: Theories and Strategy* (Westport, CT: Praeger, 1995) p. 162. Inbal Rose, *Conservatism and Foreign Policy During the Lloyd George Coalition 1918–1922* (Abingdon UK: Taylor & Francis, 1999) pp. 169–70.

50. Jellicoe also visited India, New Zealand and Canada to advise on naval defence

51. Joseph Moretz, *The Royal Navy and the Capital Ship in the Interwar Period: An Operational Perspective* (London: Frank Cass, 2002) p. 37; The four-volume 'Jellicoe Report' is in the National Archives of Australia: 'Admiral of the Fleet Viscount Jellicoe – Naval mission to Australia May– August 1919'. Correspondence re, including – Letter dated 2nd May 1919 to Lord JELLICOE from acting Prime Minister, Australia (Navy File No. 19/060) 694427.

52. Rose, *Conservatism and Foreign Policy During the Lloyd George Coalition*, p. 169.

53. Erik Goldstein, 'The Evolution of British Diplomatic Strategy for the Washington Conference', in Erik Goldstein (ed.), *The Washington Conference 1921–22: Naval Rivalry, East Asian Stability and the Road to Pearl Harbour* (London: Frank Cass, 1994) p. 14. One of a planned class of four battlecruisers, Hood of the projected 'Admiral class', was commissioned in May 1920 – she was to be Britain's last completed battlecruiser. Mounting a main armament of eight 15in. (381mm) guns, and displacing some 46,000 tonnes, Hood was, at 262.1 metres (860ft) in length, the largest capital ship in the world at the time of her commissioning.

54. Richard Worth, *Fleets of World War II* (Cambridge, MA: Da Capo, 2001) p. 93; Ian Johnston and Rob McAuley, *The Battleships* (Osceola, WI: MBI, 2001) p. 113.

55. The canon of literature on the Singapore Naval Base and associated strategy is massive. Personal favourites include: Hamill, *Strategic Illusion* (note 43 above); Brian Farrell and Sandy Hunter (eds.), *Sixty Years On: The Fall of Singapore Revisited* (Singapore: Eastern Universities Press, 2002); and W. David MacIntyre, *The Rise and Fall of the Singapore Naval Base* (Hamden, CT: Archon, 1979).

56. Harry H. Ransom, 'The Battleship Meets the Airplane', *Military Affairs* 23/1 (Spring 1959) p. 21.

57. Eugene P. Trani and David L. Wilson, The Presidency of Warren G. Harding ((Lawrence: Regents Press of Kansas, 1977) p. 151. For an account of the context within which the election of Harding took place see Wesley M. Bagby, The Road to Normalcy: The Presidential Campaign and Election of 1920 (Baltimore: Johns Hopkins Press, 1962).

58. Philip H. Love, *Andrew W. Mellon: The Man and His Work* (Whitefish, MT: Kessinger, 2003) p. 47

59. Steven R. Weisman, *The Great Tax Wars: Lincoln to Wilson – The Fierce Battles over Money and Power That Transformed the Nation* (New York: Simon & Schuster, 2002) p. 351.

60. William R. Braisted, 'The Evolution of the United States Navy's Strategic Assessments in the Pacific, 1919–31', in Goldstein, *The Washington Conference 1921–22*, p. 103.

61. Hughes had resigned as an associate justice of the Supreme Court in order to campaign, unsuccessfully, against Wilson in the 1916 presidential election and was, following his term under Harding and, after 1923, Calvin Coolidge, to go on to have a distinguished

legal career as Chief Justice of the Supreme Court following his appointment to the post by President Herbert Hoover in 1930. See Betty Glad, *Charles Evans Hughes and the Illusions of Innocence: A Study in American Diplomacy* (Urbana: University of Illinois Press, 1966); Robert Sobel, *Biographical Directory of the United States Executive Branch, 1774–1989* (New York: Greenwood Press, 1990) pp. 187–8.

62. For an excellent account of the Washington Naval Conference and its context and consequences see Chapter 2 of: Herbert P. LePore, *The Politics and Failure of Naval Disarmament 1919–1939: The Phantom Peace* (Lewiston, NY: Edwin Mellen Press, 2003).

63. Niall A. Palmer, *The Twenties in America: Politics and History* (Edinburgh: Edinburgh University Press, 2006) p. 77.

64. William H. Honan, *Bywater: The Man Who Invented the Pacific War* (London: Macdonald, 1990) p. 90; See also Goldstein, 'The Evolution of British Diplomatic Strategy for the Washington Conference', in Goldstein,. pp. 28–9. HMAS Australia was decommissioned on 12 December 1921. On 12 April 1924 the battlecruiser was scuttled off Sydney. See Michael Wilson, *Royal Australian Navy Major Warships: Profile No. 1* (Marrickville, NSW: Topmill, no date) p. 5.

65. Allen W. Dulles, *The Craft of Intelligence* (New York: Harper & Row, 1963) p. 62. For an account of the US cryptanalysis organisation of the time see Herbert O. Yardley, *The American Black Chamber* (Laguna Hills, CA: Aegean Park, 1931). For a biography of Yardley see David Kahn, *The Reader of Gentlemen's Mail: Herbert O. Yardley and the Birth of American Codebreaking* (New Haven, CT: Yale University Press, 2004).

66. 'Treaty Between Japan and China for the Settlement of Outstanding Questions Relative to Shantung', *American Journal of International Law* 16/2, Supplement: Official Documents (April 1922), pp. 84–94.

67. Anne Cipriano Venzon (ed.) *General Smedley Darlington Butler: The Letters of a Leatherneck, 1898–1931* (New York: Praeger, 1992) pp. 286–7, n. 1; Hans Schmidt, *Maverick Marine: General Smedley D. Butler and the Contradictions of American Military History* (Lexington: University Press of Kentucky, 1987) p. 194; C. Martin Wilbur, 'The Nationalist Revolution: from Canton to Nanking, 1923–28', in John K. Fairbank and Denis Twitchett (eds) *The Cambridge History of China, Volume 12, Republican China, 1912–1949* (Cambridge: Cambridge University Press, 1983) p. 706; Marjorie Dryburgh, *North China and Japanese Expansion 1933–1937: Regional Power and the National Interest* (Richmond, UK: Curzon Press, 2000).

68. James L. McClain, *Japan: A Modern History* (New York: Norton, 2001) p. 397.

69. 'An Appreciation of the Value of Singapore to Australia', Document in the Australian Archives; Series: A981/1; Item: DEF 331 Pt. 2. Title: Defence Singapore, p. 1. This document is undated, but from its contents it can be located in 1936. It speaks of the 'recent London conference regarding Naval armaments', which could mean either the First London Naval Conference of 1930 or the Second London Naval Conference, which took place in 1936. However it also mentions that 'Germany has attracted considerable attention, and caused no little anxiety, by designing a capital ship of a smaller type'. This can only mean the three Panzerschiffe of the Deutschland class, or 'pocket battleships' as they were popularly known in Britain, which were launched between 1931 and 1934. The treaty arising out of the second conference, the Second London Naval Treaty, was signed on 25 March 1936.

70. 'An Appreciation of the Value of Singapore to Australia', pp. 1–2.

71. Ibid., p. 2.

72. Admiral Sir Herbert Richmond, *Statesmen and Sea Power* (Oxford: Clarendon Press, 1946), p. 328.

73. Commander Russell Grenfell, *Sea Power in the Next War* (London: Geoffrey Bles, 1938) p. 165.

74. Gordon Rottman, *World War II Pacific Island Guide: A Geo-Military Study* (Westport, CT; Greenwood, 2002) p. 174.

75. Harry A. Gailey, *Bougainville: The Forgotten Campaign, 1943–1945* (Lexington: University of Kentucky Press, 2003) p. 79. Burton Wright III, *Eastern Mandates* (US Army Campaigns of World War II) (Washington, DC: US Army Center of Military History, 1993) p. 9.

76. Martin Gilbert, *In Search of Churchill: A Historian's Journey* (London: HarperCollins, 1994) p. 174.

77. See the final chapter of Frederick Quinn, *The French Overseas Empire* (Westport, CT; Praeger: 2000) pp. 219–64.

78. See, for example, Peter C. Smith, *Task Force 57: The British Pacific Fleet, 1944–45* (London: William Kimber, 1969). For an American perspective see Samuel Eliot Morison, *History of United States Naval Operations in World War II, Vol. 14: Victory in the Pacific 1945* [1960] (Urbana: University of Illinois Press, 2002) pp. 102–7.

79. Alan Powell, *The Third Force: ANGUA's New Guinea War, 1942–46* (Melbourne: Oxford University Press, 2003) p. 82. ANGUA was an acronym for the 'Australian New Guinea Administrative Unit'.

80. Morison, Vol. 14, p. 104.

81. The term originates, I think, with Benjamin Disraeli, who almost used it at a speech in the Free Trade Hall, Manchester, on 3 April 1878. In criticising his Liberal opponents' policy and attitude towards India, Disraeli argued that it had been proven with 'mathematical demonstration to be the most costly jewel in the Crown of England.' See W. F. Moneypenny and George E. Buckle, *The Life of Benjamin Disraeli: Earl of Beaconsfield*, 6 vols (New York: Macmillan, 1910–20) Vol. VI, pp. 191–2; Sneh Mahajan, *British Foreign Policy 1874–1914: The Role of India* (London: Routledge, 2002) p. 34.

82. John Ramsden, *Man of the Century: Winston Churchill and his Legend since 1945* (New York: Columbia University Press, 2002) p. 416. The text of the ANZUS Treaty can be found at: http://australianpolitics.com/foreign/anzus/anzus-treaty.shtml.

83. Peter Clarke, *The Last Thousand Days of the British Empire* (London: Allen Lane, 2007).

84. See, for example: Philip Murphy, *Party Politics and Decolonisation: The Conservative Party and British Colonial Policy in Tropical Africa, 1951–1964* (Oxford: Clarendon Press, 1995).

85. Peter Winzen, *Das Kaiserreich am Abgrund: Die Daily-Telegraph-Affaere und das Hale-Interview von 1908* [*The Empire at the Abyss: The Daily-Telegraph Affair and the Hale-Interview of 1908*] (Stuttgart: Franz Steiner, 2002) p. 346.

86. See Arnold H. Leibowitz, *Defining Status: A Comprehensive Analysis of United States Territorial Relations* (Dordrecht, NL: Martinus Nijhoff, 1989).

87. Edward Gibbon, *An Essay on the Study of Literature: Written Originally in French, now first Translated into English* (London: T. Becket and P. A. De Hondt, 1764) p. 1.

88. Dr Ana Maui Taufe'ulungaki, Director of the Institute of Education at the University of the South Pacific in Fiji, during her keynote address at the Fourth biennial 'Pacific Spirit' conference held at the Waipuna Hotel and Conference Centre, Auckland, on 3-4 March 2004. See: Ana Maui Taufe'ulungaki, 'Pacific Spirit' in *Alcohol.org.nz* (Alcohol Advisory Council of New Zealand/te Kaunihera Whakatupato Waipiro o Aotearoa) Vol. 5, No. 1, June 2004. p. 10. Also available online at: http://www.alac.org.nz/ InpowerFiles/ALACsMagazine/DocumentWithImage.Document.1359.3d38dc9d– 0270–4ca9–9201–6ec734bf4fb8.pdf.

Bibliography

A Note on Internet Sources
Those who have perused the notes in this work will have probably noticed that a good many Internet sources have been utilised. Indeed, the world wide web, despite the transient and impermanent nature of some of its content, can be a powerful aid in the quest for historical information.

Some particularly useful and interesting websites that readers might like to visit are: German Prisoners of War in Japan, *The Hindu* online, The Peterhof Palace, Royal Engineers Museum, the Sokehs Rebellion, Centenary of German Annexation of the Carolines, Tsingtao Brewery, The US Naval Historical Center, and Yala National Park.

I last checked the URLs on 17 July 2009, and hopefully, not too many will be out of date by the time this is printed. The bibliography has however been restricted to printed works, as these are permanent and one does not usually receive a message stating 'unable to open' when one tries to gain access.

Documents and Collections

Australian War Memorial, Canberra
'An Appreciation of the Value of Singapore to Australia.' Series: A981/1; Item: DEF 331 Pt. 2. Title: Defence Singapore.

National Library of Australia, Canberra
Alfred Deakin, Papers. 1804–1973. MS 1540.
Ronald Craufurd Munro Ferguson, Papers. 1912–1935. MS 696. National Library of Australia.

The British Library, London
Balfour Papers. Add MSS 49683–49962.

German Federal Archive, Koblenz
Pacific War Plans, BA/MA Reichs-Marine 5/v 5955.

National Archives UK, Kew
'Admiralty: Historical Section: Records used for Official History, First World War.' ADM 137.
Barnardiston, Brig.-Gen. N. W. 'Operations at Tsing Tau: Reports by.' WO 106/667.
Japan. Code 23 / Code W23 File 86–4026. Document 345 'Abstracts of Newspapers.' FO 371/3816.
Japan's Declaration of War against Germany, and Capture of Tsingtao. FO 228/2306.
'Japanese and Chinese maps and literature relating to operations at Tsingtau.' WO 106/668.
'Japanese participation in North China (Tsing Tau): Original Transcripts.' WO 106/661.

McKenna, Reginald. Imperial Conference on Defence: Admiralty Memorandum of 20 July 1909. CAB 37/100/98.

'Map of Tsingtau showing the Defences during the Siege'. MPI 1/546/16.

'Memorandum by the General Staff', 4 November 1905. CID 38/10/79.

Nash, G and Gipps G.'Narrative of the Events in Connection with the Siege, Blockade, and Reduction of the Fortress of Tsingtau', ADM 137/35.

'Notes of the Proceedings of a Conference at the Admiralty On Tuesday, 10th August 1909, between Representatives of the Admiralty and of the Government of the Commonwealth of Australia to Consider a Scheme for the Establishment of an Australian Navy', in *Imperial Conference: Proceedings* ,Vol. I. CAB 18/12A.

National Archives US, Washington, DC

'Japanese Naval Activities during European War', 11 December 1918; Office of Naval Intelligence, Record Group 38.4.3 Communications with Naval Attaches, U-4-B, 11083.

'Official Report of Japanese Naval Activities during the War', 11 December 1918, translation of official statement issued by Japanese Navy Department on 8 December 1918; Office of Naval Intelligence, Record Group 38.4.3 Communications with Naval Attaches, U-4-B, 11083.

'Operations - Japanese Navy in the Indian and Pacific Oceans during War 1914–1918', Office of Naval Intelligence, Record Group 45, Subject File 1911–1927, WA-5 Japan, box 703, folder 10, NND 913005.

Published Works and Collections

Boyce, D. G. (ed.). *The Crisis of British Power: The Imperial and Naval Papers of the Second Earl of Selborne, 1895–1910* (London: The Historians' Press, 1990).

Brace, Alfred M. 'With the Germans in Tsingtau: an Eye Witness Account of the Capture of Germany's Colony in China', in *The World's Work: A History of Our Time*, Volume XXIX, November 1914–April 1915, pp. 634–77.

British Documents on Foreign Affairs: Reports and Papers from the Foreign Office Confidential Print, Series E, Asia, 1914–1939, Part II, From the First to the Second World War (Frederick, MD: University Publications of America, 1991).

British and Foreign State Papers, 1897–1898, Volume 90 (London: HMSO, 1901).

Churchill, Randolph S. *Winston S. Churchill: Young Statesman 1901–1914*, Companion Volume II, Part 3, 1911–1914 (London: Heinemann, 1969)

Dobson, Sebastian (Introduction). *The Russo-Japanese War: Reports from Officers Attached to the Japanese Forces in the Field*, 5 vols, reprint edition with an Introduction by Sebastian Dobson (Bristol, UK: Ganesha Publishing, 2000).

Dugdale, E. T. S. (Selected and Trans.) *German Diplomatic Documents, 1871–1914*, Volume III, *The Growing Antagonism, 1898–1910* (New York: Harper & Brothers, 1930).

Ellis, Major Earl H. USMC. *Advanced Base Operations in Micronesia* [Fleet Marine Force Reference Publication (FMFRP) 12–46. Department of the Navy – Headquarters US Marine Corps] (Washington, DC: US Government Printing Office, 1992).

Gooch, G. P. and Temperly, H. W. V. (eds) *British Documents on the Origins of the War, 1898–1914*, 11 vols (London: HM Stationery Office, 1926–38).

Hancock, W. D. (ed.). *English Historical Documents* (London: Eyre & Spottiswoode, 1977).

Hansard – The Official Report of the Proceedings of [the UK] Parliament (London: HMSO, various dates).

International Court of Justice, The. *Case Concerning Certain Phosphate Lands in Nauru (Nauru v. Australia) Volume I, Application: Memorial of Nauru*, 2003.

Jäckh, Ernst (Ed.). *Kiderlen-Wächter, der Staatsmann und Mensch: Briefwechsel und Nachlaß [Kiderlen-Wächter, the Statesman and the Man: Correspondence and Private Papers]*. 2 Vols. (Stuttgart: Deutsche Verlags-Anstalt, 1924).

Jacob, E. A. *Deutsche Kolonialpolitik in Dokumenten: Gedanken und Gestalten der letzten fünfzig Jahre* [German Colonial Politics in Documents: Thoughts and Patterns from the Last Fifty Years] (Leipzig: Dieterich, 1938).

Lansing, Robert. *Papers Relating to the Foreign Policy of the United States: The Lansing Papers, 1914–1920*, 2 vols (Washington, DC: Government Printing Office, 1939–40).

Link, Arthur S. (ed.). *The Papers of Woodrow Wilson*, 69 vols (Princeton, NJ: Princeton University Press, 1966–94) Volume 36, *January–May 1916*, p. 120.

Merchant Shipping (Losses) House of Commons Paper 199, 1919 (London: HMSO, 1919).

Millard, Thomas F. 'Punishment and Revenge in China', *Scribner's Magazine*, 29 February 1901.

Morison, Elting E. (ed.). *The Letters of Theodore Roosevelt*, 8 vols (Cambridge, MA: Harvard University Press, 1951–54).

Mulligan, Timothy P. *M2089: Selected German Documents from the Records of the Naval Records Collection of the Office of Naval Records and Library, 1897–1917.* (Washington, DC: National Archives and Records Administration, 2006).

Parliamentary Papers: House of Commons (London: HMSO, various dates).

Rhodes James, Robert (ed.). *Winston S. Churchill: His Complete Speeches, 1897–1963*, 8 vols (New York: Chelsea House Publishers, 1974).

Roosevelt, Theodore. *Addresses and State Papers: Including the European Addresses*, Executive Edition, 8 vols (New York: Collier & Son, 1910).

Seager II, Robert and Doris Maguire (eds). *Letters and Papers of Alfred Thayer Mahan*, 3 vols (Annapolis, MD: Naval Institute Press, 1975).

Snyder, Louis L. (ed.). *Documents of German History* (New Brunswick, NJ: Rutgers University Press, 1958).

Staatsarchiv, Das (trans. Adam Blauhut). *Sammlung der offiziellen Aktenstücke zur Geschichte der Gegenwart [Collection of Official Documents Relating to Contemporary History]* (Leipzig: Duncker & Humblot, 1891).

'Treaty Between Japan and China for the Settlement of Outstanding Questions Relative to Shantung', *The American Journal of International Law*, Vol. 16, No. 2, Supplement: Official Documents, April 1922.

Wilson, Woodrow. Message to Congress, 63rd Congress, 2nd Session, Senate Doc. No. 566 (Washington, DC: Government Printing Office, 1914).

Books and Other Printed Works

Abelshauser, Werner et al. *German Industry and Global Enterprise: BASF: The History of a Company* (Cambridge: Cambridge University Press, 2003).

Aisin-Gioro Pu Yi (trans. WJF Jenner). *From Emperor to Citizen: The Autobiography of Aisin-Gioro Pu Yi* (Peking: Foreign Languages Press, 1964).

Alden, Carroll Storrs and Earle, Ralph. *Makers of Naval Tradition* (London: Ginn & Company, 1925).

Alexander, Roy. *The Cruise of the Raider 'Wolf'* (London: Jonathan Cape, 1939).

Altham, Edward A. *The Principles of War Historically Illustrated* (London: Macmillan, 1914).

Anderson, Eugene N. *The First Moroccan Crisis, 1904–1906* (Chicago: University of Chicago Press, 1930).

Andrew, Christopher. *Theophile Delcassé and the Making of the Entente Cordiale: A Reappraisal of French Foreign policy, 1898–1905* (London: Macmillan, 1968).

Andrews, E. M. *The Anzac Illusion: Anglo-Australian Relations during World War I*, reprint edition (Cambridge: Cambridge University Press, 1994).

Anon. *Handbook on Japanese Military Forces: War Department Technical Manual TM-E 30–480* (Washington, DC: War Department, 1944).

Anon. 'Portable Railways', *Scientific American Supplement* No. 446 New York, 19 July 1884.

Anon. 'Before Gallipoli-Australian Operations in 1914', *Semaphore: Newsletter of the Sea Power Centre, Australia*, Issue 7, August 2003.

Asquith, Herbert Henry. *The Genesis of the War* (New York: George H. Doran, 1923).

Assmann, Kurt. *Die Kämpfe der Kaiserlichen Marine in den deutschen Kolonien* [The Struggle of the Imperial Navy in the German Colonies] (Berlin: Mittler, 1935).

Atkinson, C. T. *The History of the South Wales Borderers 1914–1918* [1931] (Uckfield, UK: Naval & Military Press, 2002).

Aydelotte, William Osgood. *Bismarck and British Colonial Policy: The Problem of South West Africa 1883–1885* (Philadelphia: University of Pennsylvania Press, 1937).

Bach, John. *The Australia Station: A History of the Royal Navy in the South West Pacific, 1821–1913* (Kensington: New South Wales University Press, 1986).

Bade, James N. *Von Luckner: A Reassessment. Count Felix von Luckner in New Zealand and the South Pacific. 1917–1919 and 1938* (Frankfurt: Peter Lang, 2004).

Bagby, Wesley M. *The Road to Normalcy: The Presidential Campaign and Election of 1920* (Baltimore: Johns Hopkins Press, 1962).

Bailey, Paul John. *China in the Twentieth Century* (Oxford : Blackwell, 2001).

Bailey, Thomas A. 'Dewey and the Germans at Manila Bay', *The American Historical Review*, Vol. 45, No. 1, October 1939.

Balfour, Sebastian. *The End of the Spanish Empire, 1898–1923* (Oxford: Clarendon, 1997).

Ballendorf, Dirk Anthony. 'Earl Hancock Ellis: A Marine in Micronesia', *Micronesian Journal of the Humanities and Social Sciences*, Vol. 1, no. 1–2, December 2002, pp. 9–17.

Barraclough, Geoffrey. *From Agadir to Armageddon: Anatomy of a Crisis* (New York: Holmes & Meier, 1982).

Barclay, Sir Thomas. *New Methods of Adjusting International Disputes and the Future* (London: Constable, 1917).

Barlow, Ima C. *The Agadir Crisis* (Hamden, CT: Archon Books, 1971).

Barrie, D. S. M. *A Regional History of the Railways of Great Britain*, Volume XII *South Wales* (Newton Abbot, UK: David & Charles, 1980).

Bauer, Wolfgang. 'Tsingtao's Trade and Economy from the Japanese Occupation in 1914, until the End of the 1920s', *The Asiatic Society of Japan Bulletin No. 1*, January 1996.

Beasley, W. G. *Japanese Imperialism 1894–1945* (Oxford: Oxford University Press, 1987).

Behr, Edward. *The Last Emperor* (New York: Bantam Books, 1987).

Bennett, Geoffrey. *Naval Battles of the First World War*, revised edition (London: Penguin, 2002).

Bennett, Geoffrey. *Coronel and the Falklands* [1962], revised edition (Edinburgh: Birlinn, 2001).

Bennett, Judith A. 'Holland, Britain, and Germany in Melanesia', in K. R. Howe, Robert C. Kiste and Brij V. Lal (eds), *Tides of History: The Pacific Islands in the Twentieth Century* (Honolulu: University of Hawaii Press, 1994).

Benton, Elbert Jay. *International Law and Diplomacy of the Spanish-American War* (Baltimore: John Hopkins, 1898).

Beresford, Lord Charles. *The Break-Up of China: With an Account of Its Present Commerce, Currency, Waterways, Armies, Railways, Politics, and Future Prospects* (New York: Harper & Brothers, 1900).

Bergere, Marie-Claire (trans. Janet Lloyd). *Sun Yat-sen* (Stanford, CA: Stanford University Press, 1998).

Berghahn, V. R. *Germany and the Approach of War in 1914*, second edition (London: Palgrave Macmillan, 1993).

Berghahn, V. R. *Imperial Germany, 1871–1918: Economy, Society, Culture and Politics* (Oxford: Berghahn Books, 2005).

Berman, Sheri. *The Social Democratic Moment: Ideas and Politics in the Making of Interwar Europe* (Cambridge, MA: Harvard University Press, 1998).

Binder-Krieglstein, E. Baron. *Die Kämpfe des Deutschen Expeditionskorps in China und ihre militärischen Lehren* [The Battles of the German Expeditionary Corps in China and their Military Lessons] (Berlin: E. S. Mittler, 1902).

Bismarck, Otto Fürst von. *Die Gesammelten Werke* [The Collected Works], 15 vols (Berlin: Stollberg, 1924–35).

Blue, Gregory. 'Opium for China: the British Connection', in Timothy Brook and Bob Tadashi Wakabayashi, *Opium Regimes: China, Britain, and Japan, 1839–1952* (Collingdale, PA: Diane, 2000).

Boehmer, Elleke. *Empire Writing: An Anthology of Colonial Literature 1870–1918* (Oxford: Oxford University Press, 1998).

Boemeke, Manfred Franz et al. *Anticipating Total War: The German and American Experiences, 1871–1914* (Cambridge: Cambridge University Press, 1999).

Borkin, Joseph. *The Crime and Punishment of IG Farben* (London: Andre Deutsch, 1979).

Boyne, Walter J. *Clash of Wings: World War II in the Air* (New York: Simon & Schuster, 1994).

Brackman, Arnold C. *The Last Emperor* (New York: Scribners, 1975).

Braisted, William. *The United States Navy in the Pacific 1897–1909* (Austin: University of Texas Press, 1958).

Braisted, William R. 'The Evolution of the United States Navy's Strategic Assessments in the Pacific, 1919–31,' in Erik Goldstein (ed.), *The Washington Conference 1921–22: Naval Rivalry, East Asian Stability and the Road to Pearl Harbour* (London: Frank Cass, 1994).

Brands, H. W. *Bound to Empire: The United States and the Philippines* (Oxford: Oxford University Press, 1992).

Breck, Edward. 'Review of *The World Crisis* by Winston S. Churchill', *The American Historical Review*, Vol. 29, No. 1, October 1923.

Bredon, Juliet. *Sir Robert Hart: The Romance of a Great Career* (London: Hutchinson, 1909).

Bridge, Admiral Sir Cyprian. *The Art of Naval Warfare: Introductory Observations* (London: Smith, Elder, 1907).

Bromby, Robin. *German Raiders of the South Seas* (Sydney: Doubleday, 1985).

Bromley, Michael L. *William Howard Taft and the First Motoring Presidency, 1909–1913* (Jefferson, NC: McFarland, 2003).

Brooks, Barbara J. 'Peopling the Japanese Empire: the Koreans in Manchuria and the Rhetoric of Inclusion', in Sharon A. Minichiello (ed.), *Japan's Competing Modernities: Issues in Culture and Democracy, 1900–1930* (Honolulu: University of Hawaii Press, 1998).

Brown, Arthur Judson. *New Forces in Old China: An Inevitable Awakening*, second edition (New York: F. H. Revell, 1904).

Brown, D. K. *The Grand Fleet: Warship Design and Development 1906–1922* (Annapolis, MD: Naval Institute Press, 1999).

Brownell, Will and Billings, Richard N. *So Close to Greatness: A Biography of William C. Bullitt* (New York: Macmillan, 1987).

Buell, Raymond Leslie. *The Washington Conference: A Dissertation presented to the Faculty of Princeton University in Candidacy for the Degree of Doctor of Philosophy* (New York: D. Appleton, 1922).

Bülow, Prince Bernhard von (trans. Marie A. Lewenz). *Imperial Germany*, third impression, (London: Cassell, 1914).

Bülow, Prince Bernhard von (trans. F A Voight). *Memoirs of Prince von Bülow: From Secretary of State to Imperial Chancellor 1897–1903* (Boston: Little, Brown, 1931).

Burdick, Charles B. *The Japanese Siege of Tsingtau* (Hamden, CT: Archon, 1976).

Burdick, Charles B. and Moessner, Ursula. *The German Prisoners-of-War in Japan, 1914–1920* (Lanham, MD: University Press of America, 1984).

Burton, David H. *William Howard Taft, Confident Peacemaker* (Philadelphia: Saint Joseph's University Press, 2004).

Bywater, Hector C. *Navies and Nations: A Review of Naval Developments Since the Great War* (London: Constable 1927).

Carroll, Brian. *Australia's Prime Ministers: From Barton to Howard* (Stanmore, NSW: Cassell Australia, 1978).

Cavinder, Fred D. *Amazing Tales from Indiana* (Indianapolis: Indiana University Press, 1990).

Cecil, Lamar. *Wilhelm II: Emperor and Exile, 1900–1941* (Chapel Hill: University of North Carolina Press, 1996).

Chan Lau Kit-Ching, *Anglo-Chinese Diplomacy in the Careers of Sir John Jordan and Yüan Shih-kai 1906–1920* (Hong Kong: Hong Kong University Press, 1978).

Chang Kia-ngau *China's Struggle for Railroad Development* (New York: The John Day Company, 1943).

Charmley, John. *Splendid Isolation? Britain and the Balance of Power 1874–1914* (London: Hodder & Stoughton, 1999).

Chi, Madeleine. *China Diplomacy 1914–1918* (Cambridge, MA: Harvard University Press, 1970).

Chisholm, Geo G. 'The Resources and Means of Communication of China', in *The Geographical Journal*, Vol. 12, No. 5, November 1898, pp. 500–19.

Choi Jeong-soo. 'The Russo-Japanese War and the Root-Takahira Agreement', in *The International Journal of Korean History*, Vol. 7, February 2005, pp. 133–63.

Churchill, Winston S. *The World Crisis 1911–1918*. 2-vol. edition (London: Odhams, 1938).

Churchill, Winston S. *Great Contemporaries* (London: Odhams Press, 1949).

Clarke, Peter. *The Last Thousand Days of the British Empire* (London: Allen Lane, 2007).

Clements, Kendrick A. *The Presidency of Woodrow Wilson: American Presidency Series* (Lawrence: University Press of Kansas, 1992).

Cocker, Mark. *Rivers of Blood, Rivers of Gold: Europe's Conquest of Indigenous Peoples* (New York: Grove Press, 2001).

Cohen, Warren I (ed.). *The Cambridge History of American Foreign Relations*, 4 vols. (Cambridge: Cambridge University Press, 1993).

Coletta, Paolo E. *The Presidency of William Howard Taft* (Lawrence: University Press of Kansas, 1973).

Connaughton, Richard. *The War of the Rising Sun and Tumbling Bear*, paperback edition (London: Routledge, 1991).

Craig, Gordon A. *Germany 1866–1945* (Oxford: Oxford University Press, 1988).

Crankshaw, Edward. *The Fall of the House of Hapsburg* (New York: Viking, 1963).

Creswell, William. 'Captain Creswell's Views on Result of Imperial Conference, 16 November 1909', in G. L. Macandie, *The Genesis of the Royal Australian Navy: A Compilation* (Sydney, NSW: Government Printer, 1949)

Crouch, Tom D. *Wings: A History of Aviation from Kites to the Space Age* (New York: W. W. Norton, 2003).

Croft, Henry Page. *The Path of Empire* (London: John Murray, 1912).

Cullis, Roger. 'Technological Roulette – A Multidisciplinary Study of the Dynamics of Innovation' (University of London PhD Thesis, 1986).

Cunneen, Chris. *King's Men: Australia's Governors-General from Hopetoun to Isaacs* (Sydney: Allen & Unwin Australia, 1984).

Curtis, Lionel. *The Problem of the Commonwealth* (London: Macmillan, 1916).

Curtius, Friedrich (ed.) (trans. George W. Chrystal). *Memoirs of Prince Chlodwig of Hohenlohe Schillingsfürst*, 2 vols (London: William Heinemann, 1906).

Dahlhaus, Carl. *Nineteenth-Century Music* (Berkeley and Los Angeles: University of California Press, 1989).

Daniels, Josephus. *Annual Report of the Secretary of the Navy, 1916* (Washington, DC: Government Printing Office, 1916).

Daunton, M. J. *Coal Metropolis: Cardiff 1870–1914* (Leicester, UK: Leicester University Press, 1977).

Davila, James and Soltan, Arthur. *French Aircraft of the First World War* (Stratford, CT: Flying Machines Press, 1997).

Davis, Clarence B. and Gowen, Robert J. 'The British at Weihaiwei: A Case Study in the Irrationality of Empire', *The Historian*, Vol. 63, 22, September 2000, pp. 87–104.

Davis, Mike. *Late Victorian Holocausts: El Niño Famines and the Making of the Third World* (New York: Verso Books, 2002).

Delmendo, Sharon. *The Star-Entangled Banner: One Hundred Years of America in the Philippines* (New Brunswick, NJ: Rutgers University Press, 2004).

Deseyne, Alex. *De Kust Bezet 1914–1918* [The Coast Occupied 1914–1918] (Nieuwpoortsesteenweg, Belgium: Provincial Domain of Raversijde, 2007).

Dewey, Adelbert M. *The Life and Letters of Admiral Dewey from Montpelier* [Vermont] *to Manila* (New York: Barnes & Noble World Digital Library, 2003).

Dewey, George. *Autobiography of George Dewey: Admiral of the Navy* (New York: Scribners, 1913).

Dillon, E. J. 'The Chinese Wolf and the European Lamb', *Contemporary Review* 79, May 1901, pp. 1–31.

Dillon, Michael. *China: A Historical and Cultural Dictionary* (London: Curzon Press, 1998).

Di Nunzio, Mario R. (ed.). *Woodrow Wilson: Essential Writings and Speeches of a Scholar-President* (New York: New York University Press, 2006).

Dixon, T. B. *The Enemy Fought Splendidly* (Poole, UK: Blandford Press, 1983).

Doenecke, Justus D. 'The United States and the European War, 1939–1941: A Historiographical Review', in Michael J Hogan (ed.), *Paths to Power: The Historiography of American Foreign Relations to 1941* (Cambridge: Cambridge University Press, 2000).

Doerries, Reinhard R. 'From Neutrality to War: Woodrow Wilson and the German Challenge', in William N. Tilchin and Charles E. Neu (eds), *Artists of Power: Theodore Roosevelt, Woodrow Wilson, and Their Enduring Impact on US Foreign Policy* (Westport, CT: Praeger, 2006).

Dreyer, Edward L. *China at War, 1901–1949* (London: Longman, 1995).

Dryburgh, Marjorie. *North China and Japanese Expansion 1933–1937: Regional Power and the National Interest* (Richmond, UK: Curzon Press, 2000).

Duiker, William J. *Cultures in Collision: The Boxer Rebellion* (San Rafael, CA: Presidio Press, 1978).

Dulles, Allen W. *The Craft of Intelligence* (New York: Harper & Row, 1963).

Duranti, Alessandro. *A Companion to Linguistic Anthropology* (Malden, MA: Blackwell, 2004).

Dyal, Donald H. et al. *Historical Dictionary of the Spanish American War* (Westport, CT: Greenwood Press, 1996).

Eckart, Wolfgang U. *Medizin und Kolonialimperialismus: Deutschland 1884–1945* [Medicine and Colonial Imperialism: Germany 1884–1945] (Vienna: Ferdinand Schoeningh, 1997).

Edho Ekoko, A. 'The British Attitude towards Germany's Colonial Irredentism in Africa in the Inter-War Years', in *Journal of Contemporary History*, Vol. 14, No. 2, April 1979, pp. 287–307.

Eksteins, Modris. *Rites of Spring: The Great War and the Birth of the Modern Age* (Boston: Houghton Mifflin, 1989).

Elleman, Bruce A. *Wilson and China: A Revised History of the Shandong Question* (Armonk, NY: Sharpe, 2002).

Ellis, A. F. *Mid Pacific Outposts* (Auckland, NZ: Brown & Stuart, 1946).

Ellis, John. *Eye-Deep in Hell: Trench Warfare in World War I* (Baltimore: Johns Hopkins University Press, 1976).

Elman, Benjamin A. *A Cultural History of Civil Examinations in Late Imperial China* (Berkeley and Los Angeles: University of California Press, 2000).

Epps, Garrett. *Democracy Reborn: The Fourteenth Amendment and the Fight for Equal Rights in Post-Civil War America* (New York: Henry Holt, 2006).

Esherick, Joseph W. *The Origins of the Boxer Uprising* (Berkeley and Los Angeles: University of California Press, 1987).

Esthus, Raymond A. *Theodore Roosevelt and Japan* (Seattle: University of Washington Press, 1966).

Evans, David and Peattie, Mark. *Kaigun: Strategy, Tactics, and Technology in the Imperial Japanese Navy, 1887–1941* (Washington, DC: US Naval Institute, 1997).

Evans, Richard J. *The Coming of the Third Reich* (New York: Penguin, 2004).

Fabian, Hans. 'Aeronautical Research Comes into Being During the Time of Empire', in E. H. Hirschel, H. Prem and G. Madelung, *Aeronautical Research in Germany: From Lilienthal Until Today* (Berlin: Springer, 2004).

Farrell, Brian and Hunter, Sandy (eds). *Sixty Years On: The Fall of Singapore Revisited* (Singapore: Eastern Universities Press, 2002).

Feng Djen Djang, *The Diplomatic Relations Between China and Germany since 1898* (Shanghai: Commercial Press, 1936).

Ffestiniog Railway Company, *Rheilffordd Ffestiniog Guide Book* (Porthmadog, Wales: Ffestiniog Railway Company, 1997).

Feuchtwanger, Edgar. *Imperial Germany 1850–1918* (London: Routledge, 2001).

Fischer, Gerhard. *Enemy Aliens: Internment and the Homefront Experience in Australia, 1914–1920* (Brisbane: University of Queensland Press, 1989).

Fischer, Steven Roger. *A History of the Pacific Islands* (London: Palgrave Macmillan, 2002).

Fitzmaurice, Lord Edmond. *The Life of Granville George Leveson Gower, Second Earl Granville 1815–1891*, 2 vols (London: Longmans Green, 1905).

Foster, Robert J. *Social Reproduction and History in Melanesia: Mortuary Ritual, Gift Exchange, and Custom in the Tanga Islands* (Cambridge: Cambridge University Press, 1995).

Frame, Tom. *No Pleasure Cruise: The Story of the Royal Australian Navy* (Sydney: Allen & Unwin, 2005).

Franklin, Robert. *The Fringes of History: The Life and Times of Edward Stuart Wortley* (Christchurch, UK: Natula, 2003).

French, David. 'The Royal Navy and the Defence of the British Empire, 1914–1918', in Keith Neilson and Elizabeth Jane Errington (eds), *Navies and Global Defense: Theories and Strategy* (Westport, CT: Praeger, 1995).

Friedewald, Michael. 'The Beginnings of Radio Communication in Germany, 1897–1918', *Journal of Radio Studies*, Vol. 7, No. 2, 2000, pp. 441–63.

Fryer, Peter. *Private Case-Public Scandal* (London: Secker & Warburg, 1966).

Fung, Edmund S. K. *The Military Dimension of the Chinese Revolution: The New Army and Its Role in the Revolution of 1911* (Vancouver: University of British Columbia Press, 1980).

Gailey, Harry A. *Bougainville: The Forgotten Campaign, 1943–1945* (Lexington: University of Kentucky Press, 2003).

Gardner, Nikolas. *Trial by Fire: Command and the British Expeditionary Force in 1914* (Westport, CT: Praeger, 2003).

Gartzke, Kapitän Leutnant. *Der Aufstand in Ponape und seine Niederwerfung durch S. M. Schiffe "Emden", "Nürnberg", "Cormoran", "Planet"* [The Rebellion on Ponape and its Suppression by SMS *Emden*, *Nürnberg*, *Cormoran* and *Planet*] Nach amtlichen Berichten zusammengestellt von Kapitän Leutnant Gartzke [From the Official Reports of Lieutenant Captain Gartzke] (Berlin: Marine Rundschau, 1911).

Gates, John Morgan. *Schoolbooks and Krags: The United States Army in the Philippines, 1898–1902* (Westport, CT: Greenwood Press, 1973).

Gerard, James W. *Face to Face with Kaiserism* (London: Hodder & Stoughton, 1918).

Gewald, Jan-Bart. 'Learning to Wage and Win Wars in Africa: A Provisional History of German Military Activity in Congo, Tanzania, China and Namibia' (ASC Working Paper 60/2005) [A working paper presented at the conference 'Genocides: Forms, Causes and Consequences' held in Berlin, 13–15 January 2005].

Gewald, Jan-Bart. 'Colonial Warfare: Hehe and World War One, the wars besides Maji Maji in south-western Tanzania' (ASC Working Paper 63/2005) [A working paper first presented at the symposium, 'The Maji Maji War 1905 – 1907: Colonial Conflict, National History and Local Memory', held at the Wissenschaftskolleg zu Berlin, 30 March – 1 April 2005].

Gibbon, Edward. *An Essay on the Study of Literature: Written Originally in French, Now First Translated into English* (London: T. Becket and P. A. De Hondt, 1764).

Giessler, Klaus-Volker. *Die Institution des Marineattachés im Kaiserreich* [The Institution of the Imperial Marine Attachés] (Boppard am Rhein: Boldt, 1976).

Gilbert, Martin. *Winston S. Churchill: Companion Volume III, Part 1 July 1914–April 1915* (Boston: Houghton Mifflin, 1973).

Gilbert, Martin. *The Challenge of War: Winston S. Churchill 1914–1916* (London: Minerva, 1990).

Gilbert, Martin. *The First World War: A Complete History* (New York: Henry Holt, 1994).

Gilbert, Martin. *In Search of Churchill: A Historian's Journey* (London: HarperCollins, 1994).

Gillespie, Oliver A. *Official History of New Zealand in the Second World War 1939–45: The Pacific* (Wellington, Department of Internal Affairs: War History Branch, 1952).

Gimblett, Richard H. 'Reassessing the Dreadnought Crisis of 1909 and the Origins of the Royal Canadian Navy', in *The Northern Mariner/Le Marin du nord*, IV, No. 1, January 1994, pp. 35–53.

Glad, Betty. *Charles Evans Hughes and the Illusions of Innocence: A Study in American Diplomacy* (Urbana : University of Illinois Press, 1966).

Glatzer, Ruth. *Panorama einer Metropole: Das Wilhelminische Berlin* (Berlin: Siedler, 1997).

Godley, Michael R. *The Mandarin-Capitalists from Nanyang: Overseas Chinese Enterprise in the Modernisation of China 1893–1911* (Cambridge: Cambridge University Press, 2002).

Goldstein, Erik. 'The Evolution of British Diplomatic Strategy for the Washington Conference', in idem (ed.), *The Washington Conference 1921–22: Naval Rivalry, East Asian Stability and the Road to Pearl Harbour* (London: Frank Cass, 1994).

Gómez Núñez, Severo. *The Spanish American War: Blockades and Coast Defense* (Washington, DC: Government Printing Office, 1899).

Gooch, G. P. and Temperly, H. W. V. (eds). *British Documents on the Origins of the War, 1898–1914*, 11 vols (London: HM Stationery Office, 1926–1938) Volume III, *The Testing of the Entente 1904–6*.

Gordon, G. A. H. 'The British Navy, 1918–1945', in Keith Neilson and Elizabeth Jane Errington (eds), *Navies and Global Defense: Theories and Strategy* (Westport, CT: Praeger, 1995).

Gottberg, Otto von. *Die Helden von Tsingtau* (Berlin: Ullstein, 1915).

Gottschall, Terrell D. *By Order of the Kaiser: Otto von Diederichs and the Rise of the Imperial German Navy 1865–1902* (Annapolis, MD: US Naval Institute Press, 2003)

Bibliography

Gow, Ian. *Military Intervention in Pre-War Japanese Politics: Admiral Kato Kanji and the 'Washington System'* (London: Routledge, 2004).

Gowen, Herbert H. *An Outline History of China*, 2 vols (Boston: Sherman, French & Co., 1913).

Gray, J. A. C. *Amerika Samoa* (Annapolis, MD: US Naval Institute, 1960).

Greger, Rene. *Die Russische Flotte im Ersten Weltkrieg 1914–1917* (Munich: J. F. Lehmanns, 1970).

Grenville, John A. S. and Young, George B. *Politics, Strategy, and Diplomacy: Studies in Foreign Policy, 1873–1917* (New Haven, CT: Yale University Press, 1966).

Grey of Falloden, Viscount. *Twenty-Five Years: 1892–1916*, 2 vols. (London: Hodder & Stoughton, 1925).

Grey, Jeffrey. *A Military History of Australia* (Cambridge: Cambridge University Press, 1999)

Griffiths, Ieuan L. 'African land and Access Corridors', in Dick Hodder, Sarah J. Lloyd and Keith McLachlan (eds), *Land Locked States of Africa and Asia* (London: Frank Cass, 1998).

Hagan, Kenneth J. *This People's Navy: The Making of American Sea Power* (New York: Free Press, 1991).

Hall, John Ashley. *The Law of Naval Warfare*, revised and enlarged edition (London: Chapman & Hall, 1921).

Halstead, Murat. *Life and Achievements of Admiral Dewey from Montpelier* [Vermont] *to Manila* (Chicago: Dominion, 1899).

Halvorsen, Peter F. 'The Royal Navy and Mine Warfare, 1868–1914', in *The Journal of Strategic Studies*, Vol. 27, No. 4, December 2004, pp. 685–707.

Hamill, Ian. *Strategic Illusion: The Singapore Strategy and the Defence of Australia and New Zealand, 1919–1942* (Singapore: Singapore University Press, 1981).

Hankey, Lord. *Diplomacy by Conference: Studies in Public Affairs 1920–1946* (London: Ernest Benn, 1946).

Hanlon, David L. *Remaking Micronesia: Discourses over Development in a Pacific Territory, 1944–1982* (Honolulu: University of Hawaii Press, 1998).

Hannesson, Rögnvaldur. *Investing for Sustainability: The Management of Mineral Wealth* (Boston, MA: Kluwer, 2001).

Hardach, Gerd. 'Defining Separate Spheres: German Rule and Colonial Law in Micronesia', in Herman J. Hiery and John M. MacKenzie (eds), *European Impact and Pacific Influence: British and German Policy in the Pacific Islands and the Indigenous Response* (London: I. B. Tauris, 1997).

Hargreaves, Reginald. *Red Sun Rising: The Siege of Port Arthur* (London: Weidenfield & Nicolson, 1962).

Harter, Jim. *World Railways of the Nineteenth Century: A Pictorial History in Victorian Engravings* (Baltimore: John Hopkins University Press, 2005).

Hattendorf, John B. 'Admiral Prince Louis of Battenberg (1912–1914)', in Malcolm H. Murfett (ed.), *First Sea Lords: From Fisher to Mountbatten* (Westport, CT: Praeger, 1995)

Heller, Bernard. *Dawn or Dusk?* (New York: Bookman's, 1961).

Henderson, W. O. 'Germany's Trade with Her Colonies, 1884–1914', in *The Economic History Review*, Vol. 9, No. 1, November 1938, pp. 1–16.

Henderson, W. O. *Studies in German Colonial History* (London: Frank Cass, 1962).

Hermann, David G. *The Arming of Europe and the Making of the First World War* (Princeton, NJ: Princeton University Press, 1996).

Herring, Peter. *Yesterday's Railways: Recollections of an Age of Steam and the Golden Age of Railways* (Newton Abbot, UK: David & Charles, 2002).

Hershatter, Gail. *Dangerous Pleasures: Prostitution and Modernity in Twentieth-Century Shanghai*, reprint edition (Berkeley, CA: University of California Press, 1999).

Herwig, Holger H. *Politics of Frustration: The United States in German Naval Planning, 1889–1941* (Boston: Little Brown 1976).

Herwig, Holger H. *'Luxury Fleet': The German Imperial Navy 1888–1918* (London: George Allen & Unwin, 1980).

Hevia, James Louis. *English Lessons: The Pedagogy of Imperialism in Nineteenth-Century China* (Durham, NC: Duke University Press, 2003).

Hezel, Francis X. *Strangers in Their Own Land: A Century of Colonial Rule in the Caroline and Marshall Islands* (Honolulu: University of Hawaii Press, 1995).

Hiery, Hermann Joseph. *The Neglected War: The German South Pacific and the Influence of World War I* (Honolulu: University of Hawaii Press, 1995).

Hiery, Hermann Joseph. *Das Deutsche Reich in der Sudsee (1900–1921): Eine Anndherung an die Erfahrun- gen verschiedener Kulturen* [The German Empire in the South Seas (1900–1921): An Approach to the Experiences of Different Cultures] (Göttingen: Vandenhoeck & Ruprecht, 1995).

Hilditch, A. N. 'The Capture of Tsingtau (Nov. 7) Japan Expels Germany from the Far East', in Charles F Horne (ed.), *Source Records of World War I*, 7 vols, Volume. II, *1914–The Red Dawning of 'Der Tag'* (New York: Edwin Mellen Press, 1997).

Hill, Howard C. *Roosevelt and the Caribbean* (New York: Russell and Russell, 1965).

Hoffman, Paul. *Wings of Madness: Alberto Santos-Dumont and the Invention of Flight* (New York: Theia Press, 2003).

Holmes, Lowell D. (ed.). *Samoan Islands Bibliography* (Wichita, KS, Poly Concepts, 1984).

Honan, William H. *Bywater: The Man Who Invented the Pacific War* (London: Macdonald, 1990).

Hough, Richard. *The Fleet That Had to Die* (New York: Viking Press, 1958).

Hovgaard, William. *Modern History of Warships* (New York: Spon & Chamberlain, 1920).

Hsu, Immanuel C. Y. *The Rise of Modern China*, 6th edition (New York: Oxford University Press USA, 1999).

Huff, W. G. *The Economic Growth of Singapore: Trade and Development in the Twentieth Century* (Cambridge: Cambridge University Press, 1994).

Hughes, Helga. *Germany's Regional Recipes: Foods, Festivals, Folklore* (Iowa City, IA: Penfield, 2002).

Hugüenin, C. Oberleutnant im III. See-Bataillon [First Lieutenant III Naval Battalion]. *Geschichte Des III. See-Bataillons* [History of the III Naval Battalion] (Tsingtaü: Adolf Haupt, 1912).

Hull, Isabel V. *Absolute Destruction: Military Culture and the Practices of War in Imperial Germany* (Ithaca, NY: Cornell University Press, 2004).

Hunt, Barry D. *Sailor-Scholar: Admiral Sir Herbert Richmond 1871–1946* (Waterloo, ON: Wilfrid Laurier University Press, 1982).

Ichisada Miyazaki (trans. Conrad Schirokauer) *China's Examination Hell: The Civil Service Examinations of Imperial China* (New Haven, CT: Yale University Press, 1976).

Iikura, Akira. 'The "Yellow Peril" and its Influence on Japanese-German Relations', in

Christian W. Spang and Rolf-Harald Wippich (eds), *Japanese-German Relations, 1895–1945: War, Diplomacy and Public Opinion* (London: Routledge, 2006).

Ikle, Frank W. 'The Triple Intervention: Japan's Lesson in the Diplomacy of Imperialism', *Monumenta Nipponica* 22, no. 1–2, 1967, pp. 122–31.

Ireland, Bernard. *Jane's Battleships of the 20th Century* (New York: HarperCollins, 1996).

Jarausch, Konrad H. *The Enigmatic Chancellor: Bethmann Hollweg and the Hubris of Imperial Germany* (New Haven, CT: Yale University Press, 1973).

Jarausch, Konrad H. and Geyer, Michael. *Shattered Past: Reconstructing German Histories* (Princeton, NJ: Princeton University Press, 2003).

Jefferies, Matthew. *Imperial Culture in Germany, 1871–1918* (New York: Palgrave Macmillan, 2003).

Jerrold, Douglas. *The Royal Naval Division* (London: Hutchinson, 1923).

Jingchun Liang, *The Chinese Revolution of 1911* (Jamaica, NY: St John's University Press, 1972).

Johnston, Ian and McAuley, Rob. *The Battleships* (Osceola, WI: MBI, 2001).

Jonas, Manfred. *The United States and Japan: A Diplomatic History* (Ithaca, NY: Cornell University Press, 1984).

Jonas, Manfred. *The United States and Germany: A Diplomatic History* (Chapel Hill: University of North Carolina Press, 1992).

Jones, A. Phillip. *Britain's Search for Chinese Cooperation in the First World War* (New York: Garland, 1986).

Jones, Chester Lloyd. *The Caribbean since 1900* (New York: Prentice Hall, 1936).

Jones, Jefferson. *The Fall of Tsingtau, With a Study of Japan's Ambitions in China* (Boston: Houghton Mifflin, 1915).

Jose, Arthur W. *The Royal Australian Navy 1914–1918*, 9th edition (Sydney: Angus & Robertson, 1941) Volume IX of C. E. W. Bean (ed.), *The Official History of Australia in the War of 1914–1918*, 12 vols, various editions (Sydney: Angus & Robertson, 1941)

Jover, José María. *Política, diplomacia y humanismo popular: Estudios sobre la vida española en el siglo XIX* (Madrid: Turner, 1976).

Kahn, David. *The Reader of Gentlemen's Mail: Herbert O. Yardley and the Birth of American Codebreaking* (New Haven, CT: Yale University Press, 2004).

Kajima Morinosuke, *The Diplomacy of Japan, 1894–1922*, 3 vols. (Tokyo: The Kajima Institute of International Peace, 1976). Volume III [The First World War, Paris Peace Conference, Washington Conference].

Kane, Robert B. *Disobedience and Conspiracy in the German Army, 1918–1945* (Jefferson, NC: McFarland, 2002).

Karau, Mark D. 'Wielding the Dagger': *The MarineKorps Flandern and the German War Effort, 1914–1918* (London: Praeger, 2000).

Keegan, John. *The Price of Admiralty: The Evolution of Naval Warfare* (New York: Viking, 1989).

Kenji Shimada, *Pioneer of the Chinese Revolution: Zhang Binglin and Confucianism* (Stanford, CA: Stanford University Press, 1990).

Kennedy, Paul M. *The Samoan Tangle: A Study in Anglo-German-American Relations, 1878–1900* (New York: Barnes & Noble, 1974).

Kennedy, Paul M. *The Rise and Fall of the Great Powers: Economic Change and Military Conflict from 1500 to 2000* (New York: Random House, 1987).

Kennedy, Paul M. 'Imperial Cable Communications and Strategy, 1870–1914', in idem (ed.), *The War Plans of the Great Powers, 1880–1914* (London: Allen & Unwin, 1979).

Killen, John. *The Luftwaffe: A History* (Barnsley, UK: Pen & Sword, 2003).

King, F. H. *Farmers of Forty Centuries: Organic Farming in China, Korea and Japan* (Madison, WI: F. H. King, 1911).

Kitchen, Martin. *A History of Modern Germany 1800–2000* (Oxford: Blackwell, 2006).

Klussmann, Niels and Malik, Arnim. *Lexikon der Luftfahrt* (Berlin: Springer, 2004).

Koch, H. W. *A History of Prussia* (London: Longman, 1978).

LaFargue, Thomas F. *China and the World War* (Palo Alto, CA: Stanford University Press, 1937).

LaFeber, Walter. *The American Search for Opportunity, 1865–1913* (Cambridge: Cambridge University Press, 1993).

Lambert, Nicholas A. 'Admiral Sir Arthur Knyvett-Wilson, VC (1910–1911)' and 'Admiral Sir Francis Bridgeman-Bridgeman (1911–1912), in Malcolm H Murfett, (ed.), *First Sea Lords: From Fisher to Mountbatten* (Westport, CT: Praeger, 1995).

Lambert, Nicholas A. 'Admiral Sir John Fisher and the Concept of Flotilla Defence, 1904–1909', *The Journal of Military History*, Vol. 59, No. 4, October 1995, pp. 639–60.

Lambert, Nicholas A. 'Economy or Empire? The Fleet Unit Concept and the Quest for Collective Security in the Pacific, 1909–1914', in Keith Neilson (ed.), *Far-flung Lines: Studies in Imperial Defence in Honour of Donald Mackenzie Schurman* (London: Frank Cass, 1997).

Lambert, Nicholas A. *Sir John Fisher's Naval Revolution* (Columbia: University of South Carolina Press, 1999).

Lamont-Brown, Raymond. *Tutor to the Dragon Emperor: The Life of Sir Reginald Fleming Johnston at the Court of the Last Emperor* (Stroud, UK: Sutton, 1999). Lampe, Wilhelm Otto. 'The Kiel Canal', in Renate Platzoder and Philomene Verlaan (eds), *The Baltic Sea: New Developments in National Policies and International Cooperation* (The Hague: Kluwer Law International, 1996).

Lanzin Xiang, *The Origins of the Boxer War* (London: Routledge Curzon, 2002).

Leibowitz, Arnold H. *Defining Status: A Comprehensive Analysis of United States Territorial Relations* (Dordrecht, NL: Martinus Nijhoff, 1989).

LePore, Herbert P. *The Politics and Failure of Naval Disarmament 1919–1939: The Phantom Peace* (Lewiston, NY: Edwin Mellen Press, 2003).

Leonhard, Jörn. 'Construction and Perception of National Images: Germany and Britain, 1870–1914', in Daniel Gallimore and Dimitrina Mihaylova (eds) *The Linacre Journal*, No. 4: 'The Fatal Circle': Nationalism and Ethnic Identity Into the 21st Century', 2000, pp. 45–68

Lerman, Katharine A. *The Chancellor as Courtier: Bernhard von Bülow and the Governance of Germany, 1900–1909* (Cambridge: Cambridge University Press, 1990).

Lerman, Katherine A. 'Some Basic Statistics for Germany, 1815–1918', in Mary Fulbrook (ed.), *German History since 1800* (London: Edward Arnold, 1997).

Levene, Mark. *The Rise of the West and the Coming of Genocide*, 4 vols, Volume II *Genocide in the Age of the Nation State* (London: I. B. Tauris, 2005).

Lewis, Jay. 'Imperialism Yesterday and Today', *Workers' Liberty*, Issue 63, July 2000. pp. 15–17.

Liddell Hart, B. H. *History of the First World War* [1934] (London: Pan Books, 1972).

Lieberthal, Kenneth. *Governing China: From Revolution Through Reform* (New York: W. W. Norton, 1995).

Liliencron, Luiz von. *Die Deutsche Marine: Unter Zugrundelegung des neuen Flotteng-esetzes* [The German Navy: Using the New Fleet Law] (Berlin: Mittler, 1899).

Lilley, James R. with Lilley, Jeffrey. *China Hands: Nine Decades of Adventure, Espionage, and Diplomacy in Asia* (New York: Public Affairs, 2004).

Link, Arthur S. *Woodrow Wilson and the Progressive Era, 1910–1917* (New York: Harper, 1954).

Linn, Brian McAllister. *Guardians of Empire: The US Army and the Pacific, 1902–1940* (Chapel Hill: University of North Carolina Press, 1999).

Liu, Gretchen. *Singapore - A Pictorial History 1819–2000* (Abingdon, UK: Routledge, 2001).

Lloyd George, David. *War Memoirs*, 2-vol. edition (London: Odhams, 1938).

Lochner, R. K. (trans. Thea and Harry Lindauer). *The Last-Gentleman-Of-War: The Raider Exploits of the Cruiser Emden* (Annapolis, MD: US Naval Institute Press, 1988).

Love, Philip H. *Andrew W. Mellon: The Man and His Work* (Baltimore: F. H. Coggins, 1929).

Lowe, John. *The Great Powers, Imperialism, and the German Problem 1865–1925* (London: Routledge, 1994).

Lowe, Peter. *Great Britain and Japan 1911–1915: A Study of British Far Eastern Policy* (London: Macmillan, 1969).

Luckner, Graf. *Seeteufels Weltfahrt: Alte und neue Abenteuer* (Gütersloh: Bertelsmann, 1953).

Ludwig, Emil. (trans. Ethel Colburn Mayne). *Wilhelm Hohenzollern: The Last of the Kaisers* [1925] (Whitefish, MT: Kessinger Publishing, 2003).

Lutz, Hermann (trans. E. W. Dickes). *Lord Grey and the World War* (London: Allen and Unwin, 1928).

Lyon, David. *The First Destroyers* (London: Caxton Editions, 2001).

McBeth, Brian S. *Gunboats, Corruption, and Claims: Foreign Intervention in Venezuela, 1899–1908* (Westport, CT: Greenwood, 2001).

McClain, James L. *Japan: A Modern History* (New York: W. W. Norton, 2001).

McCord, Edward A. *The Power of the Gun: The Emergence of Modern Chinese Warlordism* (Berkeley and Los Angeles: University of California Press, 1993).

Mackenzie, S. S. *Rabaul: The Australians at Rabaul: The Capture And Administration of the German Possessions in the Southern Pacific*, 10th edition, (Sydney: Angus & Robertson, 1941) Volume X of C. E. W. Bean (ed.) *The Official History of Australia in the War of 1914–1918*, 12 vols, various editions (Sydney: Angus & Robertson, 1941).

Mackey, Richard William. *The Zabern Affair 1913–1914* (New York: University Press of America, 1991).

MacIntyre, W. David. *The Rise and Fall of the Singapore Naval Base* (Hamden, CT: Archon, 1979).

MacKinnon, Stephen R. *Power and Politics in Late Imperial China: Yuan Shi-kai in Beijing and Tianjin, 1901–1908* (Berkeley and Los Angeles: University of California Press, 1980).

Mahajan, Sneh. *British Foreign Policy 1874–1914: The Role of India* (London: Routledge, 2002).

Mahan, Alfred Thayer. *The Influence of Sea Power upon History, 1660–1783* [1890] (Boston, MA: Adamant Media Corporation, 2002).

Mahan, Alfred Thayer. *The Influence of Sea Power upon the French Revolution and Empire, 1793–1812* [1892] 2 vols (Boston, MA: Adamant Media Corporation, 2002).

Mahan, Alfred Thayer. *Naval Strategy* (London: Sampson Low, Marston, 1911).

Mahan, Alfred Thayer. *Naval strategy compared and contrasted with the principles and practice of military operations on land: lectures delivered at US Naval War College, Newport, RI, between the years 1887 and 1911.* Reprinted facsimile of the 1911 edition (Oxford: Greenwood Press, 1975).

Mamdani, Mahmood. *When Victims Become Killers: Colonialism, Nativism, and the Genocide in Rwanda* (Princeton, NJ: Princeton University Press, 2002).

Marder, Arthur J. *From the Dreadnought to Scapa Flow: The Royal Navy in the Fisher Era*, 5 vols. Volume I, *The Road to War 1904–1914* (New York: Oxford University Press, 1961).

Marder, Arthur J. *Old Enemies, New Friends: The Royal Navy and the Imperial Japanese Navy* (Oxford: Clarendon Press, 1981).

Martin, W. A. P. *The Awakening of China* (New York: Doubleday, Page, 1907).

Massie, Robert K. *Dreadnought: Britain, Germany and the Coming of the Great War* (New York: Random House, 1991).

Meaney, Neville. *Australia and the World: A Documentary History from the 1870s to the 1970s* (Melbourne: Longman Cheshire, 1985).

Meldrum, Andrew. 'German Minister says Sorry for Genocide in Namibia', *The Guardian* (London), 16 August 2004.

Meleisea, Malama et al. *The Cambridge History of the Pacific Islanders* (Cambridge: Cambridge University Press, 1997).

Millard, Thomas F. *Our Eastern Question* (New York: Century, 1916).

Miller, Edward S. *War Plan Orange: The US Strategy to Defeat Japan, 1897–1945* (Annapolis, MD: US Naval Institute Press, 2007).

Miller, Geoffrey. *Superior Force: The Conspiracy behind the Escape of Goeben and Breslau* (Hull, UK: Hull University Press, 1996).

Miller, J. Martin. *China: The Yellow Peril at War With the World* (Chicago: Wabash, 1900).

Miller, Stuart Creighton. *Benevolent Assimilation: The American Conquest of the Philippines, 1899–1903* (New Haven, CT: Yale University Press, 1982).

Millett, Allan R. 'Assault from the Sea: The Development of Amphibious Warfare between the Wars – the American, British, and Japanese Experiences', in Williamson Murray and Allan R. Millett (eds), *Military Innovation in the Interwar Period* (Cambridge: Cambridge University Press, 1996).

Mitchell, Nancy. 'The Height of the German Challenge: The Venezuela Blockade, 1902–03', *Diplomatic History*, Vol. 20, No. 2, Spring 1996, pp. 185–209.

Mitchell, Nancy. *The Danger of Dreams: German and American Imperialism in Latin America* (Chapel Hill: University of North Carolina Press, 1999).

Mombauer, Annika. *Helmuth von Moltke and the Origins of the First World War* (Cambridge: Cambridge University Press, 2001).

Mombauer, Annika. 'Wilhelm, Waldersee, and the Boxer Rebellion', in Annika Mombauer and Wilhelm Deist (eds), *The Kaiser: New Research on Wilhelm II's Role in Imperial Germany* (Cambridge: Cambridge University Press, 2003).

Mommsen, Wolfgang J. (trans. Michael S. Steinberg), *Max Weber and German Politics, 1890–1920* (Chicago: University of Chicago Press, 1984).

Moneypenny, W. F. and Buckle, George E. *The Life of Benjamin Disraeli: Earl of Beaconsfield.* 6 vols (New York: Macmillan, 1910–20) Volume VI.

Moretz, Joseph. *The Royal Navy and the Capital Ship in the Interwar Period: An Operational Perspective* (London: Frank Cass, 2002).

Morison, Samuel Eliot. *History of United States Naval Operations in World War II*, Volume 7 *Aleutians, Gilberts and Marshalls, June 1942–April 1944* [1951] (Urbana: University of Illinois Press, 2002).

Morison, Samuel Eliot. *History of United States Naval Operations in World War II.* Volume 14 *Victory in the Pacific 1945* [1960] (Urbana: University of Illinois Press, 2002).

Morris, Edmund. "'A Matter of Extreme Urgency": Theodore Roosevelt, Wilhelm II, and the Venezuela Crisis of 1902', *Naval War College Review*, Vol. 55, No. 2, Spring 2002, pp. 73–85.

Morse, Hosea Ballou. *The International Relations of the Chinese Empire: The Period of Subjection 1894–1911* (London: Longmans, Green, 1918).

Morton, W. Scott and Lewis, Charlton M. *China: Its History and Culture*, 4th edition (New York: McGraw-Hill, 2005).

Mosse, W E. *The German-Jewish Economic Elite, 1820–1935: A Socio-Cultural Profile* (Oxford: Clarendon Press, 1989).

Moynihan, Daniel Patrick *Secrecy: The American Experience* (New Haven, CT: Yale University Press, 1999).

Mücke, Hellmuth von. *The Emden-Ayesha Adventure: German Raiders in the South Seas and Beyond, 1914* (Annapolis, MD: USNaval Institute Press, 2000).

Munro, Dana G. *Intervention and Dollar Diplomacy in the Caribbean, 1900–1921* (Princeton, NJ: Princeton University Press, 1964).

Murphy, Philip. *Party Politics and Decolonisation: The Conservative Party and British Colonial Policy in Tropical Africa, 1951–1964* (Oxford: Clarendon Press, 1995).

Mutsu, Munemitsu (ed. and trans. Gordon Mark Berger). *Kenkenroku: A Diplomatic Record of the Sino-Japanese War, 1894–95*, reprint edition (Tokyo: University of Tokyo Press, 1995).

Nakamura, Jekizo (trans. J. A. Irons), 'Assault on the Central Fort, Tsingtao Campaign, 1914', Report in the US Army Military Research Collection at US Army Military History Institute, Carlisle Barracks, PA (no date).

Nerger, Karl August. *SMS Wolf* (Berlin: Scherl, 1918).

Newbolt, Henry. *History of the Great War Based on Official Documents by Direction of the Historical Section of the Committee of Imperial Defence.* Volume IV *Naval Operations* (London: Longmans, Green, 1928).

Ngoh, Victor Julius. *History of Cameroon Since 1800* (Limbé, Cameroon: Presbook, 1996).

Nicolaou, Stéphane. *Flying Boats and Seaplanes: A History from 1905* (Osceola, WI: MBI, 1998).

Nish, Ian. *Japanese Foreign Policy 1869–1942* (London: Routledge & Kegan Paul, 1977).

Nish, Ian et al. *Anglo-Japanese Relations 1892–1925*, 6 vols (London: Palgrave Macmillan, 2003).

Nish, Ian. *Collected Writings (Part 1)* (London: Routledge Curzon, 2001).

Nofi, Albert A. *The Spanish-American War: 1898* (Conshohocken, PA: Combined Books, 1996).

Noriko, Kawamura, *Turbulence in the Pacific: Japanese-US Relations during World War I* (Westport, CT: Praeger, 2000).

Norregaard, B. W. *The Great Siege: The Investment and Fall of Port Arthur* (London: Methuen, 1906).

Noyes, J. K. *Colonial Space: Spatiality in the Discourse of German South West Africa 1884–1915* (Reading, UK: Harwood, 1992).

Nozhin, E. K. (trans. A. B. Lindsay, ed., E. J. Swinton). *The Truth about Port Arthur* (London: John Murray, 1908).

Nuhn, Walter. *Kolonialpolitik und Marine: Die Rolle der Kaiserlichen Marine bei der Gründung und Sicherung des deutschen Kolonialreiches 1884–1914* [Colonial Policy and the Navy: The Role of the Imperial Navy in the Establishment and Protection of the German Colonial Empire 1884–1914] (Bonn: Bernard & Graefe, 2003).

Ober, W. B. 'Obstetrical events that shaped Western European history', *Yale Journal of Biology and Medicine* 65, May–June 1992, pp. 201–10.

O'Brien, Phillips Payson. *British and American Naval Power: Politics and Policy, 1900–1936* (Westport, CT: Praeger, 1998).

Offner, John L. *An Unwanted War: The Diplomacy of the United States and Spain Over Cuba, 1895–1898* (Chapel Hill: University of North Carolina Press, 1992).

Oksiloff, Assenka. *Picturing the Primitive: Visual Culture, Ethnography, and Early German Cinema* (New York: Palgrave, 2001).

Olcott, Charles S. *The Life of William McKinley*, 2 vols (Boston: Houghton Mifflin, 1916).

Olivier, David H. *German Naval Strategy, 1856–1888: Forerunners of Tirpitz* (London: Frank Cass, 2004).

O'Reilly, Bernard. *Life of Leo XIII from an Authentic Memoir Furnished by His Order: Written with the Encouragement, Approbation and Blessing of His Holiness the Pope* (Sydney: Oceanic Publishing, 1887).

Ory, Pascal. *1889 La Mémoire des siècles: L'Expo universelle* (Paris: Editions Complexe, 1989).

Otte, T. G. '"The Baghdad Railway of the Far East": The Tientsin–Yangtze Railway and Anglo-German Relations, 1898–1911', in T. G. Otte and Keith Neilson, *Railways and International Politics: Paths of Empire, 1848–1945* (Abingdon, UK: Routledge, 2006).

Overlack, Peter. 'The Force of Circumstances: Graf Spee's Options for the East Asian Cruiser Squadron in 1914', *Journal of Military History*, Vol. 60, No. 4, October 1996, pp. 657–82

Overlack, Peter. 'German War Plans in the Pacific, 1900–1914', *The Historian*, Vol. 60, No. 3, 1998, pp. 579–93.

Owen, Douglas. *Declaration of War: A Survey of the Position of Belligerents and Neutrals with Relative Considerations of Shipping and Marine Insurance during War* (London: Stevens and Sons, 1889).

Ozaki, Yukio (trans. Fujiko Hara) *The Autobiography of Ozaki Yukio: The Struggle for Constitutional Government in Japan* (Princeton, NJ: Princeton University Press, 2001).

Padfield, Peter. *The Great Naval Race: Anglo-German Naval Rivalry 1900–1914* (Edinburgh: Birlinn, 2005).

Padje, Willem-Alexander van't. 'The "Malet Incident", October 1895: A Prelude to the Kaiser's "Kruger Telegram" in the Context of the Anglo-German Imperialist Rivalry', in Geoff Eley and James Retallack (eds), *German Modernities, Imperialism, and the Meanings of Reform, 1890–1930: Essays for Hartmut Pogge von Strandmann* (Oxford: Berghahn, 2003).

Paine, Lauran. *Britain's Intelligence Service* (London: Robert Hale, 1979).

Paine, S. C. M. *The Sino-Japanese War of 1894–1895: Perceptions, Power, and Primacy* (Cambridge: Cambridge University Press, 2002).

Pakenham, Thomas. *The Scramble for Africa* (London: Abacus, 1992).

Palmer, Alan. *The Kaiser: Warlord of the Second Reich* (London: Weidenfield & Nicolson, 1978).

Palmer, Niall A. *The Twenties in America: Politics and History* (Edinburgh: Edinburgh University Press, 2006).

Pardoe, Blaine. *The Cruise of the Sea Eagle: The Amazing True Story of Imperial Germany's Gentleman Pirate* (Augusta, GA: Lyons Press, 2005).

Peattie, Mark R. *Nan'yō: The Rise and Fall of the Japanese in Micronesia, 1885–1945* (Honolulu: University of Hawaii Press, 1988)

Perkins, Dexter. *The Monroe Doctrine 1867–1907* (Baltimore: Johns Hopkins, 1937).

Perras, Arne. *Carl Peters and German Imperialism 1856–1918: A Political Biography* (Oxford: Clarendon Press, 2004).

Peterson, V. G. and Tseng Hsiao. 'Kiao-chau', in Robert V. Andelson (ed.), *Land-Value Taxation Around the World* (Malden, MA: Blackwell, 2000).

Philbin, Tobias R. *The Lure of Neptune: German-Soviet Naval Collaboration and Ambitions, 1919–1941* (Columbia: University of South Carolina Press, 1994).

Phillips, Kevin P. *The Cousins' Wars: Religion, Politics, and the Triumph of Anglo-America* (New York: Basic Books, 1999).

Phillipson, Coleman. *International Law and the Great War* (London: T. Fisher Unwin, 1915).

Pitt, Barrie *Coronel and Falkland: Two Great Naval Battles of the First World War* [1960] (London: Cassell, 2004).

Pleshakov, Constantine. *The Tsar's Last Armada: The Epic Voyage to the Battle of Tsushima* (New York: Basic Books, 2002).

Plüschow, Gunther. *Die Abenteuer des Fliegers von Tsingtau: Meine Erlebnisse in drei Erdteilen* [The Adventures of the Tsingtau Flier: My Experiences in Three Continents] (Berlin: Ullstein, 1916).

Plüschow, Isot and Gunther Plüschow. *Deutscher Seeman und Flieger* (Berlin: Ullstein, 1933).

Pomerantz-Zhang, Linda. *Wu Tingfang (1842–1922): Reform and Modernization in Modern Chinese History* (Hong Kong: Hong Kong University Press, 1992).

Ponsonby, Sir Frederick (ed.). *Letters of the Empress Frederick* (London: Macmillan, 1929).

Pooley, A. M. (ed.). *The Secret Memoirs of Count Tadasu Hayashi* (New York and London, G. P. Putnam's Sons, 1915).

Porter, Major-General W. The *History of the Corps of Royal Engineers*, Volume II (London: Longmans, Green, 1952).

Potter, Pitman B. 'Origin of the System of Mandates under the League of Nations', *The American Political Science Review*, Vol. 16, No. 4, November 1922, pp. 563–83.

Powell, Alan. *The Third Force: ANGUA's New Guinea War, 1942–46* (Melbourne: Oxford University Press, 2003).

Pratt, John T. *War and Politics in China* (London: Jonathan Cape, 1943).

Prentiss, Augustin M. *Chemicals in War: A Treatise in Chemical Warfare* (New York: McGraw-Hill, 1937).

Price, Ernest Batson. *The Russo-Japanese Treaties of 1907–1916 Concerning Manchuria and Mongolia* (Baltimore: The John Hopkins Press, 1933).

Putnam, William Lowell. *The Kaiser's Merchant Ships in World War I* (Jefferson, NC: McFarland, 2001).

Quinn, Frederick. *The French Overseas Empire* (Westport, CT: Praeger, 2000).

Ramsden, John. *Man of the Century: Winston Churchill and his Legend since 1945* (New York: Columbia University Press, 2002).

Rangarajan, Sadhu Prof. V and Vivekanandan R. *The Saga of Patriotism: Revolutionaries in India's Freedom Struggle* (Bangalore: Sister Nivedita Academy, 2004).

Ransom, Harry H. 'The Battleship Meets the Airplane', *Military Affairs*, Vol. 23, No. 1, Spring 1959, pp. 21–7.

Reichs-Marine-Amt, *Forschungsergebnisse S.M.S. 'Planet' 1906/7, Band 1: Reisebeschreibung* (Berlin: Karl Sigismund, 1909).

Reid, Gilbert. 'The Neutrality of China', *The Yale Law Journal*, Vol. 25, No. 2, December 1915,

Reynolds, David. *Britannia Overruled: British Policy and World Power in the Twentieth Century* (Harlow, UK: Pearson, 2000).

Rice, Howard. *The Fire of Komwonlaid Cape: The Story of Sokehs Rebellion* (Pohnpei, FSM: Division of Historic Preservation & Cultural Affairs, 1998).

Rich, Norman. *Friedrich von Holstein: Politics and Diplomacy in the Era of Bismarck and William II*, 2 vols (Cambridge: Cambridge University Press, 1965).

Richmond, Admiral Sir Herbert. *Statesmen and Sea Power* (Oxford: Clarendon Press, 1946).

Robbins, Commander Charles B. 'German Seacoast Defences at Tsingtao, 1914', *The Coast Defence Journal*, Vol. 21, Issue 2, May 2007, pp. 85–90.

Rodwell, C. H. review of 'The German Colonial Claim by L. S. Amery', *International Affairs* (Royal Institute of International Affairs 1931–1939), Vol. 18, No. 5, September– October 1939, p. 693.

Rogers, Robert F. *Destiny's Landfall: A History of Guam* (Honolulu: University of Hawaii Press, 1995).

Röhl, John C. G. *Germany Without Bismarck: The Crisis of Government in the Second Reich, 1890–1900* (Berkeley and Los Angeles: University of California Press, 1967).

Röhl, John C. G. (trans. Terence F. Cole). *The Kaiser and his Court: Wilhelm II and the Government of Germany* (Cambridge: Cambridge University Press, 1994).

Röhl, John C. G. *Young Wilhelm: The Kaiser's Early Life, 1859–1888* (Cambridge: Cambridge University Press, 1998).

Röhl, John C. G. (trans. Sheila de Bellaigue) *Wilhelm II: The Kaiser's Personal Monarchy, 1888–1900* (Cambridge: Cambridge University Press, 2004).

Röhr, Albert. *Handbuch der deutschen Marinegeschichte* [Manual of German Naval History] (Oldenburg: Gerhard Stalling, 1963).

Røksund, Arne. *The Jeune Ecole: The Strategy of the Weak* (Leiden, Netherlands: Brill, 2007).

Rose, Inbal. *Conservatism and Foreign Policy during the Lloyd George Coalition 1918–1922* (Abingdon, UK: Taylor & Francis, 1999).

Roth, Guenther. *The Social Democrats in Imperial Germany: A Study in Working-Class Isolation and National Integration* (Totowa, NJ: Bedminster Press, 1963).

Rottman, Gordon. *World War II Pacific Island Guide: A Geo-Military Sudy* (Westport, CT: Greenwood, 2002).

Rubinger, Richard. 'Education in Meiji Japan', in Wm. Theodore de Bary, Carol Gluck and Donald Keene (eds) *Sources of Japanese Tradition*, 2 vols (New York: Columbia University Press, 2003).

Sack, Peter. 'The "Ponape Rebellion" and the Phantomisation of History', *Journal de la Société des océanistes*, Vol. 104, No. 1, 1997, pp. 23–38.

Sagan, Scott D. '1914 Revisited: Allies, Offense, and Instability', in Michael E Brown, Owen R. Coté Jr., Sean M. Lynn-Jones and Steven E. Miller (eds) *Offense, Defense, and War* (Cambridge, MA: The MIT Press, 2004).

Salesa, Damon. 'Samoa's Half-Castes and Some Frontiers of Comparison', in Ann Laura Stoler, *Haunted by Empire: Geographies of Intimacy in North American History* (Durham, NC: Duke University Press, 2006).

Samuels, Richard J. *'Rich Nation, Strong Army': National Security and the Technological Transformation of Japan* (Ithaca, NY: Cornell University Press, 1994).

Saxon, Timothy D. 'Anglo-Japanese Naval Cooperation, 1914–1918', *Naval War College Review*, Vol. 53, No. 1, Winter 2000, pp. 62–92.

Schiefel, Werner. *Bernhard Dernburg 1865–1937: Kolonialpolitiker und Bankier im wilhelminischen Deutschland* (Zurich: Atlantis, 1974).

Schirmer, Daniel B. and Shalom, Stephen Rosskamm (eds), *The Philippines Reader: A History of Colonialism, Neocolonialism, Dictatorship, and Resistance* (Boston: South End Press, 1987).

Schmidt, Hans. *Maverick Marine: General Smedley D. Butler and the Contradictions of American Military History* (Lexington: University Press of Kentucky, 1987).

Schoen, Walter von. *Auf Vorposten für Deutschland: Unsere Kolonien im Weltkrieg* [On Germany's Outposts: Our Colonies in the World War] (Berlin: Ullstein, 1935).

Schoenbaum, David. *Zabern 1913: Consensus Politics in Imperial Germany* (London: George Allen & Unwin, 1982).

Schoonover, Thomas. *Uncle Sam's War of 1898 and the Origins of Globalization* (Lexington: University Press of Kentucky, 2003).

Schrecker, John E. *Imperialism and Chinese Nationalism: Germany in Shantung* (Cambridge, MA: Harvard University Press, 1971).

Schrecker, John E. *The Chinese Revolution in Historical Perspective* (Westport, CT: Greenwood Press, 1991)

Schriffin, Harold Z. *Sun Yat-sen and the Origins of the Chinese Revolution* (Berkeley and Los Angeles: University of California Press, 1970).

Schroeder, Wilhelm (ed.) (trans. Richard S. Levy) *Das persönliche Regiment: Reden und sonstige öffentliche Äusserungen Wilhelms II* [The Personal Regime: Speeches and Public Expressions of Wilhelm II] (Munich: Birk, 1912).

Schütz, Julius von (trans. Hubert Herbert Grenfell). *Gruson's Chilled Cast-Iron Armour* (London: Whitehead, Morris & Lowe, 1887).

Schwabe, Kurd. *Dienst und Kriegsführung in den Kolonien und auf überseeischen Expeditionen* [Service and War Guidance in the Colonies and on Overseas Expeditions] (Berlin: Mittler, 1903).

Schweinitz, Hans Lothar von. *Briefwechsel des Botschafters* [Exchange of letters of Ambassador] *General von Schweinitz* (Berlin : Reimar Hobbing, 1928).

Scott, Ernest. *Australia during the War*, 7th edition (Sydney: Angus & Robertson, 1941) Volume XI of C. E. W. Bean (ed.), *The Official History of Australia in the War of 1914–1918*, 12 vols, various editions (Sydney: Angus & Robertson, 1941).

Seagrave, Sterling. *Dragon Lady: The Life and Legend of the Last Empress of China*, reprint edition (London: Vintage, 1993).

Seeley, Sir John Robert. *The Expansion of England: Two Courses of Lectures* (Boston: Little, Brown, 1883).

Seligmann, Matthew S. *Rivalry in Southern Africa, 1893–99: The Transformation of German Colonial Policy* (London: Palgrave Macmillan, 1998).

Semenoff, Vladimir. *Rasplata* [The Reckoning] (London: John Murray, 1909).

Semenoff, Vladimir. *The Battle of Tsushima Between the Japanese and Russian Fleets, Fought on 27th May 1905* (New York: E. P. Dutton, 1912).

Shinji Ishii. 'The Fall of Sei-Tō (Tsing-Tao) and its Aftermath', *Asian Review: Journal of the Royal Society for India, Pakistan, and Ceylon*, Nos. 13–16. January – May 1915, pp. 17–21.

Shinji Suzuki and Masako Sakai. 'History of Early Aviation in Japan', a paper [AIAA 2005–118] presented to the 43rd AIAA [American Institute of Aeronautics and Astronautics] Aerospace Sciences Meeting and Exhibit, 10–13 January 2005, Reno, Nevada, USA.

Sieche, Erwin F. 'The Kaiser Franz Joseph I Class Torpedo-rams of the Austro-Hungarian Navy', *Warship 1995* (London: Conway Maritime Press, 1995).

Sims, Philip. 'German Tsingtao Mounts Photographs', *The Coast Defence Journal*, Vol. 20, Issue 4, November 2006, pp. 77–80.

Smith, Alson. J. *A View of the Spree: The Extraordinary Career of the American Grocer's Daughter Who Became a 'Sanctified Pompadour'* (New York: John Day, 1962).

Smith, Arthur H. *China in Convulsion*, 2 vols (New York: F. H. Revell, 1901).

Smith, Captain Bernard. 'The Siege of Tsingtau', *The Coast Artillery Journal*, November–December 1934, pp. 405–19.

Smith, Peter C. *Task Force 57: The British Pacific Fleet, 1944–45* (London: William Kimber, 1969).

Smith, Woodruff D. *The Ideological Origins of Nazi Imperialism* (Cary, NC; Oxford University Press USA, 1989).

Sobel, Robert. *Biographical Directory of the United States Executive Branch, 1774–1989* (New York: Greenwood Press, 1990).

Solzhenitsyn, Alexander. *August 1914: The Red Wheel*, 3rd printing (New York: Farrar, Straus & Giroux, 2000).

Sondhaus, Lawrence. *The Naval Policy of Austria-Hungary 1867–1918: Navalism, Industrial Development and the Politics of Dualism* (West Lafayette, IN: Purdue University Press, 1994).

Sondhaus, Lawrence. *Naval Warfare, 1815–1914* (London: Routledge, 2001).

Sösemann, Bernd. 'Forms and Effects of Public Self-Display in Wilhelmine Germany', in Annika Mombauer and Wilhelm Deist, *The Kaiser: New Research on Wilhelm II's Role in Imperial Germany* (Cambridge: Cambridge University Press, 2003).

Sowell, Thomas. *Ethnic America: A History* (New York: Basic Books, 1981).

Spender, J. A. *Fifty Years of Europe: A Study in Pre-War Documents* (London: Cassell, 1933).

Sprigade, P. and Moisel M. (eds). *Deutscher Kolonialatlas mit Jahrbuch: Herausgegeben auf Veranlassung der Deutschen Kolonialgesellschaft* [German Colonial Atlas and Yearbook:] (Berlin: Ernst Vohsen, 1905–18).

Startt, James D. *Woodrow Wilson and the Press: Prelude to the Presidency* (New York: Palgrave Macmillan, 2004).

Steele, David. *Lord Salisbury: A Political Biography* (London: Routledge, 2005).

Steinberg, John W. et al. (eds) *The Russo-Japanese War in Global Perspective: World War Zero* (Leiden, Netherlands : Brill Academic Publishers, 2005).

Steinmetz, George. '"The Devil's Handwriting": Precolonial Discourse, Ethnographic

Acuity, and Cross-Identification in German Colonialism', *Comparative Studies in Society and History*, Vol. 45, Issue 1, January 2003, pp. 41–95.

Steinmetz, George. 'From "Native Policy" to Exterminationism: German Southwest Africa, 1904, in Comparative Perspective', in Paper 30, *Theory and Research in Comparative Social Analysis*, Department of Sociology, UCLA (Los Angeles: University of California, 2005).

Steinmetz, George. 'Precoloniality and Colonial Subjectivity: Ethnographic Discourse and Native Policy in German Overseas Imperialism. 1780s–1914', in Diane E Davis (ed.) *Political Power and Social Theory*, Volume 15 (Oxford: Elsevier Science, 2002).

Stephenson, Charles. *The Admiral's Secret Weapon: Lord Dundonald and the Origins of Chemical Warfare* (Woodbridge, UK: Boydell Press, 2006).

Stevens, David. 'HMAS Australia: a Ship for a Nation', in David Stevens and John Reeve (eds), *The Navy and the Nation: The Influence of the Navy on Modern Australia* (Crows Nest, NSW: Allen & Unwin, 2005).

Stevenson, Robert Louis. *A Footnote to History: Eight Years of Trouble in Samoa* (New York: Charles Scribner's Sons, 1892),

Stevenson, Robert Louis. *Vailima Letters: Being Correspondence Addressed by Robert Louis Stevenson to Sidney Colvin, November 1890–October 1894* (London: Methuen, 1895).

Stoecker, Helmuth. 'Cameroon 1906–1914', in idem (ed.) (trans. Bernd Zöllner) *German Imperialism in Africa: From the Beginnings until the Second World War* (London: Hurst, 1986).

Stoecker, Helmuth and Nimschowski, Helmut. 'Morocco 1898–1914' in Helmuth Stoecker (ed.) (trans. Bernd Zöllner) *German Imperialism in Africa: From the Beginnings Until the Second World War* (London: Hurst, 1986).

Stone, Norman. *The Eastern Front 1914–1917* (New York: Charles Scribner's Sons, 1975).

Strachan, Hew. *The First World War*, Volume 1 *To Arms* (Oxford: Oxford University Press, 2003).

Strachan, Hew. *The Outbreak of the First World War* (Oxford: Oxford University Press, 2004).

Sumida, Jon Tetsuro. 'British Naval Operational Logistics, 1914–1918', *The Journal of Military History* Vol. 57, No. 3, 1993, pp. 447–80.

Sumino, Lila. 'L'Avion: l'Envol du Japon', *Asia: Journal collégien et lycéen d'établissements français de la zone Asie-Pacifique*, No.2, December 2006, p. 4.

Sumner, Ian. *German Air Forces 1914–18* (Oxford: Osprey, 2005).

Taliaferro, Jeffrey W. *Balancing Risks: Great Power Intervention in the Periphery* (Ithaca, NY: Cornell University Press, 2004).

Tampke, Jurgen (ed.). *Ruthless Warfare: German Military Planning and Surveillance in the Australia-New Zealand Region Before the Great War* (Canberra: Southern Highlands Publishers, 1998).

Tatsuji, Takeuchi. *War and Diplomacy in the Japanese Empire* (Chicago: Allen & Unwin, 1936).

Taylor, A. J. P. *The Struggle for Mastery in Europe 1848–1945* (Oxford: Oxford University Press, 1954).

Terrill, Ross. *The New Chinese Empire* (Sydney: University of New South Wales Press, 2003).

Thiele, Erdmann (ed.). *Telefunken nach 100 Jahren: Das Erbe einer deutschen Weltmarke* [Radio after 100 years: The Legacy of a Global Brand] (Berlin: Nicolai, 2003).

'Times, The' Correspondents of. *The Times History of the War*, Volume II (London: The Times, 1915).

Tirpitz, Grand Admiral von. *My Memoirs*, 2 vols (London: Hurst & Blackett, 1919).

Tomes, Jason. *Balfour and Foreign Policy: The International Thought of a Conservative Statesman* (Cambridge: Cambridge University Press, 2002).

Torrance, David. *The Scottish Secretaries* (Edinburgh: Birlinn, 2006).

Townsend, Mary E. 'The German Colonies and the Third Reich', *Political Science -Quarterly*, Vol. 53, No. 2, June 1938, pp. 186–206.

Trani, Eugene P. and Wilson, David L. *The Presidency of Warren G Harding* (Lawrence: Regents Press of Kansas, 1977).

Trask, David F. *The War with Spain in 1898* (New York: Simon & Schuster, 1981).

Tretyakov, Lieutenant General N. A. *My Experiences at Nan-Shan and Port Arthur with the Fifth East Siberian Rifles* (London: Hugh Rees, 1911).

Trotter, A. 'Friend to Foe? New Zealand and Japan: 1900–1937', in Roger Peren, (ed.) *Japan and New Zealand: 150 Years* (Palmerston North: New Zealand Centre for Japanese Studies, Massey University, on behalf of the Ministry of Foreign Affairs, Tokyo, in association with the Historical Branch, Dept. of Internal Affairs, Wellington, 1999).

Tuchman, Barbara W. *The Zimmerman Telegram* (New York: Viking Press, 1956).

Tucker, Spencer C. *The Great War 1914–18* (Bloomington: Indiana University Press, 1999).

Tucker, Spencer C. (ed.) *Who's Who in Twentieth Century Warfare* (London: Routledge, 2001).

Tunnicliffe, M. D. 'The Fleet We Never Had', *Canadian Naval Review*, Volume 2, Number 1, Spring 2006, pp. 16–20.

Turk, Richard W. *The Ambiguous Relationship: Theodore Roosevelt and Alfred Thayer Mahan* (Westport, CT.: Greenwood Press, 1987).

Unger, J. Marshall. *Literacy and Script Reform in Occupation Japan* (New York: Oxford University Press, 1996.

Van der Leeuw, Charles. *Oil and Gas in the Caucasus and Caspian: A History* (Richmond, UK: Curzon Press, 2000).

Van der Vat, Dan. *The Last Corsair: The Story of the Emden*, revised edition (Edinburgh: Birlinn, 2001).

Venzon, Anne Cipriano (ed.). *General Smedley Darlington Butler: The Letters of a Leatherneck, 1898–1931* (New York: Praeger, 1992).

Venzon, Anne Cipriano. *From Whaleboats to Amphibious Warfare: Lt. Gen. 'Howling Mad' Smith and the US Marine Corps* (Westport CT: Praeger, 2003).

Vollerthun, Waldemar. *Der Kampf um Tsingtau: eine Episode aus dem Weltkrieg 1914/1918 nach Tagebuchblättern* [The Battle for Tsingtau: an Episode from the World War of 1914–18 from the Pages of a Diary] (Leipzig: Hirzel, 1920).

Voskamp, Carl Johannes. *Aus dem belagerten Tsingtau* [In besieged Tsingtau] (Berlin: Society of Evangelical Missions, 1915).

Waldeyer-Hartz, Hugo von. *Der Kreuzerkrieg 1914–1918: das Kreuzergeschwader, Emden, Königsberg, Karlsruhe, die Hilfskreuzer* [The Cruiser War 1914–18: The Cruiser squadron … the Auxiliary cruisers] (Oldenburg: Gerhard Stalling, 1931).

Walton, Joseph. *China and the Present Crisis: With Notes on a Visit to Japan and Korea* (London: Sampson Low, Marston, 1900).

Walters, R. H. *The Economic and Business History of the South Wales Steam Coal Industry, 1840–1914* (New York: Arno Press, 1977).

Walworth, Arthur. *Woodrow Wilson*, 2 vols (New York: Longmans, Green, 1958).

Ward, Kyle Roy. *In the Shadow of Glory: The Thirteenth Minnesota in the Spanish-American and Philippine-American Wars, 1898–1899* (St Cloud, MN: North Star, 2000).

Warner, Marina. *The Dragon Empress: The Life and Times of Tz'u-hsi, Empress Dowager of China, 1835–1908* (New York: Macmillan, 1972).

Waters, S. D. *The Royal New Zealand Navy* (Wellington: Department of Internal Affairs, 1956)

Welles, Benjamin. *Sumner Welles: FDR's Global Strategist, a Biography* (New York: St Martin's Press, 1997).

Weisman, Steven R. *The Great Tax Wars: Lincoln to Wilson – The Fierce Battles over Money and Power That Transformed the Nation* (New York: Simon & Schuster, 2002).

Wertheimer, Mildred S. *The Pan-German league, 1890–1914* (New York: Columbia University Press, 1923).

Wetzler, Peter. *Hirohito and War: Imperial Tradition and Military Decision Making in Prewar Japan* (Honolulu: University of Hawaii Press, 1998).

White, John Albert. *Transition to Global Rivalry: Alliance Diplomacy and the Quadruple Entente, 1895–1907* (Cambridge: Cambridge University Press, 2002).

Wilbur, C. Martin. 'The Nationalist Revolution: from Canton to Nanking, 1923–28', in John K. Fairbank and Denis Twitchett (eds), *The Cambridge History of China*, Volume 12, *Republican China, 1912–1949* (Cambridge: Cambridge University Press, 1983).

Wilhelm II, Emperor of Germany, 1888–1918 (trans. Thomas R. Ybarra), *The Kaiser's Memoirs* (New York: Harper & Brothers, 1922).

Wilson, Michael. *Royal Australian Navy Major Warships: Profile No. 1* (Marrickville, NSW: Topmill, no date).

Winzen, Peter. *Das Kaiserreich am Abgrund: Die Daily-Telegraph-Affaere und das Hale-Interview von 1908* [The Empire at the Abyss: The Daily-Telegraph Affair and the Hale-Interview of 1908] (Stuttgart: Franz Steiner, 2002).

Witcover, Jules. *Sabotage at Black Tom: Imperial Germany's Secret War in America, 1914–1917* (Chapel Hill, NC: Algonquin, 1989).

Witte, Count (ed. A Yarmolinsky). *The Memoirs of Count Witte* (London: William Heinemann, 1921).

Wood, James. *History of International Broadcasting*, 2 vols (London: Peregrinus, 1992).

Woodhead, H. G. W. and Bell, H. T. M. *The China Year Book* (Shanghai: North China Daily News & Herald, 1914).

Worth, Richard. *Fleets of World War II* (Cambridge, MA: Da Capo, 2001).

Wright, Burton III. *Eastern Mandates (US Army Campaigns of World War II)* (Washington, DC: US Army Center of Military History, 1993).

Wright, Quincy. *Mandates under the League of Nations* (Chicago: University of Chicago, 1930).

Yang Xiao, 'Liang Qichai's Political and Social Philosophy', in Chung-Yin Cheng and Nicholas Bunnin, *Contemporary Chinese Philosophy* (Malden, MA: Blackwell, 2002).

Yardley, Herbert O. *The American Black Chamber* (Laguna Hills, CA: Aegean Park, 1931).

Yates, Keith. *Graf Spee's Raiders: Challenge to the Royal Navy 1914–1915* (Annapolis, MD: Naval Institute Press, 1995).

Yoichi Hirama, 'The Anglo-Japanese Alliance and the First World War', in Ian Gow, Yoichi Hirama and John Chapman (eds), *History of Anglo-Japanese Relations, 1600–2000*. Volume III *The Military Dimension* (Basingstoke, UK: Palgrave Macmillan, 2003).

Yongling Lu and Hayhoe, Ruth, 'Chinese Higher Learning: the Transition Process from Classical Knowledge Patterns to Modern Disciplines, 1860–1910', in Christophe Charle, Jürgen Schriewer, Peter Wagner (eds) *Transitional Intellectual Networks: Forms of Academic Knowledge and the Search for Cultural Identities* (Frankfurt: Campus, 2004).

Young, E. F. 'Tethered Balloons – Present and Future' a paper [AIAA-1968–941] presented to the Aerodynamic Deceleration Systems Conference of the AIAA [American Institute of Aeronautics and Astronautics], 23–25 September 1968, El Centro, California, USA.

Young, William. *German Diplomatic Relations 1871–1945: The Wilhelmstrasse and the Formulation of Foreign Policy* (New York: iUniverse, 2006).

Zarrow, Peter. *China in War and Revolution, 1895–1949* (London: Routledge, 2005).

Index

Entries in **bold** indicate graphics